D1321107

BIM for Facility Managers

IFMA
IFMA Foundation

Paul Teicholz, Editor

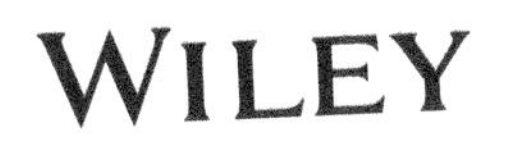

Cover illustrations: (left) reproduced by permission of Ecodomus, Inc.
(right) reproduced by permission of Autodesk, Inc.

Cover design: Anne Michele Abbott

This book is printed on acid-free paper. ♾

Published by John Wiley & Sons, Inc., Hoboken, New Jersey

Published simultaneously in Canada

Library of Congress Cataloging-in-Publication Data

BIM for facility managers / IFMA, IFMA Foundation ; Paul Teicholz, editor.
pages cm
Includes index.
Includes bibliographical references.
ISBN 978-1-118-38281-3 (hardback: alk. paper); 978-111-8-41762-1 (ebk.); 978-111-8-42067-6 (ebk.); 978-111-8-43423-9 (ebk.) 1. Building information modeling.
I. Teicholz, Paul M., editor. II. IFMA Foundation.
TH438.13.B56 2013
658.2—dc23

2012045250

Printed in the United States of America

10 9 8 7 6 5 4 3 2

Contents

Preface

"It's all about the data." That expression is a good starting point for this book. In this case, "data" refers to the massive amounts of information needed by facility managers for their work and the systems that provide the basis for effective and efficient facility management. This book describes current best practices to support the integration of BIM with FM systems and how to collect the data needed to support this integration. The emphasis in on what the owner and FM staff need to know to ensure that these practices are used on new projects. Leadership by the owner is provided by specific contract terms, and these are discussed in the chapter on legal issues.

The use of BIM to support design and construction practice is spreading rapidly, and with it a growing emphasis on more collaboration among the project team earlier in the development process. While this book does not focus on how to use BIM, it does illustrate the importance of FM participation in the early stages of a project. This will help ensure that the correct data is collected at the right times during the project and that each participant knows what is expected of them. It will also ensure that at the end of the project, there will be a successful start to the operation and maintenance of the facility. The case histories illustrate these work processes and show that in these early days of BIM FM integration, there is much to learn for all involved.

WHY A BOOK ABOUT BIM FOR FACILITY MANAGERS

The motivation for writing this book was to provide a thorough and consolidated guide to help professionals and students in the building industry learn about the opportunities for significant owner benefits that can be obtained from this new use for BIM and how to achieve these benefits. Owners today are just beginning to implement BIM FM integration, and the software and standards needed for this integration are in relative early stages of development. However, this should not stop owners and FM managers from implementing these systems and learning as much as they can about the approaches that are effective. The knowledge and experience of others that are captured in this book will help provide this education. The International Facility Management Association (IFMA) is doing many things to help its members understand BIM FM integration including this book, conference presentations and journal articles and a social networking site.

The case histories reported in this book record the difficulties and frustrations that can occur in early efforts. The lessons learned from these should help others avoid some of these difficulties, which arise from lack of experience and planning, and false expectations. If this book can help readers avoid these frustrations and costs, it will have served a useful purpose.

The contents of the book were provided by academics and professionals with exceptional backgrounds in BIM FM integration. We make no claim that the book is objective in terms of judgments on the importance of implementing BIM FM integration; however, the results to date are very promising. We have made every effort to ensure the accuracy and completeness of the facts and figures presented and to ensure that the problems are brought forward so that they can provide lessons to others.

WHO IS THIS BOOK FOR AND WHAT IS IN IT

This book is directed to owners and operators of buildings, their FM staffs, the AEC professionals that design, build, and commission buildings, the product manufacturers who provide equipment of all types that is needed for providing services in a building, and students of the AEC/FM industry. All of these people have a role to play in the successful implementation of BIM with FM. As described earlier, the collaboration of the project team working with an educated and effective owner is a primary ingredient to successful implementation.

The book contains the following chapters:

1. Chapter 1 first describes the inefficiencies associated with current FM practice and shows the significant costs caused by lack of information integration to building owners at each stage of the life cycle. It then introduces the main concepts of BIM FM integration and how they are employed. It then attempts to calculate a rough return on investment of this integration and show the costs and benefits involved.

2. Chapter 2 provides an overview of BIM technology and the emerging new developments that will play an important role in BIM FM integration. This chapter is intended for those not fully familiar with BIM and the various approaches used to link it with FM systems.
3. Chapter 3 contains information about owner guidelines for BIM FM integration with primary emphasis on the GSA guidelines. This chapter will help owners understand what needs to be addressed in contracts and BIM execution plans that guide the professionals in the project team.
4. Chapter 4 provides owners with legal guidance on what issues the contract documents need to cover on a project involving the use of BIM (with or without FM integration). These include:
   - What is in the model and its contractual status
   - Ownership of the model
   - Intellectual property ownership
   - Issues with interoperability and data exchange

Chapter 4 also contains an example of contract language for a project with FM integration.

5. Chapter 5 describes COBie (construction operations building information exchange) and how it should be used to collect building data, when each type of data should be collected, what naming standards can be used and how this information can be input to FM systems. COBie is a primary standard that has been developed for BIM FM integration and is an important part of practice. An increasing number of public and private owners are requiring the use of COBie on their projects. Thus, learning how to do this properly and effectively is very important.
6. Chapter 6 contains six case studies that document BIM FM integration for a wide variety of public and private owners. Readers are encouraged to read these studies carefully to gain an appreciation of the technologies that were used, the problems that had to be addressed and the benefits that were achieved. These are all early examples and none had progressed far enough to experience many of the projected benefits of integration. However, there are clear indications from some of the studies that good results can be expected based on the quality of data integration achieved. The introduction to this chapter outlines the major features of each case study to help readers identify those of particular relevance.
7. Appendix A contains a list of all the acronyms used in the book with the exception of special U.S. government-related abbreviations, which are defined when first encountered in case study 4.

8. Appendix B contains a list of all the software packages that are mentioned in the text together with their Web references. This should help the reader find more information about specific software if desired.

HOW TO USE THIS BOOK

Many readers will find this book a useful resource when they are confronted with a new requirement or idea relating to BIM FM integration, e.g., COBie. If this is the case, then reading the relevant chapter would be the most direct approach. If a general understanding is desired, then starting with Chapter 1, "Introduction," would be most useful for the background presented there. The chapters have been sequenced to provide knowledge from more general to more detailed. This should make it easier to absorb the content if read in this sequence. For a reader who had a good general understanding, it might be useful to start at the case studies in Chapter 6. These are quite detailed and will provide some deep insights for those with adequate background. No one study covers all aspects of the BIM FM integration process, but they do provide insights into the problems that need to be addressed and the training and educational needs to support these systems.

However you choose to read this book, we hope that it will suit your needs for useful information and ideas and will more than repay your time and effort.

Acknowledgments

The research and writing of this book involved contributions from many professionals and academics. We are deeply indebted to those who wrote significant chapters in this book including Louise Sabol (Chapter 2), Kymberli A. Aguilar and Howard W. Ashcraft (Chapter 4), and William East (Chapter 5). The case studies were written by both graduate students and professionals. Some required efforts from both sources before they reached maturity. The graduate students did this work in partial fulfillment of courses taught by Professor Kathy Roper in the Integrated Facility Management Program at the School of Building Construction Georgia Institute of Technology and Professor Charles Eastman in the School of Architecture at the same university. The individuals responsible for each case study are credited at the start of each study. Of particular note is Angela Lewis, who wrote three of the case studies and made helpful contributions throughout the book. The case studies were made possible through the very generous contributions of the project participants who corresponded with us extensively and shared their understanding and insights. Many thanks are due to Igor Starkov of EcoDomus, who made helpful suggestions and supplied a number of excellent figures for the book.

Special mention should be made of the support from IFMA for this book. In particular, Eric Teicholz (my brother) and Michael Schley, in their positions on the IFMA board of directors and IFMA Foundation Board of Trustees, guided the production of this book and facilitated its content. They helped solve technical and administrative problems at every stage of development, for which I am very grateful.

I would like to thank Kathryn Malm Bourgoine, the senior acquisitions editor at John Wiley & Sons, who encouraged the writing of this book and worked closely with IFMA to resolve the problems associated with its creation. In addition, Amy Odum, senior production editor did an excellent job of steering this book through the editing and production process.

The International Facility Management Association and the IFMA Foundation thanks our sponsors. This work would not have been possible without their support.

Silver Sponsor

Autodesk®

WWW.AUTODESK.COM

Bronze Sponsors

FM:Systems

WWW.FMSYSTEMS.COM

Graphic Systems

WWW.GRAPHICSYSTEMS.BIZ

Chapter Abstracts

CHAPTER 1: INTRODUCTION

This chapter begins with a description of current FM practice and the inefficiencies caused by poor data storage and lack of interoperability among the information systems that are used for design, construction, and facility management. These were documented In December 2004 National Institute of Standards & Technology (NIST) study titled *Cost Analysis of Inadequate Interoperability in the U.S. Capital Facilities Industry* (NIST GCR 04-867).

The second section of this chapter then identifies how BIM FM integration can address these problems and calculates the return on investment (ROI) that can be achieved by an investment in this technology and its associated processes. The results are rather startling: ROI is about 64 percent, with a payback period of 1.56 years.

CHAPTER 2: BIM TECHNOLOGY FOR FM

This chapter provides an in-depth view of BIM technology and how it is being used for FM applications. It assumes that the reader is familiar with the use of BIM for architecture and construction applications and focuses on the specific capabilities needed to support FM. There is a discussion of the benefits that can be gained, problems that need to be addressed, and the emerging technologies that will enable better support of FM needs.

CHAPTER 3: OWNER BIM FOR FM GUIDELINES

An owner needs to know what to ask for from the project team in order to get useful results for FM. This chapter presents a selection of owner guidelines that have been developed by public and private agencies that are used to specify their goals and expectations at each stage of the design, construction, and turnover process. All of the guidelines require that the project team develop a BIM execution plan (BEP) that specifies how the team will meet their requirements. A less experienced owner is advised to either hire a consultant or work with a knowledgeable contractor, architect, or engineer on their first or second projects to increase the likelihood of good results. Software vendors that market BIM FM integration applications are another source of practical knowledge. As in every other complex field, experience is an important component of success.

The General Services Administration (GSA) guidelines are presented in considerable detail as this agency has devoted a large effort involving both internal and external experts to define their goals, work processes, and information standards. Reviewing this standard will provide the user with a good understanding of the problems that need to be addressed by an owner, although they may not choose to use the same solution to these issues.

A selection of owner BIM guidlelines are summarized to give a picture of the variations that currently exist among agencies. Since BIM FM integration is relatively new, not all guidelines cover the requirements for this integration. However, it is likely that almost all will in the future.

CHAPTER 4: LEGAL ISSUES WHEN CONSIDERING BIM FOR FACILITIES MANAGEMENT

This chapter addresses four main issues, from a legal perspective, that owners implementing BIM for FM should consider:

1. What is in the model and its contractual status?
2. Ownership of the model
3. Intellectual property ownership
4. Issues with interoperability and data exchange

In addition, the chapter discusses three additional issues: (1) whether the use of BIM will increase liability of the other parties, (2) how an integrated project delivery (IPD) environment affects reliance on BIM, and (3) whether insurance will cover the parties' respective BIM-related work. All of these issues should be considered at the outset of the project and addressed with good contractual language.

CHAPTER 5: USING COBie

This chapter begins by describing the motives behind the COBie project. The spreadsheet format for COBie is described. Steps to implement COBie at a facility management office and ongoing work complete this chapter. The authoritative source for information about COBie is the Whole Building Design Guide's COBie web site, where technical documentation, example models, and instructional videos can be found.

COBie is the only open-source approach to collecting FM data over the design, construction, and turnover phases of a project. It is being required for use by an increasing number of owners who desire open-source solutions. A COBie file (now in version 2.4) can be generated from a number of BIM modeling systems, and there are tests performed by the buildingSMART alliance (bSa) to test the completeness and accuracy of systems that write and read COBie files (COBie Challenge). These are described in this chapter.

This chapter provides a good introduction to COBie and how it can be implemented. There are many COBie information sources on the BSa web site that provide additional information (www.buildingsmartalliance.org).

CHAPTER 6: CASE STUDIES

This chapter consists of six case studies that cover a wide range of BIM FM integration. These are all early efforts by owners who are implementing (or still testing) BIM FM integration for the first time. However, these are detailed studies that provide a realistic picture of the problems and benefits that can be expected. The studies cover a wide range of owner and building types. In almost every study, the owners leaned on the expertise of their project team to learn what needed to be done and how to train their own people to take over after projects were completed. In every case except one, the owner intended to implement BIM FM on future projects.

The reader is encouraged to review these studies in detail to gain the benefits of the lessons learned at these projects.

APPENDIX 1: GLOSSARY OF ACRONYMS USED IN THE BOOK

This appendix contains a list of the many acronyms that were used in this book. Each acronym is also defined when first used within a chapter or case study.

APPENDIX 2: LIST OF SOFTWARE VENDORS MENTIONED IN THE BOOK

Each software vendor that is mentioned in the book is listed here with a Web address where more information can be found. The location in the book (by chapter or case study) is also referenced.

Introduction

1

Paul Teicholz

MANAGEMENT SUMMARY

Figure 1.1 summarizes the main benefits that an owner can expect from integrating building information modeling (BIM) and facility management (FM). These are explored in further detail later in this chapter, and the rest of the book explains the technology and processes that can be used to achieve this goal. The primary goal of this book is to help owners and practitioners understand how to successfully implement BIM FM integration to achieve the benefits shown in this diagram.

This chapter begins with a description of current FM practice and the inefficiencies caused by poor data storage and lack of interoperability among the information systems that are used for design, construction, and facility management. These were documented in a December 2004 National Institute of Standards & Technology (NIST) study titled *Cost Analysis of Inadequate Interoperability in the U.S. Capital Facilities Industry* (NIST GCR 04-867). The additional cost of interoperability represents about 12.4 percent of total annual cost, which is significant as this occurs over the operational life of the building.

The second section of this chapter then identifies how BIM FM integration can address these problems and calculates the return on investment (ROI) that can be achieved by an investment in this technology and its associated processes. The results are rather startling: ROI is about 64 percent, with a payback period of 1.56 years. While the assumptions made in this analysis are tentative,

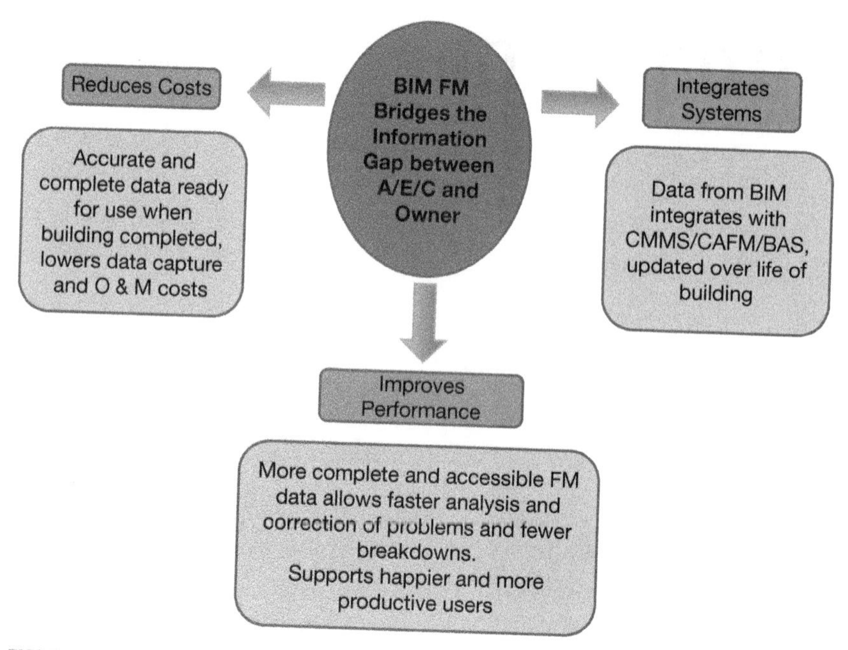

FIGURE 1.1 Summary of the main benefits that can be achieved by BIM FM integration.

they are quite conservative, and the results indicate that BIM FM integration, when done correctly, can provide very significant owner benefits. These benefits come from savings in the collection of data over the design and construction process rather than waiting until the completion of the building, and the intelligent use of a digital database of building information that allows FM managers and staff to make better and faster maintenance decisions and provide higher-quality building performance. The same database can also support more informed use of the building and its modifications over its life. These are very significant issues for all owners and operators of buildings.

The remainder of the chapter describes what can be found in the remaining five chapters of the book so that the reader can determine the best approach to reading this book based on their interests and background.

PROBLEMS WITH CURRENT FM PRACTICE

When one considers the extensive documentation of information needed for effective maintenance and operation of most facilities, it is clear that finding efficient ways to collect, access and update this information is very important. Most existing buildings have this information stored in paper documents (rolls of drawings from the architect and engineers, folders of equipment information for each type of equipment, file folders of maintenance records, etc.). This documentation is normally contractually requested by the owner and handed over after the building is already in use, often months later, and stored in some basement office where it is difficult to access. This is illustrated in Figure 1.2a and 1.2b showing actual storage of FM documents.

FIGURE 1.2a Picture of document storage for FM information after turnover by the contractor.
Courtesy EcoDomus, Inc.

FIGURE 1.2b Picture of document storage for FM information after turnover by the contractor.
Courtesy EcoDomus, Inc.

In December 2004 NIST published a study titled *Cost Analysis of Inadequate Interoperability in the U.S. Capital Facilities Industry* (NIST GCR 04-867).[1] This often-cited analysis of the cost impacts of the lack of data interoperability on architects, engineers, contractors, and owners was the first serious effort to quantify these impacts on all stakeholders and over the building life cycle. A quote from this report summarizes the impacts on owner/operators of problems described earlier:

> An inordinate amount of time is spent locating and verifying specific facility and project information from previous activities. For example, as-built drawings (from both construction and maintenance operations) are not routinely provided and the corresponding record drawings are not updated. Similarly, information on facility condition, repair parts status, or a project's contract or financial situation is difficult to locate and maintain.

For the owner who has decided to use a computerized maintenance management system (CMMS), it is necessary to transfer this equipment and other building information into digital files. Normally, this is done manually by the FM personnel as time permits. Thus, effective use of the system is delayed until it contains the necessary data and these data have been checked for accuracy and completeness. A similar comment applies to the use of computer-aided facility management (CAFM) systems. The cost and time associated with entering, verifying, and updating the information in these systems contributes to the costs identified in this report.

Section 6.5 (pp. 6–16, 17) of this report discusses the additional costs that impact owner/operators. While this is too detailed to reproduce here, the data are summarized in Tables 1.1 and 1.2 and illustrated in Figure 1.3.

We see that owners and operators represent about two-thirds of all these costs, and that they occur over all phases of the life cycle, with most of this cost in the operations and maintenance phase (57.5 percent).[2] The added cost for operations and maintenance (O&M) is $0.24 per SF or, based on the 2009 International Facility Management Association (IFMA) Maintenance Survey,[3] or 12.4 percent of total annual mean O&M costs,[4] which is significant as this occurs over the operational life of the building.

Table 1.2 shows that avoidance and mitigation form the bulk of the costs incurred by owner/operators.

[1] Available at www.nist.gov/manuscript-publication-search.cfm?pub_id=101287.

[2] The unit costs for the design and construction phases are based on 1,137 million SF of new construction in 2002. The unit costs for O&M are based on 38,600 million SF of new and existing buildings.

[3] Available at www.ifma.org/resources/research/reports/pages/32.htm

[4] This survey shows that the mean maintenance cost of all types of facilities is $2.22 per SF (in 2007 dollars). This equates to $1.97 in 2002 dollars (comparable to those in the NIST paper).

TABLE 1.1 2002 Costs of Inadequate Interoperability by Stakeholder Group, by Life-Cycle Phase (totals in millions, unit costs in dollars) Based on Table ES-2 of NIST 04-867 Study

Stakeholder Group	Planning, Design, and Eng. Phase	Construction Phase	Operations and Maint. Phase	Total	Pct. of Total
Architects and Engineers	1,007.2	147.0	15.7	1,169.8	7.4%
Per square foot (SF)	0.89	0.13		1.02	
General Contractors	485.9	1,265.3	50.4	1,801.6	11.4%
Per SF	0.43	1.11			
Special Fabricators and Suppliers	442.4	1,762.2		2,204.6	13.9%
Per SF	0.39	1.55			
Owners and Operators	722.8	898.0	9,072.2	10,648.0	67.3%
Per SF	0.64	0.79	0.23	1.66	
Total	2,658.3	4,072.4	9,093.3	15,824.0	100.0%
Per SF	2.34	3.58	0.24	6.16	
Pct. of Total	16.8%	25.7%	57.5%	100.0%	

Note: Sums may not add to totals due to independent rounding.

TABLE 1.2 2002 Costs of Inadequate Interoperability by Cost Category by Stakeholder Phase (totals in millions) Based on Table ES-3 of NIST 04-867 Study

Cost Category	Avoidance Costs	Mitigation Costs	Delay Costs	Total	Pct. of Total
Architects and Engineers	485.3	684.5	—	1,169.8	7.4%
General Contractors	1,095.4	693.3	13.0	1,801.7	11.4%
Special Fabricators and Suppliers	1,908.4	296.1	—	2,204.5	13.9%
Owners and Operators	3,120.0	6,028.2	1,499.8	10,648.0	67.3%
Total	6,609.1	7,702.0	1,512.8	15,824.0	100.0%
Pct. of Total	41.8%	48.7%	9.6%	100.0%	

Note: Sums may not add to totals due to independent rounding.

HOW BIM FM INTEGRATION CAN ADDRESS CURRENT PROBLEMS

The short answer to the current problems previously described is: integration of data systems over the life cycle of a facility. The data needed to support a given phase of the life cycle needs to be entered just once in the level of

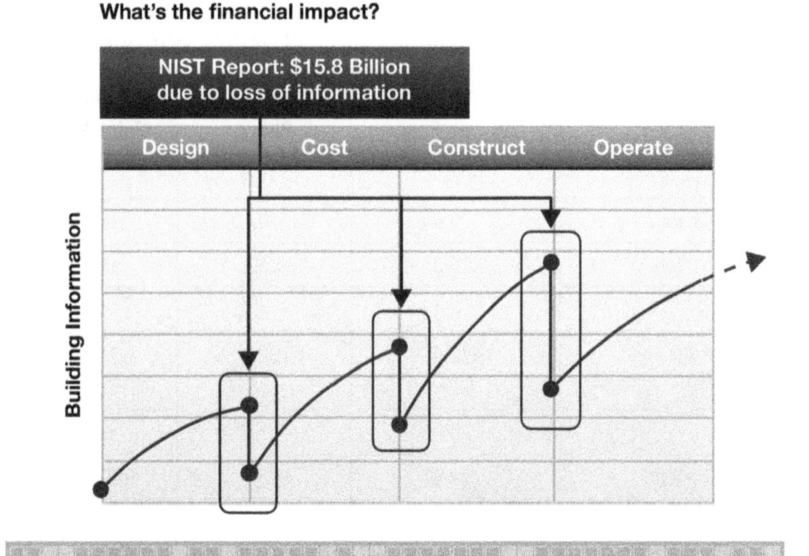

FIGURE 1.3 Loss of value as information is lost and reentered from phase to phase of the building life cycle (adopted from NIST report).
Courtesy FM:Systems

detail and accuracy that is available at that time. After that point, additional information is added as needed and at the appropriate level of detail. By the time commissioning of the building is completed, the data needed for O&M should be available for use in an accurate and usable form. This description of an ideal approach ignores many of the realities that make it difficult to achieve this goal. However, these details are covered in this book, and the reader will find that there are good solutions to this integration problem that should improve over time.

NEED FOR GRAPHICS AND DATA VARIES OVER THE LIFE CYCLE

Figure 1.4 illustrates the idea that the need for graphics is highest during the design phase and the need for detailed data is least. During conceptual design, BIM model creation systems are used to visualize the shapes, spaces, and generic objects (equipment, windows, systems, etc.). As the project progresses from conceptual to detail design, engineering analysis of various types requires more data about the materials, spaces, equipment, and so on that will be used in the building. During construction, even greater data and level of detail for cost estimation, procurement, coordination, constructability, and installation are needed. Finally, as the equipment

What do owners really need?

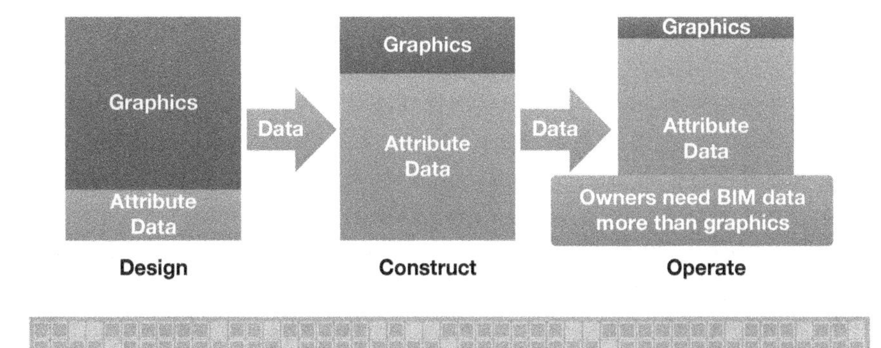

FIGURE 1.4 Mix of graphics and data changes over the facility life cycle.
Courtesy FM:Systems

is installed and systems are tested, the final information about these elements of the project become available and need to be entered into the system. One method of collecting these data is shown in Figure 1.5, where an iPad is being used to view a selected location (see left-hand menu that shows the Mechanical Room CB1021 is selected at the top with its properties shown on the right side). The user can then add a document, an attribute, or create an issue for the selected space (location). Similar properties are edited for assets and equipment.

FIGURE 1.5 Shows an iPad being used to enter equipment information after installation.
Courtesy EcoDomus

NEED FOR INTEROPERABILITY BETWEEN SYSTEMS

Clearly, all of the data is not entered into one model or one system. This therefore requires the interoperability of systems so that data can be communicated from upstream systems for downstream use. During operations and maintenance the FM data as well as the graphic data needed for FM use must be updated to reflect the changes. Once again, interoperability is the key. We will find that there are multiple approaches to achieving this flow of data, including use of open standards such as the Construction Operations Building information exchange (COBie) and proprietary approaches that integrate directly to specific BIM, CAFM, and CMMS systems. Figure 1.6 illustrates the data flows that need to be supported. This diagram shows alternative approaches to integration. In this figure, the FM Software platform can be any system used by facility managers that requires building data such as CMMS, CAFM, BAS, and so on.

One integration option is for users to develop a spreadsheet to capture the equipment and related data needed for FM and then either enter this directly into a CMMS system via an import mechanism. This approach may appear to be easier and faster to implement on small projects, but it lacks the formal structure

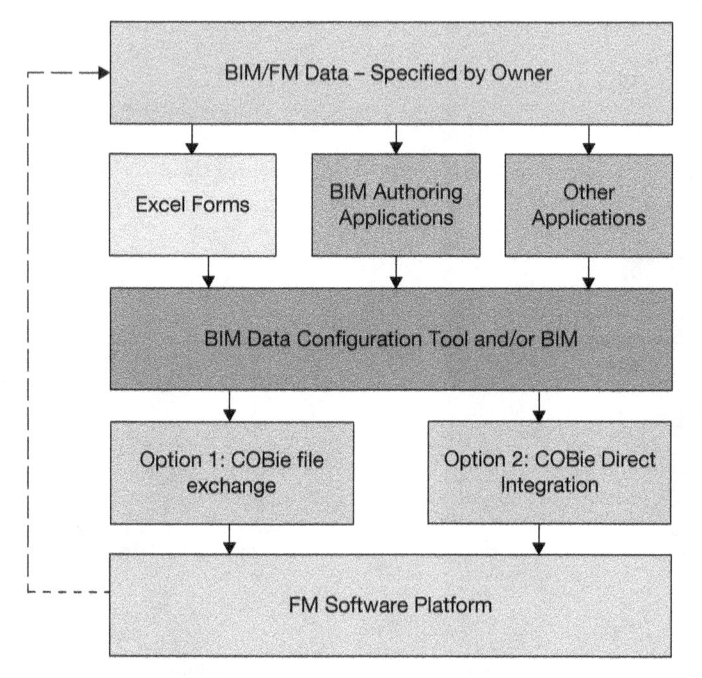

FIGURE 1.6 Alternative data paths to integrate BIM with FM.
Source: GSA BIM for FM Guidelines

of other approaches and has a higher error rate because there is no validation of the data being entered.

A second option is to use COBie, which is an open standard supported by the buildingSMART alliance. This standard specifies how all types of building and equipment data can be captured and what naming standards are appropriate for each kind of data (e.g., OmniClass codes for equipment). Using this option does not require integration with BIM as the COBie data can be imported into a CMMS program. But this option would not, for example, provide graphic data to show where equipment was located.

A third option is to take advantage of proprietary links between BIM modeling systems and FM support systems to create two-way links between these systems. EcoDomus is such a system and is being used to support facility managers who desire graphic views integrated with FM data (see Figure 1.7).

A fourth option is to directly integrate a CMMS system with a BIM modeling system using the BIM application programming interface (API). This provides an effective integration of both systems where graphics data is updated in BIM and FM data is entered into COBie and/or directly into the CMMS system. Another option is

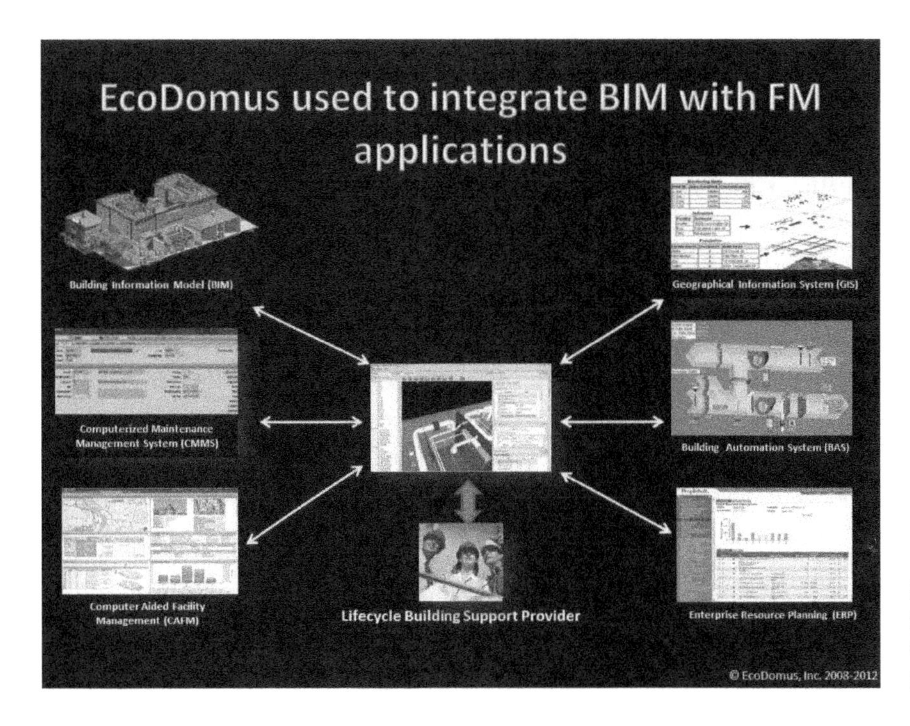

FIGURE 1.7 Example of graphic integration with FM data relating to a work order.
Courtesy EcoDomus

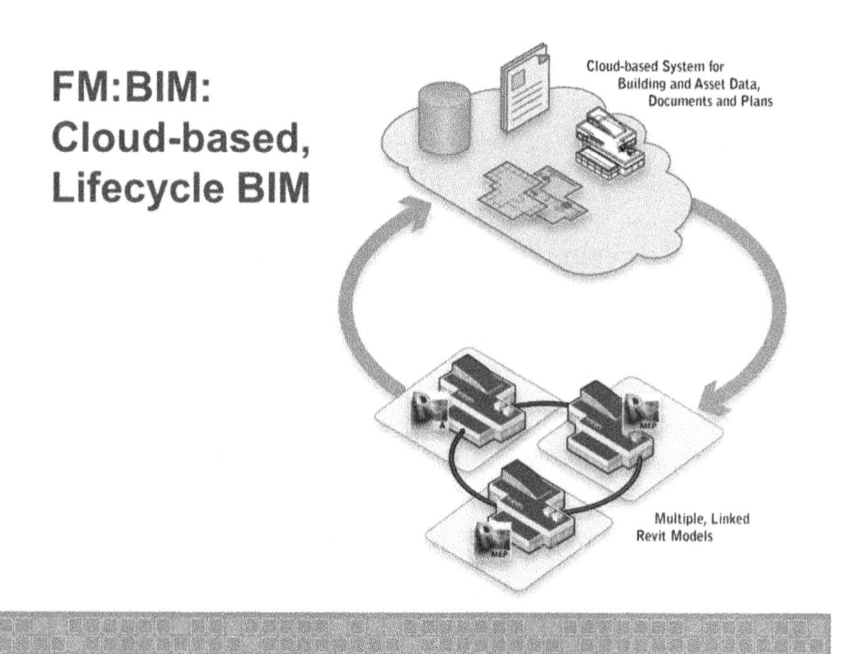

FIGURE 1.8 Direct integration of BIM and CMMS systems supported by cloud-based servers and accessed using a browser.
Courtesy FM:Systems

to support the data content on cloud-based servers that can be accessed at any location using a browser (see Figure 1.8).

OWNER BENEFITS OF BIM FM INTEGRATION

Streamlines Handover and More Effective Use of Data

A key benefit of integrating BIM with FM is that key data regarding spaces, equipment types, systems, finishes, zones, and so on can be captured from BIM and does not have to be reentered into a downstream FM system. For example, a COBie file can be extracted from the BIM model and then imported into a CMMS system. This avoids data entry cost, and generates higher-quality data. Then, as a detailed construction model is developed to document the as-built condition, additional information about equipment assemblies, ductwork, piping, electrical systems, and so on can be added to the model. This data will also be incorporated in the CMMS system, either via a COBie import or through direct integration with BIM. Finally, as equipment is installed, the equipment serial numbers can be recorded and entered into the COBie data. The result is a fully populated FM system that can be used when the building is commissioned. The

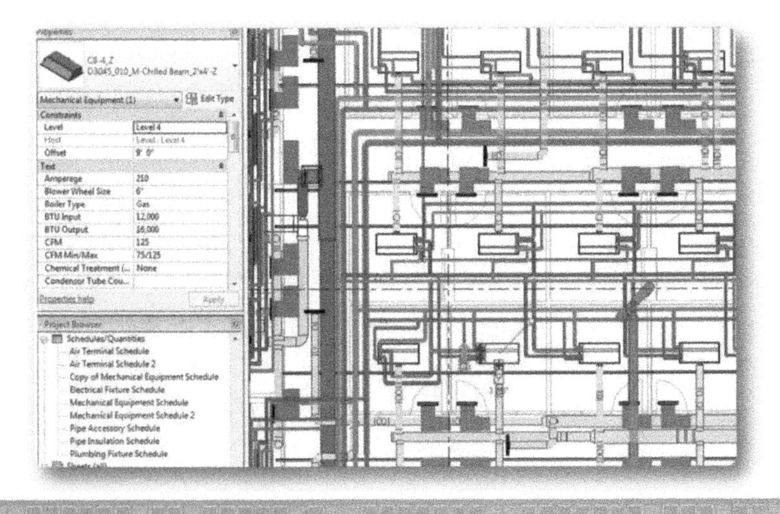

FIGURE 1.9 Shows a BIM model view of air-handling systems.
Courtesy FM:Systems

benefits to FM staff that help them understand how to operate and maintain the building are significant. Several of the case studies included in this book (see Chapter 6) illustrate this benefit and describe the processes that were used to achieve it. In Figure 1.9 we see a detailed BIM model of the systems in a building. This information can then be used with equipment data to plan maintenance after it has been linked to CMMS (see Figure 1.10).

Benefits during the Life of the Building

There are very significant cost benefits that should result from an integrated system providing accurate and complete information, including the following:

- Improved workforce efficiency because of the availability of better information when it is needed (in the office or field) rather than requiring FM staff to spend time looking up information on drawings, equipment documents, and other paper records.
- Reduced cost of utilities (energy and water) because of improved maintenance data that support better preventive maintenance planning and procedures. Building mechanical equipment will operate much more efficiently when properly maintained.

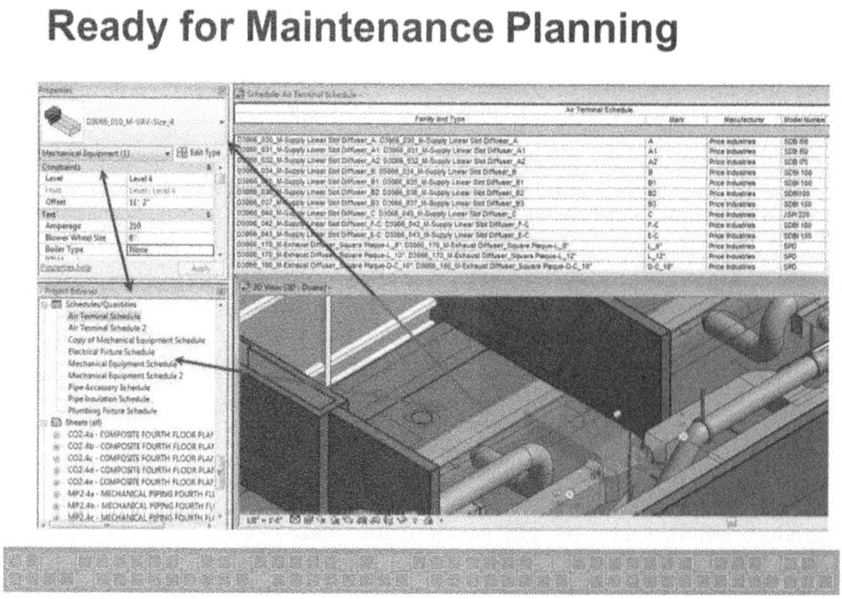

Ready for Maintenance Planning

FIGURE 1.10 That same system data is now linked to equipment data in CMMS and can be used for maintenance planning.
Courtesy FM:Systems

- Reduction in equipment failures that cause emergency repairs and impact tenants.
- Improved inventory management of parts and supplies and better tracking of asset and equipment histories.
- Longer equipment lives supported by more extensive use of PM rather than breakdown maintenance. This reduces the cost of equipment replacement in the same way that proper auto maintenance extends an auto's life and provides more reliable service.[5]

These benefits all contribute to lowering facility total cost of ownership (TCO) and providing better customer service.

[5] The following information was reported by Jim Whittaker, president of Facility Engineering Associates, P.C. (FEA). A government agency that manages and operates facilities across the United States has 578 buildings of various types on the West Coast with an estimated area of 7 million square feet and a current replacement value (CRV) of $2.5 billion ($366/SF). By automating and generating good preventive maintenance programs and using CMMS to manage and track performance they were able to optimize their capital asset replacement decisions and extend asset/equipment useful life (EUL) by an average of 9.8 years over an average industry EUL value of 18.6 years (a remarkable increase of 53 percent). This extension applies to roughly 60 percent of the total asset value. Thus, extending the life of these assets represents an estimated ownership savings of $28.4 million per year or about $4.09/SF/yr or 1.12 percent of the CRV per year, a very impressive result.

It should be noted that the case histories in this book were not able to verify all these benefits because no project had used their integrated system for sufficient time to measure the ongoing benefits previously described. Thus, they remain reasonable but not yet substantiated by these case studies.

Integrated System Can Be Used to Plan Enhancements to Building

Buildings are continually changing; spaces are used for different functions, equipment is replaced, systems are modified, and so on. If the BIM FM system is kept up to date as these changes occur, it can serve as an accurate record of current conditions. FM staff will not need to search through drawings and other documents or break through walls or ceilings to determine actual conditions. By training the FM staff to maintain the system as conditions change, much better planning data is available and better decisions can be made. The cost of renovation projects will also be reduced by reducing the uncertainty that contractors must deal with when bidding on projects. Thus, the investment in BIM FM integration can provide benefits over the entire life of the facility.

Calculating ROI in BIM FM Integration

Making some reasonable and conservative estimates and combining these with data from the 2009 IFMA Survey of Maintenance Data, it is possible to calculate a rough return on the investment in the effort to collect the data needed for BIM FM integration. The significant advantages identified above can then be quantified and put in some perspective.

1. Base cost estimates on a typical office headquarters with 400,000 gross SF with 346,620 rentable SF (ratio of 1.154 GSF/RSF) with a useful life of 25 years. This building type was chosen because it has by far the largest number of responses in the IFMA survey cited above (431 out of 1,419 or 30 percent) and thus represents the most reliable data.
2. Initial costs to create integrated system:
   This includes the investment in systems, data collection and verification, training, and related expenses needed to support integrated BIM FM: roughly $100,000 (based on personal interviews with industry professionals).
3. Ongoing costs to maintain integrated system with updated information to reflect changes to building and its equipment: 1 FTE at $125,000/yr (fully burdened) working 25 percent of time on this activity: $31,250 per year. This percentage is an average over the year and will vary from 0 to 100 percent, depending on the number of changes that need to be entered.

4. Initial savings resulting from less labor effort required to gather the information about spaces and equipment. This data is available at the start of building occupancy because it has been captured during the design and construction process rather than after building turnover. This saving avoids the cost of two months for two FM people doing initial data gathering of building maintenance data: $41,667.
5. Ongoing savings from a number of sources:
   a. Assumed cost of O&M (from 2009 IFMA survey) mean value $1.98 per GSF (or $2.28 per rentable SF).
   b. O&M savings assuming that better access to accurate information will save 0.5 hours per work order, with 1,600 work orders per year and a total burdened labor rate of $50/hr. This yields a savings of $40,000 per year or $0.10 per GSF.
   c. Assumed utility costs (from 2009 IFMA survey) mean value $2.39 per GSF.
   d. Utility cost savings assuming that improved maintenance and performance of equipment will reduce energy costs of at least 3 percent. This yields a savings of $28,680 per year or $0.07 per GSF.
   e. The total costs for O&M and Utilities are $1,746,295 per year or $4.37 per GSF.
   f. The total savings per year is $68,680 or $0.17 per GSF, which represents 3.93 percent of these costs.
6. ROI calculations:
   a. Net initial investment is $100,000 reduced by $41,667 of initial savings, yielding a one-time investment of $58,333.
   b. Annual savings over the 25-year lifetime of the building is $68,680 – $31,250 = $37,430/yr.
   c. If we assume an owner interest rate of 6% on invested funds, the present value of $37,430 per year over 25 years is $478,481.
   d. This must be reduced by the initial cost to yield a net present value = $420,148.
   e. This can also be expressed as an internal ROI of 64 percent.
   f. The payback period for the net investment = $58,333 / $37,430 = 1.56 years.

Granted these are rough calculations, but they are based on the best data the author could obtain at this time. The reader is invited to calculate revised data based on his or her own data. The preceding results, however, exclude potential "soft" savings from better comfort (temperature and humidity controls), fewer breakdowns, better inventory control of spares, extension of life for equipment, and use of combined model for remodeling and upgrades. Thus, the results should be conservative. Even if the calculated result is off by a factor of 4, which is quite unlikely, it warrants adoption of BIM FM. There is little risk on the downside (except from lack of knowledge) and considerable room for real benefits. Clearly, this is an investment where understanding what is desired and having a clear plan to achieve these results are critical requirements.

BIM Technology for FM

2

Louise Sabol

Director of Technology Solutions, Design + Construction Strategies, Washington, DC

BUILDING INFORMATION MODELING (BIM)

Building information modeling is a software technology gaining rapid acceptance throughout the architecture, engineering, and construction (AEC) industry. BIM provides a visually and dimensionally accurate three-dimensional digital representation of a building (Figure 2.1). It also is a database, offering the capability to track data attributes for the components that comprise the building model.

Building information models describe the three-dimensional geometry, objects, and attributes of a physical facility. The core of BIM is the building geometry, but BIM also is a structured information base of nongraphic data that provides detailed information about the building components. In the building information model, a wall exists as a wall, a boiler is a boiler—all objects have lifelike identity and attributes. They can be sorted, counted, and queried. BIM is a significant advancement in technology over computer-aided design (CAD), the software for drawing and documentation that has been in use for over 20 years (Figures 2.2a and Figure 2.2b). Current development and use of BIM resides primarily in the design sector, and increasingly among contractors and builders.

FIGURE 2.1 Building information model.
Courtesy Design + Construction Strategies

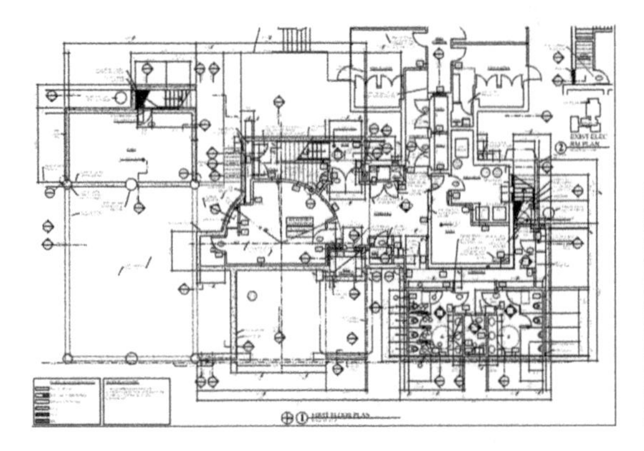

FIGURE 2.2a Traditional CAD documents are difficult to interpret.
Courtesy Design + Construction Strategies

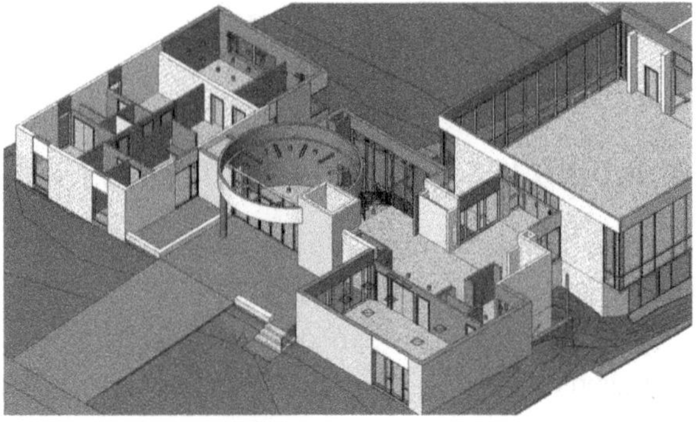

FIGURE 2.2b A 3D BIM provides an improved means of describing a building, leading to improved process efficiencies.
Courtesy Design + Construction Strategies

Because BIM is a data application with the inherent ability to affiliate data fields with the objects that comprise the model, it facilitates a wide range of capabilities that include quantity take-offs, cost estimating, space and asset management, and performing energy analyses, along with a plethora of other applications.

BIM can also incorporate parametric capabilities that allow components in a model to have attributes or parameters that define relationships with other components.

For example, a door object will be dependent upon or relate to a wall object. An effective BIM application manages the relationships of all components embedded in a model, along with their individual characteristics. This can be a very powerful tool for expediting change management.

Aside from being a powerful data application, BIM technology has the potential to enable fundamental changes in project delivery, promising to support a more integrated, efficient process. As a highly collaborative, data-rich environment, BIM has the inherent capability to reduce costs and promote efficiencies in the following manner:

- *Early decision making.* BIM allows earlier evaluation of building performance so that decisions and changes can be made with a reduced impact to time and costs.
- *Improved accuracy.* The accuracy of the model fosters more effective communication between the diverse parties involved in building projects and reinforces understanding. This reduces errors and changes throughout the design and construction process. The parametric capabilities of BIM allow for the consistent, coordinated representation of the model in all views and drawing outputs.
- *Rapid quantification.* The model can automatically generate quantities and report on data, producing estimates and workflows more efficiently and quickly than conventional processes.
- *Robust analytics.* BIM can be used to support complex analysis, including such tasks as clash detection, scheduling and sequencing (termed *4D modeling*), and energy analysis, and helps clarify decision making, resolve issues, and reduce delay in project processes.
- *Improved coordination.* BIM allows contractors and the multiple subcontractors involved in a construction project to virtually construct the building, identifying potential conflicts or clashes between building systems that would otherwise result in costly change orders if discovered in the field.
- *Improved project delivery.* BIM provides the capability to deliver a more coherent, structured, and complete body of data at project turnover.

BIM is a complex technology based on a collaborative approach to project production and facilities management. Organizations intent on deploying and leveraging BIM fully will need to evaluate and adopt new business processes in addition to the technology. Sharing, integrating, tracking, and maintaining a coherent building information model will affect all processes and participants that interact with that data.

BIM FOR FACILITY MANAGEMENT (FM)

BIM has been used most extensively in design and construction. Adoption and use for FM is a complex issue and is less straightforward than in AEC. There is no institutionalized "best practice" for using BIM in the FM sector. The use of any software technology, including BIM, in FM varies depending on organizational mission and the requirements of the facilities infrastructure supporting it. The informational needs of most facilities organizations are also quite diverse. An alphabet soup of enterprise data systems—computer-aided facility management (CAFM), CAD, integrated workplace management system (IWMS), computerized maintenance management systems (CMMS), enterprise resource planning (ERP), enterprise asset management (EAM), along with stand-alone software applications like spreadsheets currently support a wide range of information requirements in the facilities management arena.

Facility managers are continually faced with the challenge of improving and standardizing the quality of the information they have at their disposal, in order to meet day-to-day operational needs, as well as providing reliable data to building owners for life-cycle management and ongoing capital planning. An emerging technology, BIM is poised to offer a new level of functionality for managing buildings and the physical assets within them, in addition to similar benefits for FM, compelling firms in the building management industry to rapidly adopt BIM.

BIM technologies offers facilities managers and building owner/operators a powerful means to retrieve information from a visually accurate, virtual model of a physical facility. Unlike AEC professionals, these individuals are not necessarily trained in reading drawings, or able to retrieve pertinent data from an agglomeration of as-built documents. The technology is also fostering interactive information development and is capable of supporting the full building life cycle from planning through operations and maintenance. BIM will not necessarily replace the wide range of information technologies in use by facilities organizations but can support, leverage, and enhance them. Advantages of BIM for FM include:

- Unified information base, providing a building owner's manual.
- Effective support for analyses, particularly for energy and sustainability initiatives.
- Location-aware model of equipment, fixtures, and furnishings, replete with data.
- Support for emergency response and security management and scenario planning.

The business needs within a facilities management organization have very different requirements, workflows, and users than the AEC business needs for design and construction projects. As buildings become strategic assets in addition to financial assets, data retrieval to track spending and building performance is increasingly important. Aspects of building performance that can be monitored within a building information model may include work orders, space allocations, asset management, energy efficiency, security operations, and many other activities. Priorities for what is to be tracked in a BIM will vary with the organization. Although BIM authoring applications do not natively support facilities management, BIM can potentially be leveraged to facilitate many building life cycle requirements, some of which include:

- *BIM templates for efficient project development.* Organizations that have well-developed project standards can foster significant efficiencies in project development and execution by providing smart BIM templates to project teams. These customized templates can automate the population of building information models with project-specific program data that specify space and/or asset requirements. Hospitals (Figure 2.3), retail establishments, hotels, and corporate offices are some of the many organizations that can leverage standards with BIM reducing the current inefficiency of manual cross-checking and verification that are prevalent during project development.

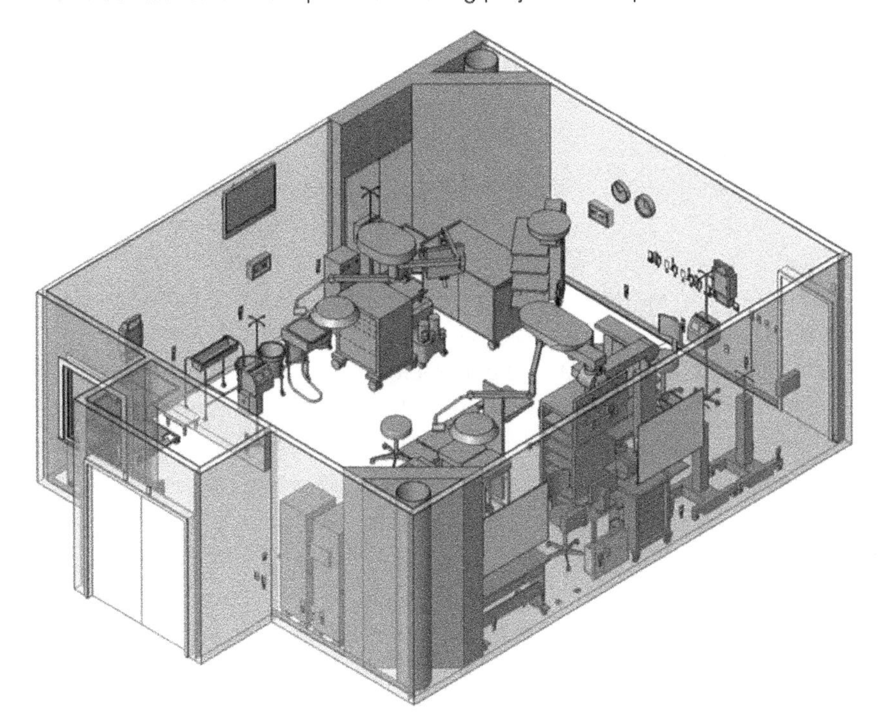

FIGURE 2.3 3D BIM template for an operating room. (U.S. Military Health Service).
Courtesy Design + Construction Strategies

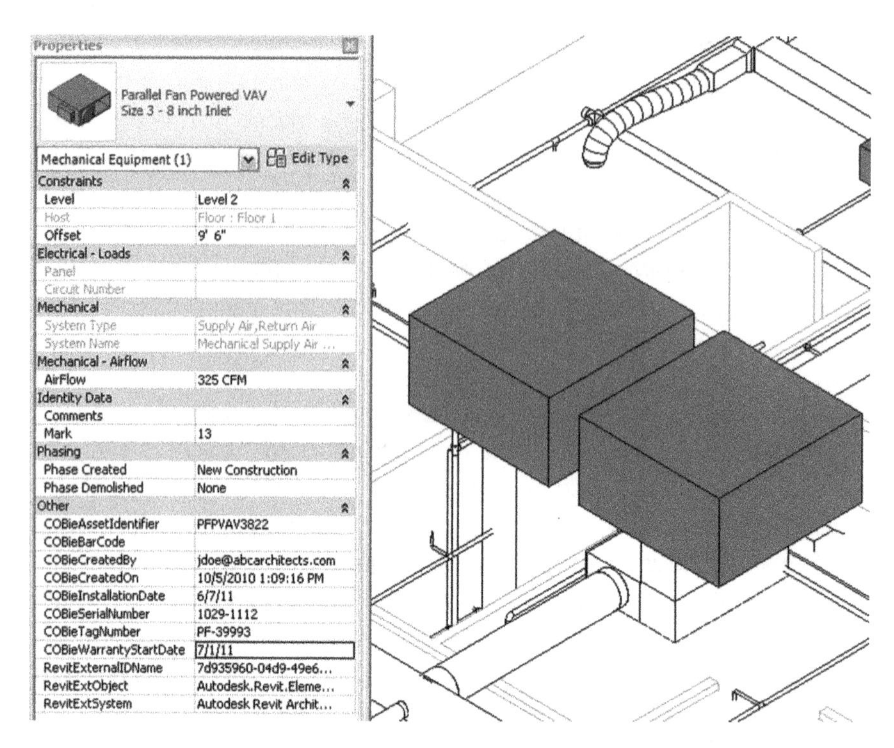

FIGURE 2.4 BIM mechanical component and COBie data.
Courtesy Design + Construction Strategies

- *Regularized project delivery.* Project BIMs can be defined and developed to incorporate organizational data to support facilities management data needs after project turnover. COBie[1] offers one framework for organizing building information delivery at turnover. Organizations might also chose to develop more specific mechanisms to meet their defined needs using various means, some of which include BIM software add-in applications (Figure 2.4).
- *Space management.* BIM incorporates real-life 3D spaces and objects and tracks attributes for these components. It can accommodate custom space management requirements and space measurement rules. BIM applications can also be extended to offer additional capabilities such as automated rules checking. Also, BIM offers a more intuitive display of space layouts, (Figure 2.5) supporting better management and communication of space assignments and change scenarios.
- *Visualization.* BIM's powerful capabilities for visualization, along with its extended capabilities to display potential changes over time (4D BIM), can effectively

[1] For more information on COBie or Construction Operations Building Information Exchange, visit the Whole Building Design Guide web site at www.wbdg.org/resources/cobie.php.

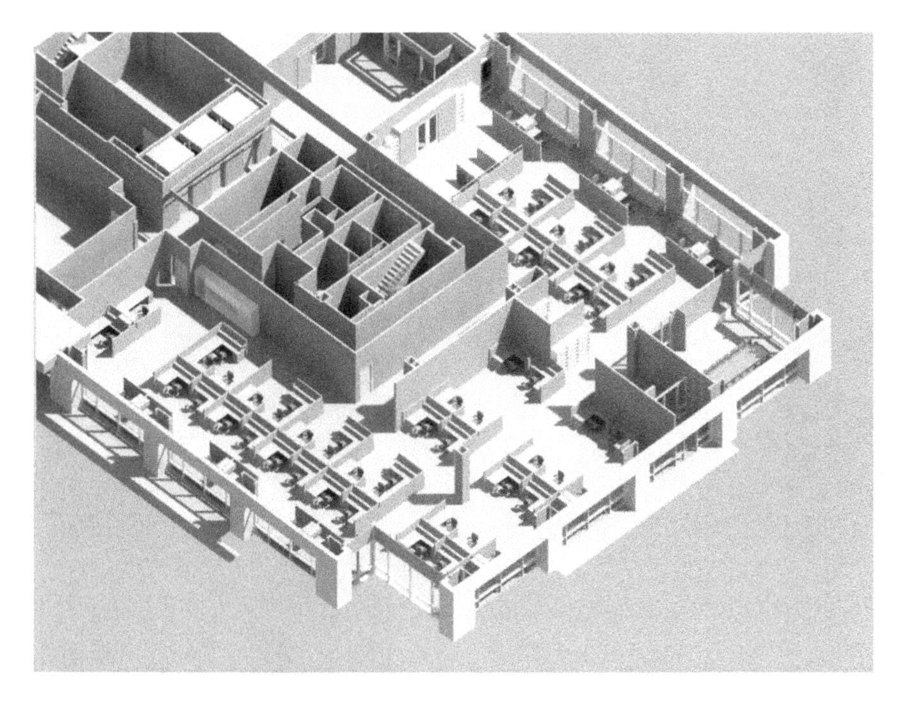

FIGURE 2.5 Spatial BIM model with furniture assets.
Courtesy Design + Construction Strategies

communicate critical building issues, especially in regard to scheduling and sequencing. Additional BIM decision support capabilities include clash detection, rules checking and validation, change tracking over time, and dynamic walkthroughs simulating proposed designs (Figure 2.6).

- *Energy and sustainability management.* Organizations are facing increased demand to increase the energy efficiency and sustainability of their facilities. BIM is well positioned to support a range of analytics, from conceptual energy analysis (Figure 2.7) to detailed engineering. It also can provide a means to track data and component information required for achieving a certification of sustainability for a building (Leadership in Energy and Environmental Design [LEED]). It can also support in-operation simulation, to help analyze the effect of system changes or renovations and retrofits.
- *Emergency management/security.* Since BIM provides an accurate three-dimensional representation of a building, it can assist in analyzing and planning for emergency response requirements and security measures. The technology offers many analytic capabilities that can provide 3D simulations of areas of concern, and provide support on range of issues, such as analyzing exit corridors and choke points, evaluating blast zones and setbacks, establishing surveillance camera cones of vision, among other uses. (Figure 2.8).

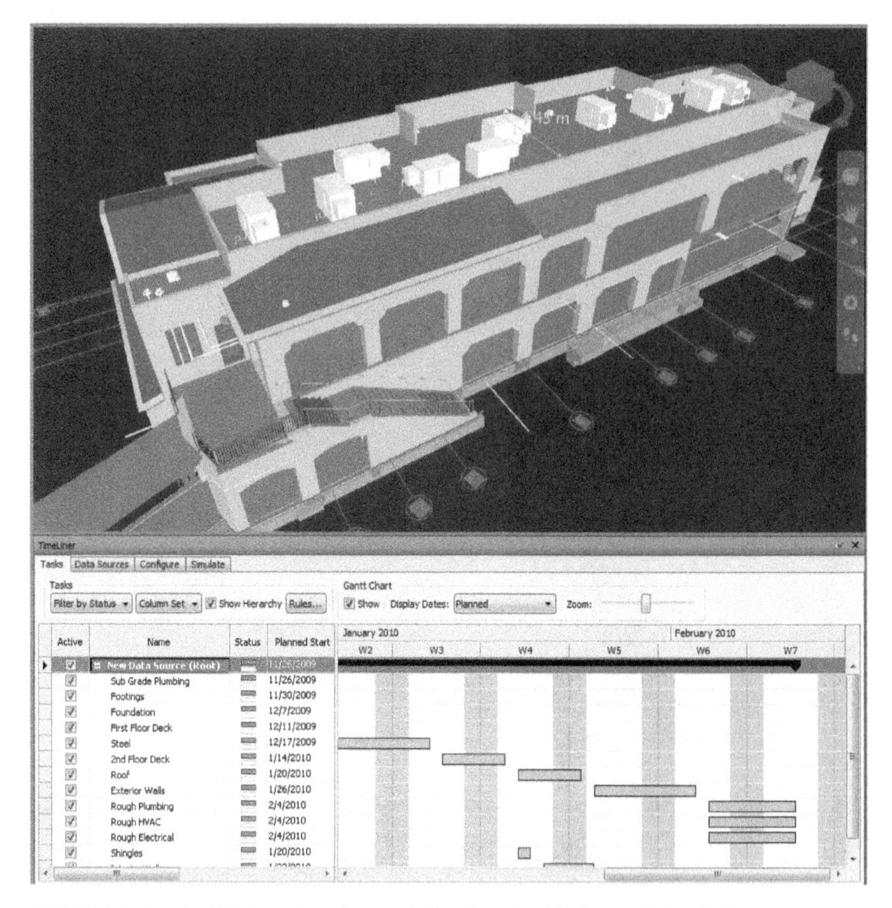

FIGURE 2.6 Autodesk Navisworks software 4D Timeline schedule feature linking BIM with project schedule.
Courtesy Design + Construction Strategies

- *Display of real-time data.* Some of the newest technologies being developed for BIM applications incorporate the capability to display real-time data analysis as gathered from sensors, directly on the geometry of the building model. This powerful capability not only allows for more intuitive feedback from an analysis (such as displaying lighting levels or temperature readings in a color range [Figure 2.9]) but stands to position BIM as a 3D visual portal capable of accessing both static and dynamic data on building components.

FM BIM will, without a doubt, need to integrate with multiple enterprise data systems, including existing facilities systems, geographic information systems, building automation systems, and even ERP systems. BIM will need to coexist with current CAD systems for some time to come. Organizations will need to develop BIM deployment plans and organizational standards to set the groundwork for successful

FIGURE 2.7 Thermal analysis (produced in Autodesk Ecotect).
Courtesy Design + Construction Strategies

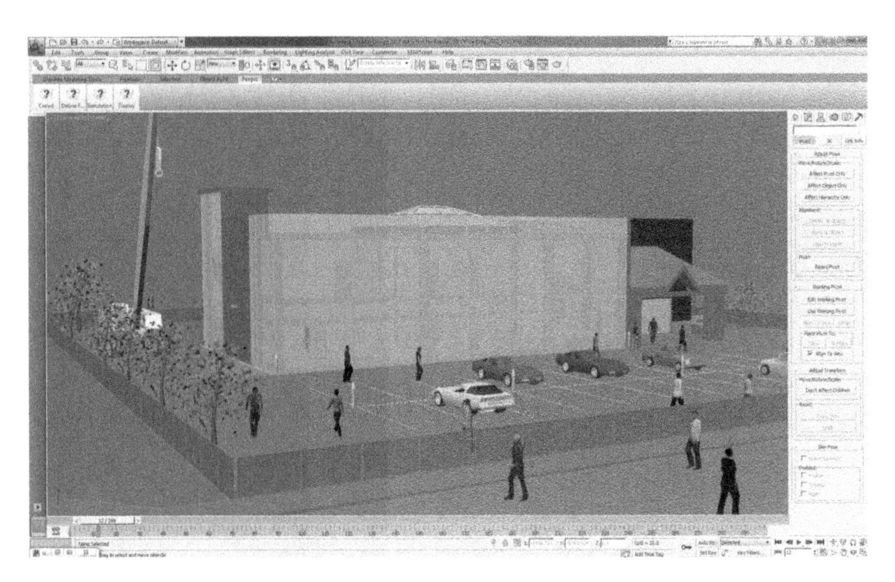

FIGURE 2.8 Simulation of human movement in a 3D model environment employing Autodesk Project Geppetto.
Courtesy of Design + Construction Strategies

FIGURE 2.9 Temperature sensor data displayed on a BIM model of an office building (Autodesk Research).

deployments of the technology. BIM applications will need to be more versatile for FM use, and incorporate different functionality and more datacentric facilities than the software employed by AEC practitioners. There is a critical need for a methodology and BIM definition that supports the rapid creation of BIM models for existing facilities. These are not design or construction models, but 3D visual data entities that support the information and workflow requirements of existing facilities with agility.

Laser scanning is an emerging technology that can serve to accurately capture the physical geometries of existing buildings in data files called *point clouds*. To support this data, many new and increasingly sophisticated software applications are also being developed that can interpret laser scan point cloud data into surfaces and objects, thus helping to speed the workflow for developing accurate and realistic 3D building models. Laser scanning can accurately capture complex geometries, such as piping runs, mechanical equipment room layouts, and other as-built conditions that would take enormous and often prohibitive manual efforts to document. These capabilities are incremental and not complete solutions.

New developments for FM BIM might include the development of rule sets to support improved information validation. These data sets would help automate BIM model checking, such as validating a delivered project model against the project program or evaluating exiting in the model against code requirements, among other use cases.

Also on the development horizon are BIM server applications. These technologies would extend beyond the current BIM authoring applications, with functionality to support, distribute, and manage BIM on an enterprise basis; capabilities to manage multiple building models and to provide support at an enterprise-level for multiple users, administer secure access, manage updates and version control, distribute multiple potential locations, and provide capabilities to exchange data with external enterprise information systems. Commercial software applications and tools that support building information modeling for FM are rapidly evolving. Sources for more information on current offerings can be found on webzines, technical conferences, and blogs.[2]

STANDARDS AND DATA EXCHANGE

Standards for data exchange in the building and facilities industry are undergoing development in order to support new information workflows and enabling technologies such as BIM. The National Building Information Model Standard (NBIMS), under the direction of the buildingSMART alliance (see references), is developing open standards to guide adoption and use of the technology. This guidance aims to establish standard definitions for building information exchanges.

Within the NBIMS efforts, several core components are being developed. Among these developments are *industry foundation classes* or IFCs, which are an open data format intended to facilitate the transfer and integrity of information between intelligent building models (Figure 2.10) and the information systems that play a role in building management. The buildingSMART alliance is responsible for the

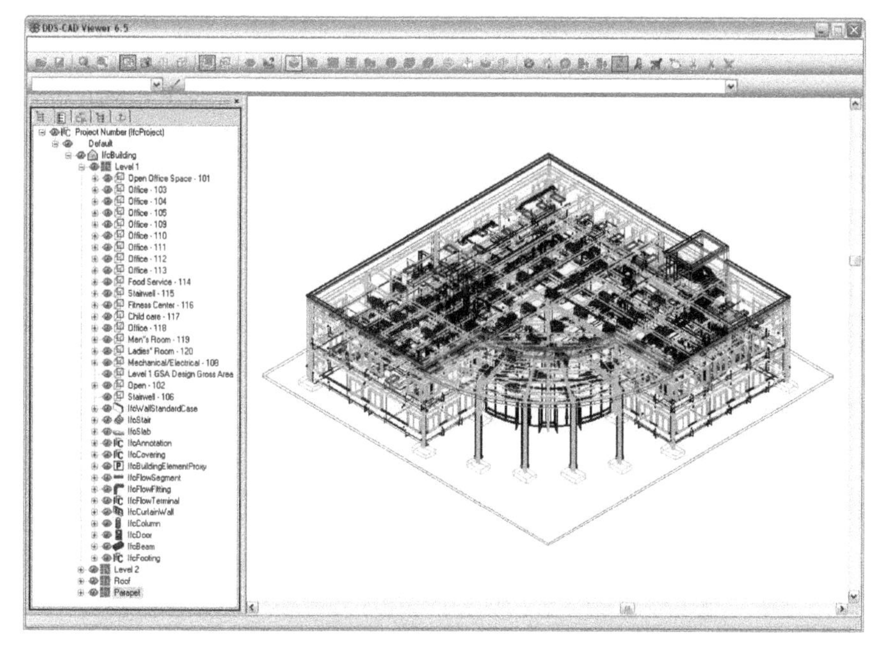

FIGURE 2.10 IFC-format building information model (displayed in an IFC viewing application).

Courtesy Design + Construction Strategies

[2] AECbytes, an online webzine authored by Lachmi Khemlani, is one such source. It can be found at www.aecbytes.com. Of note, this resource has reviewed BIM for FM software, which provides a good comparison of current applications on the market with varying capabilities for FM. See www.aecbytes.com/feature/2011/BIMforFM.html.

adoption of the IFC format for BIM data exchange since it is a vendor-independent, open-standard format that offers a framework to accommodate the many interdisciplinary information exchanges occurring during the building life cycle.

Building information models are the containers of data for a physical facility. The buildingSMART alliance (bSa) standards support user-driven initiatives for defining the information streams that will make the information model relevant to the facilities organizations for their business uses. NBIMS supported processes include developing sets of data exchange requirements termed *IFC model view definitions* or MVDs. These are subsets of the IFC schema and detail specific sets of exchange requirements, for example, a structural exchange.[3]

The Construction Operations Building information exchange (COBie) is one notable bSa initiative, sponsored and undertaken by the Engineering Research and Development Center (ERDC), U.S. Army Corps of Engineers, to improve project data delivery to owner/operators. COBie is a framework for organizing data developed and accumulated during the course of a building project for delivery to facilities owners and operators involved in life-cycle management (Figure 2.11). The COBie development project is evolving and is now in its second major version update, COBie2.

Although COBie may eventually provide a structure for the seamless transfer of data from BIM applications to FM data systems (IWMS, CAFM, or CMMS systems), in today's practice, COBie relies on organizing data in two forms: (1) a series of structured and related spreadsheets, and (2) as a bSa MVD. COBie information is compiled during different phases of a project by multiple participants: architects, engineers, constructors, specifiers, fabricators, and others. Only some of the data required in a typical COBie deliverable is, or can be, developed within a BIM authoring application. BIM software vendors are supporting the COBie framework by offering plug-in applications to support data development, including Bentley, ArchiCAD, Vectorworks, and Autodesk for its Revit BIM application.

Frameworks for organizing data for building projects have been around for years but have increased importance as we progress with BIM and the need to regularize and structure building information we develop and manage with technology. UniFormat has been a classification scheme used in North America but was developed long before digital buildings and workflows were initiated. Commercial BIM applications include default capabilities to assign UniFormat codes for model

[3] See the buildingSMART web site for additional information on IFC standards development and use, at http://buildingsmart.com/standards/ifc

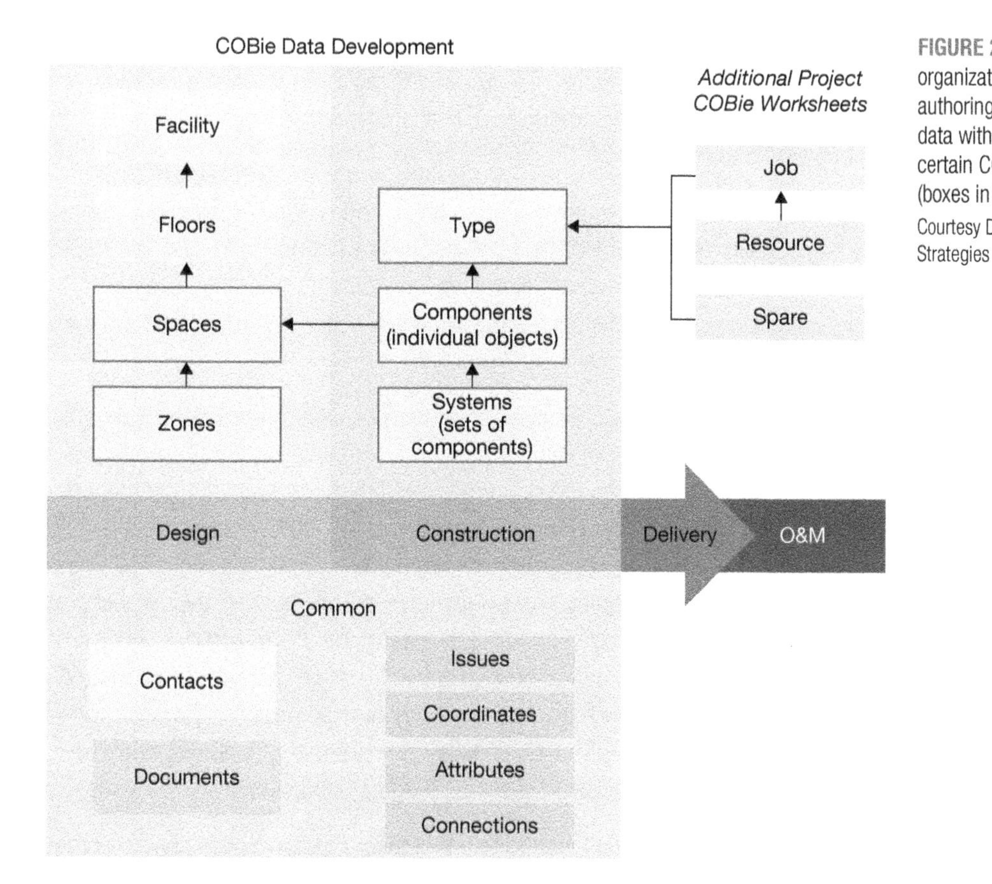

FIGURE 2.11 COBie organizational framework. BIM authoring applications affiliate data with model geometry for certain COBie components (boxes in blue).

Courtesy Design + Construction Strategies

components. OmniClass is a newer classification structure being developed for the construction industry. It supports the demand for highly articulated product information in BIM format.[4]

CHALLENGES OF BIM FOR FM

BIM is undergoing rapid adoption in the AEC industry but is still a young technology. It is just beginning to be adopted for use in FM.

Current BIM utilization reflects its primary focus, to design and construct a building project. Commercial BIM software tools are sophisticated applications, with functionality that is directed toward compiling or "authoring" a detailed information base, from which a project can be understood, executed, and completed.

[4] See the Construction Specification Institute's web site for more information on OmniClass, at www.omniclass.org.

BIM applications include complex features to assist designers and constructors. Data entry, retrieval, and reporting—important tools for managing facilities, are generally ancillary in these authoring applications and not necessarily easy to set up or intuitive to execute.

Design and construction workflows are a small part of the FM practice. Indeed, the functionality of current BIM authoring software will not be useful to a broad portion of the facility workforce. Software applications that fully leverage BIM information for facilities will most likely diverge in function from the authoring tools currently gaining acceptance in AEC practice.

Building information models delivered at project completion are a rich information source for FM, but not all of the information is valuable on a day-to-day basis within the broad range of an FM practice, where data retrieval, change management, and tracking costs and work activity are critical. Facility managers will need to detail and prioritize their information requirements—both to delineate the scope of a project's BIM deliverables and to define what to include in their working or FM building models, based on what can reasonably be maintained over time based on available resources and workflows. Components of BIM information bases that can be leveraged separately or collectively for facilities include a range of information subsets of BIM such as asset management, space management, sustainability and energy management, and egress and security management.

Maintaining building information models will require organizations to develop organizational BIM guidelines that both detail BIM project delivery requirements and define its usage within the facility practice. Deploying BIM within organizations that have many existing buildings in their portfolios will require a coherent road map and strategy as well. Many organizations maintain inconsistent inventories of building information, which may include CAD, scanned drawings, physical drawings, and point cloud files. Throwing BIM into the mix, without a strategy, will lead to waste, redundancy, and unsupportable needs of information maintenance.

There are many functional details and commercial software technologies that need further evolution to fully support BIM use in facilities management. Central among these will be software applications to maintain and manage BIM for organizational access—providing features such as versioning, user access, and privilege control and security. BIM requirements for data interoperability with enterprise systems is a complex topic, since facilities information systems are widely divergent, and will be a key issue with deploying BIM within FM.

For facilities organizations that choose to maintain an active inventory of BIM files in the native format of BIM authoring applications, it may be of concern that BIM software is not inexpensive. Also note that BIM application vendors are generally releasing new updates of their software packages on a fairly frequent update and revision cycle, at least annually. These facts may not dovetail well with the more static needs and budget constraints of an FM practice. Maintaining the currency of BIM files over time will be an issue for consideration for FM. Organizations will have to periodically, if not regularly, upgrade their BIM files to more current versions (if using commercial BIM software) since many vendors do not support backward compatibility between software versions. Maintaining currency of software versions to sync with outside contractors can be another hurdle for organization that have a lengthy procurement cycle, or that choose to maintain older BIM authoring software.

Many facilities organizations find it challenging to keep their CAD plans up to date, if they indeed have a consistent and up-to-date inventory in CAD format. Maintenance of a BIM inventory will be no easier. BIM brings along the additional challenge of updating affiliated data and object relationships, along with any (3D) geometry modifications. BIM authoring software is very complex, more so than CAD, requiring advanced user skills to master and employ. Facilities organizations might be challenged to keep adequately skilled BIM talent in-house, perhaps choosing to contract out any BIM updating or authoring requirements.

Current facilities organizations have many sources of data, often overlapping. The goal of integrating BIM will not be to add another information system, but to help regularize data delivery, clarify data ownership, and ease access to validated data. Technologies and work processes to support and fully integrate BIM with the range of applications and data repositories within facilities organizations will be an ongoing challenge as the technology is adopted within organizations.

Many questions have yet to be resolved with BIM technology in FM practice. For example, should an organization maintain a discreet, live BIM and extract, translate, and load data from it to an external enterprise data system, or will BIM pull information from a relational database from an existing enterprise system? How can those links be automated and easily managed? What software tools and systems can best leverage BIM for FM? Can BIM offer a new, intuitive means to unify disparate building information streams into a single, visual information portal?

BIM is a robust information technology, offering a lot of potential for facilities management. It is doubtful that it will be the single, game-changing application for FM; the design and construction arenas have learned that multiple applications with specific targeted capabilities is the best route to develop and utilize BIM data. The next few years will see facilities professionals and solutions vendors work in multiple arenas to leverage BIM's promise in order to deliver better information management to facilities management.

FM BIM IN PRACTICE: HEALTHCARE BIM CONSORTIUM'S INITIATIVES

Some efforts to extend BIM into facilities management are focused toward improving building information delivery at project turnover and defining standards, workflows, and tools to accommodate those exchanges.

The Healthcare BIM Consortium (HBC) has been created by health care owners[5] with the goal of finding and developing solutions for interoperability in order to fully support the facility life-cycle management (FLCM). A central focus of this effort will be to leverage BIM across the building life cycle and facilitating a seamless data transfer of relevant data across disciplines and among stakeholders in the process.[6]

Health care facilities are some of the most complex building types to build and maintain. In the current project development process, there are significant chokepoints in the process, where data is not easily exchanged between project participants. BIM is viewed as an enabling technology that can support an efficient, consolidated data framework for developing and managing health care facilities information for the full life cycle. Extending BIM for FM will involve capabilities to seamlessly pass organizational requirements in to the building information model; develop, analyze, and check the model during project development; and, at turnover, deliver a robust, integrated BIM from the project team to the owner/operator (Figure 2.12).

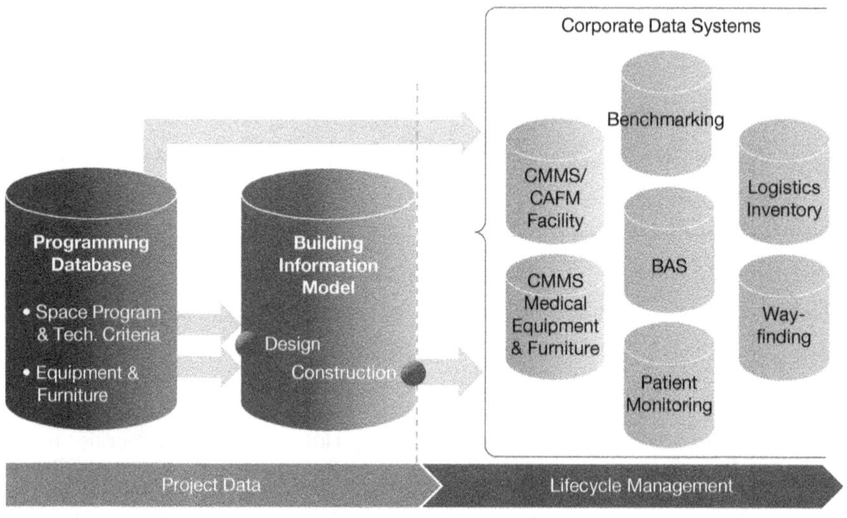

FIGURE 2.12 Data flow from health care planning systems to BIM, and at project turnover, to corporate systems. Chokepoints for data exchange currently exist during the project phase, where data is imported to BIM and at turnover, where information is delivered to the facility manager.

Adapted from slides created by Russ Manning/DoD MHS-PPMD

[5] This initiative is a project under the aegis of the bSa. See the bSa web site for more information at www.buildingsmartalliance.org/index.php/projects/activeprojects/162.

[6] For more information on MHS BIM initiatives, visit their web site at www.mhsworldclassfacilities.org/home/bim.

One of the most powerful capabilities of BIM is its potential to rapidly provide an accurate, detailed representation and inventory of a building, its components, and affiliated data. Hospital construction projects typically consist of hundreds of rooms, each containing a substantial quantity of equipment and furnishings. Automating the population of a building information model can save an enormous amount of project development time and also provide the capabilities to validate data, quantify project progress, and deliver complete and detailed project data to project participants and, ultimately, the client.

The Department of Veterans Affairs (VA) and the Department of Defense's Medical Health Service (MHS) are exploring automated tools to export data from their facilities planning programs into BIM models. These BIM add-in applications will also validate the model at any time during the design process against the project program. One BIM vendor[7] has developed a Revit add-on application that provides users with the capability to upload space and equipment data from the project program into the Revit model. Each room specified in the program has a list of equipment that is required to be contained within it. The software assists the Revit user in adding the required room to the project model, and then populates the room with equipment objects required by the program. The tool also provides the capability to run validation checks at any time to highlight rooms that might be out of compliance with the program and itemize missing equipment.

Figures 2.13 through 2.16 show a few snapshots of functions accomplished with the SEPS BIM Tool within Autodesk Revit. The VA and MHS use a medical facility planning data program called SEPS, which develops a detailed program for the new building. The SEPS BIM Tool reads this program's list of rooms and required equipment and specifications into Revit. Figure 2.13 shows a list of the program rooms that have been read into the workspace. The user selects rooms in the BIM and queues the SEPS BIM Tool to populate the space with the required equipment objects and specifications. Figure 2.14 shows how a compliance check, run with the tool, would highlight rooms (in green) that have the correct equipment objects. Figure 2.15 shows a 3D view of equipment objects (mass geometry) that have been placed in the BIM. In Figure 2.16, a rendered 3D view of an operating room in the BIM shows where, later in the project, initial mass objects have been replaced with more detailed versions.

A full life-cycle BIM will offer numerous benefits to facility owners. As BIM matures, additional workflows similar to those offered by SEPS BIM Tool will be introduced

[7] Autodesk's SEPS BIM Tool.

FIGURE 2.13 Room listings required by the project program, and affiliated equipment. Displayed in the Revit SEPS BIM Tool interface.
Courtesy Design + Construction Strategies

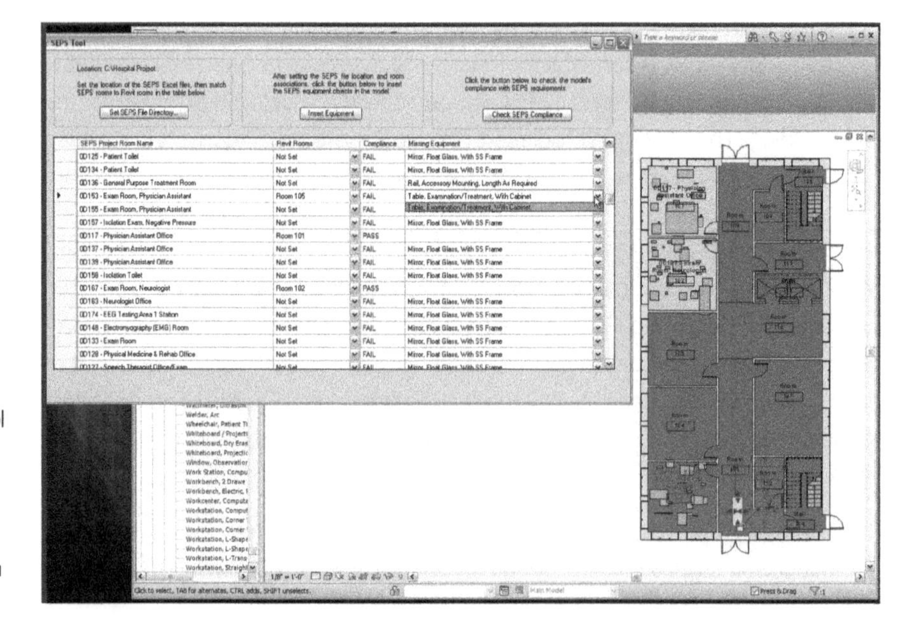

FIGURE 2.14 SEPS BIM Tool compliance check interface menu, with color-coded results displayed within the BIM application.
Courtesy Design + Construction Strategies

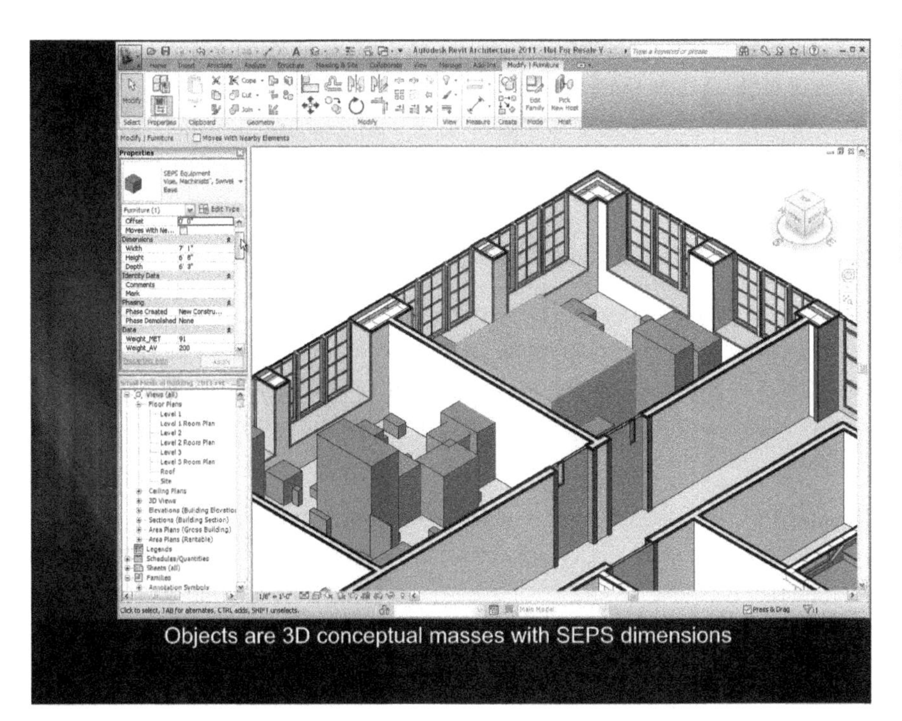

FIGURE 2.15 3D view showing equipment placed in the project model's rooms as mass objects, with data attributes attached (from the project program).
Courtesy Design + Construction Strategies

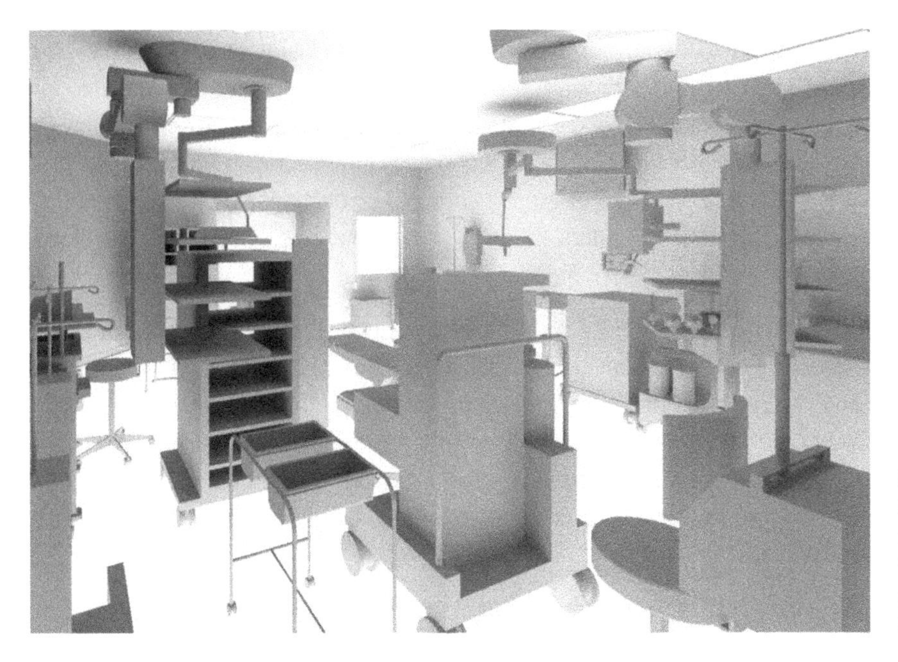

FIGURE 2.16 3D rendering of detailed SEPS equipment models that can be refined as the project progresses.
Courtesy Design + Construction Strategies

into practice. BIM's capability for automating workflows can reduce hundreds of hours of tedious data entry and cross-checking by the project team. It also provides quicker and more reliable validation of the project data model contributing greatly to improved project efficiencies.

EMERGING TECHNOLOGIES AND BIM

BIM is an evolving technology, undergoing rapid adoption throughout the building industry and continuing to integrate many new features and enhance capabilities. Innovations in the broader realm of information technology are also poised to support the complex, data-driven requirements for managing the building life cycle with BIM.

This section provides an overview on a few, important technologies that will enhance the capabilities of BIM—if not in current practice, certainly soon. Readers interested in available vendor solutions should search the Internet to access the most current market developments.

Cloud Computing

There are many definitions of what *cloud computing* comprises, but in essence, it's a set of pooled computing resources and services delivered over the Web. Cloud technologies are being adopted in many areas of information technology (IT), including those for supporting the AEC FM industry. Fueling the growing capabilities for cloud services is the increasingly fast infrastructure available for handling Internet data, along with decreased cost in cloud services. Key providers of cloud services include major technology firms, such as Amazon, Google, Microsoft, and IBM, and they are expanding their offerings. The term *infrastructure as a service* (IaaS) refers to the IT infrastructure services offered by cloud providers.

A private, as opposed to a public, cloud is an IT infrastructure configured to support a single organization. The cloud is generally centralized within one data center (or premise), and supported with a fast, large-capacity network. A private cloud can reside within a company or be leased from a service provider. There are multiple strategies to configure private clouds to meet the specific requirements of an organization and transition some, or all, of a firm's IT operations to "the cloud."

BIM applications and data typically reside primarily on user's desktops (clients) and on shared servers within an organization's intranet, but vendors are expanding cloud-based offerings. The expanding use of building information modeling, subsequent growth in data supporting BIM, and increasingly complex interactivity involved with collaborative BIM practices is driving organizations employing BIM to improve IT infrastructures to support the technology. Enterprise BIM frameworks will increasingly rely on cloud architectures.[8]

Cloud-based environments offer multiple advantages. They can decrease the in-house IT requirements for a firm, reducing the deployment and system management time burdens for company staff, as well as the investment in new and refreshed hardware. Additionally, security, business continuity, and disaster recovery requirements can be shifted to the cloud provider.

There are some disadvantages to cloud services. Organizations concerned about their security and privacy or those requiring a high degree of control over their infrastructure may not be comfortable handing over their data to a third party. A true comparison of costs may be hard to achieve—companies will have to carefully evaluate service plans and details for each offering. The flexibility and integration capabilities of cloud services also must be carefully evaluated as well.

An additional term affiliated with cloud computing is *software as a service* (SaaS). These applications are hosted on the Web and accessed by subscription users via a browser. BIM vendors are also positioning their coordination and collaboration applications for the cloud as SaaS applications. The cloud's capability to scale up and support more computationally intensive applications is providing a compelling platform to support BIM-related analytics such as computational fluid dynamics (CFD), used in mechanical and structural engineering, or advanced rendering and visualization. BIM usage will differ for FM users, but as BIM capabilities for FM advance, the potential to support intensive analyses such as real-time commissioning could be accommodated by cloud-based services. Core BIM authoring applications are not SaaS based but can be hosted in a private cloud infrastructure (IaaS).

Mobile Computing for FM

Mobile and wireless technologies are democratizing information access throughout all facets of modern life and will enhance the information environments within the building industry as well. Facilities management includes many diverse activities, such as inventories, inspections, repair, maintenance, and alterations, occurring throughout a facility.

[8] The buildingSMART alliance has identified cloud service concept as an important strategy for BIM. See the Next Steps in its Stakeholder Activity Model project at www.buildingsmartalliance.org/index.php/nbims/about/bimactivities/.

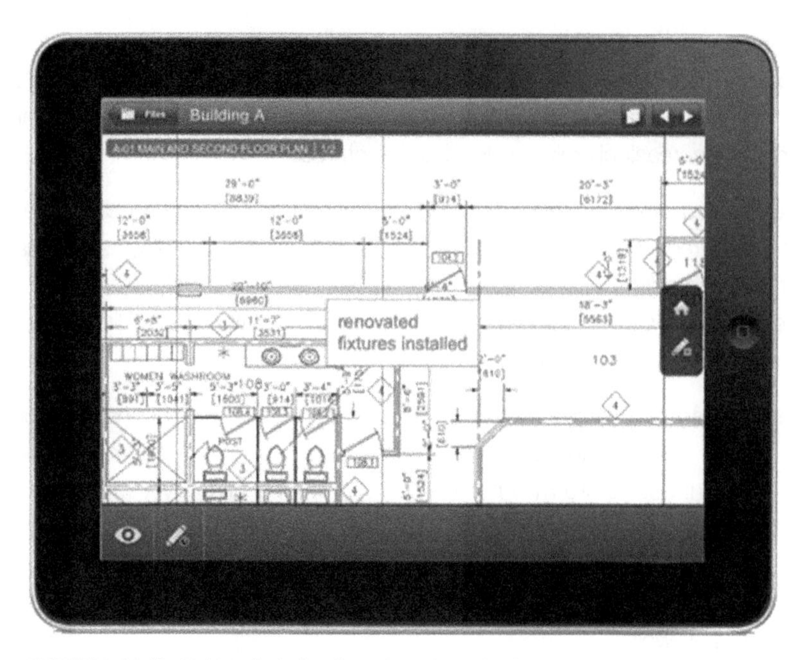

FIGURE 2.17 iPad tablet displaying floor plan, with red-lining, commenting capabilities.
Image by author

Mobile technology will provide a means of retrieving, collecting, updating, and sharing information to support these activities, where and when they are occurring. This will not only provide enhanced support for the tasks at hand but improve the currency of information maintained by the organization. Figure 2.17 illustrates an example of mobile technology use.

At present, building information modeling centers primarily on BIM authoring applications,[9] which are desktop-centric applications. The practice of BIM will differ for facilities management, whose requirements are focused more on the retrieval and update of building data. The development of FM BIM servers, portals, and BIM-capable IWMS applications will also fuel development of lightweight client apps and provide field access to a host of valuable information—work order data, repair plans, videos, and parts data are just some of the items retrievable from enterprise systems. Wireless mobile devices will be a key component of this infrastructure.

Mobile apps that support building-related activities are increasingly available. Most of the current BIM-related apps (or in most cases, 3D CAD) function primarily as model viewers. Annotation and markup features are also becoming available. Vendor sites and the apps store for devices are the best place to check for current app offerings.

[9] Such as Autodesk Revit, Bentley, AECOsim, and Graphisoft ArchiCAD.

Mobile and RFID Technologies

Radio-frequency identification (RFID) is a wireless noncontact system that transmits information from a tagged object to a scanning device. Although similar to bar codes, RFID tags do not require a direct line of sight to be read, can be read faster and at greater distances, and are more rugged and often reusable.

Construction companies are using BIM along with mobile and RFID technologies to expedite their project processes. A significant use of these technologies is in tracking project materials from the design and detailing phase (in BIM), through fabrication and into construction. Using RFID tracking is helping to foster innovative efficiency practices in the industry, notably Lean Construction,[10] and are returning real cost savings to project stakeholders.

RFID offers facilities managers a means to tag and track assets. Since BIM, at its core, is a database, an RFID identifier can be affiliated to any component in the model. Mobile technologies can enhance this capability, by accessing that BIM data and displaying it to FM users on their mobile device. This can be useful for various scenarios: displaying assets behind walls, under floors, or above ceilings while in a space; displaying assets missing from rooms but resident in the model of-record; and tracking staging locations for assets during renovations, among many more.

Mobile and Cloud Technologies

Mobile cloud computing refers to an infrastructure where both the storage and the processing of data happen outside of the mobile device. Some examples of mobile cloud computing in use today include mobile Gmail and Google maps. BIM vendors are configuring their collaboration applications for the cloud and publishing apps to support mobile devices.[11]

The cloud may soon become a disruptive force in mobile computing, eventually becoming part of the default infrastructure supporting the data operation behind mobile applications.

An industry example of the use of, and expansive growth in, mobile and cloud technologies for the AEC industry can be seen in the software provider Vela Systems. Founded in 2005 from a base of research done at the MIT Center for Real Estate and the Harvard Graduate School of Design, the company centers its software offerings on delivering information to professionals in the field. In

[10] For more information, visit the Lean Construction Institute web site at www.leanconstruction.org.

[11] Reference Autodesk's Buzzsaw and Bentley's ProjectWise software applications.

2012, Autodesk, Inc. acquired Vela and will integrate the mobile technologies with its BIM and project management software offerings.[12]

AUGMENTED REALITY

Virtual reality (VR) is a computer simulation of a real environment. Many people are familiar with VR from computer gaming or online applications like Second City. Augmented reality (AR) takes this a step further—it is the use of VR in combination with the real world to provide an "enhanced experience" for the user. AR can be an immersive environment, where a user with headgear or goggles "moves" through a 3D virtual scene. Alternatively, AR can present a view of the real world, with data layered on top of a real-life scene.

Microsoft's Kinect is a motion-sensing input device for the Xbox video game console. It enables users to control and interact with the Xbox 360 without the need to touch a game controller, through a natural user interface using gestures and spoken commands. The device has a software development kit with which many developers are building customized applications. The lowered cost entry point from the Kinect is fueling a new route for creative development of new approaches in viewing 3D data, interactively. This technology could be developed to allow users to navigate through 3D building models interactively, similar to environments provided in game engines (Figure 2.18).

FIGURE 2.18 BIM model imported into the Unity game engine, with navigation capabilities provided by the Kinect device.

Image from prototype developed by DCStrategies. Courtesy Design + Construction Strategies

[12] Currently, the Autodesk 360 family of hybrid cloud-based and on-premises software solutions.

FIGURE 2.19 Tablet device displaying ducting above ceiling from a BIM.
Image by author

AR and mobile applications are being developed to provide diverse information uses, from locating restaurants to navigating the New York subway.[13] These technologies offer intriguing capabilities for building-related activities, such as displaying energy use data on the building façade as you walk around the facility's perimeter, viewing the installed ductwork above a ceiling from a BIM model on a tablet as you walk through a room (Figure 2.19), seeing the underground utility information for an infrastructure BIM as you walk across the parking lot, listing asset records as you inspect a room (Figure 2.20), and many other intriguing possibilities. As this article is written, none of these tools are commercially available, but tablet technology is improving rapidly, and they could be available shortly.

SENSOR DATA

Optimizing the comfort and efficiency for an operational building is complex, requiring well-defined zones that are tuned to its human occupants, equipment, and their interactions and use. Sensors are delivering detailed information about

[13] See "Top 15 Augmented Reality Apps for iPhone and iPad" *PCWorld* webzine, April 10, 2012; www.pcworld.com/article/253530/top_15_augmented_reality_apps_for_iphone_and_ipad.html.

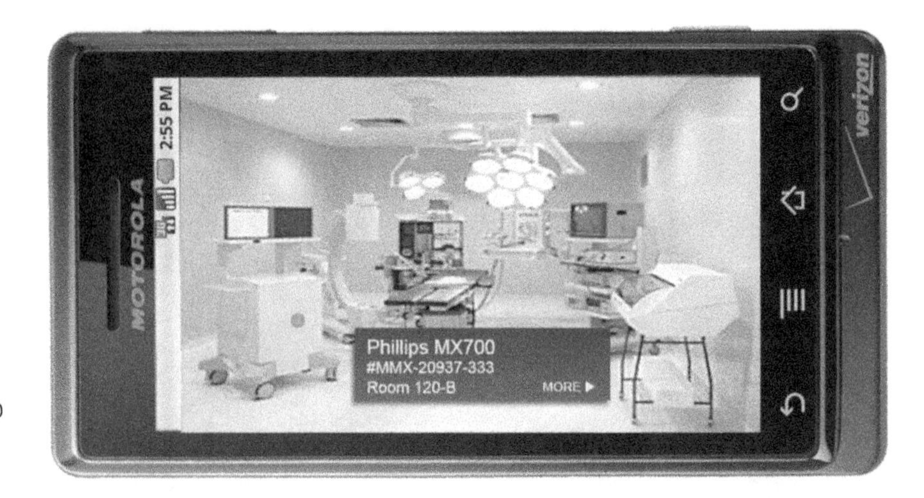

FIGURE 2.20 Prototype augmented reality asset app on smartphone.
Image by author

the operation of the building, as it is occurring in real time. However, sensor systems produce a tremendous amount of data. As capabilities for handling large data sets improve, methods to view, analyze, and evaluate the data will provide improved decision support for facility managers.

BIM can provide a visual framework to display performance data. Presently, this is done with complex model simulations, such as CFD analytics conducted to test the design for mechanical and structural systems in a building design. Building models could also provide a 3D framework on which real-time data performance feedback, such as power use, could be displayed.[14] Capabilities to aggregate and analyze complex building performance behavior will also support capabilities to perform more accurate system modifications and assist processes such as continuous commissioning throughout the building life cycle.

BIM COMPONENT DATA

New technologies and applications are changing business practices for AEC FM professionals. In conjunction with new technical innovations, a burgeoning ecosystem of information "products" is emerging that will support

[14] For one detailed technical article, see "Big Data from the Built Environment" by Azam Khan and Kasper Hornbaek, from the SIGCHI Conference of 2011, www.autodeskresearch.com/pdf/large309a-khan.pdf.

automated workflows with detailed data resources. These data repositories can provide detailed data for a range of activities, a few examples of which include climate databases to support energy analysis, geographic information system (GIS) map services that provide base data for a range of location-bases analytics, and, for BIM, manufacturers' libraries of component objects for use in model development.

Prebuilt models of building components will help AEC teams accelerate the design process and deliver high-quality, as-built drawings to owners. Data-rich, geometrically accurate component models will support multiple workflows, including energy and sustainability analyses; quantity take-offs and cost estimating; security analysis; fire and life safety calculations; and so on. For use with FM, component models that contain accurate and complete data will provide information previously filed away in data sheets or product manuals (Figures 2.21a and 2.21b).

One prominent vendor-based resource hosting BIM component models is the Autodesk Seek[15] cloud-based Web service, containing model components, drawings, and specifications developed by product manufacturers. Traditional building product resources are also providing BIM collateral. McGraw-Hill Sweets Network, long a provider of product information to the AEC industry, hosts a growing library of proprietary building models,[16] as does ARCAT,[17] a company providing resources for building product specifications.

STANDARDS

To help align the selection of building material, products, and equipment with new practices and technologies, the Specifiers' Properties information exchange (SPie) project[18] is being developed to establish standards for equipment data. Its objective is to create a set of product templates that can be used by manufacturers to export product data into an open-standard format to be used by designers, specifiers, builders, owners, and operators.

[15] See the Autodesk Seek web site at http://seek.autodesk.com/.

[16] See the Sweets BIM Collection at http://construction.com/BIM/.

[17] See the web site for Arcat, Inc.'s BIM object library at www.arcat.com/bim/bim_objects.shtml.

[18] The effort is being coordinated by CSI, National Institute of Building Science's buildingSMART alliance, SCIP, and USACE Engineer Research and Development Center. See the project web site for the most up-to-date developments, at www.buildingsmartalliance.org/index.php/projects/activeprojects/32.

(a)

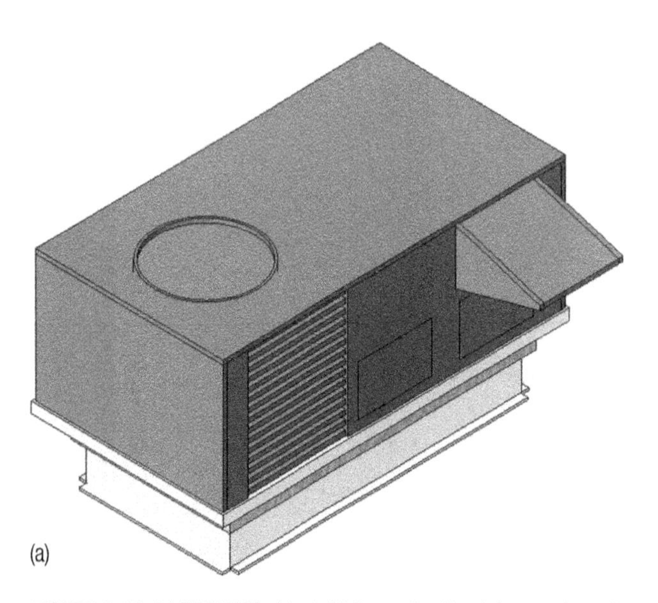

(b)

Constraints	
Clearance Bottom	1' 2"
Level	Level 1
Host	Level : Level 1
Offset	0' 0"
Construction	
Right Economizer	☑
Left Economizer	☑
Curb Exists	☑
Convenience Outlet	☑
Clearance<Generic Models>	Include Clearance
Electrical	
Convenience Outlet Voltage	115.00 V
Electrical - Loads	
Panel	
Circuit Number	
Plumbing	
Actual Heater Gas Flow	0 GPM
Actual Condensate Drain Flow	0 GPM
Mechanical	
System Classification	
System Name	
Mechanical - Airflow	
Actual Supply Air Flow	0 CFM
Actual Return Air Flow	0 CFM
Identity Data	
Serial Number	
Comments	
Mark	98
Phasing	
Phase Created	New Construction
Phase Demolished	None
Energy Analysis	
Variable Air Volume Integrate...	0.000000
Constant Volume Integrated ...	0.000000
Analysis Results	
Total Static Pressure	0.0000 in-wg
Staged Furnace Steps	0
Staged Furnace Output	300000.00 Btu/h
Staged Furnace Input	375000.00 Btu/h
Sensible Cooling Capacity	0.00 Btu/h
Return Air Dry Bulb Tempera...	0.00 °F
Outdoor Air Wet Bulb Tempe...	0.00 °F
Nominal Voltage	0.00 V
Design Supply Air Flow	0 CFM
Cooling Nominal Input Power	0.00 W
Cooling Air Temperature On ...	0.00 °F
Actual Exhaust Air Flow	0 CFM
Other	
CTRL Output Step 3	900000.00 Btu/h
CTRL Output Step 2	600000.00 Btu/h
CTRL Output Step 1	300000.00 Btu/h
CTRL Input Step 3	112500.00 Btu/h
CTRL Input Step 2	750000.00 Btu/h
CTRL Input Step 1	375000.00 Btu/h
CTRL Curb Height	1' 2"

FIGURE 2.21 (a) BIM HVAC object; (b) Properties (data). Images by author.

REFERENCES

buildingSMART. http://buildingsmart.com/Construction Operations Building information exchange (COBie). Whole Building Design Guide. www.wbdg.org/resources/cobie.php

International Alliance for Interoperability. www.iai-interoperability.org, including the IFC, Industry Foundation Classes specifications: www.iai-international.org/Model/IFC(ifcXML)Specs.html

National 3D-4D Building Information Modeling Program. U.S. Government Services Administration (GSA). www.gsa.gov/portal/content/105075

OmniClass, A Strategy for Classifying the Built Environment. www.omniclass.org

Open BIM Standards for Communication Throughout the Facilities Industry. buildingSMART alliance, a council of the National Institute of Building Sciences. www.buildingsmartalliance.org/

Veterans Administration Building Information Lifecycle Vision. www.cfm.va.gov/til/bim/BIMGuide/lifecycle.htm

Owner BIM for FM Guidelines

3

Paul Teicholz

INTRODUCTION

For owners and facility management (FM) staff who wish to implement the use of building information modeling (BIM) for the life-cycle requirements of buildings (new and remodels or renovations), there is a need to understand the goals of linking BIM to FM. These involve careful planning of how BIM will be used for modeling and capturing the geometry and data, how data will be collected and by whom during design, construction and commissioning, what naming standards will be used, how the data will be organized so that they can be linked (or imported) into the FM systems used for the building, and then how the FM staff should be involved in this process to maximize the effectiveness of the results. These are all very significant efforts that involve planning, monitoring, education, and follow-through. This chapter introduces owner BIM for FM guidelines that cover these issues (and more) to introduce the reader to how they can be addressed. These guidelines were selected because they represent a cross-section of owner types (U.S. government, state government, and private) and cover many different types of buildings (offices, laboratories, hospitals, and academic facilities). Despite these differences, they have much in common, and all are focused on creating owner value from the data in BIM models (with emphasis on the information component of BIM) and how these data can be integrated with building management systems. These include computerized maintenance management systems (CMMSs), computer-aided facility management (CAFM), energy management systems (EMSs), and geographic information systems (GISs).

The General Services Administration (GSA) Guidelines are presented in the greatest detail because they represent the most comprehensive approach to linking BIM to FM requirements. These guidelines are among the first to be used on actual projects where contractual requirements specified how BIM was to be used, how FM data was to be collected and transmitted or integrated with FM systems (including the use of the Construction Operations Building information exchange [COBie]), how the as-built BIM model was to be updated as modifications to the building occurred, and so on. There are also some case study results presented that give an idea of the difficulties that project teams had and how they dealt with these problems. These experiences clearly show that project teams and FM staffs are struggling to accomplish BIM FM integration and that the learning curve is a steep one.

Traditional approaches to the BIM FM integration problem have involved paper documents (drawings, equipment data, warranty document, etc.) that were given to the owner as submittals by members of the project team (mainly the GC and subcontractors), often considerably after the delivery of a building. These submittals can be all types of documents for all types of equipment that are thrown into one file, for example, "lighting fixtures," that may be 400 pages long, with no particular order.[1] The FM staff, if using CMMS to manage maintenance, then had to enter these data into the system, a time-consuming and error-prone activity. Often, it was discovered that needed information was not available or that multiple trips to the file room were required. This approach is expensive, can hinder efficient procedures for maintenance, and increases building costs. It leads to reactive rather than proactive facility maintenance. For all these reasons, a better approach is needed that exploits the data that are developed for BIM models and can be enhanced by additional data needed for FM. This information is developed during design, construction, and commissioning and is an excellent reason for facility managers to be involved in these processes. This collaboration is greatly enhanced by nontraditional procurement practices such as integrated project delivery (IPD). The building standards presented here cover both traditional and nontraditional approaches.

[1] To avoid this problem, owners need to insist in their guidelines that providers split the documents by type (i.e., Product Datasheet, Warranty Manual, Installation Instructions, Parts Diagram, etc.) and by each product type (COBie:Type).

Following the detailed description of the GSA Guideline for BIM FM integration, other BIM guidelines are summarized. Most of these focus primarily on the use of BIM during design and construction and touch only slightly on BIM FM integration. This focus reflects the early implementation of BIM for these early stages of the building life cycle. However, there is some discussion of BIM FM integration, and more can be expected in the future.

GSA GUIDELINES

The BIM for FM Guidelines developed by the GSA,[2] working with a team of inside and outside consultants, is part of a series of eight that cover the use of BIM over the life cycle of a building. The GSA Guides are more advanced than many other guidelines and represent a work in progress and their experience provides feedback from GSA projects. These are as follows (see www.gsa.gov/portal/content/103735):

- 01: Overview
- 02: Spatial Program Validation
- 03: 3D imaging
- 04: 4D Phasing
- 05: Energy Performance and Operation
- 06: Circulation and Security Validation
- 07: Building Elements
- 08: Facility Management (the guide being reviewed here)

The BIM for FM Guideline (08) includes five sections as follows:

- Section 1: BIM and FM—Overall vision and objectives for using BIM for facility management.
- Section 2: Implementation Guidance—Implementation guidance to GSA associates and consultants.
- Section 3: Modeling Requirements—BIM object and attribute requirements for use during FM.
- Section 4: Technology Assessment—Technology requirements for creating and using BIMs for FM.
- Section 5: Pilot Projects—Description of pilot projects for BIM and FM.
- Section 6: Biography

We now present an overview of each of the preceding sections.

[2] The description of the GSA BIM for FM Guidelines that follows is extracted in abbreviated form from the document available on the Web.

BIM and FM—Overall Vision and Objectives for Using BIM for Facility Management

This section makes the business case for using BIM for FM and describes the data requirements to support GSA business needs. Figure 3.1 illustrates their vision of integrating BIM with FM systems to support the life-cycle data needs of a building.

The GSA's vision is to streamline how BIM is used in support of BIM FM integration throughout the facility's life cycle from planning through operations. A central facility repository will be a key component in managing the facility information. The central facility repository plans to integrate and house 3D object parametric data; mechanical, electrical, and plumbing (MEP) system layouts; asset management data; facility management data; building materials and specifications; 2D data; laser scanning data; and real -time sensor data and controls. Through the central facility repository, it is envisioned that buildings'

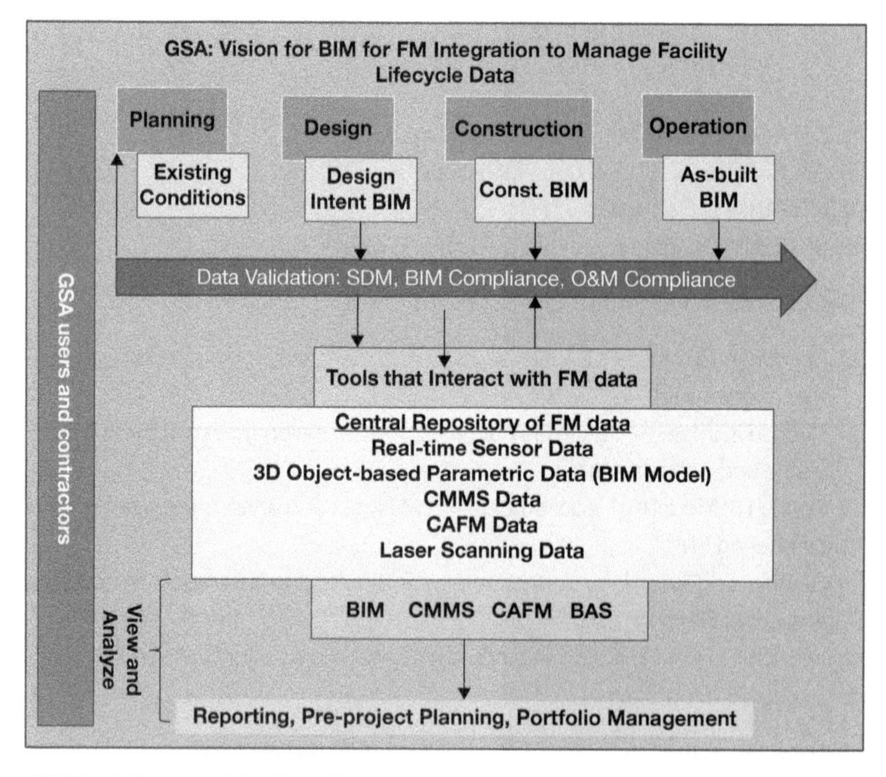

FIGURE 3.1 Illustrates their vision of integrating BIM with FM systems to support the life-cycle data needs of a building.

Source: BIM Guide Series 08- Facility Management V1

BIMs would be managed and maintained for all types of projects. Furthermore, operations and maintenance (O&M) personnel would be able to view the BIMs. Software tools would "sit on top" of the central facility repository to provide security, search and view capabilities, version control, notifications on updates, and analysis and reporting.

While the needs of each owner agency are similar, there can be unique requirements for a given owner not specifically covered in this section (e.g., the need for unique sensor data to monitor vibration). However, because the GSA is the largest property owner in the United States and manages 362 million square feet in 9,624 buildings located in all 50 states and 6 U.S. territories, it is highly likely that the GSA encounters almost all building FM requirements. To allow them to meet this wide range of needs, they have developed three tiers of requirements.

Tier 1

Tier 1 applies to all buildings, both new and renovations. It is mandated because of the significant benefits of an accurate 3D geometric model to many downstream users. These include the value of being able to calculate accurate areas of spaces, floor covering types for maintenance contracts, and being able to identify locations of building systems and equipment concealed in walls or above ceilings without opening those walls or ceilings.

Tier 1 requires:

- BIM models must have the objects listed below in a valid 3D geometry representation that are needed to support facility management. These objects shall be provided in both native BIM-authoring formats and open-standard formats such as industry foundation class (IFC) and COBie.

The required objects include:

- All objects required by BIM Guide Series 02 (spatial requirements for spaces, walls, doors, windows, slabs, columns, beams)
- Ceilings
- Lighting systems, fixtures, and equipment
- Communication systems and equipment
- Electrical systems and equipment
- Mechanical systems and equipment
- Plumbing systems and equipment
- Irrigation systems and equipment
- Fire protection systems and equipment

- Vertical and horizontal transportation equipment
- Furniture and specifications
- Specialty systems and equipment

  Project teams shall develop a BIM Execution Plan outlining how these BIM requirements will be met.

Tier 2

Tier 2 applies to larger and more complex buildings. Equipment inventories or facility equipment lists form the basis for many facility management activities. Equipment inventories are used for equipment condition assessments, energy management, emergency response, warranties, manpower calculations, and so forth. Operations and maintenance incurs additional time, manpower, and costs with inaccurate or lack of equipment inventories. The failure to properly track equipment inventories reduces the reliability of project scope and cost estimates, impairs emergency response, and degrades the ability to make executive decisions.

Tier 2 requires:

- Equipment information—globally unique identifier (GUID) machine interpretable unique identifier that provides a link between BIM and an FM system (including building automation system [BAS], energy management system [EMS], computerized maintenance management system [CMMS], etc.), make, model, serial number, warranty information, and maintenance instructions. The project teams in conjunction with Public Building Service (PBS) Service Center will define the list of equipment types that are required in the BIM Execution Plan.

Tier 3

Tier 3 is applied as an optional requirement. If as-designed BIM with energy analysis is captured, the data can eventually be integrated with a facility BAS, enabling model-based analysis and optimization. Ideally, the energy analysis would enable building operators to understand when and how actual performance differs from predicted performance. This allows a feedback loop of lessons learned and troubleshooting. During operations, it enables building operators to understand how the building was intended to be operated to achieve optimum performance. Feedback regarding the actual operation of the building will then become critical to creating more realistic and accurate energy predictions during design.

Tier 3 requires:

- As-designed BIM with energy analysis predictions.

Implementation Guidance to GSA Associates and Consultants

Implementing BIM for FM requires the following:

Identify Project Opportunities

GSA associates are encouraged to gather appropriate team members (e.g., project manager, facility manager, spatial data manager, regional BIM champion) to discuss potential opportunities for capturing FM data and getting this data into FM systems.

Define an Implementation Strategy

Defining an implementation strategy consists of defining what information will be required, how it will be used, and when the FM information will be collected and by whom. If an existing facility will be subject to a small renovation, then it may not be practical to create a BIM model. In this case, it still may be possible to create an equipment inventory that can be used for CMMS. Each case must be evaluated separately.

Assessing how the project delivery approach (traditional design/bid/build, design/build, or other alternative project delivery methods) will affect the contractual responsibility for information delivery. Requirements and contract language must be geared to the scope and responsibilities of the respective parties. Under a traditional project delivery approach, there will be multiple contracts and multiple responsible parties for BIM development and deliverables. In this case, the A/E and the contractors would each have BIM and COBie deliverables defined in their contracts. Alternative project delivery approaches, such as Design/Build (D/B), Construction Manager at Risk (CMR), and Integrated Project Delivery (IPD) blur the distinctions between the design and construction teams. In the cases of D/B or D/B-B, a single entity would be responsible for the delivery of the information required for facility management.

Standardize the Identification, Classification, and Coding of Equipment

One early lesson learned from pilot projects (GSA FM Guideline Section 5) is the importance of standardizing what information is required, what that information is called (e.g., asset identification number) and the allowable terminology for that information. For example, the equipment identification consists of the standard equipment acronym and a sequence number.

In one pilot project, HNTB received an export of 1,018 Maximo records in .xls format for Building 105 in the GSA's Good Fellow Complex in St. Louis, Missouri (see www.hntb.com for more background). One of the goals of the project was to match the Maximo records to the corresponding equipment in a Revit BIM. Despite a comprehensive review of existing building documentation as well as field verification efforts, HNTB was able to match only 176 out of 1,018 Maximo records (17 percent) in the BIM model. They recommended that the integration of CMMS and BIM required more standardization and structuring of the data within both systems.

Create a BIM Execution Plan (BEP)

At project initiation, it is necessary to create a BEP. This provides a master information/data management plan and assignment of roles and responsibilities for model creation and data integration. The BEP brings together the modeling and attribute requirements defined in Section 3 with the format requirements (COBie, IFC, etc.), the current extent of BIM implementation for the facility, and the project-specific conditions and work processes to ensure that GSA receives the FM information it requires. The project team member(s) holding a contract with the GSA have the responsibility to produce the BEP. Project-specific BEPs should be developed for new construction, major renovation, and larger scope and dollar small projects. As project conditions change, the BEP should be continually developed and be used as a means to keep the various contractors use of BIM consistent.

The BEP content includes the following:

- BEP Overview
- Project Information
- Key Project Contacts
- Project Goals/BM Uses
- Organizational Roles/Staffing

BIM Process Design (Determine When and by Whom Information Will Be Created)

On new construction, the A/E is responsible for the building configuration, accommodation of the spatial program, sizing of building systems (structure, MEP/FP) and location and specification of major equipment. This information is developed during design. Details of the building systems and sometimes the enclosure system, as well as specific product details are provided by the trade contractors and fabricators and developed during construction. However, in alternative project delivery approaches, responsibilities may change and some tasks, such as detailing building systems, may be performed earlier in the design/build process. In addition, there is equipment information generated during commissioning by the Commissioning contractor. The COBie specification assigns specific information to be entered by the A/E and the contractor. (See the discussion of COBie deliverables from design, construction and commissioning starting on page 61.)

Best practice in the construction phase for BIM use is for the designer, construction manager or a third party to create the base building BIM (architectural and structural components) and for the trade contractors to create BIM models for the systems they are fabricating. These are the Construction models, which are merged to form the Coordination model. By resolving building system conflicts in the Coordination model, the construction team can minimize field problems and improve budget and schedule conformance. In order to perform accurate interference checking, the Construction BIMs are updated throughout construction. An important point is that the various trades should build to the model, to ensure that coordination benefits are achieved. For this reason, the coordinated Construction BIMs represent an immediate, extremely complete, accurate and useful physical description of the building to support a broad range of facility management activities. For traditional (Design/Bid/Build) delivery, the contractor must provide an updated project BEP, BIM, and COBie deliverables.

Establishing the Responsible GSA Party for Monitoring Compliance with the BEP and Validating the Completeness and Quality of the Deliverables

Quality control checks on BIM models are performed at key project milestones defined in the BEP and incorporated into the contractor's Quality Service Plan (QSP) and Construction Quality Control (CQC) Plan. The quality control checks occur across the project lifecycle. GSA develops the means and methods to properly enforce contract BIM requirements throughout the project delivery and O&M process. This includes enforcement of standards and guidelines (e.g., attributes, naming conventions) and assurance that the virtual building is being maintained in conjunction with the constructed building at designated project checkpoints. The GSA is also developing a Virtual Design and Construction (VDC) scorecard to measure the quality of BIM use and compliance on projects. The scorecards will be evaluated at project milestones defined in the BEP.

One early lesson learned from pilot projects is the importance of standardizing what information is required, what that information is called (e.g., asset identification number) and the allowable terminology for that information. For example: The equipment identification consists of the standard equipment acronym and a sequence number. The integration of CMMS and BIM requires more standardization and structuring of the data within both systems. Today CMMS systems are not standardized nor do all regions use a CMMS. At this time, a national team within GSA is collaborating with regions to develop and implement a national CMMS. However, standardizing the system without standardizing the data will be ineffective. Accurate inventories are critical for a CMMS, and validation of the GSA's PBS equipment inventory is needed before loading data to the CMMS.

The GSA is working toward a comprehensive, standard list of building element and equipment types, and their attributes. A number of GSA internal as well as industry-wide initiatives have partially addressed this issue. The GSA's National Equipment Standard Team (NEST) has done considerable work to standardize the identification, classification, collection, and coding of equipment within facilities across the regions.

Specifiers' Properties information exchange (SPie) is a National Institute of Building Sciences (NIBS)/buildingSMART alliance project to create an open schema to allow manufacturers to export product data into a format that can be consumed by designers, specifiers, builders, owners, and operators. This initiative aims to turn specifications into property sets that can be applied to the appropriate BIM objects. The focus is on the properties needed for specification, discovery, selection, and verification of products against those specifications. (See http://projects.buildingsmartalliance.org/files/?artifact_id=3143.)

Modeling Requirements—A Record BIM

While design and construction BIMs are produced throughout the project life cycle, this section of the *GSA Guide* focuses on the modeling requirements for a record BIM, which is submitted at project turnover to document the final as-constructed building and is archived as part of the project record. The as-built BIM is an editable copy of the record BIM that is maintained by the GSA for updates to the building and systems configuration.

Equipment attributes required for facility management activities, such as manufacturer, capacities, model number, and so on should be submitted in the current version of the COBie format. Section 3.3 describes the minimum GSA COBie requirements. It is important to note that this information will be entered by various project team members at various points in the design and construction phases. Project teams should define how COBie requirements will be met in the project BEP.

HIGH-LEVEL MODELING REQUIREMENTS

BIM Authoring Applications

Project teams are required to use BIM authoring applications that are IFC compliant to meet GSA BIM requirements.[3] The BIM authoring application, at a minimum, should be able to create IFCs in compliance with the coordination view, spatial program validation view (BIM Guide Series 02), and COBie. BIM authoring applications, unlike traditional CAD applications, enable project teams to provide object intelligence for building elements. CAD applications that primarily focus on producing printed or plotted drawings, often referred to as 2D CAD applications, are generally not adequate for a BIM design process and do not satisfy the BIM requirements in this guide. Further, 3D functionality in a CAD application does not automatically imply that the system is capable of producing a BIM. Project teams should consult with the GSA Central Office to determine if a software application will meet GSA BIM requirements.

The ability of BIM authoring applications to manage components and spaces with complex geometric shapes varies. In some situations, IFC BIM export from a BIM authoring application may fail to preserve such complex shapes or to capture all of the attributes of an object. This could be a limitation in some applications' level of support for the IFC standard. BIM modelers should work with their BIM authoring vendor to understand if any such limitations exist in the IFC export to be used for submission to the GSA. Limitations that may affect submissions to the GSA shall be documented in the BEP.

BIM Model Structure

The model structure (or containment hierarchy) of BIM is normally generated by the BIM authoring application. Users have little if any possibility to influence it. In situations where the user can define the model containment hierarchy, it should be structured as in the IFC data model. Typically, spaces and building elements

[3] See http://en.wikipedia.org/wiki/Industry_Foundation_Classes for a general introduction to IFC standards and how they are supported.

are contained in a building floor, building floors are contained in buildings, buildings are contained in a site, and a project can contain one or more sites. In the submission to the GSA's Office of Design and Construction (ODC), the site object is optional (in which case the building is contained directly by the project). Spaces can also be members of one or more zones (e.g., daylighting; [HVAC]; or even an organizational department).

In general, the BIM authoring application will manage this for the BIM modeler, but it is important to be aware of this containment hierarchy to better understand the requirements for developing a BIM. As always, BIM modelers are encouraged to consult with their BIM authoring application vendor for more information if this topic is unclear.

Asset Identification Number

A major feature that differentiates CAD from BIM is the fact that BIM provides a computable description of a building. The life-cycle view of a BIM requires tracking what changes are made, when and by whom, over the life of the facility. To be useful, changes must be tracked at the element or component level, not at the file level. Thus, each object within a BIM needs to have a unique identity that can be referenced as changes occur. Within the software community, this unique identifier is implemented as a GUID. The concept is that a GUID is a totally unique number—one that will never be generated twice by any computer in existence. While each generated GUID is not guaranteed to be unique, the total number of unique keys is so large that the probability of the same number being generated twice is very small.

GUIDs are typically managed by the software and not under control of the user. Some early BIM adopters discovered that certain BIM analysis applications "recreated" the model and assigned all new GUIDs to the BIM objects. COBie has omitted inclusion of a GUID to make spreadsheet entry easier. Thus, to ensure that the GSA and its consultants and contractors can manage each BIM object's unique identifier, each equipment object shall have an asset identification number in addition to the GUID. This will enable a given object to be uniquely identified over the life cycle of the building model.

DESIGN, CONSTRUCTION, AND RECORD BIMS

Throughout the project, various types of BIMs are created and modified. Project teams will start with the design intent BIM, move to multiple construction BIMs, and, ultimately, create a record BIM. At the end of construction, there are multiple, building system–specific construction BIMs. Typically, the architectural and the structural models are those produced by the design team with minor modifications. In the case of a steel structure, a fabrication model may be available. The MEP/FP models are frequently produced by the trades using very specialized CAD-based software packages that interface with cost estimating, inventory, and/or fabrication systems. As the BIM models are created for the project, the project team should follow the BEP in demonstrating how the virtual building is being maintained in conjunction with the constructed building at designated project checkpoints.

Required BIM Objects and Properties

Objects

The following object types are required in the record BIM submitted to the GSA:

- All objects required by BIM Guide Series 02
- Ceilings
- Lighting systems, fixtures, and equipment
- Communications systems and equipment
- Irrigation system and equipment
- Furniture manufacturers and specifications
- Electrical systems, equipment, and clearances
- Mechanical systems, equipment, insulation, and clearances
- Plumbing systems, equipment, insulation, and clearances
- Fire protection systems, equipment, and clearances
- Specialty systems, equipment, and clearances

Object Properties

The minimum set of properties that should be associated with each required BIM equipment object:

- Equipment GUID
- Equipment asset identification number
- Space primary key (i.e., object location)

Space objects must include GSA space properties, as defined in *GSA BIM Guide Series 02*.

National Equipment Standard

The GSA is currently developing a national equipment standard that will enable the GSA to leverage equipment data through the facility life cycle. For more information about this standard, see www.bing.com/search?q=GSA+National+Equipment+Standard&pc=ZUGO&form=ZGAIDF.

Organization of Record BIMs

Record BIMs need to be partitioned by floor and building system. The structural model should be partitioned to include the slab for the relevant level up through the framing for the level above. To allow visualization of the MEP/FP systems at each level, the slab at the level above should not be included. If the building floor plate is very large, then additional partitioning may be advisable. A composite model can always be assembled from multiple submodels. Organization of models shall be determined by the project team and documented in the BEP.

Modeling Precision

The system of measure for modeling PBS new construction projects is hard metric (e.g., 250 mm). For modeling renovation and alteration projects, it can be soft metric (e.g., designations such as 1 inch or 25.4 mm in which metric equivalents are attached to International System of units [SI]). Measurement accuracy shall be in accordance with the PBS CAD Standard (June 2010).

Consistent Units and Origin

In order to properly register all building models in 3D space, a common coordinate system and units must be used. Models used to represent a single building will use a common reference point, for example, 0, 0, 0 for the southwest exterior finish of the ground floor, with north being the top of a sheet or screen view.

Prior to Submittal of Record BIMs

Prior to submittal of record BIMs the following actions are required:

- Verify that all construction BIMs (building, structure, finishes, and building systems) represent as-built conditions, including architectural supplemental instructions, Change Notices, and field changes and include the minimum attributes required by the GSA.
- Create, for each discipline or system, a record BIM for each floor of the building. Save in native format of authoring application.
- Verify that the record BIMs for each floor register in X, Y, and Z dimensions.
- MEP/FP BIMs: Verify that primary keys correspond to those in equipment inventory.

- Create an .ifc version of each record BIM.
- Create a composite model of the record BIMs in .ifc format.

Maintaining and Updating As-Built BIMs

Record BIM serves two purposes: to document the as-constructed building and components for use in future projects and O&M activities, and as the project record archive. The as-built BIM is maintained by the GSA to capture building and component updates throughout the facility's life cycle.

What needs to be maintained in the BIM versus externally?

For the most part, nongeometric data about a facility will be more easily accessed and updated if maintained in a database external to the parametric model. A common unique identifier for each item of interest must be maintained in the BIM authoring application model and the database to maintain association. Additional attributes may be included in the BIM authoring application model by designers or contractors to meet their own needs, such as generating wall, window, and door schedules and extracting quantities for cost estimating.

COBIE SUBMITTALS

COBie is an open standard approach to handing design and construction information over to facility management. The Army Corps of Engineers and NASA have been the primary developers of COBie, with several other agencies (including GSA) adopting this open standard. For the current version of COBie and a more detailed explanation, please visit the Whole Building Design Guide (www.wbdg.org/resources/cobie.php) and chapter 5.

COBie provides an open standard format for capturing project data, particularly equipment data, when it is generated during the design, construction, and commissioning phases. COBie minimizes information exchange loss and associated costs from the physical handover of project information at the end of a project. COBie maximizes the chances of receiving relevant information in a timesaving manner. It has been demonstrated through NIBS sponsored "COBie Challenges"[4] that COBie data can be imported into a facility management system such as a CMMS to update and track facility asset data.

[4] The COBie Challenge consists of a series of tests performed by the BbuildingSMART Aalliance that validate whether software conforms to the COBie standard (either to receive or generate COBie data). For more information, see www.buildingsmartalliance.org/index.php/newsevents/proceedings/cobiechallenge/ and Chapter 5.

Not all attribute information must be in a BIM, but required information should be transferred via COBie-compliant files. Required COBie space, zone, and equipment data must be linked to the objects in the Record BIMs. A common primary key should be assigned in both COBie and the model to link the BIM objects to their associated attributes. Project teams shall document how they will comply with COBie requirements in their BIM execution plan.

The COBie-compliant Excel file consists of 16 separate spreadsheets or worksheets that capture project data from different facility life cycle phases. Details of these spreadsheets can be found at the web site referenced earlier. They are also discussed in Chapter 5.

Minimum COBie Requirements

For GSA, a COBie deliverable, in accordance with current COBie standards, shall be submitted for all projects that involve space, zone, building systems, or equipment changes.

The COBie deliverable should contain attribute data for all BIM objects required by the GSA project team, as outlined in the BIM execution plan. The record BIM and the COBie deliverable should contain the same equipment primary key, equipment identification, and space primary key for each BIM equipment object. The equipment primary key and the equipment identification link the equipment attribute data in the COBie deliverable to the BIM equipment object in the record BIM. Electronic copies of product information and shop drawings shall be linked to the model.

Creating COBie Deliverables

COBie deliverables can be created and updated one of four ways:

- Manually entering data in the COBie spreadsheet
- Extracting BIM attribute data into a COBie-compliant file.
- Direct use of COBie-compliant software.
- Exporting an IFC file with correctly structured property sets.

The method selected for creating and updating the COBie deliverable should be defined in the BEP. Project teams should consider the capabilities and resource requirements among the different methods to deliver COBie data when determining which method to use.

Standardized terminology is required. This is a source of potential problems, and GSA project teams should consult their regional BIM champion or Central Office BIM program for COBie templates and specifications.

TECHNOLOGY REQUIREMENTS

Central Repository of Facility Information

The key to using BIM effectively for facility management is the establishment of a centralized repository of facility data. The data may actually be stored in multiple, linked repositories, but the data must serve as a centralized resource available to all appropriate users.

Infrastructure

Software tools and communication links must be responsive if users are expected to access and maintain facility information in a central repository. Necessary technology infrastructure includes:

- Adequate, high-speed data storage
- Adequate server capacity
- Adequate desktop computer processing capacity
- Adequate numbers of software licenses
- Adequate network bandwidth
- Responsive license servers

Security

All facility management information and FM BIMs should be maintained inside GSA firewalls. However, external repositories, accessible to the GSA, A/Es, and construction teams, are needed to allow copies of design, construction, record, and as-built BIMs to be made available to project teams, to permit the sharing and collaborative updating of the project models, and to support the submission of the as-built BIMs and other electronic deliverables. These repositories must meet security requirements for sensitive but unclassified (SBU) information.

Functionality

From the project process through the update and maintenance of facility information throughout the life cycle, there are a number of different technology requirements:

- During project execution, the design and construction teams need the ability to collaborate on the development of the facility model. Multiple groups within the GSA, including Design & Construction and Spatial Data Management, also need to be able to monitor progress and compliance to GSA requirements throughout this process.

- At project closeout, the facility information must be handed over and uploaded into the central facility repository inside the GSA firewall.
- During the O&M phase, tools are needed to update the as-built BIMs and synchronize those updates with activity in the CMMS and equipment inventory database, as well as with eSmart (GSA's 2D drawing repository).

THE VISION: TECHNOLOGY OVERVIEW

This section describes GSA's vision for an integrated store of data to support BIM and FM functions. It is still in development, and a conceptual diagram can be found in Appendix A of the GSA BIM for FM Guidelines.

TECHNOLOGY CHALLENGES

This section discusses current technology challenges and provides recommendations for immediate implementation.

Multi-User Update

New construction projects will provide the initial facility information. That information will be updated in two ways:

1. Exchanging data with other GSA systems
2. Capturing changes resulting from both small projects and major renovations

Within any facility, multiple change activities will overlap. Therefore, the multi-user access requirements are quite complex. If multiple users have modified the same data, whose changes take precedence? Should it be the last user to check in? What if that is old data whose check-in was delayed, rather than data that represents the latest building modification? It is for this reason that check-out typically locks the data and permits the check-in of changes to that data by only one user.

Increasingly, BIM software products support access to and updating of building information at the component level. However, only one user has update access at any one time. There are a few products that support Web services for updates. This scenario would permit something like database record locking, with the lock being released the moment the change transaction is completed. This appears to be the direction in which the industry is moving.

Management of Updates

Today, most BIM data, particularly the geometric information, is managed at best at the level of a checked out and locked set of components. Managing updates of the as-built BIM in the environment of many GSA facilities, where there are multiple, overlapping major renovations; small projects; and maintenance activities underway simultaneously, is challenging.

Project conditions that pose additional difficulties include:

- When should the project data replace the official existing conditions information?
- How can a project model for a specific area of a building be inserted into the overall model? How can such an update be accomplished while accurately managing the primary keys of GSA-required COBie objects so that primary keys of:
  - Items that remain are unchanged.
  - Items that are removed during the project are removed from other systems (e.g., CMMS).
  - New items are identified and transferred to other systems.

Recommendations are:

- Project work should not be incorporated into the as-built BIM for the overall facility or CMMS until such time as the construction is complete and the project's as-built BIMs have been checked and accepted.
- The A/E should produce a report indicating the primary keys of COBie objects that will remain and those that will be removed as a result of the project.
- The contractor should ensure that primary keys on items remaining are not changed in the as-built BIMs. This will be a difficult requirement to get across, but it will be possible to validate that primary keys are unchanged based on the A/E's report.
- The incorporation of the project as-built BIM into the overall facility as-built BIM cannot be completely automated at this time, unless the renovation is so extensive that an entire as-built BIM file can be replaced. In other circumstances, an experienced and knowledgeable BIM user will need to knit the modifications into the existing fabric of the building. This is currently the case with FM CAD as well.

Multi-User Access and Viewing

Access to facility information can be facilitated through 3D visualization. However, BIM authoring tools are not the correct application to provide this access to users who need view-only access. Easy-to-navigate, low-cost, or free viewers are preferred.

Similarly, capturing and extracting needed facility data (attributes) using a BIM authoring tool becomes cumbersome and difficult to manage. The BIM file size becomes very large and slow to manipulate with all the required facility data. Every user requires high-powered hardware and access to and training in expensive BIM authoring tools.

Vendor-Neutral Options

GSA is committed to the interoperability of data as a strategic management issue to ensure GSA's access to building information over the life of the capital asset. This implies that there are vendor-neutral options. The GSA National Equipment Standard Team has suggested that capturing design and construction data in an open, ODBC-compliant database format supports GSA's policy on vendor neutral software. This format provides for easy interoperability with similar database-structured facility management systems.

Recommendations are:

- Use the COBie file to synchronize as-built project data with CMMS and other facility management systems.
- Use the equipment primary key to link BIM equipment objects with external equipment data that is created by multiple project and O&M activities.
- Use the current version of the COBie file.

Multiple Paths for Data Transfers

With current technology, there are some limitations as noted above, but also many opportunities for harvesting useful BIMs and linked data for facility management. Figure 3.2 shows some of these alternatives.

EMERGING TECHNOLOGY: MODEL SERVERS

There is an emerging class of BIM software product referred to as "model servers." These provide the functionality discussed earlier in section 4.2. A number of GSA pilot projects are examining this category of technology. A preliminary list of desired model server capabilities (many of which are not met by currently available capabilities) includes:

- Manages models in IFC format.
- Manages related files in multiple formats.

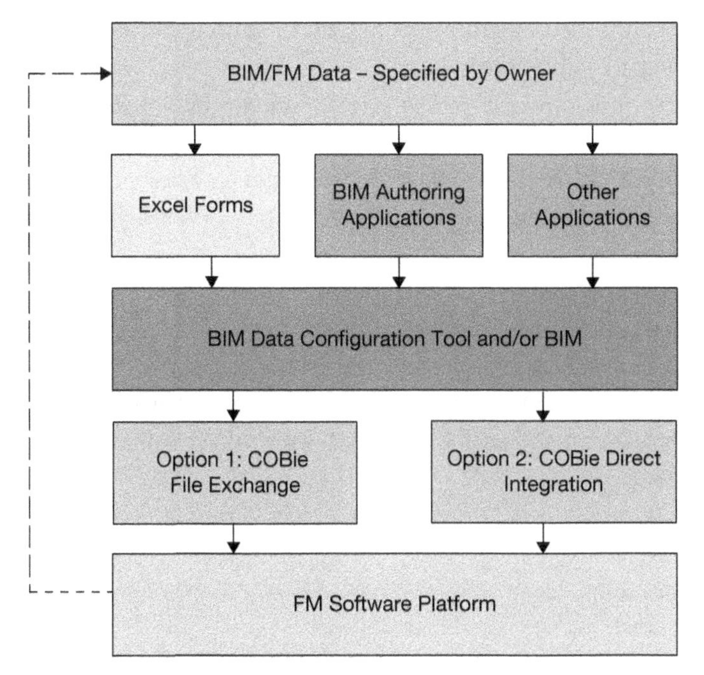

FIGURE 3.2 Alternative Paths for Data Transfer
Image courtesy Onuma, Inc. with edits by GSA

- Manages associated object properties in ifcXML format.
- Assigns an object's GUID as an explicit property.
- Provides viewers for all formats managed.
- Allows volumes and/or components of a model to be associated with a particular project.
- Project properties include start/end date range.
- Supports queries such as:
  - Find all projects that have affected this part (volume) of the building in the last <number> years.
  - Find any projects scheduled to affect this part of the building between <date range>.
  - Find any maintenance projects currently under way in this part of the building.
  - Find all changes that have been made to this branch of the HVAC system since the building was constructed.
- Allows model elements associated with a project to be copied to a "working model."
- Can notify other users who have copies of any of the same model elements.

- Can use Web Services to permit the model to be updated in real time on a component-by-component basis.
- Has the ability to update the primary model by "checking in" project models:
- Can route check-in data through validation and compliance checks.
  - Can compare the incoming model to the current version and identify changes.
- Changes to geometry.
- Changes to properties, including primary keys.
- Can replace each (and only) changed components with a new version.
- Can maintain an audit trail for each version of each component.
- Can apply a status to each model checked in, at a minimum:
  - Pending
  - Current
  - Archive
- Can notify other users who have copies of any of the changed components or properties.
- Has ability to perform real-time and batch updates of models and component properties based on data transfers from other systems.
- Provides integration tools for automating such updates.
- May incorporate tools for direct model update.
- Has the ability to perform coordinate transformations (translation and rotation) so that a project with a local coordinate system can be accurately registered to a building, campus, city, and so forth.
- Is compliant with the Federal Information Security Management Act of 2002 (FISMA) based on GSA security category mappings.

PILOT PROJECTS FOR BIM AND FM USING GSA GUIDELINES

At the time these guidelines were published, the initial projects that were under way using these guidelines (to at least a partial extent) were in the early stages of project delivery. The project results and lessons learned were, as a result, preliminary. However, the author has asked the GSA BIM Champions[5] at 3 of these projects to respond to a series of questions about their experiences. These will be summarized here to illustrate the major problems and successes that have been experienced thus far (through July 2012).

[5] Designated people within the GSA who are knowledgeable about BIM and lead in its implementation at project sites at GSA offices.

Peter W. Rodino Federal Building Modernization, Newark, New Jersey

DESCRIPTION OF PROJECT

The American Recovery and Reinvestment has authorized $146 million for this 16-story building's first major upgrade in its 41-year history. Completed in 1968, the 526,609-gross-square-foot Rodino Federal Building, located in the heart of Newark's civic center, is the largest federal building in the state of New Jersey.

The upgrade will construct a new glass curtain wall over the existing precast façade, which will transform the structure's outward appearance. GSA will also renovate the interior offices spaces. While the building has received partial asbestos abatement in the past, this project will provide for abatement in the balance of the building.

SUSTAINABLE FEATURES

To provide for a more energy efficient building, this project has a goal of achieving U.S. Green Building Council's LEED® Silver designation. System enhancements in the structure will focus on high-performance lighting, cooling plant, and air handling units. In addition, the new glass curtain wall will create an energy-efficient dual-curtain wall. The GSA anticipates that these features will reduce overall energy use by approximately 32 percent.

TIMELINE

Bridging documents are completed.

Design/build contract award is completed.

Construction work began in October 2010.

Twelfth floor renovation completed, tenant relocated back March 2012.

Fourteenth floor renovation completed, tenant relocated back February 2012.

Completion is anticipated for spring 2015.

CONTRACTOR INFORMATION

In August 2009, the GSA awarded the firm of Dattner Architects of New York a $3.45 million contract modification to begin preliminary design work and bridging

(Continued)

documents on this project. In addition to its own efforts on the project, Dattner also employed the services of nine other local companies as subcontractors and consultants. Bovis Lend Lease of Princeton, New Jersey, is providing construction management services and is contracting with five additional local firms as subconsultants on the project. The modernization of the Rodino Federal Building will be completed under a design/build contract. A general construction contractor will be brought onto the project via that award.

Bridging architect: Dattner Architects, New York City

Design/build contractor: Tocci/Driscoll Joint Venture, Woburn, Massachusetts

Architect of record: KlingStubbins, Cambridge, Massachusetts, and Philadelphia

Construction manager: Lend Lease, Ewing, New Jersey

GOALS OF BIM FM INTEGRATION

The Rodino project is serving as a pilot project to link design and construction data to FM activities, and help to educate GSA associates in different BIM uses. The pilot project team includes the GSA regional BIM champion, the GSA building manager, the GSA project manager, the GSA contracting officer, the BIM consultant, and the design/build construction contractor.

The scope of effort on this project includes limited-scope HVAC modernization and new construction The project used design/build project delivery. BIMs were created during the design phase. The teams will use COBie data format to transfer facility data, as the facility management systems and file formats have not been identified, and the Onuma System to validate the COBie deliverables. The A/E of record is creating four design intent BIMs, which are split by discipline: interior architectural, exterior architectural, structural, and MEP/FP. Figure 3.3 illustrates the data flows on this project.

QUESTIONS AND RESPONSES FROM THE GSA REGIONAL BIM CHAMPION ON THIS PROJECT[6]

1. What kinds of data are you collecting during the design and construction phases?

   COBie data were collected during these phases.

[6] Ilana Hellmann, PE, LEED AP, Engineer/Project Manager, Design and Construction Division (2PCD), GSA Public Buildings Service, Northeast and Caribbean Region.

(Continued)

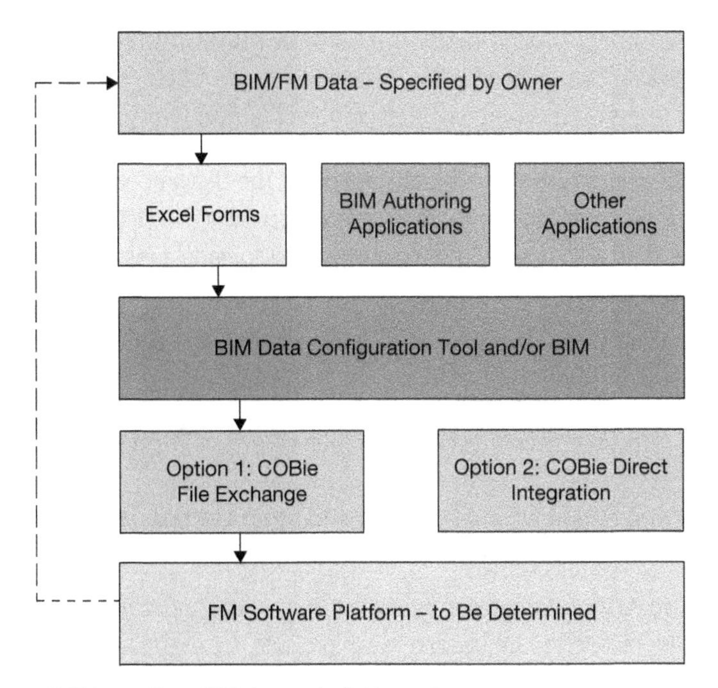

FIGURE 3.3 Flow of FM data on the Rubino project.

2. Were these data requirements specified in the contract? If not, how were they specified?

   Data requirements were not specified in the original design/build contract; they were added by modification with a specification for data and FM deliverables.

3. Was BIM used for design and construction, and if so, was it also used for FM data?

   BIM was not used by our bridging designer. BIM is being used by our design/build contractor; a BIM execution plan was part of the proposal for the design/build contract. To leverage this, we added a BIM FM requirement by modification after contract award. BIM is being used to aggregate FM data.

4. Were FM staff involved during the early stages of design? If not, when did they get involved?

   FM staff were involved during design, as well as during development of the specification for the BIM FM modification. We invited our FM staff to

(Continued)

participate in our team workshop at which we discussed the BIM FM scope and deliverables to develop the modification.

5. How are you collecting the data?

   We are using COBie as the data standard. The design/build contractor is using a variety of tools to gather the data, populating the Revit model, using Vela to enter field data, and using customized spreadsheets to collect some data at the subcontractor level.

   We are using the Onuma Planning System to verify the data and aggregate it into COBie format.

6. What naming standards are you using for the data (spaces, equipment types, etc.)

   We are conforming to the National Equipment Standard developed by the GSA (not yet implemented).

7. How are you communicating this data to the CMMS and other CAFM systems used (or planned to be used) on your projects, for example, COBie or other methods?

   The plan is to use COBie. We haven't gotten this far yet. COBie is a requirement of the BIM FM scope of work for the design/builder.

8. What have been the biggest problems you have had in specifying and collecting and communicating this data?

   The biggest issue in specifying the data was determining what data was truly important to our building maintenance staff. Secondary to that was the issue with getting the building staff to decide in advance to use a specific CMMS system.

   The design/build contractor has indicated that collecting the data in a timely fashion has been an issue for them and that data collection has been much more labor intensive than they had anticipated. They have also had issues with subcontractors taking responsibility for providing field-level data.

9. Have you experienced any benefits from the use of this data for commissioning or use by facility managers?

   Not up to commissioning just yet.

Bishop Henry Whipple Federal Building, 1 Federal Drive, Fort Snelling, MN 55111-4080

Project Size: Approximately: 618,000 square feet (with major replacement of mechanical, electrical, plumbing, and fire/life safety systems throughout the building, utilizing it to incorporate geothermal technology).

Total ARRA Funding: $160 million

Scheduled Completion: 2014

GOALS OF PROJECT

The GSA is replacing the old, inefficient heating, ventilation, and air conditioning system at the Bishop Henry Whipple Federal Building in Fort Snelling with a state-of-the-art heating and cooling system that uses geothermal ground wells. This system will be one of the largest installed in the upper Midwest and will be about 72 percent more efficient than traditional electric heating and air conditioning systems.

The building's mechanical, electrical, plumbing, and fire safety systems will also receive a major overhaul. Some of these components date to the original 1960s construction. The building's interior and exterior lighting systems will also be replaced.

The savings for the new lighting system is estimated at about 20 percent of the building's current lighting energy consumption. Energy savings for the overall project are projected to be about 30 percent of current annual energy costs. The total price for the Whipple project is estimated at $158 million.

The goals of this renovation include the energy efficiency described above and the following:

- Link the as-built BIM data to facility management systems.
- Identify and provide the critical data for BAS/CMMMS.
- Provide electronic version of the as-built data linked with 3D elements in BIM model.
- Identify design systems and zones in the BIM model to improve facility management and operations.

The BIM models were initially created by the A/E team during the design stage. However, BIM models were developed to be the as-built BIM model by incorporating

(Continued)

changes made during construction for both graphics and data. Utilizing the BIM integration sessions, all team members used their collaborative efforts to reflect the as-built conditions and ensure the accuracy of the model.

QUESTIONS AND RESPONSES FROM THE GSA REGIONAL BIM CHAMPION ON THIS PROJECT[7]

1. What kinds of data are you collecting during the design and construction phases?

During design, we collect some of COBie information that relates to design (Watt, BTU, etc.). We call it "Design element." We also try to identify "Design Systems and Zones." This kind of information should be provided by the design team. During the construction phase, we collect the other items of COBie (manufacture, model number, warranty, etc.), as-built conditions, and also the close-out documentation (shop drawings, product information, etc.)

2. Were these data requirements specified in the contract? If not, how were they specified?

These data requirements are sometimes included in GSA contracts. However, the contract language is very generic and vague. No specifics in detail. For example, we specify the as-built documentation as part of the final deliverable at the end of project. However, we don't specify how it should be organized, formatted, and connected with the 3D model. It is a big problem, and the range of interpretation is too wide. The contract language has to be specific on the requirements when it is associated with BIM.

3. Was BIM used for design and construction, and if so, was it also used for FM data?

For all my projects, BIM was used for design and construction. Yet most of the design teams have used BIM as a supplemental tool to AutoCAD. Many firms felt comfortable with AutoCAD and they had little knowledge and experience of how to maximize the benefit of BIM. They used BIM software, but they completed the model without an integrated process. [There was] no input from contractor or owner. Almost every team used BIM for collision detection.

We required COBie to collect FM data. However, it required tremendous time and efforts from GC and subs. Consequently, it cost more to GSA to

[7] Richard Gee, LEED AP, GSA Chicago, IL 60604.

(Continued)

collect FM data. COBie requirements weren't part of the original contract, but were added.

4. Was the FM staff involved during the early stages of design? If not, when did they get involved?

   GSA FM staff was involved during the design stage but found no benefits. They offered few contributions. Most of FM staff lost interest and found no purpose in being part of design team. They dropped out. However, the FM staff was more involved during the construction stage. They particularly showed enthusiasm and interest during the as-built model phase and close-out documentation.

5. How are you collecting the data?

   COBie is a primary vehicle for the FM data. We also have a template that the design and construction team are supposed to fill out. Usually, GC coordinates with the subs for data collection. GSA gets the COBie data as part of the deliverable.

6. What naming standards are you using for the data (spaces, equipment types, etc.)?

   GSA has own naming convention, National Equipment Standards.[8]

7. How are you communicating this data to the CMMS and other CAFM systems used (or planned to be used) on your projects, for example, COBie or other methods?

   COBie is being used for now. We have not yet exported COBie to CMMS. Prior to that, we need to make determination as to which CMMS or CAFM to use. The decision has not been made in my region.

8. What have been the biggest problems you have had in specifying and collecting and communicating these data?

   COBie, along with BIM, is a new requirement to many design and construction firms. Their unfamiliarity with COBie often causes confusion, misdirection, and incorrect interpretation. It creates a hardship among team members when there is no integrated process among the design team, construction team and owner. Many design teams often work on 3D models without proper communication and coordination. As a result, they often do not deliver what owner has specified. The same often applies to the

[8] These are provisional standards currently being reviewed by GSA. Version 0.5 of this standard can be found at http://www.scribd.com/doc/83975104/PBS-GSA-National-Equipment-Standard-Guide-2011-03-21#page=8.

(Continued)

contractors. There is no way to specify detailed requirements in BIM, like specifying the line weight for each layer in AutoCAD. The team needs to communicate and coordinate about the model on a regular basis. Also, there has to be a clear definition of what FM data entails, what the as-built model entails, and how the closeout documents are connected with the model. Currently, these interpretations and expectations differ from one team to another.

9. Have you experienced any benefits from the use of this data for commissioning or use by facility managers?

   Not yet, but we are going in that direction. It is the goal of the GSA BIM program to have a full implementation of BIM in facility management.

Camden Annex Lifecycle and NASA Projects

BACKGROUND OF CAMDEN BIM FOR FM AND ENERGY MANAGEMENT PILOT PROJECT

The Camden Federal Courthouse Complex consists of two buildings, the post office and courthouse building, and a courthouse annex. The buildings are attached through a link-way. The building identified as the post office and courthouse building is located at 401 Market Street, and consists of five floors and a basement, encompassing approximately 99,924 GSF. The annex building, located at 400 Cooper Street, consists of six floors, a basement, a sub-basement, and a penthouse, encompassing approximately 185,896 GSF.

This project will focus on the Annex building.

GOALS OF THIS PROJECT

The Camden BIM for FM and Energy Management Pilot objective is to provide previously unavailable tools to facilities managers and building engineers by integrating currently disparate BIM, CMMS, and BAS building information systems into a single application. For facilities managers, reports will include but not be limited to planned versus actual energy performance of the building, building floors, building zones, building rooms, and building equipment. These reports will also provide the location of the equipment, the service history of the equipment, and warranty information about the equipment. For building engineers, a tablet device will be utilized in the field to instantaneously access location, performance, service, and warranty information and access operations and maintenance documents of equipment. This information can be shown spatially in a BIM model, allowing the building engineers to better understand the relationships between and locations of building floors, zones, rooms, tenants, systems, system components, and energy sensors. (For a more detailed description and illustration of these goals, see https://sites.google.com/a/gsa.gov/camden-bim-pilot/?pli=1.)

QUESTIONS AND RESPONSES FROM THE GSA REGIONAL BIM CHAMPION ON THIS PROJECT[9]

1. What kinds of data are you collecting during the design and construction phases?

[9] Steve DeVito, Project Technology Specialist, GSA Public Buildings Service, 20 N 8th Street, Philadelphia, PA 19107.

(Continued)

Design Phase

Spatial Programming Data

- Building name
- Building number
- Floor (and/or level)
- Department
- Subdepartment
- Space name—English name and abbreviation
- Room number—wayfinding room number
- Room number—construction document number (for builder use)
- Space code—agency room code
- Unique space ID (computer generated)—GUID
- Space type—OmniClass Table 13 (www.omniclass.org/)
- Space type—Uniformat
- Space measurement
- Net square footage (NSF)
- Department net square footage (DNSF)
- Department gross square footage (DGSF)
- Building gross square footage (BGS)

Facility Data

- Facility and floors are defined.
- Spaces should be classified using OmniClass.
- Net area is provided (gross area is generated by Revit).
- Spaces' boundaries should be properly connected.
- MEP model should have spaces identical to the Revit Architectural model and all life-cycle-targeted MEP equipment should be assigned to spaces.
- Equipment should be assigned to proper families, that is, a pump should belong to mechanical equipment, not to electrical.
- Zones should be defined in the BIM model and consist of spaces.
- Zones should have categories assigned.
- Types should have name, category (OmniClass), description, and asset type.
- Components should have name, description, type, and space.
- Systems should have name, category (OmniClass), and component.

Construction Phase

- Type information updated by providing the following attributes:
  - Manufacturer

(Continued)

  - Model number
  - Warranty information (parts and labor and duration), replacement cost
- Information updated by providing the following attributes:
  - Serial number
  - Installation date
  - Warranty start date
  - Optional tag number or barcode
  - Spare parts provided for types
  - Attributes provided for types and components

Commissioning Phase

- Documents assigned (uploaded) to corresponding BIM objects (types, components, spaces, facility).
- Attributes corrected based on real measurements.

2. Were these data requirements specified in the contract? If not, how were they specified?

   Yes, the answer above is from actual contract language.

3. Was BIM used for design and construction, and if so, was it also used for FM data?

   Yes for NASA AOB1 and IESB (still in design). Camden CH involved modeling existing conditions as it was existing building.

4. Was the FM staff involved during the early stages of design? If not, when did they get involved?

   Yes, FM staff was involved as early as project planning.

5. How are you collecting the data?

   CMMS System and Inventory Spreadsheet.

6. What naming standards are you using for the data (spaces, equipment types, etc.)?

   - Spaces—GSA Spatial Assignment Guide/OmniClass/Uniformat
   - Equipment-OmniClass

7. How are you communicating this data to the CMMS and other CAFM systems used (or planned to be used) on your projects, for example, COBie or other methods?

   We are using EcoDomus FM.

(Continued)

8. What have been the biggest problems you have had in specifying and collecting and communicating this data?

   - For facility managers/mechanics: Lack of understanding of BIM/experience with BIM projects/hands-on skills using BIM software.
   - For BIM specialists: Lack of understanding of facility managers/mechanics' standard practices/workflows and lack of hands-on skills using CMMS/CAFM systems.
   - Perceived difficulty in using new technology or new processes. Lack of trust in using unproven technologies or processes.
   - Lack of standards in facility managers/mechanics' classification of and management of equipment/documents.
   - Some standards have been developed by local key personnel, and these were based on their specific experience, not on industry standards.

9. Have you experienced any benefits from the use of this data for commissioning or use by facility managers?

Both the facility managers and O&M contractors see great value in implementing the EcoDomus middleware solution, which will integrate all above facilities data with predictive energy model, energy management system (Automated Logic), and CMMS system (Corrigo). This middleware will be used on iPads and laptops in the field by both managers and mechanics.

OTHER BIM GUIDELINES

There are an increasing number of BIM Guidelines from federal, state, academic, and private sources. In this section, we briefly summarize these and provide Internet sources where further information can be found.

BIM Planning Guide for Facility Owners

Name	BIM Planning Guide for Facility Owners
Source	Penn State University, Computer Integrated Construction Research Program, Department of Architectural Engineering Contact: Professor John Messner Principal PI jmessner@engr.psu.edu Document can be downloaded at http://bim.psu.edu
Sponsored by	Charles Pankow Foundation, US DoD Military Health System, Kaiser Permanente, US Dept. of Veteran Affairs, Penn State Office of Physical Plant
Date released	April 2012
Applies to	Total building life cycle but with greater emphasis on design and construction.
Comments	The guideline provides an excellent overview of the use of BIM and how an owner should plan for desired results from the start of a project with a careful BIM execution plan. The guideline emphasizes the organization and technology needs of an overall plan and covers the following planning elements: strategy, uses for BIM, process to achieve these uses, information needs, software and hardware infrastructure, and personnel requirements. There are sample forms and examples of use. There are some comments on support for FM requirements, including the use of COBie.

National BIM Standard—United States™ Version 2

Name	National BIM Standard—United States™ Version 2 (NBIMS-US V2)
Source	National Institute of Building Sciences, buildingSMART alliance Contact: Mr. Dana K. "Deke" Smith, FAIA Executive Director, Building Seismic Safety Council and buildingSMART alliance deke@dksic.net Document can be downloaded at http://www.nationalbimstandard.org/. Additional tools available to members of buildingSMART alliance. Copyright statement: www.nationalbimstandard.org/copyright.php.

(Continued)

Sponsored by	National Institute of Building Sciences, buildingSMART alliance
Date Released	Version 1 issued in December 2007 (not a consensus product) May 2012 (initial documents only)
Applies to	Total building life cycle
Comments	These standards are designed for two specific audiences: software developers and vendors, and practice documents for implementers who design, engineer, construct, own, and operate the built environment. Two sections within the standard provide the software developer with the necessary information: Reference standards: This set of standards provides a data dictionary, data model, Web-based exchange, and structures and identifiers for building data and information. These were developed by other allied standards organizations. Examples include ISO 16739 (IFC) and OmniClass. Exchange information standards: This section sets standards for data management, assurance, validation, as well as exchange concepts. It defines the design of exchanges for specific types of data related to building analysis; and includes Construction Operations Building information exchange (COBie) and GSA exchanges. These were written and balloted by the NBIMS-US project committee. Guidance standards: This section is targeted at practitioners and includes items such as the Project Execution Guide. A consensus approach (voting) is used for all adopted material to ensure a broad base of support. Content primarily provided by associations coordinating various aspects of the facilities industry. Future input from other countries is also encouraged. Updates with new content issued annually. Changes will ultimately be on a five-year cycle.

Wisconsin BIM Guidelines and Standards for Architects and Engineers, v2

Name	Wisconsin BIM Guidelines and Standards for Architects and Engineers, v2
Source	State of Wisconsin, Department of Administration Division of State Facilities Contact: Bill Napier, Wisconsin Department of Administration bill.napier@wisconsin.gov Document can be downloaded at www.doa.state.wi.us/dsf/masterspec_view_new.asp?catid=61&locid=4
Sponsored by	Division of Facilities Development, Department of Administration

(Continued)

Date Released	July 2012
Applies to	Design, construction, and project turnover
Comments	The guideline emphasizes Reference to the National BIM Standard version 2, Section 5 Practice Documents as a best practice guide. It requires that the A/E submit a BIM execution plan (BEP) that covers all execution and deliverables specified in the standards. It requires the use of BIM for design with a separate model for each discipline with a specified level of development (LOD) that can be expressed in an open IFC format to facilitate turnover to the State of WI. It also requires energy analysis and comparative cost analysis of design options. The BIM models are required to be submitted at designated milestones during the project and updated to reflect as-built conditions. There is no discussion of BIM/FM integration, which will be covered in a separate guideline to be issued in the fall of 2012.

LACCD BIM Standards, v3

Name	LACCD BIM Standards, v3
Source	Los Angeles Community College District Contact: Michael Cervantes/Jim Youngblood michael.cervantes@build-laccd.org/jim.youngblood@build-laccd.org Document can be downloaded at http://standards.build-laccd.org/cgi-bin/projects/dcs/extensions/viewer/code/viewer_client.pl?command=MANUAL_INDEX
Sponsored by	Division of Facilities Development, Department of Administration
Date released	April, 2010 (revised to version 3)
Applies to	Design, construction, and project turnover; design/build; design/bid/build
Comments	The guideline emphasizes the use of BIM for design and construction each discipline requiring a separate model that can be expressed in an open IFC format to facilitate turnover to the LACCD so that they can be incorporated into a district-wide GIS. It also requires energy and water analysis and 4D analysis of construction schedules. It does not require 5D cost estimates from the BIM models at this time. There are specific requirements for a BIM execution plan that specify the need for a virtual design and construction (VDC) manager. The BIM models are required to be updated during construction to reflect as-built conditions. There is no discussion of BIM/FM integration at this time, although turnover files are being linked to the modeled elements. Pending Revision v4 of the BIM standards may include a COBie requirement.

Legal Issues When Considering BIM for Facilities Management

4

Kymberli A. Aguilar

Senior Counsel, Hanson Bridgett LLP

and Howard W. Ashcraft

Partner, Hanson Bridgett LLP, and Procure Workshop Chair for NBIMS Version 2.0

INTRODUCTION

Building information modeling (BIM) evokes images of 3D visualizations, fly-throughs, and animations, but the strength of BIM is that it is just data. And these data can be abstracted, computed, and viewed in many different ways. BIM has demonstrated this power by reshaping how buildings are designed and constructed. But much of the same data can be used to simulate and manage the building itself and attributes of BIM elements can be augmented with facility management information. The result, better operations and management, can be far more important than the gains achieved by using BIM to design and construct the project. And unlike the design and construction phases, the information needs of facility managers continue for the life cycle of the facility (Jordani 2010, p. 13).[1]

Although progress has been made, efficient transfer of design and construction information to CMMS systems is still developing (using COBie standards for file

[1] This article indicates that 85 percent of the life cycle cost of a facility occurs after construction is completed.

transfer and/or direct integration). Building automation systems (BASs) generally are not interoperable with the construction BIM model, although some data exchange may be possible. A National Institute of Standards and Technology (NIST) study[2] found massive waste looking for, validating, and recreating facility information. There are substantial opportunities for improvement.

If the appropriate model input data is specified at the outset and the facility is constructed per the model (which can be verified during construction and turnover), an owner will have an accurate as-built model that that will include most, if not all, information the facility manger would need to take over and operate the building, including energy and other performance data. Indeed, if data needed for facility management is properly specified and integrated into the model, it becomes an invaluable tool that can be used by the owner for building life-cycle management. The data in the model can then be channeled, often by an open standard like COBie,[3] into a variety of downstream facility software management systems. Through the use of middleware, it can also be integrated with geographic information systems (GISs) and BASs, which allows the facility manager an increased ability to analyze operational data, including energy efficiency and Leadership in Energy and Environmental Design (LEED) compliance, and have a more holistic approach to capital asset management. Although BIM for facility management (FM) is still in its infancy, capturing and efficiently using digital information about a facility and its assets and systems is valuable to all parties involved in a project; contractors and designers can extend their services by responding to the need, and owners can receive a return on their BIM investment for the life of the facility.

Full life-cycle BIM is inherently collaborative—which is a departure from traditional approaches to design and construction.[4] To reduce potential risks, business practices and legal standards have favored compartmentalizing roles and responsibilities with minimal data exchanges. However, these liability concerns and uncertainty regarding intellectual property issues have impeded BIM adoption and have been used to justify limiting BIM. Although these concerns directly affect

[2] In fact, the NIST Interoperability Study, NIST GCR 04-86, indicated that two-thirds of the $15.8 billion lost are due to inadequate interoperability that occurs during the operation and maintenance phases (see Jordani, 2010, p. 13). The NIST study can be downloaded here: fire.nist.gov/bfrlpubs/build04/PDF/b04022.pdf. This study is discussed in greater detail in Chapter 1 of this book.

[3] COBie has been described as "an open standard for capture and delivery of digital data as it is created during design, construction, and commissioning for use in operations" (Jordani, 2010, p. 15). For more information about COBie, see the buildingSMART alliance web site: www.buildingsmartalliance.org/index.php/projects/activeprojects/25.

[4] Project delivery methods, such as integrated project delivery and the more collaborative versions of design/build, are leading a trend toward more collaboration, interactivity, and data exchange.

the designers and contractor, they indirectly affect the owner because reluctance to share BIM information dilutes its value to the owner. Fortunately, these issues can be effectively addressed by careful planning and contract drafting.

This chapter addresses four main issues, from a legal perspective, that owners implementing BIM for FM should consider:

1. What is in the model and its contractual status.
2. Ownership of the model.
3. Intellectual property ownership.
4. Issues with interoperability and data exchange.

In addition, the chapter discusses three additional issues: (1) whether the use of BIM will increase liability of the other parties, (2) how an integrated project delivery (IPD) environment affects reliance on BIM, and (3) whether insurance covers the parties' respective BIM-related work. All of these issues should be considered at the outset of the project and addressed with good contractual language.

HOW WILL THE MODEL(S) BE USED?

Ask and You Shall Receive

To get what you want, you need to ask for it. The request, however, should be detailed enough to ensure the desired result without including unnecessary information. This holds true in many contexts, but none more so than in a construction project that uses BIM from design through operations. From an FM perspective, the most difficult and important challenge is clearly specifying the data you need to have input into the model and the information to be exported from the model. To determine that information, owners must have an understanding of how the model will be used.

The level of information in the model(s) and the protocols for their use and management depends on how the model(s) will be used. Thus, the participants should outline the planned uses to allow all parties to understand how they should create and manage their data. If facility management is an intended use, the owner will need to determine whether data will be used for (1) operations and maintenance, (2) capital improvement planning, and/or (3) BASs.

The first two are what an owner might typically think of as common uses of BIM data for facility management. But using the data in conjunction with a BAS gives an owner an invaluable tool and control over a building that was never previously possible. A BAS is an example of a distributed control system. The control system is a computerized, intelligent network of electronic devices designed to monitor and control the mechanical electronics, and lighting systems in a building. A BAS can keep the building climate within a specified range, provide lighting based on an occupancy schedule, monitor system performance and device failures, and provide e-mail and/or text notifications to building engineering/maintenance staff. When the BIM data and BAS are properly linked, the model can also be used to track energy efficiency and LEED compliance.[5]

Once the owner identifies how it intends to use the BIM data during design, during construction and thereafter, it can then assess what data should be compiled in the model to assist with these areas. This calls for owners to be even more involved at the inception of the project with BIM requirements and BIM execution plans. This will occur at two levels. First, at a contractual level, the owner should specify that the design and construction models will be enhanced with FM information, and specify the parties' responsibility for entering the data during the design phase, or later, through submittals and creation of record models. The contract should explicitly require the updating of the model to reflect as-built and as-installed conditions. Second, during development of the BIM execution plan, the owner should help define what information it expects to extract from, or manage with, the building information model. At this time, the parties should address how information can be imported into the CMMS or BAS, and whether this will be a unilateral data transfer, or a live link between systems, either directly or one that is moderated by a middleware solution. The owner's operational staff needs to be intimately involved with specifying the data required because they, and not the contractor or architect, will best know what information will be useful. Without the owner's direction, the included information may be incomplete or so awkward to use that facility managers will ignore it in favor of a simpler solution.

If the owner is uncertain how it will use the data, it may be tempted to broadly ask for "the kitchen sink" and then later determine what it actually needed. Not only does this clog the model with unnecessary information, reducing performance, but it is expensive and leads to difficulties in exporting and using the data.

[5] Historically, a significant contribution to poor facility management is the owner's lack of detailed and visual information about its buildings. Owners cannot improve the energy performance of a building if they cannot track the building's energy usage by systems, zones, spaces, equipment, etc. in comparison to the design data. This lack of reliable information causes an inefficient reaction to demand-response requests from the Smart Grid. Owners investing in LEED certification cannot identify where they are having issues without matching design specifications with actual performance. Certain companies, like EcoDomus, provide a link between BAS and BIM, created to solve these inefficiencies.

See "Sample BIM Specification" at the end of this chapter (pp. 102–106) for specification language extracted from a 30-page BIM specification for an industrial facility.

What Is the Model's Contractual Status?

Traditionally, the printed plans and specifications are the controlling documents for a construction project. In most instances, these are the only documents that can be reviewed and approved by the regulatory agencies. But if printed plans and specifications are the contract documents, then what is the contractual status of modeled information?

There are three primary options. The model may be a tool to create the plans and specifications. In this case, the model has no contractual status. But because the model contains information beyond what is shown in plans and specifications, and is presumably conflict free, it may be preferable to afford the model some legal status. In some projects, the model is granted equal status with plans and specifications. This requires defining precedence between the model and the other contract documents. The model may also be the controlling document for construction. From a facility viewpoint, this is the preferable solution because the model, if kept current during construction, contains the most complete data concerning the project.

Best practice in construction phase BIM use is for the designer, construction manager, or a third party to create the base building BIM (architectural and structural components) and for the trade contractors to create the BIMs for the systems they are fabricating. These are the construction BIMs, which are merged to form the coordination BIM. By resolving building system conflicts in the coordination BIM, the construction team can minimize field problems and improve budget and schedule conformance. In order to perform accurate interference checking, the construction BIMs are updated throughout construction (U.S. General Services Administration 2011).

An important point is that the various trades *should build to the model* to ensure that coordination benefits are achieved. If this is the case, the coordinated construction BIMs represent an immediate, extremely complete, accurate, and useful physical description of the building to inform a broad range of FM activities.

However, because the model is not the permitted document, care must be taken to ensure that the model does not alter the approved drawings. An example of this approach is included in Table 4.1.

TABLE 4.1 Example of How to Avoid Conflicts between the BIM Models and the Drawings

Status of the Building Information Model	The project will be constructed in accordance with the design and construction details illustrated in the model. Those portions of the model prepared by the architect, its consultants, any design/build subcontractors, or other design professionals are construction documents as well as any submittal or fabrication models submitted to the architect or its consultants and incorporated into the model. Those work elements and building components that are not modeled will be constructed in accordance with the details demonstrated in the 2D construction documents. Although the master and subsidiary models will show more detail for those project components that are modeled, the models must not deviate from the overall design indicated in the 2D construction documents unless the deviation is necessary to correct a design error or omission and the parties have received prior approval by regulatory authorities.
Conflicts between documents	Those portions of the model that are considered construction documents will govern all dimensional information. The 2D construction documents will govern the work elements and building components that are not modeled.
Submission of signed and stamped 2D construction documents	The 2D construction documents must be generated, reviewed, signed, and sealed by the architect of record or other appropriately licensed design professional and/or design/build subcontractor, and submitted to regulatory authorities for review and approval of permits. To the greatest extent practicable, the 2D construction documents will be generated from the model.

Placing the model within, or at the head of, the contractual document hierarchy raises significant issues regarding the portions of the model that should be considered contract documents. As noted elsewhere, projects are built from a series of interrelated models rather than a single, global model. Beyond the primary design model, there may be models related to mechanical design, structural design, structural fabrication, mechanical fabrication, and possibly others. Before contractual status is conferred, the parties should determine what is and isn't contained in the contractual model. For example, fabrication models or portions of the construction model that are created to facilitate construction might be included or excluded from the contract documents.

Once the parties have determined the various uses of the model, the necessary input and output information and what the contractual model will contain, the information should be memorialized in the appropriate contract document so that expectations are clear and can be referenced as the project progresses.

OWNERSHIP OF THE MODEL

In every project that uses BIM, ownership of the model will need to be addressed. It is important that the issue be settled because ownership of jointly created works can be problematic. For certain projects, it may not matter who owns the model as long as all parties have sufficient licensed rights to use the model(s) for project purposes. However, as the use of BIM for FM increases, there will likely be more of an insistence by owners to own the contractual model since they will be using and modifying it for many years into the future. That being said, there are three primary ownership options to be considered, all of which are workable, provided the details are correctly handled in the contract documents. Regardless of the option chosen, appropriate consideration should be given to ownership or licensing of the model for future renovation. This should be detailed in the contract with the original designers and should permit renovation or additions to the facility. To be fair, the designers should not be responsible for the model's use. The issue to be addressed will be the extent to which the new architect can rely on the modeled information.

Owner Owns Modeling Information

This option will be preferred by many institutional and public owners because they typically own information created for them, such as contract documents. As previously mentioned, it will likely be the choice for many owners who want to use the model for its many possible applications post-construction. Under this option, all of the project participants must be licensed to use the modeling information for project purposes.[6] Design professionals, at least, will also want the right to display their designs for promotional or educational purposes and may want the right to reuse elements created for the project.

The "owner owns" approach also raises the issue of what information in the model should be transferred to the owner. Even if the owner obtains title to the design model, designers should reserve ownership of their standard library elements so they can reuse their standard elements on later projects. In addition, designers should be indemnified against liability arising from later modifications and reuse of the model(s).

[6] While the ConsensusDOCS 301 BIM Addendum does not transfer ownership to the owner, it does have each party grant a limited, non-exclusive license to the other parties to use the first party's BIM contribution for the purpose of that project. See ConsensusDOCS 301 Building Information Modeling (BIM) Addendum, § 6.2. The AIA E202-2008 specifically states that no ownership right is conveyed and that unless granted in a separate license, "the right to use, modify or further transmit the model is specifically limited to the design and construction of the Project." AIA E202-2008, § 2.2, Model Ownership.

Designer Owns Modeling Information

This option is consistent with traditional American Institute of Architects (AIA) contract documents that define designs as the architect's instruments of service. The owner, the contractor, and others who need to use the information would be licensed to use the information by appropriate language in the designer's agreement. If the parties opt for this arrangement, the owner's license will need to allow for the use of the model and its data for operation and maintenance, including revisions to the project. Because the owner's license will include limited reuse, the designer should be indemnified against liability arising from subsequent modifications and reuse.

All Parties Own Whatever They Create

This approach requires cross-licensing between all parties and, thus, provisions in all of the principal contracts. Other than this additional complication, it is similar to the designer's owning the modeling information described earlier.

As a general proposition, digital information in a model can be easily copied and reused. The parties, including their subcontractors, their manufacturers and suppliers may provide proprietary designs to the model and/or trade secret information. Accordingly, they may require agreements that prevent fabrication or reuse of the design or information by others. To properly protect this type of information while still allowing collaboration, access and use of the model must be defined—either in the contract documents or as BIM management procedures (Thomson n.d., p. 13).

WHO OWNS THE INTELLECTUAL PROPERTY?

Who Owns the Design?

The fluid nature of the "model" concept creates new intellectual property issues: what is the design, where is the design, and who owns it? Current design practice uses a set of interrelated models with a primary model controlling basic geometry that is enhanced by subsidiary design and fabrication models. These models can be supported, or interact with, external analysis models, cost models, and scheduling software. In a very real sense, the design is the dynamic whole of these parts.

But if this is true, who owns this dynamic design? The theoretical answer delves deeply into intellectual property concepts of joint efforts, derivative works, and work for hire. The practical answer lies in well-drafted contract documents that predetermine who will own specific parts of the model and which parts will be licensed for use.[7]

Who Owns the Copyright?

Copyright protection attaches to original works of authorship, including "pictorial, graphic, and sculptural works."[8] A copyright allows an author of a tangible work to maintain protection over that work by prohibiting others from copying, using, or otherwise interfering with the author's ownership and use. As with other instruments of professional service, a model as a whole and its component parts are subject to copyright protection.

Traditional owner-architect agreements provide strict protections for an architect's instrument of services. For example, the AIA Document B101-2007 states that architects will "be deemed the authors and owners of their respective Instruments of Service, including the Drawings and Specifications, and shall retain all common law, statutory and other reserved rights, including copyrights."[9] AIA Document E202-2008, Building Information Modeling Protocol Exhibit, is similar to the traditional model except that it extends this protection to other parties contributing to the BIM, stating that a "Model Element Author does not convey any ownership right in the content provided."[10]

Other agreements take a more collaborative approach, allowing the contract parties to choose whether the owner receives the copyright to documents, drawings, specifications, electronic data, and other information the design professional prepares for the project.[11] ConsensusDOCS 301, Building Information Modeling (BIM) Addendum, can be used in conjunction with such a choice. In fact, the BIM Addendum points the parties to the governing contract stating, "The Project Owner's entitlement to use the Full Design Model after completion of the Project shall be governed by the Contract between the Owner and the Architect/Engineer." The BIM Addendum, like the AIA Document E202-2008, provides that contributions to the model do not deprive a contributor of its copyright.

[7] Design professionals are often concerned that their additions to BIM software's library of components will be "adopted" by others who have access to a project model. This is the high tech equivalent of copying a firm's standard details. Although reprehensible, and you can craft contract language to prohibit it, there is no practical way to quell this "borrowing," because enforcing the firm's copyright would require constant vigilance and expensive legal action.

[8] 17 U.S.C. §102(a)(5).

[9] AIA Document B101-2007, Standard Form of Agreement between Owner and Architect, § 7.2.

[10] AIA Document E202-2008, Building Information Modeling Protocol Exhibit, § 2.2.

[11] For example, see ConsensusDOCS 240, Agreement between Owner and Architect-Engineer.

The party with the ownership right, however, can decide to contract that away in whole or in part. Typically, parties will agree to provide a license, which allows limited use to another party while maintaining copyright and ultimate control. A license is permission to do something with another's property that, absent the license, would be legally actionable. See the earlier references to situations where licenses are granted to the model or portions thereof.

From an FM perspective, it is important that the owner either own the design or have a broad license to use the design information to operate, maintain, and upgrade the project facilities.

STANDARDS AND INTEROPERABILITY

CMMS software exists separately from BIM and may be maintained in several proprietary databases or maintained in Excel tables. In general, these FM databases do not directly communicate with the BIM, and to use both software platforms, there needs to be a strategy for data transfer. In some instances, there are direct paths for data transfer, such as from a BIM platform, such as Revit to a CMMS product, such as Maximo. FM data is expected to last for the life cycle of a structure and a better approach may be to export data into a developed, open-source standard that is likely to endure for the life of the structure. For FM data, this means COBie compliance.

COBie (www.wbdg.org/resources/cobie.php) is the leading open standard for maintaining FM data, particularly equipment data, and is supported to some degree by several BIM platforms. BIM specifications should almost always require the ability to export to COBie, which has been demonstrated through NIBS sponsored "COBie Challenges." It is a standard built specifically for FM data and will likely endure, and because it is a leading open source standard, future software options will likely be designed to be compatible with COBie.

A typical deliverable requirement is in the GSA BIM Guide Series 008:

> 2.2.5.2 COBie deliverables:
>
> A COBie submittal during the design phase is required. See Section 3 for more about COBie requirements.
>
> Include the following COBie worksheets: Contact, Facility, Floor, Space, Zone, Type, Component, System, Document, and Attribute.
>
> Use the same coordinate system, model origin, and units used in the BIMS.

Handover COBie submittal to the contractor for the construction phase.

Use unique asset identification numbers for COBie and corresponding BIM objects.

COBie information can be extracted from the BIM and can also be provided through COBie compliant files or from properly structured Industry Foundation Class (IFC) files. The GSA BIM Guide Series 008—GSA BIM Guide for Facility Management is a useful resource for using COBie and relating BIM to Facility Management (U.S. General Services Administration 2011). This material is described in detail in Chapter 3.

An alternative or complementary approach is to use third-party middleware to extract FM information from the BIM and to manage it within the middleware level. Middleware has two separate but related meanings. One is software that enables two separate programs to interact with each other. It runs quietly in the background, but serves as important "glue" between the server applications. Another is a software layer inside a single application that allows different aspects of the program to work together.[12] FM middleware can, among other things, create a bidirectional link between the model and other applications.

EcoDomus (www.ecodomus.com) is an example of a third-party provider of what has been termed a *BIM for FM* solution. It uses a middleware called EcoDomus FM that provides for real-time integration of BIM with BAS, FMS, and GIS with FM software. By integrating these previously separate datasets, it allows the facility manager an increased ability to analyze operational data and have a more complete approach to asset management. It also employs advanced integration with major applications like Autodesk Revit, Bentley BIM, and IBM Maximo.In addition to the use of middleware, parties can also create digital data transfer agreements to resolve miscommunication and misunderstandings that can lead to loss and liability. To reduce potential liability, digital data transfer agreements have become common, replete with liability waivers and caveats regarding use. At their extreme, these documents prohibit reliance on the electronic documents and require that the receiving party compare the digital information against hard copy documentation. But prohibiting reliance undermines the single advantage of digital information, its ability to be efficiently exchanged and repurposed. Thus, current practice is evolving to allow relying on transferred data for specifically identified uses, including FM uses.

[12] See www.techterms.com, s.v. "middleware," accessed January 2013.

WILL USING BIM INCREASE LIABILITY TO OTHER PARTIES?

Efficient use of BIM requires significant exchange of data between design, construction, and FM, thus bridging the distinctions between these disciplines. This has resulted in liability concerns that impede BIM adoptions. Design professionals have become more concerned with the possibility that they may be drawn into disputes between contractors and owners, while contractors are concerned that they will be liable for certain design elements. The FM BIM, or the FM data extracted from the BIM, becomes a new team deliverable that traces back to design and construction. Although collaborative use of BIM will likely reduce the risk of errors—and thus the parties' actual risk—the increased data exchange can broaden liability, if problems do occur. Although these liability concerns are applicable to BIM generally, as well as the use of BIM for facility management, they are important to understand because they affect the parties' willingness to exchange information that will eventually reside in the FM BIM or database.

Will Designers Have an Increased Risk?

Design professionals have long sought to distance themselves from economic disputes between the contractor and the owner. Where the contractor asserts direct claims, designers have argued they are not liable because they are not in privity (i.e., there is no contractual relationship) with the contractor and the damages sought are not recoverable due to the economic loss doctrine. These arguments have been partially successful, although the scope and exceptions to the economic loss doctrine vary between jurisdictions.

But if information is provided for another's reliance, privity is not necessary to recover economic damages. The essentials of a negligent misrepresentation claim are set forth in *Restatement of Torts, Second,* section 552, as follows:

1. One who, in the course of his business, profession or employment, or in any other transaction in which he has a pecuniary interest, supplies false information for the guidance of others in their business transactions, is subject to liability for pecuniary loss caused to them by their justifiable reliance upon the information, if he fails to exercise reasonable care or competence in obtaining or communicating the information.
2. Except as stated in Subsection (3), the liability stated in Subsection (1) is limited to loss suffered:
   a. by the person or one of a limited group of persons for whose benefit and guidance he intends to supply the information or knows that the recipient intends to supply it; and

   b. through reliance upon it in a transaction that he intends the information to influence or knows that the recipient so intends or in a substantially similar transaction.

3. The liability of one who is under a public duty to give the information extends to loss suffered by any of the class of persons for whose benefit the duty is created, in any of the transactions in which it is intended to protect them.

Thus, a data recipient can state a claim under §552 and that privity and the economic loss doctrine will have little sway. Some may say that a solution is to provide either the model or certain data with broad disclaimers of liability, discouraging reliance. In the context of a BIM model, however, reliance is paramount. Having unreliable data in the model undercuts the efficiency of BIM, not only because parties will have to verify other parties' work, but also as a collaborative tool that can be used throughout the project and into operations of the facility. It also discourages collaboration.

Although the defenses of privity and economic loss are diminished, risk is not necessarily increased. The ability to share model information between designer and contractor leads to better quality documents and the avoidance of physical clashes. Thus, designers increase their exposure by providing information, but can effectively reduce their risk by reducing the probability and severity of project failure.

Will Contractors Have Increased Liability for Defects in the Plans and Specifications?

The *Spearin* doctrine allocates defected design risk by implying an owner's warranty that plans are complete and accurate. The protection afforded contractors under the *Spearin* doctrine is based on the implied warranty from the party providing the design documents and specifications that those documents are free from defect.[13] Although initially a defensive doctrine, *Spearin* has evolved into an offensive weapon that permits contractors to recover whenever plans have errors or omissions, which is almost certain to occur in any real project. Contractors' concern is that collaboration in the design process through BIM may undermine the implied warranty behind the design documents, leaving them less protected under the *Spearin* doctrine.

[13] The Spearin court found that the one who provides the plans and specification for a construction project warrants that those plans and specifications are free from defect. See *U.S. v. Spearin* (1918) 248 U.S. 132, 136.

There is an exception to the *Spearin* doctrine for contractors who participate in the preparation of specification or other design documents.[14] In other words, if the project design incorporates material information provided by the contractor, there will be no implied warranty.[15] This occurred, for example, when a contractor agreed to design, manufacture, and test an innovative digital data recording system.[16] The contract contained detailed specifications as to the method of constructing the system, but the contractor determined that the contract would be impossible to perform using those specifications.[17] It modified the design, but was still unable to successfully execute the contract. The court denied the contractor the defense of impossibility, holding that the contractor warranted its ability to perform according to the specifications it provided.

The *Spearin* doctrine does not apply to performance specifications because the owner has not dictated how the work will be performed. Thus, the characterization as "design" or "performance" specifications determines the existence of the implied warranty–and often the result. Specifications containing performance and prescriptive elements (hybrid specifications) are fact specific and have had differing outcomes. In a fully modeled project, particularly in a collaborative project where subcontractor and vendor information is incorporated into the design, however, a court would likely turn to cases of hybrid specifications to determine whether to imply a warranty. Although the decision turns the facts, the more a contractor's involvement in the design, the less likely a warranty will be implied.

Spearin protection also extends to a contractor who discovers a patent ambiguity in the bid documents and notifies the architect or owner. A contractor's participation in reviewing the design model early on in the design process will surely increase its ability to discover defects. In such a case, however, the contractor may lose the benefit of the owner's implied warranty. One writer noted that invocation of the *Spearin* doctrine by a contractor and BIM participant as to whether an error otherwise latent should be considered patent would likely be set very high (O'Brien 2007, pp. 30, 31).

Thus, the contractor's involvement in design, which may defeat the designer's economic loss and privity defenses, may also diminish the contractor's implied warranty claims. As with the risk profile for designers, the use of BIM necessitates a shift in risk for contractors, but not necessarily an increase in overall risk.

[14] See Federal Court of Claims case *Haehn Management Co. v. United States* (1988) 15 Cl. Ct. 50, 56 , stating: "[t]he warranty of specifications can be vitiated by the involvement of industry or the contractor's participation in drafting and development of the specification absent superior knowledge on the part of the Government."

[15] *Austin Co. v. United States* (1963) 314 F.2d 518, 520.

[16] Ibid., 520.

[17] Ibid.

HOW DOES AN INTEGRATED PROJECT DELIVERY (IPD) ENVIRONMENT AFFECT LIABILITIES RELATED TO RELIANCE ON BIM?

Many of the legal issues related to reliance on BIM information are theoretically exacerbated in Integrated IPD because of the early involvement of many consultants and trades and the exchange of "incomplete work early and often." But in practice, the risk is sharply reduced because the contract between the parties explicitly waives many of the risks among them and the process greatly improves understanding and reduces the likelihood of error.

IPD agreements allocate the liabilities in several different ways. Typical approaches are to:

- Waive liabilities among at risk parties with certain defined exceptions (AIA C191 and Hanson Bridgett Standard IPD Agreement).
- Limit liability to the profit in the risk/reward pool (Sutter Health Integrated Agreement for Lean Project Delivery 2008).
- Waive liabilities for joint decisions (ConsensusDOCS 300).

There are also a variety of hybrid approaches and some except the limitation of waiver based on the availability of insurance (including AIA C191).

The limitation of liability provisions for each of the referenced documents are further detailed in this chapter, but it should be noted that both the Sutter Health Agreement and ConsensusDOCS 300 are being revised as this chapter is written.

The AIA C191 liability waiver is a complete waiver of claims subject to seven exceptions: (1) willful misconduct, (2) express warranty, (3) owner's failure to pay, (4) express indemnification, (5) failure to procure insurance, (6) damages arising from third-party liens and the like; and (7) damages covered by insurance.[18] Note that although there is a waiver of consequential damages, the agreement allows for liquidated damages.[19]

The Hanson Bridgett Standard IPD Agreement liability waiver provides that all liability between the parties, Cost Reimbursable Consultants and Cost Reimbursable Subcontractors is waived except for "Allowed Claims," which are: (1) willful default, (2) warranty, (3) project performance after final completion, (4) third-party claims, (5) owner directive, (6) owner nonpayment; (7) termination or suspension costs; (8) enforcement of indemnity obligations, (9) failure

[18] AIA C191—2009 Standard Form Multi-Party Agreement for Integrated Project Delivery, § 8.1.

[19] AIA C191—2009 Standard Form Multi-Party Agreement for Integrated Project Delivery, § 8.2.1.

to procure proper insurance coverage, and (10) enforcement of dispute resolution provisions, mechanics liens, and stop notices.[20] Although this is a private agreement, it has been used on a variety of IPD projects and has been used as a model on others.

The Sutter Health Integrated Form of Agreement (IFOA) provides that all liability of architect, CM/GC, and others participating in the IPD Team Risk Pool is limited to the amount of funds available in the pool, except that no limitation of liability is made for the following items: (1) insurance recoveries, (2) fraud or willful misconduct, (3) claims against subcontractors who are not IPD Team Risk Pool members, (4) fines or penalties assessed against an IPD Team Risk Pool member, or (5) an IPD Team Risk Pool member who abandons the project.[21] Like the Hanson Bridgett agreement, the Sutter Health IFOA has been used on IPD projects and has served as a model on others.[22]

The ConsensusDOCS 300 project risk allocation has two options: (1) "Safe Harbor Decisions" or (2) "Traditional Risk Allocation." Regardless of the option selected, there is a mutual waiver of consequential damages.[23] Under the Safe Harbor, the parties waive liability against each other for acts, omissions, mistakes, or errors in judgment arising from joint decisions made in good faith by the PMG, unless the party is in willful default of an obligation under the agreement.[24] Under the traditional risk allocation, each party remains fully liable for its own negligence and breaches of contract and warranty, but there is an option to cap designer's and constructor's liability to a specified amount for uninsurable risk.[25]

Although the mechanisms differ between the IPD contracts, all seek to create a structure that reduces the parties fear of being sued based on the free exchange of data,[26] thus limiting the quality and velocity of communication—which is

[20] Hanson Bridgett Standard Integrated Project Delivery Agreement, § 12.1–12.2.

[21] Sutter Health's Integrated Agreement for Lean Project Delivery, §33.1.

[22] For a description of how this IFOA was implemented on a recent Sutter Health Hospital project, see Eastman et al., 2011, pp. 431–479.

[23] ConsensusDOCS 300—Standard Form of Tri-Party Agreement for Collaborative Project Delivery, §3.8.2, §3.8.3.

[24] Ibid., §3.8.2.1.

[25] Ibid., §3.8.2.2.

[26] The primary reasons for limiting liability are to increase communication, foster creativity, and reduce excessive contingencies. The liability concern, and its potential harm, was neatly summarized in the commentary Intelligent Building Models and Downstream Use, Comments of the Technology in Architectural Practice Advisory Group submitted for the 2007 revisions to AIA Documents B141 and A201, AIA 2005: "We fear there will be a tendency, driven by valid concerns about liability and insurability, to prevent such use of the architect's design data. We believe this is the wrong answer and would jeopardize the future of architectural practice as we know it. . . . Obstacles to a free flow of data among the project participants should be overcome so that the architecture firm can deliver the full value of its work to the client and be rewarded commensurately."

necessary for efficient coordination of design and construction and is a major factor in creativity.[27]

The liability reduction in IPD projects has a major effect on how BIM is used. Because they benefit from liability waivers and limitations, designers are more open to sharing interim work with trade contractors and suppliers, allowing earlier cost and constructability feedback. Similarly, contractors are more willing to deeply engage in design assist if they are less concerned about assuming design liability.

IPD agreements also place all or a portion of the parties' profit at risk based on overall project outcome. If there are errors in design, the contractor's profit is reduced. If the contractor is less efficient, the architect suffers, too. This improves alignment between parties, encourages careful review of each other's work, and also removes the incentive to file claims or blame the other. Moreover, by working closely together, contractors and designers develop an understanding of each other's competency—and with little incentive to finger-point—develop trust in each other's work. It is not uncommon for IPD designers and contractors to be working in joint files, as well as freely exchanging data.

The upshot is that IPD increases the potential for liability by greatly increasing the data interchange between parties, but practically reduces the risk by changing the way work is performed and supporting the change with appropriate contract language.

DOES INSURANCE COVER BIM-RELATED WORK?

BIM raises property and liability insurance issues. The property insurance issues relate to who has rights in the model(s) (and hence has an insurable interest), and where the model(s) exist. Contracts with parties contributing to the BIM should require coverage of the BIM through electronic "valuable papers" coverage.

The liability issues are, thankfully, straightforward. Professional liability policies are clearly broad enough to cover a designer's use of BIM, which should be treated no differently than designing with computer-aided design (CAD). The two professional liability insurance provisions most likely to create coverage disputes are joint venture exclusions and means and methods exclusions. The joint venture exclusion could conceivably be applied to claims arising from projects performed under multiparty collaborative contracts if the contracts are poorly drafted. Means and methods exclusions, applicable to some policies, could apply if the design

[27] A climate of fear is not conducive to creativity and undermines intrinsic motivation (see Amabile 1998).

required, or implied, a specific, but incorrect, method. In addition, if the design professional is providing software development or Web hosting for the project, care should be taken to assure that these services are not outside the professional liability definition of the policy. Contractors engaged in BIM projects should have contractor's professional liability coverage because their design contributions in the model could conflict with the design exclusion in their commercial general liability policies.

CONCLUSION

Although all BIM projects have these issues, the success and failure of projects using BIM specifically for FM will depend to a large extent on how well the parties have defined the information to be input and exported from the model and whether the contract documents clearly define the contractual model, who owns what, and how data translation issues have been addressed. When clear expectations regarding responsibility and deliverables are set early and memorialized, the parties become comfortable with BIM road map from design through operations.

Sample BIM Specification

Record BIM

The BIM must be updated continuously throughout the construction process and must include all addenda, approved change orders, field orders, clarifications, request for information (RFI) responses, and as-built conditions. The record BIM includes the BIM at a level of detail (LOD) 500 and includes a description of the relationship of each model in the Record BIM to the others. Contractor may reference the AIA Document E202–2008 for LOD 500 description. In addition, the record BIM must be accompanied by the final versions of all fabrication and detailing models prepared by the contractor and its subcontractors. All models must be provided in native file format with a description of the software used to create the model (software manufacturer, software name, version number, and operating system used for the software).

(Continued)

Objectives

- To create a BIM(s) that contains the actual population of architectural, structural, mechanical, electrical, plumbing, and civil objects for building services such as fire and life safety, HVAC, data/communications, security, and lighting that may be utilized for building design, construction, and operation.
- To populate the critical mechanical, electrical, plumbing, and civil objects with the appropriate performance requirements and as-built information. The object attribute information that is captured will be used throughout the building life cycle and potentially integrated into owner's ArcGIS system.
- To create an accurate current-condition record of the existing building conditions.

Requirements

Contractor must update the BIM to accurately reflect all design and construction changes from the final preconstruction DBIM submitted to owner.

Contractor must create a Record Building Information Model that accurately reflects "as-built" conditions for all building systems, including but not limited to architectural, civil, structural, mechanical, life safety, and electrical systems.

The contractor must model the following:

- Underground utilities (within building footprint and 15 feet beyond its perimeter).
- Architectural models.
- Structural models.
- Mechanical, electrical, life safety, and plumbing elements limited to:
  - All fixed mechanical ducts.
  - Electrical conduit 3/4 inch (19.05 mm) or greater.
  - Plumbing and life safety piping 1/4 inch (6.35 mm) or greater.

(Continued)

- All fixtures and equipment (manufacturer, model, size, and weight).
- Equipment performance information (input/output).
- Power distribution (panels and circuits).
- Lighting.
- All piping and terminations.
- All ductwork.
- Calculation information and sustaining information tied into models views.
- Space–zone/circulation information.

The following must be defined for all systems:

- Materials.
- Finishes.
- All electrical circuiting.
- Cable trays and raceways.
- Tags.
- Labels.
- All warranty information tied to the model objects and presented in views.
- Product data/cut sheets tied to the objects.
- Maintenance schedules and operations data.

Facility Management Information

Record model must be consistent with the COBie2 Model View definition published by the National Institute of Building Science in the Whole Building Design Guide.

The contractor will assist owner in the integration of the project BIM into the owner's computerized maintenance management system (CMMS). This contractor's effort will consist of collecting, validating, updating, and exporting design, construction and commissioning data for owner's use, and if required by the contract, entering the information into owner's CMMS.

The contractor must prepare the BIM at each phase with the following defined information.

(Continued)

Construction Phase

- Type information updated by providing manufacturer, model number, warranty information (parts and labor and duration), and replacement cost.
- Component information updated by providing serial number, installation date, warranty start date, and, optionally, tag number or barcode. Installation date for major equipment will be the finish date of the corresponding schedule activity.
- Spare parts provided for types.
- Attributes provided for types and components.

Commissioning Phase

- Documents assigned (uploaded) to corresponding BIM objects (types, components, spaces, facility).
- Attributes corrected based on real measurements.

Facility Management

The BIM execution plan (BEP) must specify a workflow to identify model elements that are significant for operations and maintenance of the facility and to map data structures from owner's computerized maintenance management system (CMMS) and computer-aided facility management (CAFM) to systems attributes of the identified model elements. Where the CMMS and facility management system (FMS) data structure does not have a comparable attribute in a modeled element, the BEP should define an additional custom model element attribute to provide congruent mapping to the CMMS data structure.

The BEP should specify a workflow for transferring FM data from the BIM to the CMMS either directly or through middleware that manages the interchange of information between the record model and the CMMS.

COBie2

BIM-authoring software must support data export and import from the COBie table databases.

(Continued)

FM/BAS Integration Export

Owner currently uses Maximo by IBM as its primary CMMS. The record BIM must map Maximo input fields as required by this specification to allow CMMS data export from the Record BIM into Maximo. Mapping should follow the guidelines of USACE Engineer Research and Development Center, *COBie2 Data Import/Export Interoperability with the MAXIMO Computerized Maintenance Management System,* November 2008. Contractor must demonstrate data export into the CMMS during development of the BEP. In addition, and if required by the contract, the record BIM must be interoperable with owner-specified middleware that manages the interchange of information between the record model and the CMMS.

REFERENCES

Amabile, T. 1998. "How to Kill Creativity." *Harvard Business Review* (September–October).

Eastman, Chuck, Paul Teicholz, Rafael Sacks, and Kathleen Liston. 2011. *The BIM Handbook: A Guide to Building Information Modeling* (2nd ed.). Hoboken, NJ: John Wiley and Sons.

Jordani, David A. 2010. "BIM and FM: The Portal to Lifecycle Facility Management." *Journal of Building Information Modeling* (Spring), 13–16.

O'Brien, T. 2007. "Building Information Modeling, Sailing on Uncharted Waters." Conference paper, ABA Forum on the Construction Industry, October 2007.

U.S. General Services Administration. 2011. *GSA Building Information Modeling Guide Series: 08—GSA BIM Guide for Facility Management.* Version 1 (December). Washington, DC: U.S. General Services Administration. Available at www.gsa.gov/graphics/pbs/BIM_Guide_Series_Facility_Management.pdf (accessed January 2013).

Using COBie

5

Bill East, PhD, PE, F.ASCE

Research Civil Engineer, Engineer Research and Development Center, Champaign, IL

EXECUTIVE SUMMARY

COBie is an international standard that delivers managed asset information. COBie stands for the Construction Operations Building information exchange. Today, COBie can be created and exchanged using over 20 commercial software systems. COBie can also be created and exchanged using simple spreadsheets, if that is more helpful for the team. This chapter begins by describing the motives behind the COBie project. The spreadsheet format for COBie is described. Steps to implement COBie at a facility management office and ongoing work complete this chapter. The authoritative source for information about COBie is the Whole Building Design Guide's COBie web site where technical documentation, example models, and instructional videos can be found (East 2008).

WHY COBIE?

In 1983 a leading panel of experts convened by the National Research Council concluded that "much valuable data associated with the design, construction, and operation of a facility is lost during its life span" (National Research Council

1983). That statement is as true today as it was during the advent of modern construction practice, which began with the invention of scaled construction drawings in the Renaissance period. The impact of the loss of this design and construction information is felt in many ways that are simply part of the way that facility managers do business. Following are some examples of real stories told to me about problems that could be easily solved if design, construction, and facility information were available as secure, shared information to facility managers.

The first example is the case of a broken industrial trash compactor at a commissary on a large Army installation. To replace this trash compactor should have been a simple matter of determining what was already installed and purchasing a replacement. Had the information been available in data form, then the job would have been completed in minutes. In reality, a midlevel facility management staff member needed two days to comb through project records before the original product data for the equipment could be found.

The second example comes from needing to replace a specific part of a complex piece of equipment. The heating element of a boiler had corroded out until it was no longer safe to use. The pressure vessel part of the boiler was in good shape, but the heating element had to be replaced. There was no information on the heating element at all since the manufacturer was out of business. The original specifications for the heating element could not be found. To purchase a new heating element based on incomplete information or to wait for an entirely new boiler installation were the choices left to the facility manager.

Facility managers are often responsible for both operations and maintenance (O&M) and tenant management. The last anecdote shows the potential impact of maintaining multiple building asset records in a major hospital. Following a change to departmental assignments tenants assigned to wings or floors of buildings often make changes in the way that those spaces are used, without providing feedback to the facility management office. To compare the two different databases about spaces and their uses I randomly selected a floor and picked a room directly behind that wing's central nurse station. To my surprise the tenant management database indicated that the room was a medicine preparation area and the facility management database indicated that the same room belonged to housekeeping. The questions that arose included, "Does the janitorial staff have keys to the room in which restricted medications are kept?" and "Are the mop and bucket being kept in the same space as medicine preparation?"

While many facility management (FM) organizations have spent vast quantities of financial, organizational, and human resource capital for the purchase of complex systems to manage maintenance, operations, and assets, these systems cannot be effectively used today. This is because the introduction of technology has demonstrated the enormous expense of loading data from design and construction into maintenance management systems. A recent presentation reported that six technicians working overtime and weekends for 5 months were required to load equipment manufacturer and model information into a maintenance management system for a mid-size medical facility (Medellin 2010). Clearly, most facility managers do not have the resources to pay for such overtime and weekend work. I have personally visited facilities that employ one or more full-time data-entry clerks to enter such information. One maintenance management system software company recently reported that on a small campus of five administrative buildings cost and time savings on preventative maintenance and service orders could reach one quarter of a million dollars per year (Siorek 2010).

After a 2011 plenary presentation to a major national construction association, the president of that organization thanked me for the presentation on COBie, but then added, "You know, Bill, we know all about this problem." What struck me as so odd was the fact while an entire industry sector is acutely aware of the waste associated with problems of facility handover, they were not interested in reducing their wasted effort to effectively increase their profit and/or improve productivity.

While this chapter will address the new national standard developed specifically to streamline the delivery of managed building assets through the planning, design, and construction process, the real question for facility managers is, "Why hasn't anyone fixed this before now?" After an explanation of the COBie format, I will return to this question again to discuss an implementation checklist for a simple, step-by-step method through which facility managers may begin to gain productivity for both technical and administrative staff through the application of secure, shared, and structured building information.

HOW WAS COBIE DESIGNED?

When designing buildings, architects need to understand what activities will take place in the building, structural engineers need to know the types of loads those activities will generate, and mechanical engineers will have to know the extent to which temperature and humidity must be controlled to support these activities. In some ways, developing an information exchange standard is no different from the design of a building. There are requirements to be identified. There is a solution to be designed based on those requirements. There is a process by which the design is built and tested. Finally, the building is used by those who designed it. The development of COBie directly followed this pattern to ensure that when people were ready to use COBie, it would provide the information needed for them to maintain, operate, and manage facilities.

Determining what should be included in COBie and what should be left out is complicated because of the technological, contractual, and process constraints on the practical delivery of the required information. Rather than ignore such constraints, the design of COBie directly addresses the practicalities of scope, technology, contract, and process. The criteria used to arrive at the current scope of the COBie standard reflect current contractual requirements of different parties that enforce the delivery of construction handover information. Included in this data set is a list of managed assets initialized in design schedules, updated by the construction contractor, and finalized during commissioning processes. Product data sheets are provided by product manufacturers. System layout drawings are provided by the subcontracting fabricator. Because of the different sources of construction handover information, three projects were developed to reflect differences in the way that the information would have to be created and contractually specified.

The first of these projects, COBie, focused on replicating the current lists of managed assets and related information developed by the contractor and commissioning agent (East 2007). The second project focused on obtaining manufacturer's product data for those assets. The second project is called the Specifers' Properties information exchange (SPie), East 2012b. The third project focused on the definition of the connections among components to create system-oriented information. The third project, originally called the Equipment Layout information exchange (ELie) project has now become four separate projects covering heating, ventilating, and air conditioning (HVAC) systems; electrical systems; water distribution; and building automation systems. While this chapter focuses on COBie, more information on each of the other projects may be found on the buildingSMART alliance information exchange project pages (For a list of all active bSa projects: www.buildingsmartalliance.org/index.php/projects/activeprojects).

Managed Asset Inventory

At construction handover, the essential responsibility of facility managers is to ensure that the facility's fixed assets deliver the services needed in each of the spaces in the facility. Managed assets are those assets that require management, maintenance, consumable parts, regular inspections, and so on. Such assets are of two types. First are the assets that are typically managed through computer-aided facility management (CAFM) systems (i.e., spaces). Second are the equipment and product assets related to building services such has HVAC, electrical, water, and the like that are typically managed through a computerized maintenance management system (CMMS). Information about structures and architectural elements, to the extent that such products are actively managed, may also be included in COBie.

For the purpose of managing facility assets, the absolute location of each piece of equipment is not required. As long as equipment can be identified as within a given space, then the technician will be able to perform the required maintenance or repair activity. As a result, COBie requires all products and equipment to be identified within a specific space. Furthermore, the placement of that equipment in walls, under floors, or in plenums versus visible within the space may be included in COBie.

Knowing the properties of a given piece of equipment is also important for the facility manager. Having such information on hand can significantly reduce the time to repair or replace broken equipment. While the SPie project will ultimately allow manufactures to directly provide required information through the design and construction process, the COBie Guide provides a minimum statement of properties required for managed assets (East 2012b).

The organization of assets across multiple facilities is also of importance when obtaining COBie data. Repair and replacement decisions reviewed across an organization can improve the reliability of the entire facility inventory. Having a consolidated picture of assets across and entire campus may also result in improved staffing and management decision making. To compare information delivered on several facilities the facility manager must identify and require that assets are consistently classified.

Classification of spaces as well as equipment is also required in COBie. This allows the facility manager to more fully allocate occupants to spaces that meet their specific needs. The utilization of underallocated spaces may be adjusted. The facility manager will also be able to more quickly respond to changes in mission of tenants and emergency operations. Again, the COBie Guide provides recommendations about the types of classifications needed (East 2012b).

Operations and Maintenance Requirements

Current construction handover specifications require the delivery of information from manufacturer's regarding equipment preventative maintenance plans, startup, shutdown, and emergency operational procedures. Commissioning agents or subcontractors also prepare documents that provide operational information about entire building systems. Such information is critical since failure of a building's systems can impact building occupants if such steps are not followed. Failure to follow proper shutdown procedures on HVAC system, for example, closing dampers without first turning off fans, may cause sufficient negative pressure to collapse ductwork. Failure to follow standard operational settings, such as decreasing the proportion of outside air to recirculated conditioned air has, for example, resulted in increased rates of infection in medical facilities.

COBie organizes all task-based actions that need to be documented at construction handover into one common format of "jobs." Each job is identified as to the type of work, preventative maintenance, startup procedures, emergency operations procedures, and so on. In many cases, specialized tools, training, or materials may also be needed to complete the work. These resources are also captured. In addition to allocating correctly trained and outfitted technicians for a specific job, the facility manager may also use this information to document annual training and equipment budgets. Other O&M information contained in COBie includes warranty terms, documents, and guarantor information, and spare and consumable parts information.

Technological Constraints

An important factor in the development of any standard is making sure that the people who need to use it have the technology to enable them to produce, review, and use the information. Since the start of the personal computer age, software and media used in the design and construction industry have been rapidly changing. In many ways this change in technology, while being sold with the expectation of increasing efficiency, has directly contributed to the loss of valuable project information.

Consider that the state of the art 30 years ago was linen and ink drawings. Such documents, if kept dry and away from light, could easily last centuries. The longevity of this medium was commensurate with the expected life of a building. Now consider computer-aided drafting and design software files for buildings produced on 5.25-inch floppy disks. Five years after the receipt of those drawings, the media has likely been demagnetized, and there may not be a computer in the office able to read the files. Even if there is still a floppy disk drive, the software needed to open, update, and print those drawings is not likely to be available or supported.

The most important decision regarding technology made in the development of COBie is that proprietary standards or those that require specific media formats or software systems will not be usable over the expected life of a given facility or campus. As a result, an open international standard data exchange format was selected as the underlying format for COBie data. Using open standards allows the facility manager to secure, own, access, and update his/her information over the entire life of the project. Decisions of software can be made on the ability of that software to utilize open standard data to support facility management operations, and not on the next technology fetish.

One of the international drivers for the creation of COBie was the German state of Bavaria. Every five years the management of public buildings in Bavaria is put out for bid. A part of that bid is the transfer of information from one company's maintenance management system to the new company's system. Such a transfer before COBie was very difficult and required specialized software.

Once the decision to use open standards was made, standards for the expression of the complete set of managed facility asset information were reviewed. The only format sufficient to capture COBie requirements was found to be the industry foundation class (IFC) model. As a result, the underlying format of all buildingSMART alliance projects is an ISO standard for building information called the Industry Foundation Class, IFC, Model (ISO 26739). IFC model information is typically exchanged through a complex computer-to-computer information exchange format called STEP (ISO 10303). The formal specification of COBie is called the Facility Management Handover Model View Definition (East and Chipman 2012).

While the formal specification for COBie envisions the performance-based delivery of computer-to-computer of facility information, that day has not yet arrived. As a result COBie was developed so that the data could be easily accessible to those with no computer programming skills, using the most modest of software. As a result the spreadsheet was chosen as the format for COBie information that would be most widely presented. To ensure compliance with the underlying international standard format, a set of translation rules were used to allow software developers to translate between IFC-based formats and the spreadsheet format. For those needing the precise technical specification of COBie, including IFC mapping rules, should review the COBie Responsibility Matrix (East, Bogen, and Love 2011).

Contracting Constraints

History has shown that rarely are project owners willing to spend more during planning and design, even if the result is a more operationally efficient building. Asking for additional fee from designers and contractors to produce electronic design and construction information would, therefore, be an untenable position. As a result COBie is specifically designed to only include the delivery of information that is already found in typical design and construction contracts.

It is quite easy for the casual observer to consider that once the list of equipment is provided in electronic format that all the properties of that product could also be provided. Such an observation does not, however, take into account the practicality of the contractor obtaining product information in data, versus product data format. Without all manufacturers directly providing product data in a COBie-compatible format, contractors will have to type in product attributes. Since retyping manufacturers' product data is not currently required, there would be a significant additional cost to include such attributes in a specification for the delivery of COBie. As a result, product attribute data is necessarily left out of the basic COBie specification.

There is, however, some product data that could be required. Since COBie captures information about managed assets we can see that these managed assets will typically appear on product schedules on design drawings. The COBie Guide, released for public comment in July 2012, specifically requires that COBie file attributes about scheduled equipment match the attributes that are found on the design schedules (East 2012b). Given that the criteria is simply that the COBie information match the information found on design drawings, such a quality standard may be defensible from a contracting cost point of view.

Process Constraints

While there has been much interest in lean construction practices for builders, few have considered the impact of emerging standards, such as COBie, to eliminate wasteful administrative processes. As an example of such a wasteful process, a former research assistant employed on my team had, between undergraduate and graduate schools, the summer job of copying paper submittal documents to create O&M manuals for a large construction project. This procedure was wasteful since all the information needed to create these manuals was already processed through the contract administration process related to construction submittals. Had the electronic form of approved submittals been captured, during the submittal process, a very bright student could have been spared the mind-numbing job of making paper copies of formerly electronic documents. The typical process for documenting scheduled equipment nameplate data is by walk-through at the end of the project. This "job crawl" captures information that could have been documented at installation, startup, or testing of the equipment with very little additional effort.

The COBie process is based on a simple assumption. This assumption is that COBie data should be provided by the party who is traditionally and contractually required to create that information. The only real difference in COBie-based process is that the deliverable is a data file (or files) and not paper. Architects, for example, create designs that identify spaces and equipment. Space and equipment schedules produced in a COBie format should be directly exported to COBie from design software as simply as those design products print construction drawings. Product data sheets and other file-based information, captured through an electronic submittal process, eliminate the need for a contractor to scan such information. If the contractor, when documenting the installed and on-site equipment for payment purposes, is required to submit their report using COBie, then there will be no delay at the end of the project. In short, a new information-based process of design, construction, and handover can be supported using COBie as the information exchange format. The generic specification of what information is provided by whom and when in the facility life cycle is defined in the Life-Cycle Information Exchange Project (East 2010).

With scope, technology, contracting- and process-related decisions made in the early design phase of the COBie standard, what remained was to determine the most compact and mutually agreeable format for the delivery of managed assets and associated O&M information. The following section describes the COBie data model and explains how each of the parts of that model connect.

WHAT IS INCLUDED IN COBIE?

The overall structure of a COBie data set at the construction handover stage of a project is shown in Figure 5.1. There are three types of information in COBie. The first is information that is created by designers, shown in the blue box in Figure 5.1. The second, information created by contractors, is shown in the orange box. The third is supporting information that is created by both designers and contractors, shown in the green box.

COBie's requirements for designers reflect the two major categories of assets: spatial and equipment assets. Spaces within a building are organized by facility, floor, and then the space. There is a correlation between the idea of a Space and a physical room in COBie. If a given physical room has several functions, or different parts of it belong to different departments, then that physical space may be defined by several individual spaces. Often, the designer already identifies these differences by adding letters after a room number, such as "101-A" and "101-B." As the project progresses from design to handover, the final signage outside each

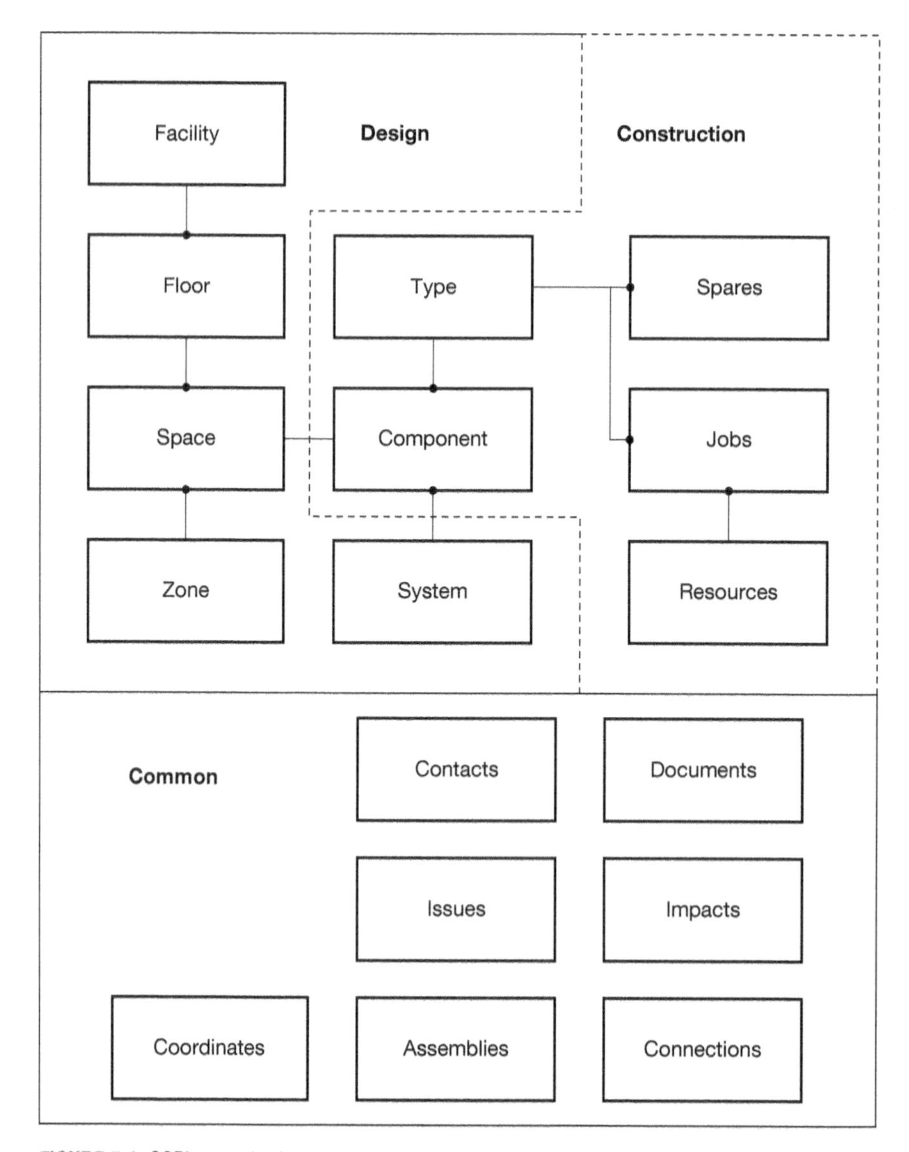

FIGURE 5.1 COBie organization.

of the rooms of the facility often does not match the room numbers provided by the designer. The contractor adds the signage information once that is known as the Space.RoomTag value.

Figure 5.2 provides an example of how spaces are organized into zones in one portion of a medical clinic building. At the top left of Figure 5.2, the name of the facility is shown as "Medical Clinic." This information is captured in the "Facility"

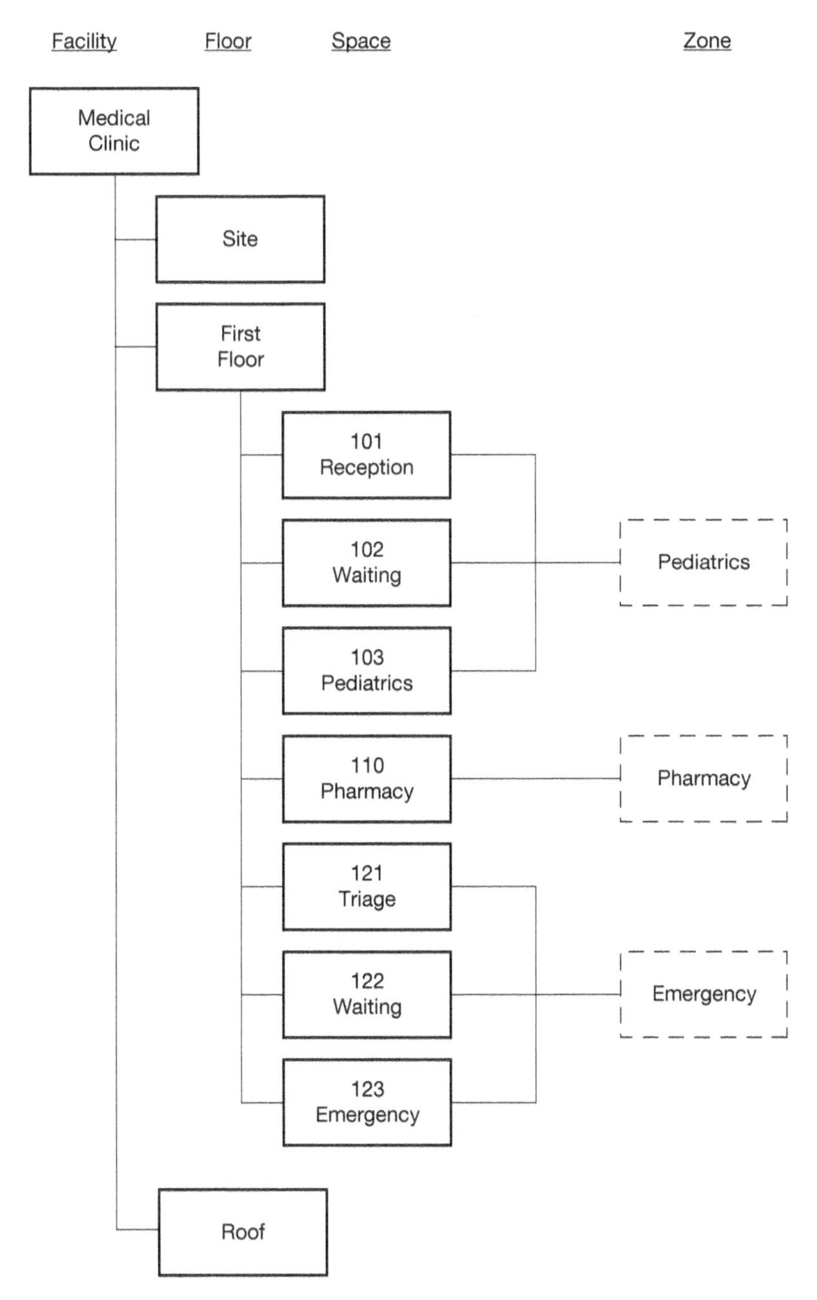

FIGURE 5.2 Spatial organization.

area of COBie. Under the facility are the different vertical slices through that facility. These are called "Floors" in COBie. As shown in the figure, even the site and the roof are listed as COBie floors. The working areas of the buildings, for example, "101 Reception," are the spaces in COBie. If we were interested in identifying some aspects of groups of rooms, we would use a COBie "zone." In the figure, the focus is on identifying the department occupying the spaces. The pediatrics department uses spaces 101 through 103. The pharmacy uses a single space, 110. The emergency department uses 121 through 123.

Groups of spaces are managed in zones; therefore, zones are found in COBie. In a given building there are always many different kinds of zones, all of which can be represented in COBie. Figure 5.2 is an example where spaces are organized by department. There could also be circulation zones that indicate public and private space and zones for spaces that reflect specific types of building services such as heating and cooling zones or fire protection zones. Each of these zones has a separate list of categories, just as the department zone in Figure 5.2 has three different categories, but all zones refer back to the same list of spaces that make up the building.

The second major category of assets in facilities is scheduled equipment and tagged products. All equipment assets are organized by the type of asset, that is, the manufacturer and model number, and then each of the individual components. During design, equipment schedules are found on the design drawings and should be fully reflected in a COBie file. Bulk items that may be reported by the contractor such as valves, switches, and dampers may need to be drawn out from notes and symbols on design drawings. Often, contractors are required to install brass tags on bulk items such as valves. Some facility managers require these tags or bar codes on all managed equipment. These tags or codes are also recorded in the Component.TagNumber and Component.BarCode fields.

To provide specific services to building occupants, equipment is organized into systems. Figure 5.3 provides a brief example of the organization of equipment in COBie. At the top left of the Figure 5.3 is the facility in which the equipment operates. The next layer of information about equipment is that of equipment Type. Equipment or product type reflects the organization of the designer's equipment and product schedules. These schedules strive to reuse the same specific type of equipment in a given facility where appropriate. This reduces the cost of the purchase of equipment on the project and reduces the cost for the construction and commissioning process. The example shown in Figure 5.3 illustrates part of the list of types for the "Medical Clinic" facility. Shown is door type A, since there will be more than a single type of door in a given building, each of the other door types will be similarly listed. The example also shows that there will be different types of pumps, a single type of air handling unit (AHU), and multiple types of windows. A real building would, of course, have many more types of equipment, so Figure 5.3 provides only a small subset. Under each equipment type are the specific instances of that equipment. As shown, there are two pumps of type A and two AHUs.

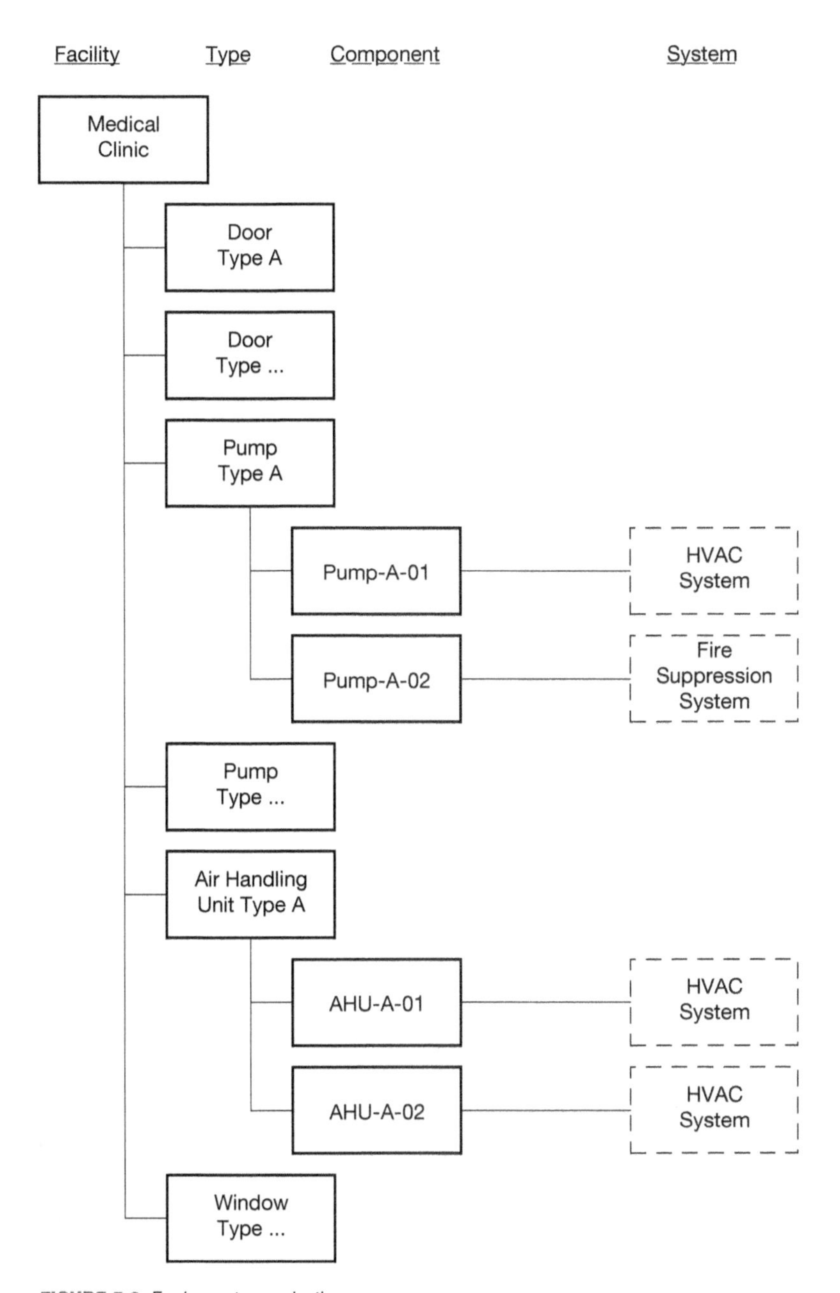

FIGURE 5.3 Equipment organization.

Equipment in a facility does not exist as a separate entity but is part of a system of components, connectors (such as pipes, ducts, and wiring), and controllers that provide a service (such as heating, cooling, fire suppression, etc.) The engineering consultants designing these systems, during the process of design, organize these services into different systems and subsystems to ensure that proper services can be delivered. To reflect that organization COBie allows these designers to identify the systems to which each component belongs. In Figure 5.3, for example, one of the pumps is used for the HVAC system and one of the pumps is used for the fire suppression system. Both AHUs are used for the heating and cooling system. The *COBie Guide* provides recommendations about the types of systems that should be captured to support facility maintenance activities, and helpful ways to categorize and name these systems to allow information to be more easily accessed (East 2012b).

Once the designer delivers COBie data at the end of the design, then the contractor's job is to augment the design data with information captured from construction. If the data provided from the designer is accurate, then to identify the make and model of a particular type of equipment, the contractor can use the information from the approved product submittals and update the designer's COBie data. Once the equipment is installed, the contractor needs only to document the installation date and serial number. Clearly, capturing such information when it is first available is a departure from paper-based processes. The benefit is that the contractor does not have to capture and possibly lose the information several times during the course of the project.

As building systems are commissioned, the contractor or commissioning agent collects the manufacturer's recommended maintenance and parts schedules as well as the system O&M information. Warranty and spare and consumable parts are also captured. It is up to the contractor or commissioning agent to complete the identification of that information in the COBie Jobs, Resources, and Spares worksheets.

IN WHAT FORMATS IS COBIE DELIVERED?

The ease with which we take for granted existing information standards hides the effort required to create and implement these standards. Those facility managers who began their careers with mainframe computers will recall difficulties in moving programs and documents from one manufacturer's computers to another's. One of the tools to resolve this issue was the development of the American Standard Code for Information Interchange, or ASCII, standard. Today, ASCII allows us to share written documents among a wide variety of devices.

At this time of transition between paper-based and information-based exchanges, facility managers need to have some understanding of the formats in which COBie can be exchanged. This knowledge will assist the facility manager in keeping track of claims and counterclaims made by the proponent of one format versus another. Those considering the use of COBie need to be aware that the information needed by the facility manager can be delivered in several different formats. As long as the information contained in the file reflects the requirements identified by the facility manager, is organized according to the COBie data model, and can be produced and consumed by the required software, that format is adequate for the transmission of COBie data. When conversations about COBie focus on the format of the file, this will reduce the time spent to ensure the quality of the result. As ASCII allows the transparent exchange of written documents, COBie and the related family of standards will allow the transmission of facility information across software and devices.

Today, there are three data formats that can be used to exchange COBie data. The first is called the Standard for the Exchange of Product, or STEP, which is an international standard found in the ISO 10303 specification. STEP files are widely used in product and industrial manufacturing and have been adapted through the additional schema requirements identified in the IFC Mode, ISO 16739. The second standard that may be used is called ifcXML. This format provides an Extensible Markup Language version of the STEP file. While these formats provide concise statements of COBie data, the formats themselves are oriented toward computer-to-computer interactions. Another of the available formats, SpreadsheetML, provides COBie information in a spreadsheet format.

Most users of COBie in the United States and the United Kingdom are familiar with the Excel spreadsheet version of COBie. This format provides a human-accessible view of facility information. Therefore, this chapter will focus on the spreadsheet version of the COBie file, knowing that other formats will be acceptable, provided that they contain the required information and can be consumed by the software needed at the FM office.

HOW IS THE SPREADSHEET FORMAT ORGANIZED?

The organization of COBie information, in spreadsheet form, occurs through a series of related worksheets. Together, these worksheets create a database of the facility describing that facilities set of managed assets. There has been extensive technical documentation on the COBie standard already published through the COBie web site (East 2008); therefore, the following descriptions provide only an introduction to the topic.

Along with each of the descriptions is an indication of the ability of commercial software to produce and/or consume that specific type of COBie information today. This information is provided to allow the facility manager to see what can be accomplished with COBie and what is possible, provided commercial software manufacturers upgrade their products, to deliver using COBie. There are several root causes to the gap between the practical and possible. These causes will be discussed in the later section discussing software testing as part of COBie Challenge events.

Common Worksheet Conventions

To simplify the organization of building information model into a spreadsheet, certain conventions were developed for COBie worksheets. These conventions, which include worksheet and field naming, field ordering, and color-coding, assist COBie users to reduce the complexity of what had not been possible before COBie. These conventions are described in the following paragraphs and documented fully in the COBie Guide (East 2012b). Examples of COBie files at different stages of project development may be found on the Common Building Information Model Files (East 2012d).

Worksheet Layout

COBie worksheets are organized to begin with the unique data element for that worksheet (the primary key) in the first column. Typically, the column is labeled "Name." Thus, the Type.Name refers to the Type worksheet, name column. The name column will always show up in the first column. The values for the rows in the name column are required to be unique.

The next set of columns contains information author history, specifically the CreatedBy and CreatedOn values. These values identify the person or company that created the data found in the COBie worksheet row. This person could be the person who was developing the COBie model, or simply the person who created the COBie file. Either way is fine as long as there is a way to get back to the person who created the information, in case there is a question.

The fourth column is typically the category of the information found in the row of data. For many of the categories of information found in a COBie file the facility manager may already have a standard set of values. Such values can be provided in the facility manager's COBie contract language and enforced through the delivery process. Having consistent categorization ensures that information about one facility can be compared with that of another facility.

The next set of columns allows information in the current worksheet, if needed, to reference information in previous COBie worksheets. Such information is very important in worksheets such as the Document and Attribute worksheets.

These worksheets provide information either external files, in the case of the Document worksheet, or specific properties, in the case of the Attribute worksheet, about COBie.Spaces, COBie.Types, and so on. Within the "reference" worksheets, the name of the previous COBie worksheet and the specific row to which the document or property refer are listed. In database terms, these can be considered to be foreign key values.

The next set of information is required fields to be provided for every record. Often, a "Description" field is required, as is the case in the Space and Type worksheets. Another example of required information, needed at a construction handover, is the model number of each specific approved type of equipment.

The next set of COBie information allows automated systems to document the specific location from which the information in the COBie file was created. Specifically, three columns are required to document the external system name, the name of the related field, and the specific identification number from which the current COBie data was drawn. While COBie data are meant to be delivered automatically from a software system, hand-created COBie models will always leave these columns blank.

Following the external information is the set of information that is identified as "as-specified." Such information is common to all the expected rows of the COBie worksheet but should be explicitly specified to ensure that the information will be used, if time is taken to record the information. An example of such a column in the Type worksheet is "Code.Compliance." This text field allows a product manufacturer or contractor to document the code compliance of the product that is installed in the facility.

Color Scheme

To reinforce the conventions described earlier, example COBie models include color-coding, reflecting the type of information found in each of the worksheets and specific data columns. Figure 5.4 shows the color-coding of an example Space worksheet. The yellow-colored columns contain required text input. The salmon-colored columns contain required values to be selected from other parts of the COBie file. For example, the Space.CreatedBy column values must be found in the Contact.Email column. The Space.Category column data is found in the Pick-List worksheet under the PickList.Facility-Category column. The Space. FloorName must be found in the Floor.Name column.

The information in the three purple columns reflects the origin of each row of data from the originating software system used to create the data. Green columns to

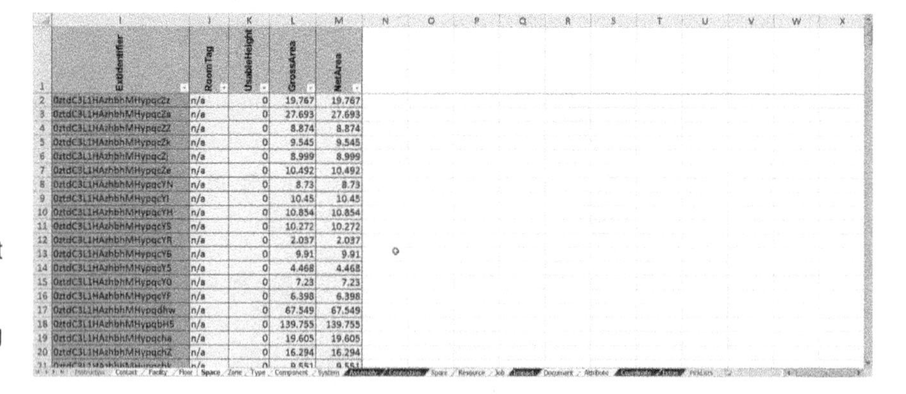

	Name	CreatedOn	Category	FloorName	Description	ExtSystem	ExtObject
2	1A01	2011-09-14T16:57:52	13-11 11 31: Reception Space	First Floor	PATIENT ADMIN. RECEPT.	Autodesk Revit Architecture 2011	IfcSpace
3	1A02	2011-09-14T16:57:52	13-15 11 34 11: Office	First Floor	RMO ANALYST	Autodesk Revit Architecture 2011	IfcSpace
4	1A03	2011-09-14T16:57:52	13-15 11 34 11: Office	First Floor	TRICARE OFFICE	Autodesk Revit Architecture 2011	IfcSpace
5	1A04	2011-09-14T16:57:52	13-15 11 34 11: Office	First Floor	TRICARE OFFICE	Autodesk Revit Architecture 2011	IfcSpace
6	1A05	2011-09-14T16:57:52	13-15 11 34 11: Office	First Floor	TRICARE OFFICE	Autodesk Revit Architecture 2011	IfcSpace
7	1A06	2011-09-14T16:57:52	13-15 11 34 11: Office	First Floor	TRICARE OFFICE	Autodesk Revit Architecture 2011	IfcSpace
8	1A07	2011-09-14T16:57:52	13-15 11 34 11: Office	First Floor	TRICARE OFFICE	Autodesk Revit Architecture 2011	IfcSpace
9	1A08	2011-09-14T16:57:52	13-15 11 34 11: Office	First Floor	PHARM. OFFICE	Autodesk Revit Architecture 2011	IfcSpace
10	1A09	2011-09-14T16:57:52	13-41 11 14 21: Restroom	First Floor	W. TOILET	Autodesk Revit Architecture 2011	IfcSpace
11	1A10	2011-09-14T16:57:52	13-51 11 21: Break Room	First Floor	LOUNGE	Autodesk Revit Architecture 2011	IfcSpace
12	1A11	2011-09-14T16:57:52	13-75 11 11: Storage Room	First Floor	JAN.	Autodesk Revit Architecture 2011	IfcSpace
13	1A12	2011-09-14T16:57:52	13-41 11 14 21: Restroom	First Floor	M. TOILET	Autodesk Revit Architecture 2011	IfcSpace
14	1A13	2011-09-14T16:57:52	13-41 11 14 21: Restroom	First Floor	STAFF TOILET	Autodesk Revit Architecture 2011	IfcSpace
15	1A14	2011-09-14T16:57:52	13-15 11 34 11: Office	First Floor	SUPER / NCOIC	Autodesk Revit Architecture 2011	IfcSpace
16	1A15	2011-09-14T16:57:52	13-41 41 99: Other Healing Spaces	First Floor	COUNSELING	Autodesk Revit Architecture 2011	IfcSpace
17	1A16	2011-09-14T16:57:52	13-75 11 11: Storage Room	First Floor	PHARM. DISP.	Autodesk Revit Architecture 2011	IfcSpace
18	1AC1	2011-09-14T16:57:52	13-51 31 11: Waiting Room	First Floor	CENTRAL WAITING	Autodesk Revit Architecture 2011	IfcSpace
19	1AC2	2011-09-14T16:57:52	13-85 11 11: Corridor	First Floor	CORRIDOR	Autodesk Revit Architecture 2011	IfcSpace
20	1AC3	2011-09-14T16:57:52	13-85 11 11: Corridor	First Floor	CORRIDOR	Autodesk Revit Architecture 2011	IfcSpace

FIGURE 5.4a Example of COBie Space worksheet (columns A through H), reproduced here in shades of gray. In the application, columns appear the following colors: A-C yellow; D-E salmon; F yellow; G-H purple.

	ExtIdentifier	RoomTag	UsableHeight	GrossArea	NetArea
2	0ztdC3L1HAzhbhMHypqcZz	n/a	0	19.767	19.767
3	0ztdC3L1HAzhbhMHypqcZa	n/a	0	27.693	27.693
4	0ztdC3L1HAzhbhMHypqcZZ	n/a	0	8.874	8.874
5	0ztdC3L1HAzhbhMHypqcZk	n/a	0	9.545	9.545
6	0ztdC3L1HAzhbhMHypqcZj	n/a	0	8.999	8.999
7	0ztdC3L1HAzhbhMHypqcZe	n/a	0	10.492	10.492
8	0ztdC3L1HAzhbhMHypqcYN	n/a	0	8.73	8.73
9	0ztdC3L1HAzhbhMHypqcYI	n/a	0	10.45	10.45
10	0ztdC3L1HAzhbhMHypqcYH	n/a	0	10.854	10.854
11	0ztdC3L1HAzhbhMHypqcYS	n/a	0	10.272	10.272
12	0ztdC3L1HAzhbhMHypqcYR	n/a	0	2.037	2.037
13	0ztdC3L1HAzhbhMHypqcY6	n/a	0	9.91	9.91
14	0ztdC3L1HAzhbhMHypqcY5	n/a	0	4.468	4.468
15	0ztdC3L1HAzhbhMHypqcY0	n/a	0	7.23	7.23
16	0ztdC3L1HAzhbhMHypqcYF	n/a	0	6.398	6.398
17	0ztdC3L1HAzhbhMHypqdhw	n/a	0	67.549	67.549
18	0ztdC3L1HAzhbhMHypqbH5	n/a	0	139.755	139.755
19	0ztdC3L1HAzhbhMHypqcha	n/a	0	19.605	19.605
20	0ztdC3L1HAzhbhMHypqchZ	n/a	0	16.294	16.294

FIGURE 5.4b Example of same COBie Space worksheet (Reproduced here in shades of gray, in the application column I appears in purple, columns J through M are green).

the right identify "as-specified" columns that, in this case have been filled out with information from the design building information model. Worksheet tabs are also identified by color-code using the yellow color for required, green for as-specified, and black for not used. Notice that, in the file provided, the Assembly worksheet is one of several worksheets that have been identified as not containing any information.

The reader may notice that values for the Space.RoomTag, Column J in Figure 5.4, are set to "n/a." In COBie, the "n/a" means "not available" or "not applicable"; this designation is equivalent to a NIL in an XML or database table. Since Figure 5.4 represents the design deliverable, the final room signage that would be found in the RoomTag column is not known. As a result, Space.RoomTag set to "n/a" reflects that the signage for the space has not yet been assigned.

Extensions

The names of each worksheet and the column headings for COBie may not be changed. The order of these headings is also fixed. That is the basis for the COBie standard. Changing the existing worksheets and columns results in nonstandard use of COBie and may result in commercial software's not being able to produce or consume data in such customized formats. While the set of specified COBie information is fixed, there are three ways to extend COBie allowed in the COBie specification. The first way is by changing the default classification tables found in COBie example files. The OmniClass (Construction Specification Institute 2008) classification tables are used, by default, in the COBie specification and in example files. If another classification scheme is required, then the values simply can be swapped for the current set.

The second way to extend the contents of COBie information is through the specification of required attribute values for specific classes of space, type, or component entities. Through this means the properties that are important for the local O&M of these assets can be identified and delivered. The third way is to include additional columns of information to the right of any existing COBie worksheet. Thus, if a new property were to be identified with every row in a worksheet, the new column could be added to the right of all the existing COBie columns. An example of such a property on the Space worksheet might be "Perimeter." This new column would allow the capture and possibly the consumption of this new column automatically. If the facility manager wanted to color-code these columns, then the COBie suggests that color-coding for extended properties for an entire worksheet be blue.

COBie Worksheet Descriptions

Figure 5.1 identifies each of the worksheets in the spreadsheet version of the COBie data standard. The following paragraphs briefly describe each of these worksheets. For complete technical documentation of COBie, the reader should review the previously referenced COBie-related web sites and COBie Guide. To compare the information that follows with an example of a COBie file, the reader may wish to review the material in conjunction with one of the many COBie sample files (East 2012d).

COBie.Instruction

COBie.Instruction is the first spreadsheet in a COBie workbook. It contains only template information but can be used to give a concise overview of the contents of a given COBie submission. The version of the COBie file and the worksheets included are listed at the top of this page. A legend at the bottom of the instruction worksheet provides the color-coding used in the remainder of the file. Color-coding is provided for hand-created COBie files published by buildingSMART alliance, but is technically not needed. As previously described, the color-coding does help people to more easily conduct a manual review the content of the file.

In many commercial software implementations of COBie, the Instructions worksheet simply reflects the default COBie workbook instructions and is not automatically customized for the specific deliverable. In some cases, the Instructions worksheet is left blank.

COBie.Contact

COBie.Contact contains the list of individuals and companies referenced during the life of the project. During design, the values relate to those people or companies creating or producing COBie data files. During construction, the information is supplemented with those entering or updating COBie data. At handover, the information is supplemented with manufacturer, supplier, and warranty guarantor information.

Contact information is generally well represented in construction software, which is where it is most important to identify manufacturer and supplier contact information.

COBie.Facility

COBie.Facility contains information about the facility being exchanged during a given COBie deliverable. Since COBie deliverables may be exchanged during planning, design, construction, handover, or operation phases, there may be differences in facility designations. Creating a standard naming convention is something that project owner should do. COBie can only reflect the identifiers that are currently used by the owner. COBie files should only contain a single facility. The COBie.Attribute worksheet can be used to provide the longitude, latitude, and rotation of the facility on the site to coordinate geospatial information with information within the facility.

All tested software is able to produce and/or consume some portion of the overall facility information.

COBie.Floor

COBie.Floor contains information about the vertical levels of the facility. Levels of traditional buildings will include the floors of the building as well as foundation and roof levels. For horizontal facilities, the levels will include regions of space outside the facility or across a campus.

All tested software is able to produce and/or consume some portion of the overall facility information.

COBie.Space

COBie.Space contains information about the horizontal organization of space within a given vertical, or floor level. Typically, but not always, spaces refer to the physical rooms within the facility as defined by the designer. Spaces have a slightly different definition within COBie to ensure that the different types of spaces, even if they are in the same room, can be captured. COBie splits large rooms into spaces if the activities or tenant has subdivided into several spaces representing different departmental waiting areas. Signage added by the contractor during construction is added to the space data after it has been installed.

All tested software is able to produce and/or use some portion of the overall facility information.

COBie.Zone

COBie.Zone contains information about the grouping of spaces organized into relevant categories that support various design or operational functions of the facility. To have a consistent result, zoning must be defined by the owner's requirements while planning the project. The *COBie Guide* provides a recommended set of zones and conventions for zone naming (East 2012b). In large, complex facilities, there are many zones and subzones. In COBie, these groups of rooms may be nested through the use of naming conventions applied by the designer, contractor, and commissioning agent as the project proceeds. Zoning refers not only to groups of spaces that share building services, but also to the functional or occupancy aspects of spaces.

Despite the clear requirement by the FM community to identify spatial zones, as documented in the COBie design requirements since 2008, not all tested software is able to produce and/or consume zoning information. This inability can be directly tied to the lack of underlying data structures that contain zoning information in tested software.

COBie.Type

COBie.Type contains information about the types of managed assets in the facility. These assets are identified during the design process and appear in design drawing schedules. Types are organized to concisely provide related lists of components, properties, and needed O&M information. The types of products to be installed during construction are defined during the design stage. Early in the design stage, the types of architectural elements to be included in the facility are documented. Later in design, the types of products required for mechanical, electrical, plumbing, and other systems are defined. During the construction submittal process, the contractor provides information about each of these equipment types. Later, testing results and O&M manuals are provided. All such information is linked to specific manufacture and model information (i.e., COBie.Types).

All tested software is able to produce and/or consume some portion of the type information. A major problem with producing software is the inability to translate the type information found on design drawings into type information found in COBie. This is often the result of problems related to design workflow, where designers often paste tabular data into design drawings for purposes of printing drawings, in lieu of ensuring that the information in the model is correct.

COBie.Component

COBie.Component contains information about the specific instances of each managed asset. The majority of such information is identified, during design, in design drawing schedules. During construction, such items require the documentation of installation dates and serial numbers. Information about bulk assets, important to O&M, are also identified by construction contractors using brass tags, bar codes, or other designations. These components are also included in the COBie.Component worksheet.

All tested software is able to produce and/or use some portion of the type information. A key problem with delivering both type and component information is that owners have been unwilling to spend the time to determine the list of mandatory types and components to be included in a COBie file. The *COBie Guide* provides a recommended set of types and components, with associated naming conventions (East 2012b).

COBie.System

COBie.System contains information to describe how groups of components are organized into relevant categories that deliver specific building services to the facility. COBie.Spaces are to COBie.Zones as COBie.Components are to COBie. Systems. While some system and zoning information will typically overlap, it is not always the case in COBie—systems of components and zones of spaces are both maintained.

Despite the clear requirement to identify component systems by the FM community, as documented in the COBie design requirements since 2008, not all tested software is able to produce and/or use system information. This inability can be directly tied to lack of underlying data structures that contain system information in tested software.

COBie.Assembly

COBie.Assembly contains information to describe the way in which products, which are themselves composed of other managed products, can be captured. In some types of assemblies this is critical, since internal components of these assemblies have different maintenance plans. An example of such an assembly is an AHU. For other types of assemblies, the subcomponents each have attributes that must be known, for example, an electrical distribution board where each internal breaker serves a specific circuit.

No software tested as of July 2012 has been demonstrated to produce assembly information.

COBie.Connection

COBie.Connection contains information about the logic connections between components. Such information is important to assist facility management staff to determine the upstream or downstream impact of their decisions when flipping a breaker or closing a valve.

No software tested as of July 2012 has been demonstrated to produce connection information.

COBie.Spare

COBie.Spare provides a mechanism through which spare parts, replacement parts, and consumable parts required for the O&M of each type of managed asset may be identified. Spare information may be provided in one row, in which case a COBie.Document record should also be found. Spare information may also be identified part by part in the Spare worksheet.

Some of the maintenance management systems have been demonstrated to consume information about spare and replacement parts and consumables.

COBie.Resource

COBie.Resource provides a mechanism through which the material, equipment, and training required for maintenance activities may be communicated.

Some of the maintenance management systems have been demonstrated to consume information about the material, equipment, and training required for job plans.

COBie.Job

COBie.Job provides a mechanism through which information about preventative maintenance, safety, testing, operational, and emergency procedures may be communicated. COBie.Job may contain a general description of a series of operations or tasks. COBie.Job may also be used to create small critical path method projects where project teams want to explicitly link resources to specific operations within a job.

The majority of maintenance management systems have been demonstrated to consume information about job plans. Few of these tools have been able to consume multistep job schedules, preferring to import large blocks of text instead.

COBie.Impact

COBie.Impact provides a mechanism through which the types of impacts that the facility has on the environment and the tenants of the facility may be captured.

No software tested as of July 2012 has been demonstrated to produce assembly information.

COBie.Document

COBie.Document provides a mechanism through which the many types of external documents may be indexed and their information may be captured.

The majority of construction and maintenance management systems have been demonstrated to capture and consume some of the information in documents related to product types.

COBie.Attribute

COBie.Attribute provides a mechanism through which the many types of attributes may be captured. Those specifying the delivery of COBie data may require specific attributes. A minimum standard for the required set of attributes to be included based on the headers of design schedule tables. The *COBie Guide* provides a minimum set of attributes that can be specified for commonly encountered product types (East 2012b).

All software has been demonstrated to produce and/or consume attribute information. Much of the attribute information currently provided from design software pertains to information needed to be sent to plotters. Given that facility managers have not specified the required attributes, the attributes that are provided are often irrelevant for FM and may not even match the attributes found on design drawing schedules.

COBie.Coordinate

COBie.Coordinate provides a mechanism through which a minimal set of point, line, and box geometry may be specified for the referenced object.

Design software has been demonstrated to produce coordinate information for space objects.

COBie.Issue

COBie.Issue provides a mechanism through which text descriptions of issues and decisions made during the related phase of the project may be captured. Issues may pertain to a single asset previously identified in the COBie file, or they may pertain to the some aspect of two assets.

No commercial software tested as of July 2012 has been demonstrated to produce issue information. Model server technologies have, however, demonstrated the production of issues such as punch lists and integrated these within COBie exchanges.

COBie.PickList

COBie.Picklist contains, for hand-developed files, the columns of values used in category and other selection lists in COBie worksheets. COBie files produced via software output often will not have any content in the COBie.PickList worksheet, or the sheet may be omitted completely.

The identification of the pick lists pertaining to facility, space, zone, component, and systems should be of primary importance to the facility manager when developing local requirements for that specific agency or facility campus.

HOW IS COBIE DELIVERED?

COBie is organized to efficiently deliver that information about managed assets during several stages during a facility life cycle. Starting with the planning of a new building and ending with the current operating condition of a facility, there are six major milestones where COBie data can be captured. The complete set of exchanges of all or partial COBie data is described in the Life-Cycle information exchange (East 2010).

As-Planned

Prior to the decision to design and construct a facility, planners and tenants develop the requirements for each new facility. For buildings, the planning process produces as one its key artifacts a "room data sheet." The room data sheet contains the list of required spaces in the facility and the characteristics and services that the space needs to provide to meet the tenant's requirements. Many large owners have well-developed space management criteria. In the case of the U.S. Department of Defense, for example, a series of unified facility criteria documents identifies each type of typical space and the furniture and equipment needed in that space (www.wbdg.org/ccb/browse_cat.php?o=29&c=4). The compilation of the set of spaces that compose a given planned building is called the space program. The compilation of the set of equipment needed for those spaces is called the equipment program.

Since COBie contains space and equipment assets, the delivery of COBie data at the as-planned stage of a project is the perfect place to start. In fact, the delivery of the as-planned COBie model as part of the design or design/build contract helps jump-start the designer to delivery COBie data in a way that is compatible with local FM practice. This is because the names of each type of space and equipment, developed from standard criteria, can be reused by the designer. The alternative is for the designer to take the room data sheets and manually transcribe some of the information into architectural floor plans. This transcription is error prone, and the information lost from planning to design is never recovered. For most projects the facility manager is never able to see the original requirements for each of the spaces because the original space and equipment program data are not transferred from planning to design.

As-Designed

During design, an early architectural COBie model and a full construction documents stage design model should be specified. The purpose of the architectural model is to verify that the space program requirements are met. Comparing the space programming COBie file and the early architectural COBie model will allow the facility manager and funding organizations to determine if the design that has been presented meets the requirements stated in relevant contract documents.

The construction documents stage design model should fully reflect the information found in the contract construction documents. Of primary interest is that the COBie file match the information found on the drawings in design schedules and related notes. These schedules would include room schedules, equipment schedules, and product schedules.

Given that different designers develop asset schedules and associated notes based on industry convention and the personal preference of the designer, additional discipline will be required by designers to provide a consistent set of shared, structured information about building assets. The first step in ensuring this consistency is to define the minimum information that should be present in the design schedules of critical managed assets. Without defining the requirement, the design and construction teams will provide customary information, which may or may not meet the needs of the facility management office.

The COBie Guide identifies the minimum set of fixed assets that should be included in the deliverable file and outlines the required properties for each type of asset (East 2012b). Furthermore, the *COBie Guide* lists COBie required managed assets in relative order of importance, from an O&M point of view. With each type of asset is the minimum set of properties that should be identified by the designer, and later by the contractor in COBie format. Ideally, these properties would also be used by the designers as the headings in design schedules found on contract drawings and as-builts.

As-Constructed

During the construction phase the construction manager, contractor, subcontractors, and commissioning agent will be working toward completing the facility. As this takes place, they should be capturing COBie data as they go. The construction manager, if using an electronic submittal register, automatically captures product data on all approved products in the facility. The construction contractor, or subs, can capture the serial number and installation date of installed equipment. During commissioning, information about installed equipment can be checked, and O&M information can also be provided.

An important reason for the facility manager to obtain a high-quality COBie model following the installation of all major equipment is that COBie information can assist maintenance staff to plan their expected personnel requirements. During construction there are, essentially, three different approaches to delivering COBie files. The FM office should determine which of these approaches would provide the most useful information given the size and scope of the facility to be built. This assessment can be made during the design review process, and the approach taken must be reflected in the construction contract to ensure that retainage can be held for failure to deliver the required information.

The first approach is a monthly submission of COBie files for equipment-heavy or industrial facilities. On such projects, contractors often have a substantial investment in on-site, but not installed, equipment to increase the contractor's cash flow. The COBie file can be used by the construction management agent to justify payment for such on-site equipment and provide a copy of that COBie file so that the facility manager can determine if any specialized training or equipment will need to be purchased for O&M of such an equipment-intensive project.

For traditional facilities that have commonly used equipment, a facility manager is primarily interested in the quantity of the equipment and the complexity of the control systems that must be operated and maintained. To assess such considerations, a COBie file for all major equipment is required from the contractor following the approval of submittals.

For commonly constructed facilities with which the FM office has significant experience, the minimum set of COBie deliverables can be provided. These deliverables would occur at the beneficial occupancy stage and the fiscal completion of construction stage.

As-Occupied

Upon being given responsibility to occupy a building prior to the completion of the project, the facility manager becomes responsible to begin O&M of that portion of the facility. The as-occupied COBie deliverable should be provided with (or before) the keys to the facility are given to the FM office. COBie information at this phase should include warranty, parts, consumables, maintenance, and operations information.

Before doing anything, the facility manager should place a copy of the COBie file and associated documents in a backup location. Once the information has been stored for future reference, the operational use of COBie data by the FM office should begin. If the FM office uses a CMMS, then the COBie file should be imported into that system. Importing COBie.Type, COBie.Component, COBie.Job, and related information will immediately allow the continuation of appropriate maintenance and operations activities.

In addition to scheduling the required jobs, the facility management staff will also want access to COBie data as they complete these tasks. COBie can be delivered to the staff in the following ways: paper, network, cloud-based, or integrated system. The following paragraphs describe the first of these three options; the integrated system is described in a later section.

The format for the information can be different for each maintenance shop depending on the facility staff's level of expertise with computers and the security posture of the facility. Sections of the COBie data and documents can be printed for those technicians or shops that demand it. For offices whose facility information should not be placed on computer networks outside the control of the facilities' information management networks, a shared network drive can be configured for each building and the COBie data placed there. Such drives should be configured to provide read-only access so that product data sheets, shop drawings, and so on can be read but not changed by authorized users.

Commercial or not-for-profit cloud-based platforms that have verified compliance with relevant security accreditation requirements, can be evaluated and selected to host COBie information and related files. While the enforcement of security controls over cloud-based applications provides a layer of complexity to the facility management process over simply creating a read-only network drive, the aggregation of COBie data across an entire campus may raise issues related to facility security.

Another use of the information delivered through COBie is for computerized-aided facility management (CAFM). Typically, such systems support the allocation of space to tenants. COBie delivers to such systems the complete list of all spaces and space area measures. In addition to the list of spaces, the characteristics of spaces are also provided through COBie. Such information provides a powerful tool to assist facility asset managers to determine where required tenant activities may be supported within a given facility.

As-Built

The as-delivered COBie model is provided at the fiscal conclusion of the construction process. This is typically months, if not years, following the actual occupancy of the facility. The delay is required to include the complete set of changes into the project and resolve any remaining punch-list items. This COBie model should only have minor deviations to the as-occupied COBie model and from the point of view of the list of spaces and managed assets; there should be little deviation from the occupancy and fiscal completion model.

As-Maintained

For COBie to ultimately be successful, it is critical that the delivery of COBie information at beneficial occupancy be the starting point and not the ending point for the use of COBie data by the facility manager. Today, there are many different processes that impact the ongoing status of COBie data. Work orders may result in use of spare parts or consumables. Service orders could require the removal of equipment and installation of replacement equipment. Renovations may demolish, move, and add new equipment. To truly determine how the COBie will change, the facility management staff must first map and understand the information flows among the variety of information systems that are currently in place.

Since decisions about information systems are complex, it is often the case that facility management offices will either be directed to use specific products or select whatever current product appears to be most able to address some individual aspect of the COBie information management life cycle. Such decisions may give the appearance of forward progress but may also result in expensive data translation and transformation efforts due to lack of adoption of open standards across all products.

SOFTWARE SUPPORTING COBIE

There is no COBie-specific software. COBie is an information exchange standard format. COBie is meant to be used by software to help the project team capture, exchange, and ultimately deliver COBie data to the facility management office. While COBie data can be captured by hand using commonly available spreadsheets, COBie has also been incorporated directly into over 20 different software products. The COBie Means and Methods web site is the national repository that describes the ability of each of these products to produce or consume COBie data, depending on the nature of the specific product (East 2012c).

Starting with the first release of COBie in July 2008, my team has directly tested software for its ability to produce COBie data. There are two types of quality testing conducted. For those products that produce COBie data files, there is a quality control test performed. For those products that consume COBie data files, there is a quality assurance test performed.

Quality control testing has two components. The first is to ensure that the format for the information produced is correct. COBie data may be provided in one of three formats: IFC, ifcXML, or SpreadsheetML. Since software developers are easily able to provide data in a specified format, there has been little difficulty obtaining compliance with data formats. Rather, problems have been the direct result of poor implementation of the COBie model, shown in Figure 5.1, within that software.

The 11 COBie Challenge events held between July 2008 and December 2011 have shown improvements in the ability of commercial software to produce the required content of the COBie model. Nevertheless, there is still work to be done. It is worth noting that COBie did not become a U.S. national BIM standard until 2012. This delay was caused by the fact that the internal configuration of design software remains, even today, oriented toward the production of paper documents. An example of the lack of compliance of existing commercial tools to the COBie format was documented in a recent COBie case studies presentation

(Carrasquillo and Love 2011). The current list of issues identified in this case study is representative of problems that will be encountered by virtually all project teams during design and construction.

For software that consumes (imports) COBie data, a quality control test cannot be accomplished without looking directly at the proprietary data formats and programming within commercial software systems. As a result, consuming COBie applications are subjected to a quality assurance test where a sample COBie file (with changes known only to the testing team) is required to be imported. The results of that import are investigated through a question-and-answer session that ensures the proper importation of the COBie data, within the scope of work accomplished by the consuming application. Examples of these checklists can be found in many of the previous COBie Challenge events available from the main COBie web site (East 2008).

INTERNAL SOFTWARE TESTING

For the facility manager, the ability of maintenance and management software to consume COBie data is of paramount importance. Since the specific software used at a given FM office is unlikely to be the exact same product and configuration as those products tested during a COBie Challenge event, it is recommended that each facility manager take the time to perform an internal COBie Challenge, using the smallest of the three standard BIM files used by my testing teams, that of the Duplex Apartment Building. The test can be as simple as creating a new building in the software being tested and using the same software to import the small Duplex model. Following the importation of the model, a side-by-side comparison of the Duplex model data with the screens generated by the software will show precisely what information was, and was not, imported. Until such tests are conducted and the reports provided back to software vendors, it is unlikely that a fully satisfactory result will be obtained by the facility manager. If, however, the test is conducted and the software vendor is responsive about correcting the import of any missing data, then the facility manager may be assured that the software will work as needed.

LEGAL IMPLICATIONS OF COBIE

Any discussion of building information modeling data, such as that found in COBie, inevitably requires addressing legal issues. Many of these discussions pertain to collaborative design processes that could result in the modification of authoritative sources. Requirements for COBie do not pertain to any such collaborative processes. The delivery of COBie data mirrors directly the contracted deliverable requirements that currently exist in design and construction contracts. Designers produce room schedules and equipment and product schedules in their existing design deliverables today. The COBie information provided by designers is intended to exactly match that information. Contractors are currently required in the general provisions of virtually all contracts to delivery operations and maintenance information. COBie simply transforms the format of that information, from paper to structured information and attached electronic documents.

The major legal issue to be resolved is that a proper specification of the quality requirements for COBie deliverables needs to be provided. Without such a quality standard, whatever data is provided in COBie-formatted files must be accepted. The specification of the contents of COBie, as is proposed in the *COBie Guide*, provides a contractible quality standard for the objective evaluation of design and construction deliverables.

Given that COBie deliverables map precisely to existing contract deliverables and define the quality of such deliverables, no legal issues have been identified regarding the requirement, delivery, or use of COBie information.

HOW TO IMPLEMENT COBIE

The best way to start using COBie for the first time is to jump in and use it to get some immediate feedback. One starting point is following the design and construction of capital projects. The second is to capture information about ongoing facility management office work orders and the like. The following checklists provide a starting point for the FM COBie team to consider when embarking on the use of COBie for the first time.

Conduct a COBie Pilot Project

- ☐ Review the capital program based on scope and project team.
- ☐ Conduct introductory meeting stating project goals.
- ☐ Identify and review design and construction processes and procedures.
- ☐ Review and update existing contracts and specifications.
- ☐ Update contracts to deliver COBie data.
- ☐ Monitor production of COBie via monthly team meetings.
- ☐ Review COBie deliverables.
- ☐ Accept COBie deliverables in lieu of paper documents.
- ☐ Import COBie data into relevant existing information technology.

Identify Opportunities for Innovation

- ☐ Provision of asset information with service orders.
- ☐ Provision of form-based data input for work orders.
- ☐ Provision of as-maintained building data for renovations and as-operated conditions.
- ☐ Consolidated maintenance and asset management functions.

Review Existing Information Technology

- ☐ Identify operations and maintenance management software.
- ☐ Identify asset management software.
- ☐ Determine the extent to which this software can consume COBie data.
- ☐ Conduct an internal COBie Challenge to verify COBie compliance.

Review Existing Management Controls

- ☐ Identify a common classification system.
- ☐ Identify equipment naming conventions.
- ☐ Identify mandatory properties for most critical assets.
- ☐ Document processes for capture of COBie data during O&M phase.
- ☐ Document processes for use authorized use of centralized COBie data warehouse.

While much attention has been paid to the development of COBie data for new facilities, the majority of the buildings in the industrialized world have already been built. At even the most aggressive facility replacement rate, the capture of COBie data for an entire campus may require decades. There has been one published study to date on technologies used for capturing COBie for existing facilities (Rojas 2010). This report demonstrates simple tools that can be used to conduct inexpensive surveys, on the average of one dollar per square foot, to capture as-built COBie data for spaces and major building assets.

Following the completion of processes for the delivery of COBie on all capital facilities, facility managers should also consider that information about assets can be captured on a daily basis as part of each service order, work order, or renovation project. The modification of contracts, procedures, and current software to have technicians document existing or changed assets should be seen as a high-value opportunity for leveraging existing maintenance personnel. Since most major equipment must be maintained on an annual basis, slight changes to include COBie documentation in all service orders could result in a complete COBie inventory within a single year.

CONCLUSIONS

COBie is a structured set of information about managed facility assets. COBie information may be exchanged in one of three open standard formats: IFC, ifcXML, and SpreadsheetML. The spreadsheet version of COBie has begun to be widely accepted since the information is clearly presented, easily understood, and can be produced and consumed by over twenty commercially developed software systems.

The need for COBie was first recognized by the National Research Council in 1983 (NRC 1983). Their findings indicated that a significant amount of information is lost between design, construction, and facility operations. Since much of the information that is lost pertains to information about managed assets, COBie can eliminate a significant amount of that information loss. The automated production of COBie during planning, design, and construction can also reduce or eliminate the need for expensive paper documentation that is so often simply discarded.

While the development of COBie reflects a decade of work, the development of the COBie information model and data formats is the easiest part of this effort. The difficult work is ahead of each facility manager as they determine how and when to conduct COBie pilot projects and organize their back office services to support not only the consumption of COBie at the end of capital projects, but the real-time delivery of as-operated facilities through the use of this same COBie standard.

It is recommended that every facility manager interested in knowing the current status of the assets for which they are responsible begin by identifying those organizational elements that should participate in the COBie transformation. Within these divisions, branches, and organizations, the facility manager must develop champions who will guide the transformation of the business practice of each of these offices.

One of the first activities that should be completed is the identification of waste associated with the loss and recreation of COBie data. The resulting estimates can be developed and presented in the amount of additional capacity that could be achieved by utilizing shared and structured information. With the projection of the expected result, pilot projects should be initiated. Comparing the actual versus the expected performance using COBie will allow the facility manager to develop the business case for organization-wide transformation that can be achieved with COBie.

FUTURE DEVELOPMENTS

While the basic skeleton of COBie and requirements for the delivery of managed assets has been completed, the hard job, implementation within the design, construction, and FM office is just beginning. There are several COBie-related projects that may help to streamline the use of COBie.

The first of these projects, called the COBieCutSheet, is aimed at transforming manufacturer's document-centric PDF product data sheets into lightweight data models. If this were accomplished information about equipment within a building could flow through the supply chain, streamlining the entire process. Before the COBieCutSheet is realized, however, data standards about the specific properties required for each type of asset must be established (attributes, units of measures, etc.). The SPie project aims to deliver such standard product templates.

A key problem when implementing COBie for those "in the trenches" is the request from upper management that a "business case" be developed. The COBieCalculator, a project whose results will be published in January 2013, will show the differences between a current document-centric business process and that which can be put in place with COBie information. Developed with simple flowcharts in Excel, the calculator can be adjusted to reflect per-project and portfolio-based savings.

A problem for implementers of heavy weight STEP and even SpreadsheetML specifications is that such specifications to not easily support the rapid software prototyping that has driven substantial technical innovation over the last decade. The COBieLite specification will be an XML specification for the delivery of COBie data. Developed using the Content Assembly Mechanism standard developed under the Organization for the Advancement of Structured Information Standards (OASIS), the COBie development team will open building information to a variety of different computer programmers and begin to unlock the potential for securely sharing building information with clients, tenants, regulators, and building occupants via any number of smart sensors and platforms.

The delivery of COBie data described in this chapter is based on the delivery of COBie data in full data sets at prescribed contractual phases. When developing COBie, the parties to these contracts should not be waiting until shortly before the required deliverable to produce the full data sets. The delivery of asset information during the life of the project can be achieved through the careful assignment of specific parties who are currently required to deliver portions of that information as part of their subcontracts or quality control processes. The specification for the life-cycle delivery of asset information is found in the Life-Cycle information exchange (LCie) project (East 2010). It is this LCie project that can help planners, designers, builders, and commissioning agents to streamline their business practices to both eliminate waste in their process and deliver a higher-quality handover data set to the facility manager.

The handover of design and construction information to the facility manager at the conclusion of a construction project is one of many different types of exchanges that take place every day across our industry. The most valuable resource to develop standards that allow our industry to move beyond the current document-based exchanges to create information-based exchanges is subject matter expertise engagement. COBie was successful as a direct result of subject matter engagement with the problem. Since the ultimate object of projects like COBie is to have them recognized as national standards, as part of the United States National Building Information Model standard, those interested in working in solving other problems should contact the buildingSMART alliance.

REFERENCES

Carrasquillo, Mariangelica, and Danielle Love. 2011. "The Cost of Correcting Design Models for Construction," http://projects.buildingsmartalliance.org/files/?artifact_id=4504 (accessed July 9, 2012).

Construction Specification Institute. 2008 "OmniClass: A Strategy for Classifying the Built Environment." www.omniclass.org (accessed July 12, 2012).

East, Bill 2012a. "Specifier's Properties Information Exchange," Buildingsmart Alliance, Http://Www.Buildingsmartalliance.Org/Index.Php/Projects/Activeprojects/32 (accessed July 9, 2012).

______. 2012b. "The COBie Guide." buildingSMART alliance, http://projects.buildingsmartalliance.org/files/?artifact_id=4856 (accessed July 9, 2012).

______. 2012c. "COBie Means and Methods." buildingSMART alliance, www.buildingsmartalliance.org/index.php/projects/cobie (accessed July 9, 2012).

______. 2012d. "Common Building Information Model Files." National Institute of Building Science, www.buildingsmartalliance.org/index.php/projects/commonbimfiles (accessed July 12, 2012).

East, Bill, Chris Bogen, and Danielle Love. 2011. "COBie Responsibility Matrix." buildingSMART alliance, National Institute of Building Sciences, http://projects.buildingsmartalliance.org/files/?artifact_id=4093 (accessed July 12, 2012).

East, Bill, and Tim Chipman. 2012. "Facility Management Handover Model View Definition." buildingSMART alliance, www.nibs.org/docs/BSADOC_COBIE/index.htm (accessed June 16, 2012).

East, E. William. 2007. "Construction Operations Building Information Exchange (COBie)." U.S. Army, Corps of Engineers, Engineer Research and Development Center, Construction Engineering Research Laboratory, ERDC/CERL TR-07-30, Champaign, IL. www.wbdg.org/pdfs/erdc_cerl_tr0730.pdf (accessed June 15, 2011).

______. 2008. "Construction Operations Building Information Exchange (Cobie)." National Institute of Building Sciences, Whole Building Design Guide, www.wbdg.org/resources/cobie.php (accessed July 12, 2012).

______. 2010. "Life-Cycle Information Exchange (LCIE)." Buildingsmart Alliance Project, National Institute of Building Sciences www.buildingsmartalliance.Org/Index.Php/projects/activeprojects/140 (accessed June 15, 2011).

Medellin, K., A. Dominguez, G. Cox, K. Joels, and P. Billante. 2010. "University Health System and COBie: A Case Study." Presented at the 2010 National Institute of Building Sciences Annual Meeting (December), Washington, DC, p. 12, http://projects.buildingsmartalliance.org/files/?artifact_id=3598 (accessed June 7, 2012).

National Research Council. 1983. *A Report from the 1983 Workshop on Advanced Technology For Building Design and Engineering*. Washington, DC: National Academy Press.

Rojas, E.; C. Dossick, and J. Schaufelberger, J. 2010. Developing Best Practices for Capturing As-Built Building Information Models (BIM) for Existing Facilities. Seattle, WA: Seattle Pacific University. Available at http://oai.dtic.mil/oai/oai?verb=getRecord&metadataPrefix=html&identifier=ADA554392.

Siorek, G., and N. Stefanidakis, 2011. "COBie Connector for ARCHIBUS." Presented at the 2011 National Institute of Building Sciences annual meeting, Washington, DC, p. 15, http://projects.buildingsmartalliance.org/files/?artifact_id=4438 (accessed June 7, 2012).

Case Studies

6

INTRODUCTION

In this chapter we present six case studies of projects in which BIM FM integration played a significant role. They represent early efforts by a variety of types of owner to gain the benefits of linking BIM to their FM systems. The case studies emphasize the planning, technologies, and coordination needed to implement successful use of BIM for FM. There is less emphasis on the use of BIM for architecture, engineering, and construction tasks, as these issues are covered in many other sources. This set of case studies was selected because they illustrate a number of different technologies that can be used to achieve these results. In addition, various types of contracts among the project participants were used. In this early stage of BIM FM integration, there is no "standard" approach to achieving good results. However, there are important guidelines that are discussed in each case study and referenced in the "lessons learned."

These case studies were written by students at Georgia Tech and USC Universities, and professionals with backgrounds in the building industry. Every effort has been made to ensure their accuracy and all have been reviewed and approved by the owners on these projects. Each case study lists the specific people who contributed to that study. Any errors that remain are the fault of the editor.

TABLE 6.1 Basic Data for Case Studies

No.	Brief Description	Type of Owner	Major Software	Phases of Project
1	MathWorks, Inc. campus in Natick, MA: Use of BIM linked to FM system for a new building on existing campus	Private corporation	AutoCAD Revit Navisworks FM:Interact	Design, construction, planning for turnover
2	Health Sciences buildings on the Texas A&M campus, College Station, TX: Use of BIM for design and construction and use of COBie to link to existing FM system	Public university	AutoCAD Revit Navisworks COBie AiM CMMS	Design, construction, collection, and turnover of COBie data to AiM, maintain
3	USC School of Cinematic Arts, Los Angeles, CA: Use of BIM for design, construction, turnover, and use of EcoDomus to link to CMMS	Private university	Revit Tekla Onuma System EcoDomus	Design, construction, turnover
4	Xavier University, Cincinnati, OH: Use of BIM for design and construction of four new buildings on campus and use of FM:Interact to link to BIM and provide CMMS data	Private university	CAD MEP Revit FM:Interact	Design, construction, turnover
5	WI state facilities, various locations, WI	State government	Revit Submittal Exchange LogMeln TMA AssetWorks	Design, construction, turnover
6	University of Chicago, Chicago, IL: Use of BIM for the renovation of the administration building: use of BIM and project-specific spreadsheet to link to existing CMMS and CAFM systems	Private university	AutoCAD Revit eBuilder Archibus Maximo	Design, construction, turnover

Table 6.1 provides a brief description of each case study, the type of owner, the major software that was used, and the phases of the project covered in the study. This table is provided to allow readers to select those case studies that are most relevant to their interests.

Case Study 1: MathWorks

Osama Aladham, Jasmin Gonzalez, Iris Grant, Kenyatta Harper, Abe Kruger, Scott Nannis, Arpan Patel, and Lauren Snedeker

MANAGEMENT SUMMARY

MathWorks, a leading developer of mathematical software for engineers and scientists, planned to add a new building to their corporate campus to accommodate the growth of the company, employees' needs, and increase client satisfaction. In both their procurement and contract language, MathWorks emphasized building information modeling (BIM) as a key factor in awarding contracts for this project. To design and construct the new building, the facilities team at MathWorks worked with Spagnolo, Gisness, & Associates, Inc. (SG&A; Core & Shell Architects), Gensler (Interior Architects), Cranshaw Construction of New England (General Contractor), van Zelm Engineers (MEP Engineers), Vico Software (BIM Consultants), FM:Systems (FM Software), ID Group (Data Center Consultant), and National Development (Developer). The collaboration of this team helped MathWorks realize its vision for a work environment similar to a college campus: fostering a corporate culture focused on innovation, learning, and teamwork. Their design, construction, and facilities management teams have proven to be effective in achieving their goals, although there are no deliverables yet in terms of quantifiable costs and benefits data.

This project highlights innovation in both the processes and technology required to support the integration of BIM and FM. Although their contract specified only a basic requirement to deliver a BIM model, during the course of the project MathWorks realized that a more detailed definition of deliverables was critical. While the GC and its team of subcontractors were very skilled at their core disciplines, there were various levels of BIM maturity across the firms. This eventually led MathWorks to ask SG&A to help them find a BIM consultant to coordinate modeling among all the parties involved during the construction phase. SG&A found Vico Software and MathWorks retained them to manage coordination. This meant that some team members had to pay Vico to create their part of the BIM model, an investment the MathWorks felt was worth its value in the long run. In total, there were five different BIM models created and linked together. The main BIM software used to coordinate construction was Autodesk Revit and MathWork's space and maintenance management system was FM:Interact, which released a major enhancement to its Revit integration in May 2012. This project was a pilot for the new technology.

New technology paves the way for process improvement by giving the project team improved methods to analyze the benefits and barriers of their traditional workflows. A natural benefit of the technology was the project's use of integrated project delivery (IPD) principles such as co-location, which took the form of weekly coordination meetings that included all parties, if not in person, then via the Web. This helped the team uncover and resolve issues before finding them in the field—avoiding potential cost and delay. In addition to accurately modeling the building systems to avoid clashes in the field during construction, data elements like equipment model, manufacturer, and other attributes were entered into the BIM models to eliminate the manual entry of operations and maintenance data after building handover. This allowed the project team to place complete and accurate FM information into the hands of the owner before occupancy.

The project faced two barriers to fully integrating BIM and FM during the construction process. The first was the learning curve involved in the transition from traditional two-dimensional construction documentation to the newer three-dimensional, data-centric process. While many architecture, engineering, and construction firms have adopted BIM, many subcontractors still work in CAD-based products, which cause problems when integrating their data. The second issue that was addressed on this project was the determination of data detail for the FM model. Because FM integration with BIM technology is still evolving, there is a need to outline the steps or guidelines required to implement these processes. Despite these barriers, the MathWorks Campus Expansion project is a well-planned attempt toward a milestone for BIM/FM technology integration (Bernardi and Donahue 2012).

GENERAL DESCRIPTION

MathWorks is a privately held company specializing in the development of mathematical computing software for engineers and scientists. Currently growing their Natick, Massachusetts campus, the expansion, shown in Figure 6.1, consists of adding a new level to an existing garage, adding a new parking garage with 855 parking spaces, and constructing a 176,000-square-foot (approximate), four-story office building. The addition also includes outside spaces, which will integrate the new and existing facilities. The goal of the project is to accommodate the growing number of staff and visitors with a building that is energy efficient and productive for its users. The new building and renovation will add 800 seats, and by

FIGURE 6.1 Construction is slated to finish in 2012. The new facility is in the foreground, while the existing facility can be seen in the left background.
Courtesy MathWorks, Inc.

completion, the total campus will accommodate 2,500 people. With this population increase, MathWorks has plans in place to improve traffic flow and navigation around the campus. The goal of the outside spaces like courtyards and a large barbecue space is to encourage equal utilization of inside and outside space. This will create a pleasant work environment and give the feel of a small college campus (Bernardi and Donahue 2012).

Project planning began in 2005 in Natick, Massachusetts. The area has a very active neighborhood association, so local community approval took about two years. Originally, MathWorks planned to move in by 2009 and fully occupy the space by 2012. However, due to the economic downturn, the process was slowed. It now plans to move into the building in December 2012 and be fully occupied within two to three years. As a privately held company, MathWorks does not disclose construction project budgets. In 2009, a company representative stated that the purchase of the existing building, land, and new construction would equal approximately $100 million (Butler 2009).

ROLE OF OWNER AND FM STAFF IN SETTING BIM AND FM REQUIREMENTS

The architect, Al Spagnolo of SG&A, championed the use of BIM from the beginning of the project. After MathWorks learned more about the technology, the creation and use of a BIM model on this project made sense to the owners. Initially, the goal was for all design work to occur in BIM, but over time it became clear that all members of the design and construction teams were not equally capable of delivering designs in BIM. Instead of one BIM model, multiple linked models detailed different aspects of the building. SG&A designed the core and shell of the building in Revit while Gensler designed the interiors. van Zelm Engineers designed the mechanical, electrical, and plumbing (MEP) systems using AutoCAD. Vico, the BIM consultant, acted as the BIM coordinator, modeling the building systems and constantly updating the models (Bernardi and Donahue 2012).

MathWorks was involved with setting the facility management requirements from the start. The facility management team is very small, consisting of only one HVAC technician, one electrical technician, and one project manager. MathWorks is currently in the process of hiring a facility manager and another project manager, and they have already added another electrical person. By the time they occupy the new building, the plan is to have doubled or tripled the team. The facility project manager who has been working on the new building has been on the design team from the start and has been dedicated to the construction for the last nine months (Bernardi and Donahue 2012).

The MathWorks team as a whole set the parameters for what data would be collected and incorporated into the model. However, one challenge was that, while everyone was recommending the use of BIM, there weren't many case studies or previous projects to draw upon for integrating BIM into FM. At first, the team's requirements were very open and vague, encouraging too much information to be incorporated into the model. Upon realizing this, the MathWorks project manager then carefully evaluated what data to collect based on what was most practical and useful for the design and future operation of the building. In the end, MathWorks required the architect, engineers, and the contractors to turn over a functional and complete BIM models and detailed the specific data points required for each type of equipment. MathWorks also provided their internal naming, numbering, and classification standards for space and assets. Because BIM is still a new and upcoming technology, some of the architecture, engineering, and construction (AEC) team members did not have the in-house expertise to create a fully functioning model. While the mechanical contractor had an in-house Revit team, they still opted to hire Vico to ensure a more precise level of detail in their BIM model. Considering the facility management aspect, equipment placement is essential. MathWorks required the equipment placement within the model to be within one inch of actual installation (Bernardi and Donahue 2012).

PROJECT CONTRACTS

In regard to contractual relationships, this is a traditional project with the owner contracting directly with the architect, engineers, and the general contractor. While the contracts are held by the owner, MathWorks still endeavored to run the project as if it were an IPD team. Collaboration was a key requirement for this project.

MathWorks did not use the industry-standard BIM contracts from existing entities like the American Institute of Architects (AIA) or Design-Build Institute of America (DBIA). The guidelines and general aspects of the contract for the BIM services were based on Indiana University's BIM Deliverable Guidelines (www.indiana.edu/~uao/iubim.html). Since this was MathWorks' first FM/BIM experience, they wrote the contract with simple and basic requirements for BIM delivery (Bernardi and Donahue 2012).

PROJECT TEAM

The MathWorks project team was comprised of several companies, the majority of which were local companies that had ties to the Boston area and were very familiar with the local regulations and codes. Table 6.2 provides a list of the key companies involved with design, construction, and facility management services. The relationship among these team members is shown in Figure 6.2.

TABLE 6.2 Key Members of Design and Construction Team

Architect—Core and Shell	Spagnolo, Gisness & Associates (GS&A)
Architect—Interiors	Gensler
General Contractor	Cranshaw Construction of New England
MEP Engineer	Zelm Engineers
BIM Consultant	Vico Software
FM Software	FM:Systems

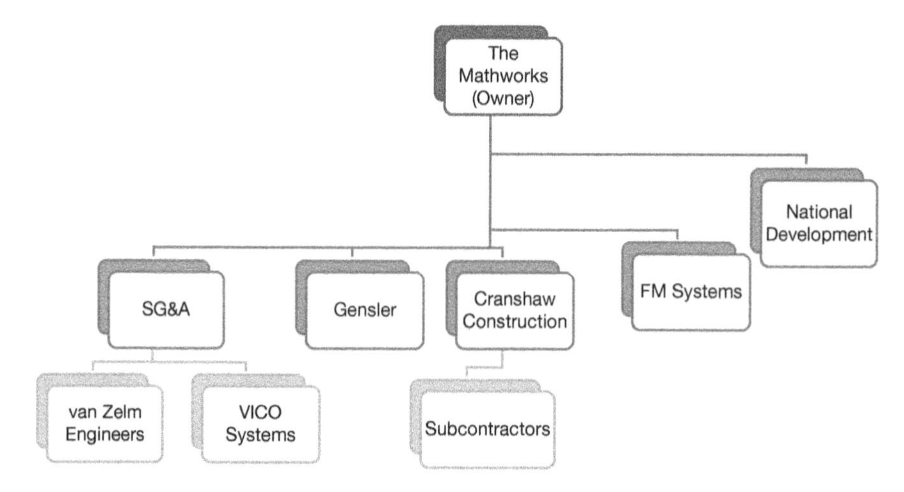

FIGURE 6.2 Contractual relationships among members of the project team.

ARCHITECT FOR BUILDINGS—SPAGNOLO, GISNESS, AND ASSOCIATES, INC. (SG&A)

SG&A is a full-service architecture firm that offers architectural, interior design, and planning services to major international corporations, development firms, and institutions. SG&A has consistently been ranked in the Top 25 interior design firms in the *Boston Business Journal's* Book of Lists, and in the top 35 of the "Area's Largest Architecture Firms" (www.sga-arch.com/). In its capacity with MathWorks, SG&A was responsible for the design of the core and shell of the building. They had previously designed the core, shell, and garage of another facility on the MathWorks campus in Natick, were familiar with the site, town, regulations, and needs of the owner. According to the owner, "They [SG&A] were the right people to go back to," and they were selected solely on a qualifications-based selection (Bernardi and Donahue 2012).

ARCHITECT FOR INTERIORS—GENSLER

Gensler is a firm of architects, designers, planners, and consultants who work on projects that range from the design of a wine label to the design of a new urban district. Gensler is a multiple winner of the Business Week/Architectural Record Awards and has recently achieved a ranking of number 1 on *Boston Business Journal*'s Largest Interior Design Firms List. They have approximately 3,000 professionals across 41 locations, but the Boston team was selected specifically for this project because of their ability to create environments that enhance organizational performance and achieve specific measurable business goals (www.gensler.com/#expertise/markets/15). The Boston team of Gensler beat out nine other teams that responded to a request for qualifications/request for proposal (RFQ/RFP) solicitation by MathWorks. They won the contract and were responsible for the design of all interiors on this project (Bernardi and Donahue 2012).

CONSTRUCTION MANAGER—CRANSHAW CONSTRUCTION

Cranshaw Construction is one of the leading builders and construction managers in the Boston Area and offer their clients estimating, preconstruction, construction scheduling, conceptual design, site selections, development, and dynamic high-quality project teams (www.cranshaw.com/). They were the only construction management firm that was considered for this project. They were chosen to provide preconstruction and construction management services for MathWorks campus expansion as a construction manager at risk and based on a qualifications-based selection process. By bringing the contractor on board as a construction manager at risk at a guaranteed maximum price (GMP), MathWorks was ensured that the project would be delivered on time and within budget. This contractual arrangement also allowed MathWorks to utilize Cranshaw's valuable preconstruction expertise and get cost feedback on intricate design features, green initiatives, and the implementation of BIM, areas in which the owner had no prior experience.

The expansion project consisted of multiple phases and included adding a fourth level to an existing precast garage, demolition of an existing 25,000-square-foot building, and the new construction and interior fit-out of a 176,000-square-foot, four-story office building. MathWorks contracted with Cranshaw, under a purchase and sale agreement that was contingent upon permit approval, for the new building, site work, and new parking garage. This agreement required both Cranshaw and the development firm, National Development, to work closely together to achieve MathWorks' goals (Bernardi and Donahue 2012).

DEVELOPER—NATIONAL DEVELOPMENT

National Development worked closely with Cranshaw Construction as a consultant of the owner during the development process, and they were utilized to set up the purchase and sale agreement, and manage permitting and other local approvals that were required. They have been recognized twice by the NAIOP Massachusetts as the region's outstanding development firm and have 25 years of experience working on development projects (http://natdev.com/development/). MathWorks selected National because of their familiarity with county codes and because they had worked on previous projects with the owner. They were the only firm considered for development and were selected on a qualifications-based selection (Bernardi and Donahue 2012).

MEP ENGINEER—VAN ZELM ENGINEERS

van Zelm, Heywood, & Shadford is an engineering firm offering mechanical and electrical engineering, sustainable design, power and utility, energy, commissioning, and planning services (http://vanzelm.com/index.htm). MathWorks bid out the engineering work on this project and received a handful of responses, of which no firm was selected. MathWorks then contacted van Zelm on a recommendation from a former employee, and after looking at the company's body of work for college institutions and owner-occupied for life spaces, it was decided that van Zelm would be a good fit for the job. The company was selected solely on a qualifications-based selection (Bernardi and Donahue 2012).

BIM CONSULTANT—VICO SOFTWARE

Vico Software is a BIM consulting firm that provides construction software and services to the construction industry throughout the country (www.vicosoftware.com/). Vico's local office in Salem, Massachusetts, was recommended by Cranshaw Construction and selected by MathWorks on a qualifications-based selection. On this particular project, they had the responsibility for coordinating all CAD and BIM documents between the owner, designers, contractor, and subcontractors. Mechanical, electrical, and plumbing (MEP) coordination was critical in this project, and all pipes over 1 inch and conduit over 1½ inches were modeled. After running the developed model, size and location conflicts were easily found and were able to be corrected throughout design development and not during construction. Vico was critical in this process, and their coordination efforts were advantageous to all parties. Figure 6.3 shows the flow of information among all parties (Bernardi and Donahue 2012).

The BIM model is subdivided into five different linked models (architectural core; shell and interior; mechanical, electrical, and plumbing; and furniture) all based on the same core and shell model from SG&A. At project completion, Vico will deliver to MathWorks a complete as-built integrated model. MathWorks will retain ownership of the BIM model after completion of the project for use for FM functions and future remodeling.

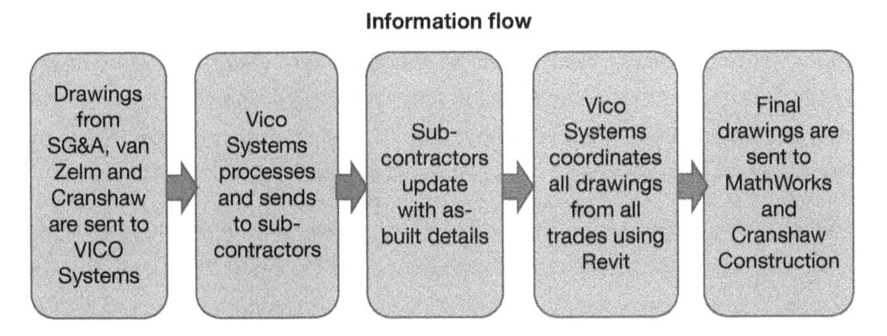

FIGURE 6.3 Vico BIM process. Vico was involved in every step of the process for the creation of and coordination of BIM models.

FM SOFTWARE—FM:SYSTEMS

FM:Systems provided Web-based software that helped to improve the management of the space and occupants while reducing costs and increasing productivity. Although they are headquartered in Raleigh, North Carolina, and not a local company, FM:Systems participated in the project and agreed to provide assistance to MathWorks for this project. FM:Systems' product team worked with MathWorks to enhance their Revit integration to meet MathWorks' requirements. MathWorks is currently using an FM:Systems product that uses AutoCAD drawings and not Revit models. Prior to occupying the new building, MathWorks will utilize the latest software from FM:Systems that allows for Revit integration (www.fmsystems.com/ and http://www.fmbim.com).

ROLE OF BIM FOR SUPPORTING FM REQUIREMENTS

As owners, the primary goal for BIM FM integration is ultimately to help better manage the facilities. With BIM FM integration, FM:Systems software can be used for a variety of functions including: calculating occupancy costs, managing space, maintenance of equipment, and documentation of possible energy savings. Building operations and maintenance will be improved because of the BIM model's ability to integrate with the facility management model in cataloging assets, keeping inventory, and establishing preventative maintenance.

In the past, MathWorks used a more reactive, manual approach to maintenance, assessing and addressing problems as they arose. One of their goals for this new integrated software is to adopt a preventive maintenance approach. FM:Systems supports preventive maintenance and asset management. The BIM model was created with equipment model, properties, and manufacturer information. MathWorks is still developing their asset list as well as the additional information they are going to use from within the BIM model. Because BIM integrated with FM is a relatively new technology, MathWorks is adapting to use this software within their facility management staff, who will be trained by FM:Systems on how to use the software and keep the Revit model updated over time.

In terms of cost, using BIM on this project was more costly than traditional CAD drafting due to the level of development necessary to support FM data handover. However, according to MathWorks' facility manager, the additional cost is "less than the cost of one typical change order" (Bernardi and Donahue 2012). As a result, MathWorks expects to realize a full return on their investment during construction by reducing the number of change orders in the field. In addition, the owners believe that the additional cost of using BIM will be significantly less than the traditional process of reentering handover data for building equipment required for maintenance management. By integrating BIM and FM, MathWorks will create a fully populated preventive maintenance program prior to taking occupancy of the building. According to MathWorks, in traditional projects, maintenance data can take months or even years to enter manually. Based on the results to date, MathWorks plans to update the two-dimensional CAD drawings of their existing facilities to BIM. This work will likely be done by in-house resources and the migration to BIM will be phased in over time.

PROJECT TECHNOLOGY

With a company whose products and services are as advanced as MathWorks, it made sense for them to be on the forefront of technological advances by using the latest in facility management software, FM:Systems. MathWorks has been using FM:Systems software, specifically FM:Interact, since 2004 for building management on the existing campus buildings. FM:Interact, however, only supported traditional two-dimensional AutoCAD drawings until 2010. Figure 6.4 illustrates the systems integration implemented by FM:Interact.

Autodesk's Revit software was the chosen BIM software for this project. Since integration between BIM and facility management software systems is a new capability, MathWorks and FM:Systems both benefited from an interactive relationship. As a result of this project, FM:Systems has recently enhanced their Revit integration software, which allows BIM data and geometry created in Revit to be used within the facility management software.

This BIM Integration Component will allow for the supervision of the Space Management module's inventory, allocations, and occupancy through Revit;

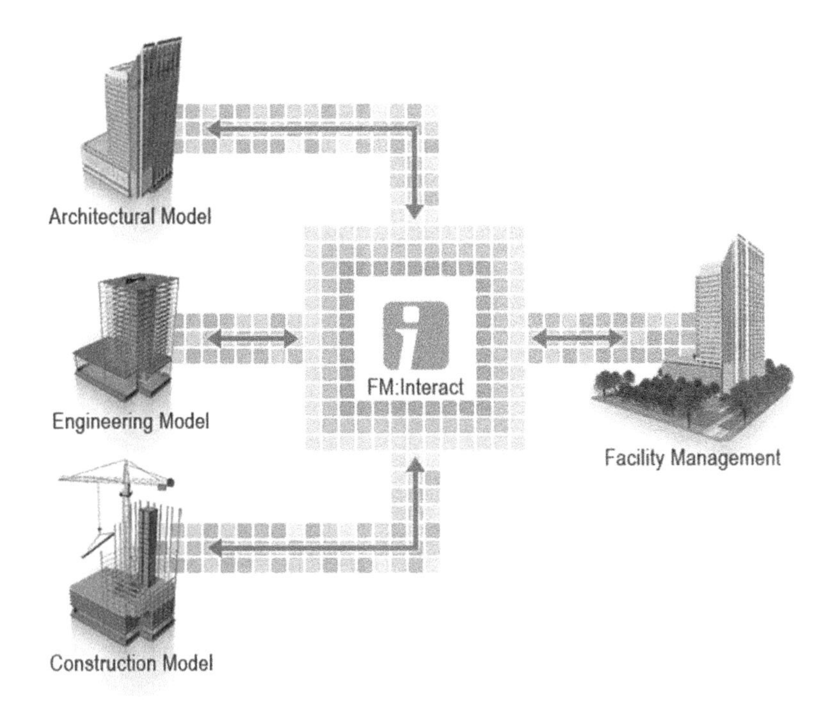

FIGURE 6.4 FM:Interact allowed facility managers online access to AutoCAD Drawings (version 8 announced in August 2010 supports Revit model access).
Courtesy FM:Systems

coordination of building systems data in the Facility Maintenance module with building components in Revit models; and the publishing of floor plans from Revit models to FM:Interact, so relevant parties can view floor plans in a web browser, as shown in Figure 6.5 (www.fmsystems.com/products/bim_revit.html).

FM:Interact coordinates real-time information to analyze and access properties, facilities, and maintenance requirements. Its three main modules are Space Management, Strategic Planning, and Asset Management. Other available modules include Real Estate Portfolio Management, Move Management, Project Management, Facility Maintenance Management, and Sustainability. The new Sustainability module can facilitate the balancing of environmental and financial impacts and assist in managing critical information on energy performance, building certifications, and sustainability projects such as energy retrofits (Khemlani 2011).

The implementation of FM:Interact has provided MathWorks with excellent results. Using the software, two facilities professionals were able to move over 500 employees in two weekends with no errors. This is an impressive feat since, without FM:Interact, the move would most likely have taken months, a larger

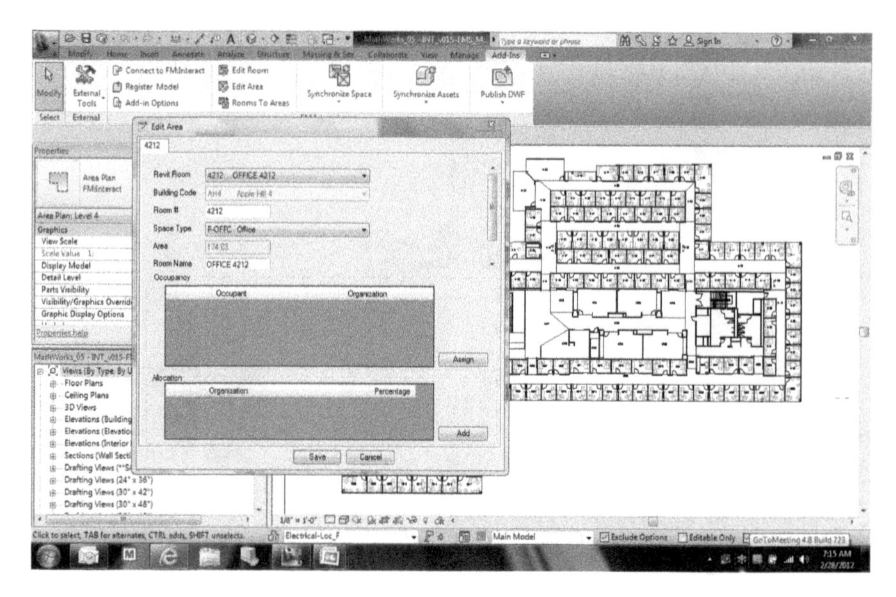

FIGURE 6.5 The interactivity of the menus should allow for ease of use and streamlining of maintenance processes.
Courtesy FM:Systems

team, and more resources. Another valuable outcome has been increased executive buy-in for the MathWorks space planning team. With the help of reports from the FM:Interact software, the conversations between the executive team and the space and planning management have turned from merely discussing the accuracy of capacity/occupancy numbers to discussing the company's need for more space and which groups would be affected, and identifying critical locations. Space Planning Manager Bob Donahue sums up the value of the software, stating, "The bottom line is that productivity has been greatly increased since implementing this technology. The ratio of time saved is ten to one; for every ten minutes we spent prior to FM:Interact we now spend only one minute. I think that speaks for itself" (www.fmsystems.com/knowledge/knowledge_cs_MathWorks.html).

COLLABORATION

The collaboration process in the built environment is the action of bringing together individuals to achieve a common goal for the betterment of all involved. In most building collaboration, this would include the owner or owner's representative of the proposed facility, the architect or design team representative, the constructor or general contractor, and possibly the facility manager. It is important to also understand that, depending on the specific type of structural proposal, other various individuals may be represented in the conceptual phase of the project during collaboration. A good example is a student representative for a new academic structure at a local university.

The MathWorks design team included Chris Bernardi, CAD/CAFM coordinator; Bob Donahue, facilities planning manager; Jeanne O'Keefe, CFO; Jack Little, CEO/president; and Alex Braginsky, director of facilities engineering and VP of operations. The facility manager was involved in the collaboration process with the design team from the conceptual stage of the project. The coordination between the facility manager and the design and construction team was encouraged by the fact that Alex Braginsky also served on the design team. Mr. Braginsky is a seasoned veteran in the industry with over 30 years' experience, and he wore multiple hats throughout the process. MathWorks' intent was to have Mr. Braginsky act as a liaison for the design and construction teams. At the same time, Mr. Braginsky also executed his responsibilities as facility manager (Bernardi and Donahue 2012).

In the collaboration process of the MathWorks case study, all of the listed design team members were involved in weekly collaboration via GoToMeeting software. This software is an interactive Web-based product that connects anyone, anywhere for conferences and online meetings. (www.gotomeeting.com/fec/) In addition to the weekly webinars, the collaboration was realized through an off-site database called Dropbox, capable of sharing all documentation and project deliverables. Dropbox is an online service that offers free hosting services for documents, photos, and videos. The appeal of this product is that it can be used from anywhere by anyone (www.dropbox.com).

Since the project is not fully completed (as of June 2012), the collaboration process between the facility manager and the design and construction team is still an evolving process. Most of the information needed for the operation and maintenance of the building is being gathered based solely upon past experience. Traditionally, this information would be composed in a set of operation and maintenance (O&M) manuals and record drawings, which would be delivered months after project completion. One major goal in this collaboration process was to have all documentation in PDF format prior to completion and project turnover. The collection of this information was done in order to assist the creation of a database within the BIM model, one of the benefits of using the FM:Systems software (Bernardi and Donahue 2012). MathWorks used the COBie standard as a reference source in creating their BIM deliverable guidelines but did not use COBie to transfer the data. Because the project team was modeling in Revit, they used FM:Systems' direct integration with Revit to synchronize the model data with their system.

The collaboration process was also driven by the BIM software. Vico Software was the hired third-party company to combine all the BIM models into one cohesive and complete model. All renderings and drawings from SG&A, van Zelm Engineers (MEP), and Cranshaw Construction go through Vico to the subcontractors. Vico in return reports back to Cranshaw for coordination work, along with MathWorks for the FM model.

METRICS

In the MathWorks case study, there were no formal metrics utilized in tracking project performance, and the contract did not require the formal use of any metrics. The proposed building is still under construction and project performance is still under evaluation. According to an interview with Chris Bernardi and Bob Donahue, some return on investment (ROI) analysis was conducted based on materials in use and construction methods. MathWorks hopes that the ROI analysis will show favorable results over a life cycle of five to seven years. MathWorks' main concern lay with creating a corporate campus that "is as efficient as possible, and to create a pleasant work environment similar to a small college campus" (Bernardi and Donahue 2012).

According to Chris Bernardi and Bob Donahue, "Meeting the new Massachusetts stretch code (www.mass.gov/eea/energy-utilities-clean-tech/energy-efficiency/policies-regs-for-ee/building-energy-codes.html), and making decisions based on an ROI of five to seven years rather than typical spec builder looking at two or three years "will give MathWorks an aggressive sustainability benefit which in their opinion goes above and beyond the LEED standards" (Bernardi and Donahue 2012). While not all the decisions made by MathWorks were justified by the ROI, MathWorks placed the emphasis on doing what made sense for the company. It's the company's belief that using BIM will promote an overall cost and performance savings for FM and building cost after occupancy. Even so, Bob Donahue with MathWorks states that having an accurate building equipment inventory that supports a proper preventive maintenance program will be well worth the additional cost incurred.

Cost savings are anticipated through the use of Navisworks for clash detection during the construction process, but the magnitude is not known yet (see example in Figure 6.6).

At this stage, it is still too early to tell exactly what savings will be realized for the overall project. The major benefits that are anticipated from integrating BIM and FM are the ability to have all information at hand for operation and maintenance

FIGURE 6.6 An example of using Navisworks for MEP/FP coordination.

of the facility prior to occupancy. MathWorks is new to the concept of facility management merged with BIM and wanted to make the transition into this practice as easy and thorough as possible. One thing MathWorks likes about BIM is there won't be a physical, hard copy O&M manual. Instead, because FM:Systems' Revit integration allows them to populate their asset inventory and maintenance schedules during design and construction, an electronic O&M manual will be delivered prior to occupancy, instead of having to wait the typical two to three months after taking ownership. In addition to the data, MathWorks will get a data CD or DVD with the BIM model and PDFs of all the files that are linked to the BIM model, and this will include material and maintenance cut sheets (Bernardi and Donahue 2012).

As the project hasn't yet reached the commissioning phase, MathWorks' facility manager feels it is too early to comment on the advantages and disadvantages of using BIM to integrate data from commissioning and FM processes. However, because their maintenance and asset management system will be populated with building equipment information prior to commissioning, Mathworks intends to gather data for commissioning and enter it into the FM:Systems. Leveraging data in the BIM model for commissioning and updating the model with actual performance data will benefit the facility when the commissioning agent confirms as built performance versus BIM specifications. Any differences will be corrected or updated in the integrated maintenance system and BIM model. For example, airflow rates will be updated in the model for ventilation (Bernardi and Donahue 2012).

Finally, the FM department plans to keep the model up to date as the building or equipment is modified. Mathworks is investing in Revit training for a staff member to keep the model geometry up to date. As the building is modified over time, Mathworks facility manager will use FM:Systems' Revit integration to synchronize current data with the model. The facility manager's goal is to keep an "as-maintained" model to facilitate documentation of existing conditions for any future modification or renewal projects for the building.

LESSONS LEARNED

The general consensus of the MathWorks design team is that until completion of construction, the evaluation of lessons learned cannot be fully known in terms of time, cost, and quality. There is an assumption that cost savings will be apparently present due to early clash detection in addition to design team collaboration efforts. To date, MathWorks has integrated the BIM model with FM:Systems' software in a test system, but they have no plans to modify the integration once connected to their live system. The biggest issue expressed from the design team is that they seemed to be flying blind throughout much of the process. A sense of academic experience was all they had to fall back on. MathWorks' design team is pioneering the industry with BIM technology that was able to interface to facility management systems.

The most critical lesson learned from this experience so far is that there were no established rules to follow. The next project is promising to be more streamlined due to the evolving process that the design team is currently learning and documenting. As stated by the design team, hopefully a major lesson learned will be the back end benefits after turnover of the project. MathWorks, as both a facility owner and operator, wants to use the best tools to manage their facilities (Bernardi and Donahue 2012).

ACKNOWLEDGMENTS

The authors of this case study would like to acknowledge students Osama Aladham, Jasmin Gonzalez, Iris Grant, Kenyatta Harper, Abe Kruger, Scott Nannis, Arpan Patel, and Lauren Snedeker for the hard work and effort put forth on this document. The case study was prepared for the BC 6400 class at Georgia Institute of Technology under the guidance of Professor Kathy O. Roper. In addition, acknowledgment and thanks go to Chris Bernardi and Bob Donahue of MathWorks and Marty Chobot of FM:Systems for their time, effort, and assistance in providing the information for this case study.

REFERENCES

Bernardi, C., and B. Donahue. 2012. Personal interview by A. Kruger, March 19, 2012.

Butler, B. 2009. MathWorks begins expansion. Worcester Business Journal Online (December 16). Retrieved from www.wbjournal.com/news45225.html.

Khemlani, L. 2011. "BIM for Facilities Management." *AECBytes* (September 30). Retrieved from www.aecbytes.com/feature/2011/BIMforFM.html.

Case Study 2: Texas A&M Health Science Center—A Case Study of BIM and COBie for Facility Management

Rebecca Beatty, Georgia Institute of Technology
Charles Eastman, Georgia Institute of Technology

Kyungki Kim, Georgia Institute of Technology
Yihai Fang, Georgia Institute of Technology

MANAGEMENT SUMMARY

The enriched data captured in building information modeling during design and construction has important uses during the full operating lifetime of a facility. The identification, capture, and processing of data useful for this lifetime has just begun. The Texas A&M Health Science Center's (TAM HSC) most recent completed project, Phase 1 in Bryan, Texas, has taken multiple steps to integrate BIM into their facility management program. This case study reviews efforts made to capture digital information about the spaces, systems, and equipment used for facility management on the HSC facilities across nine campuses. The primary focus of the case study is on the implementation of COBie on the Bryan campus location, the first campus to implement COBie. The second campus to implement COBie was in Round Rock, Texas, for a facility that was a few years old, but the FM data was intact enough to apply the process to an existing building. The long-term intent is to evaluate the benefits for new and existing facilities and to validate the predicted benefits and return on investment. Once validated, the process will be applied to other campuses and existing facilities to rebaseline and normalize their facilities management data across the enterprise.

TAM HSC is the owner/client for this project and defined the initial target requirements for the use of BIM on the project in coordination with recommendations and proposed approaches from Broaddus & Associates. The owner team (TAM HSC and Broaddus) identified the use of COBie to generate the base data for supporting preventive maintenance and facility condition analysis. The computerized maintenance management system (CMMS) selected to carry out the maintenance

This case study was developed in coursework and then expanded in the College of Architecture at Georgia Institute of Technology, under direction of Chuck Eastman.

activities was AiM (developed and sold by AssetWorks). AiM is Web based and was used to import all the existing datasets for the Bryan campus and also from the other campuses to unite them into a single integrated CMMS system. Broaddus & Associates of Austin, Texas, was the program manager for the Phase 1 project for Texas A&M University. They oversaw the design, construction, and commissioning process for the $130 million dollar Phase 1 project. Early in the project, the subject of BIM was introduced to the project team. Broaddus worked with key TAM HSC leadership to implement the COBie process for TAM HSC. The project's three main BIM objectives were (1) to deliver as-built 3D models from the construction process, (2) to deliver facilities management data in the COBie format, and (3) to facilitate the import (upload) process of the data and documents into the CMMS. TAM HSC staff also conducted a requirements analysis for an enterprise asset management system, competitively procured it, and administered the deployment and configuration of the CMMS. AiM by AssetWorks was the system selected and installed. Broaddus assisted the TAM HSC in formulating specific BIM and COBie requirements and test scenarios used in the procurement process.

This study reports on the new precedent that the project has set for the Texas A&M University System and reviews the lessons learned for future projects and how to realize the targeted integration between BIM and their CMMS system. TAM HSC was one of the first large-scale educational institutions to implement COBie in their building program all the way into their facility management application. Bryan Campus Phase 1 also serves as an example for improvement and gives a glimpse into the future for the facility management industry. Future improvements being addressed include, but are not limited to, the develop of a BIM POR (program of requirements) that is specific to TAM HSC and will allow them to further pursue BIM with consistency in the areas of campus strategy, 3D modeling criteria, FM data criteria (COBie), and utilization in AiM.

GENERAL DESCRIPTION

TAM HSC is an affiliated but separate branch of the Texas A&M University System. TAM HSC has nine campus locations throughout Texas. The most recently completed TAM HSC project is located on the southern edge of Bryan, Texas. There are three components of the Bryan campus Phase 1 project. The first is the physical construction of Phase 1, made up of three new facilities. Building models were developed within each project. The second was the implementation of COBie to facilitate an asset data set. The third is the CMMS system that was implemented and populated with data for FM use.

The Bryan campus started construction in October 2008 and the project was turned over in December 2010 per the original schedule. The Bryan campus master plan encompasses 4 million gross square feet (GSF) of planned space on a 205-acre greenfield campus. A TAM HSC goal is to develop this as a "digital campus" inclusive of building and site models as well as digital FM data for AiM. Phase 1's total expected project cost was $131,372,000. Phase 1 involved the construction of three new buildings: the central utility plant (CUP) at 12,565 GSF, which included a separate structure for the Telecom Building; a health professional building (HPEB) at 128,159 GSF; and a medical research and education building (MREB) at 127,514 GSF. The HPEB includes a 27,000 GSF simulation center, and the MREB includes a 4,100-GSF level-three biological safety Lab (BSL-3). See Figure 6.7.

These three new facilities were awarded under a competitive sealed proposal delivery method and cost $102,200,000 at initial award. The final completion cost

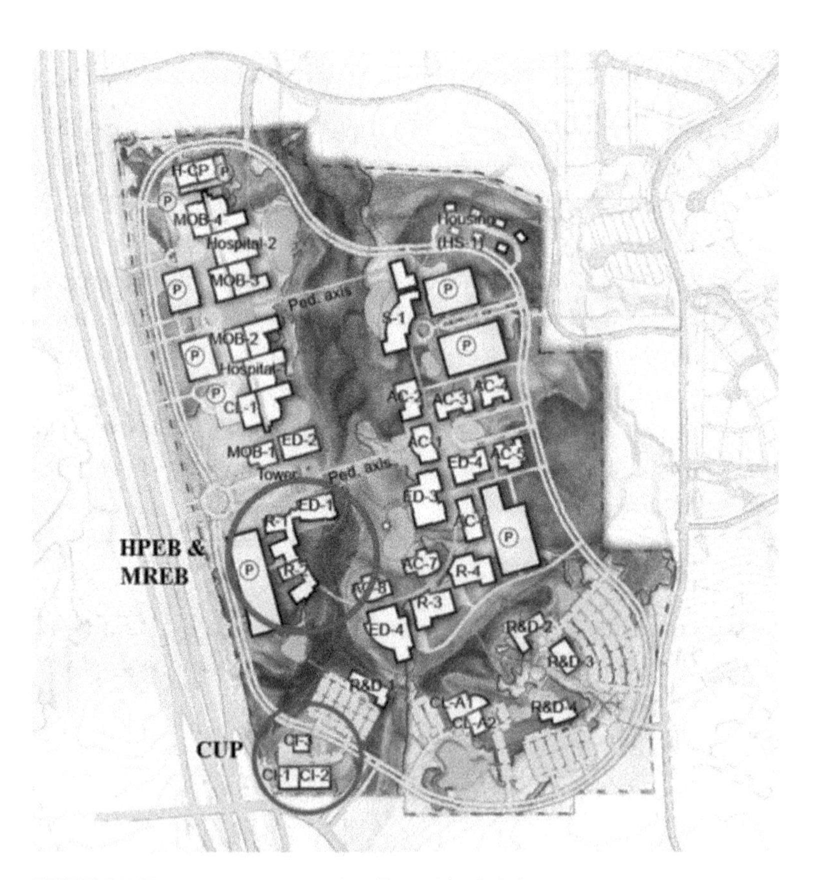

FIGURE 6.7 Bryan campus master plan. Phase 1 is circled.

FIGURE 6.8 Bryan Campus Phase 1, HPEB and MREB buildings.
Courtesy TAM HSC

was $109,451,000. The initial competitive price resulted in a significant savings (22.2 percent of the original budget) that could be allocated to further work, including all adding alternates and owner-initiated scope upgrades. These savings can be attributed to the general contractor, Satterfield & Pontikes Construction, Inc., which developed a BIM model of all three buildings prior to the bidding process (see Figure 6.8). The contractor modeled the foundations, superstructure, and exterior shell for proposal analysis and competitive pricing. From this model they were able to extract accurate quantities, make a precise cost estimate, analyze the construction schedule, and so on. This allowed them to reduce the normal contingency amount in their bid and propose the buildings at a reduced cost. The buildings function as a place for education, research, clinical, hospital, administrative, residential, and private incubator-type facilities.

The HPEB and MREB superstructures were constructed of reinforced concrete, and the CUP superstructure was constructed with a steel frame and traditional masonry walls. HPEB, MREB, and CUP have foundations made of auger-cast concrete piles (over 900). The structure was cast-in-place concrete columns and a flat slab system. The exterior was metal stud backup with masonry and stone veneer. See Figure 6.9 for the final model after interior fit-out and 3D coordination during the construction phase.

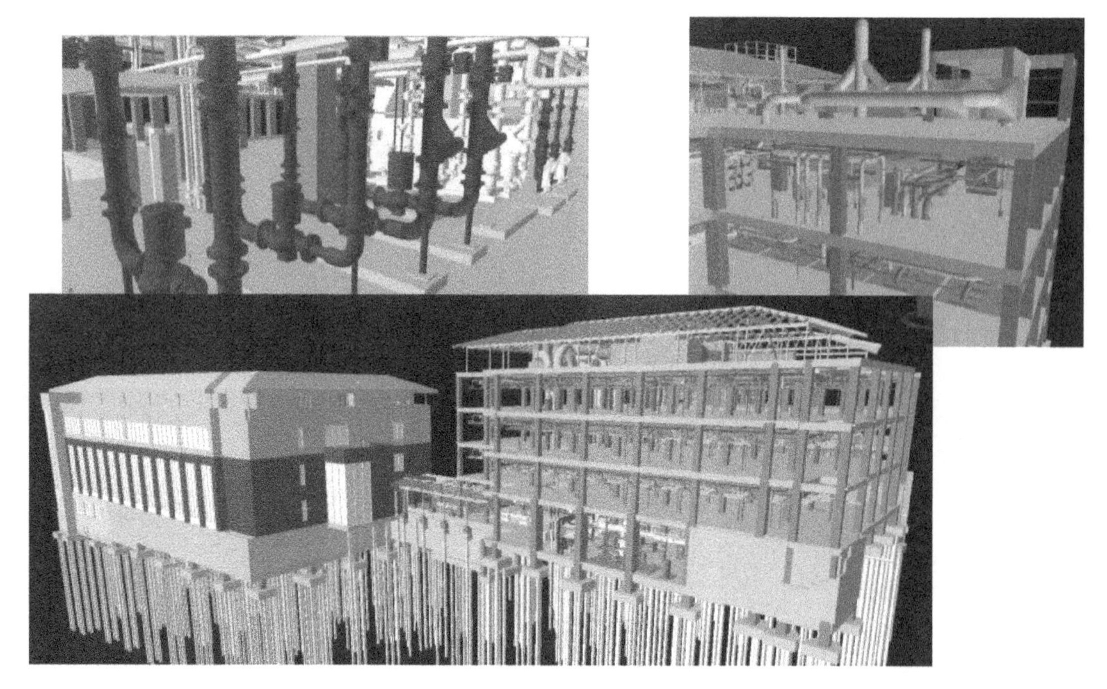

FIGURE 6.9 Revit as-built model of an equipment room on the Bryan Campus project by the general contractor.
Courtesy Broaddus & Associates

PROJECT TEAM

The project and construction team for Phase 1 at the Bryan campus is as follows:

- Architect = FKP Architects
- Engineer = Shah Smith & Associates (MEP), Hanes Whaley Associates (Structural), Mitchell & Morgan LLP (Civil)
- General contractor/BIM = Satterfield & Pontikes Construction, Inc. (S&P)
- Program manager/construction manager/COBie integrator = Broaddus & Associates

CONTRACTS

Architect/Engineer = Design contract

General contractor = Started as a construction manager at risk (CM-R)

After preconstruction, the original construction management team (not S&P) was removed from the project. The contract was then changed to a competitive sealed proposal (CSP) for the remainder of the work. COBie data was a requirement in all these contracts.

The switch to a CSP contract with the construction management team was done because a guaranteed maximum price agreement could not be reached between the original CMAR contractor and the Texas A&M System. All of the contractual arrangements subcontractors and fabricators were contracted through the general contractor's contract.

During construction, the Bryan campus Phase 1 project was modeled by the general contractor and field verified by Broaddus. S&P reconciled the entire Revit model and updated it to actual as-built conditions, including all of the site components (underground utilities, etc.). Broaddus & Associates was hired by Texas A&M University System Facilities Planning & Construction (TAMUS FPC) to be the program manager and the COBie integrator, and to implement COBie for the TAM HSC facility turnover. The COBie data was extracted from some of the architectural models by Broaddus. Further, Broaddus configured COBie data provided by the architecture and engineering teams in the contract documents and construction records. Subcontractor information was also handed over to the program manager for data integration into COBie. Broaddus & Associates first used TOKMO (now called EcoDomus) and later Onuma to add and edit data from the model to create the COBie file. The transition to the use of Onuma for the last 5 percent of the project was to enable cross-training of Broaddus staff. The success story in this switch emphasizes the interoperability of the COBie data process. The transition from one COBie configuration tool (TOKMO/EcoDomus) to another (Onuma) proves that BIM and data interoperability is paramount and can be achieved with proper planning and tools. The switch was made for training purposes alone and not related to any TOKMO challenges. Both software systems worked well. Broaddus then exported the information into a Microsoft Excel format (COBie) for turnover to the TAM HSC Facilities & Construction department. During the implementation and configuration of AiM, Broaddus provided continued support and corrections to the multiple COBie files. Numerous test uploads were conducted to verify that information was migrating to the correct cells in AiM and that documents were properly mapped to the right paths. This was also done in order to allow TAM HSC to verify where data was being imported to in AiM. Although TAM HSC staff had been reviewing the COBie files during development, the real test and confirmation happened when the data reached its intended destination in AiM. In some cases, revisions to the COBie data were required in order to "fine-tune" the process and improve how the data was displayed inside of AiM to meet TAM HSC's functional needs. After the BIM model and data turnover, TAM HSC retains ownership of the models.

AssetWorks and Broaddus & Associates collaborated to integrate the BIM data with AiM. The cost of incorporating COBie into this project was not tracked separately: it was included in the construction management fees. However, hours for configuring COBie were tracked. The estimated hours equated to about 2,400 essentially, greater than 1 FTE for 1 year. This excludes the time spent planning and coordinating before data configuration started. Formulation of an implementation strategy involved multiple discussions by TAM HSC and Broaddus staff. The estimated cost for AssetWorks to use their COBie import process within AiM was a lump sum of approximately $10,000, paying for the AssetWorks services and licensing fees. However, this cost was inclusive of the total nine-campus implementation of AiM by AssetWorks, so the COBie portion of the services cannot easily be separated because of the enterprise-wide implementation effort employed.

The COBie project at the Bryan campus location ran from May 2009 to September 2011. Set-up took place from May to October of 2009. Then, collection, structure, and updates took place from November 2009 to August 2011. Finally, import testing, review, and adjustments occurred from June 2011 to September 2011. The separate but concurrent CMMS AiM project included all nine campuses. AssetWorks implemented AiM on existing campuses by using the available information, such as AutoCAD drawings, and manually uploaded material. The Bryan campus was the initial one that incorporated a COBie data platform; work on it was completed in November 2011. Later, the HPEB building at Round Rock also used COBie; it ran from April 2011 until March 2012. The last four months (December to March) were spent in improvement efforts resulting from lessons learned from the Bryan campus, in dialogue with AssetWorks and Broaddus, dealing with upload and import testing/review (discussed below).

The owner of the project is TAM HSC, which had a direct relationship with the architect, the general contractor, and Broaddus and Associates. All of the engineers consulted directly with the architect. The subcontractors and fabricators reported to the general contractor. Broaddus & Associates also had a relationship with TOKMO (now EcoDomus) and Onuma, which was used strictly by them in order to collect and add data from the model and output COBie data. The budget savings on the Bryan campus allowed the project to also include the HPEB building at the Round Rock Campus for COBie Phase integration.

ROLE OF OWNER AND FM STAFF IN SETTING BIM AND FM REQUIREMENTS

The primary goal for BIM/FM integration for the Bryan Campus Phase 1 project was to more easily assemble the asset data into a comprehensive turnover to CMMS. TAM HSC's expectation was to use this information for maintenance and operational needs, space management, and immediate facility condition assessment

(FCA). The benefits of the adoption of BIM technology and the COBie format for information exchange in the project included:

- The ability to capture accurate/structured data as the buildings are being constructed (not after they are completed) and the ability to conduct FM data quality control and validation during construction
- The time savings and reduced effort for the in-house staff
- The assumed overall efficiency and cost savings for facilities operations
- The ability to use the BIM and asset models to plan facility upgrades
- The capability to identify the assets that needed to be included in the preventive maintenance program
- The potential for all of TAM HSC to eventually be fully converted to a digital campus with normalized FM data
- The ease of locating necessary equipment that is not straightforwardly found
- Clash detection and accessibility of asset/equipment information for FCA
- The ability to have O&M manuals, warranties, commissioning records, submittals, and other documents attached in the CMMS for reference

The TAM HSC facility management staff were direct contributors in determining the BIM deliverables from the Phase 1 Bryan campus project. Manuals, submittals, and other related documents were linked to each asset/equipment profile for usability (see Figure 6.10). Having FM functions in the BIM model can allow for easy access and better communication regarding the asset data associated with the buildings. The commissioning information was not imported back into the BIM model for this project, but was part of the defined scope for COBie data imported to AiM.

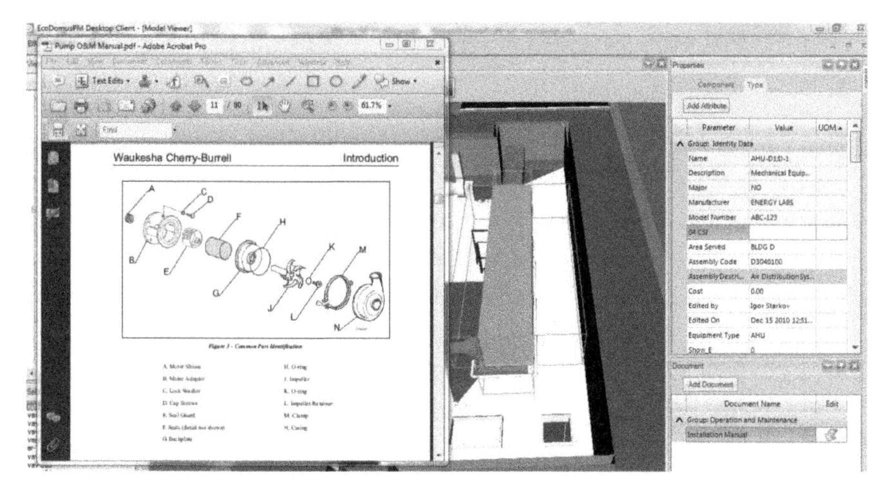

FIGURE 6.10 Example of how manuals are linked to the BIM model and accessed in PDF format.
Courtesy EcoDomus

Commissioning documents were attached at appropriate levels corresponding to equipment and systems.

Initially, TAM HSC did not know what CMMS system would best fit their program. TAM HSC FM staff networked with industry experts and attended conferences and webinars to acquire a comprehensive understanding of the practical and essential information that they should require in their deliverable. Independently obtaining such knowledge was a critical component that enabled the TAM HSC staff to establish their own guidelines and operational requirements. TAM HSC FM staff also consulted with the project architectural and engineering design firms along with the construction management team to set up parameters for implementation. The facility management functions were an integral part of developing the contents of the BIM model and the FM data (COBie) requirements. Many of these requirements evolved over the course of the project as project discovery occurred.

The TAM HSC FM staff and Broaddus started designing the data collection process by reviewing various lists of the building components and all of the assets. This started with Broaddus nominating and proposing FM data content. Then, alignment meetings were held with the FM staff to confirm the scope of work. Next, they divided the assets into categories and separated those into subcategories, using the OmniClass system from the Construction Specifications Institute. BIM models are capable of carrying large amounts of data, and determining the subset most critical to the work plan goals of TAM HSC was an important issue. They standardized how they wanted the information structured and related. TAM HSC teamed with Broaddus & Associates to define the level of detail in the facility components. There were three key areas of significance that the TAM HSC FM staff prioritized when they were evaluating which assets to include in the BIM/COBie data:

1. Preventive maintenance
2. Emergency situation regarding operations
3. The ability to facilitate a remodel

The scope of the models and COBie data sets was determined by these required FM functions. The amount of detail and specification that was included in the model was directly related to the management, maintenance, and operations of the facilities, such as the request that the BIM model contain information about pipes more than 2 inches in diameter and disregard any pipes less than 2 inches in diameter. Omitting unneeded data ensured that only details applicable to the FM staff would be incorporated in the deliverable. TAM HSC anticipated using the BIM model as an ongoing tool for life-cycle operations. The final COBie data collection process is shown in Figure 6.11, as undertaken by Broaddus & Associates. In this initial project,

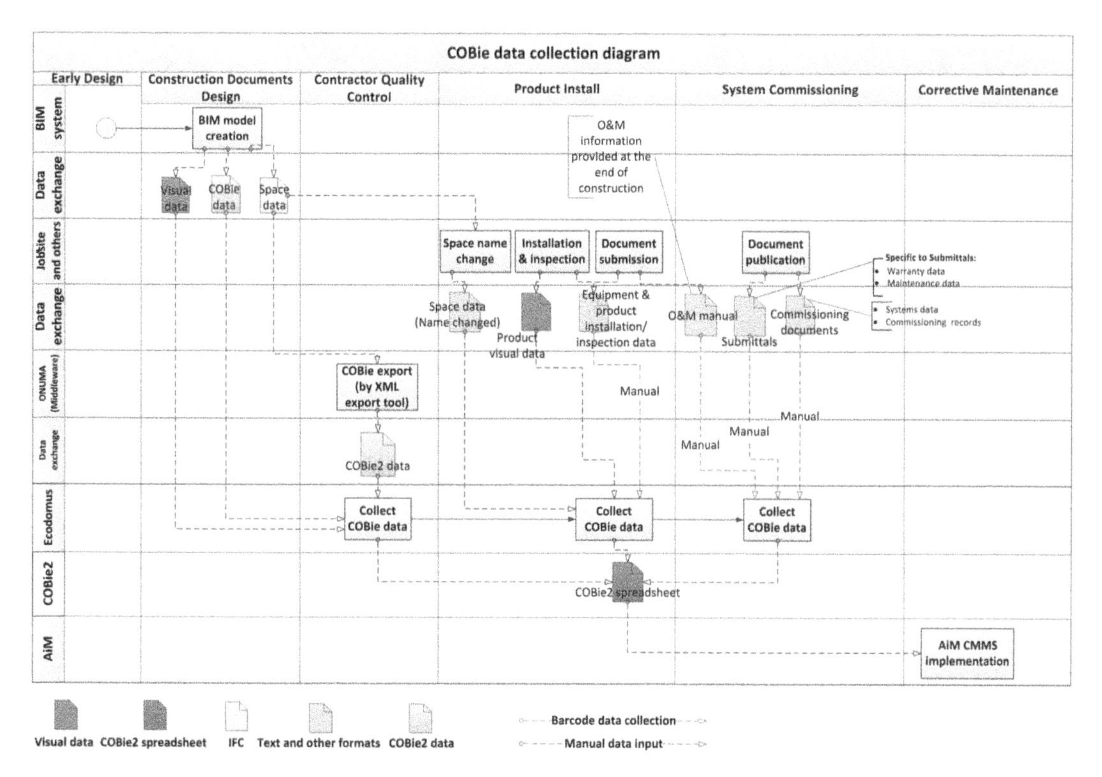

FIGURE 6.11 COBie data collection diagram.
Courtesy Broaddus & Associates

the inputs were manual. In the future, more automated links, incorporating radio-frequency identification (RFID) tags are expected to be used.

ROI

There is a short-term return, based on improved ownership transition, better "ramp-up" of staff, and fewer lost warranty opportunities. In summary, the owner's FM staff estimated that the investment made to configure the facility life-cycle management (FLCM) related data for systematic initial upload has a 100 percent first-year ROI when compared to the first cost effort of the owner's staff to research, configure, and upload the FLCM data as they find the time during the first year or longer of operations. The effort required for the owner's staff to collect configure and structure the data, to the same level and detail as was done for TAM HSC Phase 1, is typically 2× to 2.5× that of the Broaddus team because of their other responsibilities that conflict with the time needed for data collection using the BIM COBie process.

With assistance from AssetWorks, Broaddus and Associates completed a pre-analysis comparison to estimate the time that could be saved during a work order

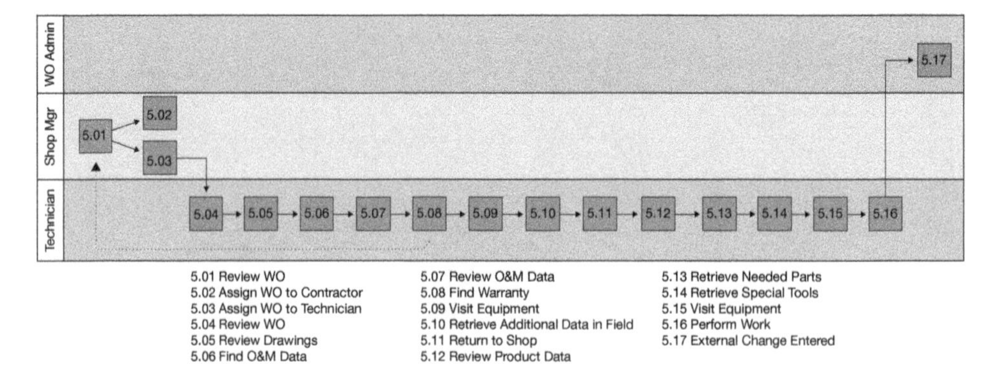

FIGURE 6.12 Pre-COBie-enabled CMMS work order process collected by surveying three campuses.
Courtesy Broaddus & Associates

TABLE 6.3 Work Order Process before COBie-Enabled CMMS

WO process BEFORE COBie-enabled CMMS				**Dallas**	**Bryan**	**McAllen**	
Activity ID	**Activity**	**Predecessor**	**Responsibility**	**Estimated Time (min)**	**Estimated Time (min)**	**Estimated Time (min)**	**Average Time**
5.01	Review WO	Start, 5.08	Shop Manager	5	5	5	5
5.02	Assign WO contractor	5.01	Shop Manager	15	12.5	16	14.5
5.03	Assign WO to technician	5.01	Shop Manager	5	5	2	4
5.04	Review WO	50.3	Technician	5	5	2	4
5.05	Review drawings	5.04	Technician	2	11	10	7.7
5.06	Find O & M	5.05	Technician	1	3	2	2.0
5.07	Review O & M	5.06	Technician	1	5	2	2.7
5.08	Find Warranty	5.07	Technician	3	2	2	2.3
5.09	Visit equipment	5.06	Technician	1	1.25	0.75	1
5.10	Retrieve product data from equipment	5.09	Technician	0.75	1.25	1	1.0
5.11	Return to shop	5.10	Technician	0.75	1.25	1	1.0
5.12	Review product data	5.08, 5.11	Technician	10	12	13	11.7
5.13	Retrieve needed parts	5.12	Technician	5	10	15	10
5.14	Retrieve special tools	5.13	Technician	3	3	2	2.7
5.15	Visit equipment	5.14	Technician	10	20	5	11.7
5.16	Perform work	5.15	Technician	45	30	60	45
5.17	External change entered	5.16	WO Admin	3	2	7.5	4.2
	Total			115.5	129.25	146.25	130.3

process by using a COBie-based process (see Figure 6.12) as opposed to the process that was being used (see Figure 6.12).

TAM HSC FM staff hoped to use COBie to reduce time in the work order cycle by having a digitally enabled CMMS system. Broaddus & Associates made predictions about how the COBie system would make the work order process more efficient, based upon interviews with FM staff. Workers were surveyed to see how long the existing process of a work order, from submission to execution, took without a COBie-enabled CMMS system. Table 6.3 reflects the time estimates before the use of COBie data, and Table 6.4 shows the estimates after the integrated system was implemented. The abridged comparison suggests that TAM HSC should realize a short period ROI with regards to the maintenance

TABLE 6.4 WO Process after COBie-Enabled CMMS

WO process AFTER COBie enabled CMMS				**Dallas**	**Bryan**	**McAllen**	
Activity ID	**Activity**	**Predecessor**	**Responsibiltiy**	**Estimated Time (min)**	**Estimated Time (min)**	**Estimated Time (min)**	**Average Time**
6.01	Review WO	Start	Shop Manager	5	5	5	5
6.02	Assign WO contractor	6.01	Shop Manager	15	12.5	10	12.5
6.03	Assign WO to technician	6.01	Shop Manager	5	5	2	4
6.04	Review WO	6.03	Technician	5	5	2	4
6.05	Review drawings	6.04	Technician	1.25	8.5	8.5	6.1
5.06	Find O & M	5.05	Technician	0.26	0.14	0.38	0.3
5.07	Review O & M	5.06	Technician	1	5	2	2.7
5.08	Find Warranty	5.07	Technician	0.25	0.25	0.25	0.3
5.09	Visit equipment	5.06	Technician	0.75	1.25	1	1
5.10	Retrieve product data from equipment	5.09	Technician	0.25	0.75	0.5	0.5
5.11	Return to shop	5.10	Technician	0.75	1.25	1	1.0
6.12	Review product data	6.05	Technician	8.5	7.5	8	8.00
6.13	Retrieve needed parts	6.12	Technician	5	10	15	10
6.14	Retrieve special tools	6.13	Technician	3	3	2	2.7
6.15	Visit equipment	6.10	Technician	10	20	5	11.7
6.16	Perform work	6.15	Technician	45	30	60	45
6.17	External change entered	6.16	External change entered	3	2	7.5	4.2
	Total			109.01	117.14	130.13	118.8

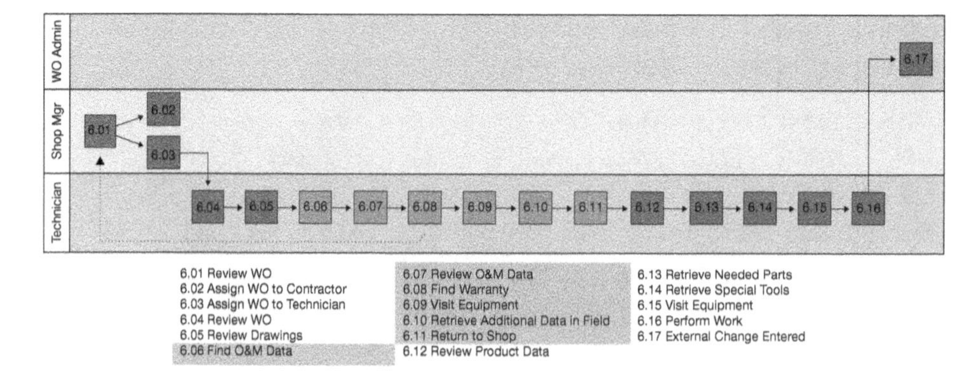

FIGURE 6.13 Predicted future work order process after COBie integration. Steps 6.06–6.11 show an anticipated compression for time spent on those portions of the process.
Courtesy Broaddus & Associates

and construction staff. The key to this workflow improvement is the consistency with which AiM can implement work orders. The CMMS allows for a consistent approach, which was not possible before an enterprise asset management program was put in place.

They next considered the activities required to process a work order currently (see Figure 6.12) with the activities required to process a work order using COBie and AiM (see Figure 6.13). The savings per work order were then expanded for the three campuses summarized in Figure 6.14.

This survey indicates that there was an anticipated 8.7 percent reduction in time spent on the work order process. This reduction is attributed to having ready

	Dallas	Bryan	McAllen	Average	Details:
Total Time per WO (Min)	115.5	129.3	146.3	130.3	Average time before COBie (from interviews)
Total Time per WO (Min)	109.0	117.1	130.1	118.8	Average time after COBie (from interviews)
Total Time per WO (Min)	6.5	12.1	16.1	11.6	Average savings per WO realized by COBie data (from interviews)
SAVING per WO (MH)	0.11	0.20	0.27	0.19	Average hour savings per WO realized by use of COBie data (from interview)
TIME SAVINGS (%)	5.6%	9.4%	11.0%	8.7%	WO time savings diveded by total time per WO
Technician Count	16.00	5.00	1.00	n/a	Amount of campus technicians available for WO's
Available Hours/Yr	24000	7500	1500	n/a	Technician count multiplied by actual FTE (1,500 MH)
Expected WO's/Yr	13210	3842	692	n/a	Available MH's divided by total time per WO
Expected MH Savings/Yr	1429	775	186	n/a	Expected WO's/Yr mulitplied by MH savings per WO

FIGURE 6.14 Survey of three campuses showing projected time saved through a BIM/COBie/AiM improved process.
Courtesy Broaddus and Associates

access to accurate and complete digital information and documents. The COBie project, along with the CMMS system, has been operational for only a short time, and there has been no further analysis to measure the actual benefits for using the COBie-enabled CMMS system (AiM). The next phase of confirmation of the benefits is for the TAM HSC FM staff to collect work order data (time durations) to allow assessment of the predicted benefits. Once that data is available, Broaddus will continue to work with TAM HSC to advance the research and confirm the predicted results with objective time measurements (the critical parameter) for the case study.

TECHNOLOGIES

The TAM HSC Phase 1 buildings at the Bryan campus is where the project team developed a detailed equipment/asset management dataset of the specified components for the new project, using as input the COBie data exchange template. TAM HSC and Broaddus selected COBie because it is a well-documented public standard. TAM HSC specified that the enterprise asset management (EAM) system was to be compatible with COBie and utilize the data developed for the new campus, as well as for data for the existing campuses. Broaddus & Associates (acting as the COBie integrator) initially used TOKMO (now named EcoDomus) as middleware throughout the majority of the project. Some of the facility-management-related data was extracted from the Architectural Revit models by Broaddus.

Additional data was supplemented by submittals (asset and building information), O&M product manuals, and field data (installation and inspection). The supplemental information was input manually or through the use of the EcoDomus and Onuma middleware. This information created a data set that was then imported into the CMMS system (AiM). This process is diagrammed in Figure 6.15. Once the data were uploaded, this enabled the facility management team to digitally manage the facility by utilizing different functions within the CMMS system, such as work orders and maintenance schedules. This automation is expected to help the FM staff schedule maintenance and track which vendors are under contract to service equipment.

Broaddus and Associates developed 95 percent of the COBie data inside EcoDomus. Most of the space data was generated during design, with the exception of the space names that changed when the wayfinding/signage package came out during the product installation stage (see COBie data collection diagram in

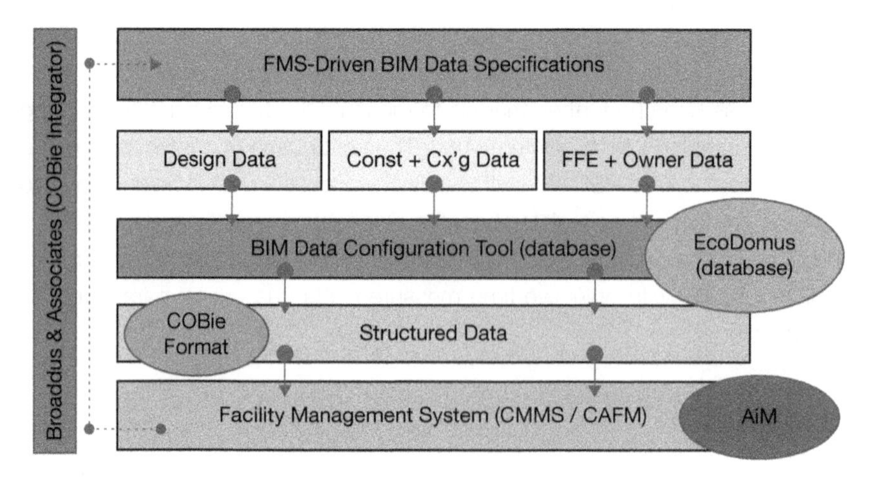

FIGURE 6.15 Information flows.
Courtesy Broaddus & Associates

Figure 6.11). Space data (floors and spaces) were imported from the Revit model into Onuma, then exported as a COBie file (via XML export tool developed by Onuma, Inc.) and imported into EcoDomus.[1] This is a good example of how BIM requires the use of multiple tools and the ability of data to be interoperable from one tool to another. About 95 percent of the way through the project, Broaddus switched over to Onuma to facilitate cross-training of Broaddus staff on multiple COBie configuration tools. Other information relative to COBie was manually entered into spreadsheets that could be uploaded to the COBie configuration tools. This facilitated data capture and provisioning from the contractor and related subs without them having to fully understand COBie. The use of the Excel (XLS) templates and simple instructions reduced a complex subject (COBie data compilation) to a simple XLS request. Then, Broaddus integrated those strings of information into the COBie data set. Thus, the concept of a COBie integrator was formed. Location data made up about 6 percent of the entire COBie effort. Equipment and product

[1] In 2010 EcoDomus was given the FIATECH CETI (Celebration of Engineering & Technology Innovation) Award for "Lifecycle Data Management and Information Integration." The FIATECH CETI web site (http://fiatech.org/ceti-award/2010-ceti-recipients) describes the award as follows: "The Texas A&M University Health Sciences Center project consisted of a $68 million health professions education building, a $60 million medical research and education building, and a central utility plant. The university wanted to use open standards, such as COBie and Omni Class, to collect data during design and construction. This project was the first large project in the world to use COBie. The savings from using the process, managed by Broaddus & Associates and EcoDomus software, reached 45 percent of the standard handover costs. In addition, EcoDomus software enabled connection of the 3D CAD model to the collect COBie dataset, enabling creation of an intelligent BIM model from the 3D CAD. Element 9 of the Fiatech Roadmap, Life-Cycle Data Management and Information Integration, focuses on the problems solved within this project."

data was generated during the product installation stage (see Figure 6.11). COBie is a generated data set that is a product of information collected from the Revit model and the middleware and then exported as an Excel spreadsheet. Equipment serial numbers were verified through the documents published in the system commissioning stage (see Figure 6.11).

There were a number of additional technologies used on the Bryan campus project. Two-dimensional AutoCAD drawings were drafted by the architect and then used by the general contractor to create a 3D model in Revit Architecture. The Revit model was then imported into Navisworks for field clash detection by S&P. The BIM capabilities of the general contractor helped them to be awarded the contract with a low bid that was 20 percent lower than the highest bid because they had a 3D model of the project, which permitted a more thorough understanding of the project and allowed them to reduce their contingency costs.

COLLABORATION AND TRAINING

The owner was a very active collaborator. TAM HSC provided indispensable information regarding the way that they expected BIM/COBie to function with regards to facility management. TAM HSC was available to address any questions that Broaddus or the general contractor asked regarding the owner's expectations for the way the information needed to perform. The advantages observed for commissioning and for FM functions are that it will ensure that proper preventive maintenance (PM) will be conducted on all assets. The FM staff will have the opportunity to pinpoint the location of an asset in the building model, and they will be capable of retrieving that asset's data, and work history. This new automation is anticipated to save a significant amount of time and reduce errors. The main disadvantages of this path are the resources that are necessary to develop a new workflow protocol and to train staff to utilize the BIM model directly from the CMMS system. The incorporation of the new BIM FM systems resulted in the TAM HSC FM staff's need to hire suitable personnel that had the proper skill set to integrate and operate the new systems. Extensive training was given at all campus locations for the existing employees. Currently, TAM HSC is responsible for the maintenance of the BIM models (Revit and Navisworks). In the future, TAM HSC FM staff might consider a service contract to maintain the model. This transition will depend on future complexity and growth. Broaddus is also providing site model update services for a recently constructed (Clinical Building 1) developer built project. This includes the site model updates and adding the building model into the "digital campus" master files.

LESSONS LEARNED

TAM HSC had the opportunity to apply some lessons learned from the completed Phase 1 Bryan campus project on the Round Rock campus. For future projects, the TAM HSC facility management staff plans on itemizing the fee structure for COBie integration so that a detailed scope of responsibilities may be referenced in the contract. This can be accomplished by formulating a BIM POR (program of requirements) that is specific to TAM HSC. The BIM POR includes criteria for the BIM execution plan (BEP) framework, 3D modeling requirements (tied to FM data needs), and FM (COBie) data requirements. Further, the BIM POR includes criteria to delineate FM data content, data format (structure), division of responsibility, and milestone timing for the deliverables.

The Bryan campus BIM/COBie project served as a prototype for the methods that will be used on future TAM HSC projects. Lessons were learned about the components that create the database, but also for the project set up and management. One of the major lessons learned was in regard to the scope and role of all of the parties in taking the project from conception to turn over. The division of responsibility, mentioned previously, delineates who the best authoring source is for the FM data. Further, it became evident that one party needed to be responsible for the configuration management of the COBie data. The process needs a "gatekeeper" to ensure that confidence in the data quality remains high and that configuration management of the data is not lost by having multiple parties making unauthorized changes to the record COBie data set during development.

The Bryan Campus BIM/COBie project was the first of its kind for TAM HSC. It taught the TAM HSC team how they will better format contracts in the future. Future projects need to have an explicit monetary amount allocated to specific tasks. The responsibilities of each party involved need to be more specific in scope and clearly defined in the contracts. The BIM POR will facilitate this process. The desired level of detail of modeled components needs to be specified in the contract. Time tracking for data collection will also be required on future projects to allow better break down of costs. Many of the requirements that the FM staff dictated were the result of discussions with the COBie integrator, so that their scope was designed at the same time it was being set into action. The next project will have a clearer set of guidelines. The specifications for the FM data process on this project were essentially as-built to the COBie data specification and format. That is, no specification existed at the start of the project. The specification was developed in order to document the resulting COBie data set.

No formal metrics were used to track project performance on the owner's part. TAM HSC relied heavily on the expertise of Broaddus and the general contractor. There was no requirement for any metrics in any of the contracts. The new system is now being used to streamline the management of TAM HSC facilities. After more experience with the new system, the BIM/COBie results will be compared against those of the other campuses that do not have BIM models and COBie data sets. When this analysis is completed, TAM HSC will have a fuller understanding of the time and cost savings and be able to calculate their actual savings and return on investment.

TAM HSC has a future goal to extend the data to support development of a system for energy management by leveraging existing models and FM data to drive the benefits of a building energy model (BEM).

AREAS OF IMPROVEMENT

TAM HSC has already identified areas for improvement through referencing Bryan campus decisions in hindsight and developing new "best practices" for the Round Rock campus COBie project. The main correction is properly defining the level of family/type data that should be included in the COBie documents. TAM HSC has identified the level of detail expected for future projects. It was difficult for the FM staff to review COBie data in the XLS format. Once the test uploads commenced, the FM staff had a much better appreciation for how the COBie data would be used in AiM. This led to adjustments and alignments to be made by Broaddus before the final data sets were turned over. It was a learning process for the TAM HSC and for Broaddus in data configuration efforts. One of the first steps in the process was to outline a list of applicable categories for the pick list. TAM HSC wanted to keep OmniClass as their standard for equipment and asset classification, but they replaced the standard numerical value with a more intuitive name so that technicians could recognize the item on asset profiles, on work orders, or while using the AiM system. An example of this would be the OmniClass classification for an air handler unit was 23-33 25 17. Using this code alone would require the technician to look it up because it is not intuitively understood what equipment group it applies to. This asset group number was changed to "AHU," which more clearly describes that the item is an air handling unit. The naming is consistent across all nine campuses.

The room spaces were identified by the code established by the Texas Higher Education Coordinating Board. OmniClass Table 21 was used for naming category/element in the COBie file, and the asset groups were identified by the OmniClass product Table 23.

Following the Bryan campus project, Broaddus had the opportunity to take some of the immediate lessons learned and apply them to the project at Round Rock campus. Part of this improvement was the ability to incorporate more concise specifications. The COBie "best practices" developed from the Bryan project were then used for higher quality data for the AiM system at the Round Rock campus.

Another area for improvement required 240 additions of "types" (serialized asset groups). These "types" were fragmented from the model number in order for the user to view both the model number and the manufacturer of the asset instead of having to navigate to a separate window. Succinct asset groups provide a better selection of groups to develop preventive maintenance (PM) procedures. A simplified example of this would be that instead of requesting maintenance on a "bathroom," the request would now be labeled "lavatory" because "bathroom" has many different components within it, "lavatory" further specifies the classification. More defined reporting is a benefit of well-defined serialized asset groups (types). The systems that were nonserialized asset groups required 60 more additions. At the Bryan campus, the assets were grouped on the basis of function (i.e., plumbing, electrical, mechanical). At the Round Rock campus, the assets were also grouped by function, but also included parent/child systems (e.g., AHU/fan motor). The advantage to this type of classification is that the system can provide information about upstream and downstream components, understanding that the fan motor is contained within the AHU. The parent/child system gives the user a map linking the source to the problem so that they will have a better understanding of the situation before deploying into the field. This knowledge will save time and energy necessary to remedy the issue.

Assets contain detailed information attributes. Round Rock incorporated attributes on a number of critical components that were not specified at the Bryan campus. Attributes include design parameters and approximately 1,800 additions were made in the improvement processes from Bryan to Round Rock. The advantage of adding the attribute information is that the user has more efficient access to drawings and documents. An example of this would be not to simply call out the AHU, but also include the tracking for the fan motor showing the manufacturer and model number. This example includes the attribute of "fan motor" as a separate entity so that if the fan motor becomes inoperable, then it is clearly identified and the information on how to fix or order a new part is given. If this were not an attribute of the AHU, then the only information given would be that the unit was broken. The technician would then need to go into the field to determine that it was the fan motor and then would need to pull up the data on the air handler to get the information needed about the fan motor.

The Round Rock campus attribute additions did not involve adding new documents, but rather dividing the existing large documents into smaller segments, so that the equipment was decomposed into multiple categories. This process resulted in the creation of more documents as items even though the actual number of original documents had not changed. The benefit of document subdivision is that there is a shorter download time and a faster, more accurate review time because the user is referencing material that is more directly relevant to the asset at hand and not the entire submittal that can encompass hundreds of pages of irrelevant data. For example, AHU submittals were broken down by model number. Instead of including all project AHU submittals in one document, these were subdivided by model number to correspond to types in COBie. TAM HSC will incorporate these adaptations in future projects.

CONCLUSION

TAM HSC has created a new precedent at the Bryan campus, not only for the Texas A&M system, but also for other organizations making the journey into digital facility management. As software, processes, and systems evolve so will the methods and standards of the industry. TAM HSC has laid a secure foundation based on their current standards and they are beginning to outline changes to process and data contents in future projects. Each facet of growth brings about an expanded understanding and accumulated knowledge for improvement for the next phase.

The current implementation of COBie and AIM was undertaken using data extracted from the BIM model but without direct linking of the asset and CMMS data with a BIM model. This is targeted by TAM HSC as a future step. It was important to TAM HSC to first specify, capture, structure, validate, and import the FM data and documents into AiM before tackling the issue of 3D model integration. That is on the horizon in the near future.

Technology is at the core of this phenomenon, but the objective could never be realized without proper human collaboration and training. As this new era in the facility management industry moves forward, it is important for the FM team not only to play the role of owners, but also to serve as leaders. Facility managers must understand the business and operational goals and objectives of their organizations and the means needed to accomplish them. They must embrace new relationships and recognize the importance of teamwork. TAM HSC describes one case where the industry is heading and how they plan to get there. This investigation not only describes the process of arrival but also the possibilities for a new threshold for the FM industry.

ACKNOWLEDGMENTS

- Mark Cervenka, facilities manager at Texas A&M Health Science Center (provided editorial support and project knowledge)
- Corey Losinski, assistant director for facilities and construction (provided editorial support and project knowledge. Special thanks for being the primary contact and middle man for gathering information.)
- Dr. Clay Hanks, director of campus operations and Texas A&M Health Science Center (provided editorial support and project knowledge)
- John Marshall, vice president at Satterfield & Pontikes Construction, Inc. (provided project information)
- Samuel Sprouse, vice president of professional services at Satterfield & Pontikes Construction, Inc. (provided project information)
- Hyde Griffith, vice president at Broaddus & Associates (provided editorial support and project knowledge)
- Matt Moore, BIM manager at Broaddus & Associates (provided project information)

Case Study 3: USC School of Cinematic Arts

Victor Aspurez
PE Assistant Director—Engineering Services, Facilities Management Services, University of Southern California; PhD student in the Sonny Astani Department of Civil and Environmental Engineering, University of Southern California

Angela Lewis, PE, PhD, LEED AP
Project Manager with Facility Engineering Associates

MANAGEMENT SUMMARY

The University of Southern California (USC) School of Cinematic Arts is an example of a successful BIM FM project that challenged current industry practice. The complex of six buildings was constructed in three separate phases, starting in 2007 to the present day. The first phase of the project used BIM in a construction centric manner. During Phase 1, the University Capital Construction Division (CCD) and Facility Management Services (FMS) really started to understand the potential value of BIM FM. Phase 2 was design BIM centric. During this phase, designers were required to leverage BIM. Phase 3 is considered facility management–centric. This phase is ongoing as this case study is written in 2012. During this phase, FM-related information from BIM is being collected from the design and construction process, as a result of following BIM Guidelines established by the university.

The major advances from the three-phase project include:

- The development of a BIM Guideline that includes a documented approach of how to use multiple common industry standards, including OmniClass, the National CAD Standard and COBie. These guidelines provide a framework for project stakeholders in the execution of their services and the completion of deliverables required to meet FM goals.
- The realization that the most significant information for FM is the data from the BIM models. The 3D graphic model is of secondary importance.
- The development of a facility management portal, created with the needs of FM personnel in mind, made it easier to find information.

The major stakeholders that largely influenced the outcome of BIM FM over the 3 phases include the primary donor; the USC Facility Management Services (FMS) team; the BIM integrator, View By View; the Architect, Urban Design Group; and a middleware software provider, EcoDomus. Additionally, university and consultant project principals played a significant role in influencing the vision and project requirements.

One of the biggest challenges during the project was finding the resources to update as-built building models after completion of construction, as required for FM purposes. These models were needed for facility management decision making and building operations troubleshooting. These FM systems (such as the building automation system [BAS]) require access to accurate real-time data. These goals cannot be satisfied by referencing 2D static as-built drawings and closeout documentation. Additional technology and human resources are needed to support the management of models and their related information. In addition new FM processes are required to support the integration of BIM with FM.

Key technologies on this project included BIM authoring software (Revit Architecture, Revit MEP, and Tekla Structures), middleware (Navisworks Manage and EcoDomus) and FM systems (facility management information system [FAMIS], Enterprise Building Integrator, and Meridian Enterprise).

The most important lessons learned include:

- New processes do not necessarily require that new types of software to be developed to replace traditional FM information systems. In some cases, it is a matter of using BIM FM more effectively along with existing FM software (CMMS, CAFM, BAS, and DMS).
- Recommendations about what practices or standards to use are often role based, e.g. a designer will favor standards that are traditionally used for design. Thus, the team determining what practices and standards to use should be representative of all key stakeholders, including those from FM.
- BIM FM is not an "out-of-the-box" product. It requires new processes, new technologies, and new lines of communication.

INTRODUCTION

The University of Southern California (USC) is located in Los Angeles, California. The School of Cinematic Arts was one of the first universities in the United States

FIGURE 6.16 Architectural style of the new School of Cinematic Arts complex: an interpretation of Southern California mission style.
Courtesy Hathaway Dinwiddie

to offer a bachelor of arts degree in film. Today, the School of Cinematic Arts has a highly ranked program with bachelor's, master's, and doctorate degrees, as well as minors. The addition of a new complex for the School of Cinematic Arts, served as a pilot to USC, for both BIM and BIM FM. The complex is located adjacent to the existing School of Cinematic Arts on the USC campus. As shown in Figure 6.16, the architectural style of the complex is an interpretation of Southern California mission style architecture with Venetian stucco and stone façade.

In 2009, the USC School of Cinematic Arts dedicated a new multibuilding complex marking the 80th anniversary of the school. By the time the final phase is complete, the three phases are estimated to cost $165 million (supplied by a donor). From the beginning it was stated that BIM was to be used to facilitate design, construction, and life-cycle management. Specifically, BIM was to be used for architectural, structural, and MEP disciplines from the start of the project and coordinated between all disciplines to improve cost and schedule control. The donor also required that the buildings be built to maximize longevity and performance and be designed for a 100-year service life.

FIGURE 6.17 New School of Cinematic Arts buildings identified by building letter.

The complex was built within three phases (Figure 6.17). The first phase consisted of the School of Cinematic Arts Building A (SCA), which was completed in 2008. This contains 137,000 square feet of classrooms, production labs, administrative offices, a 200-seat theater, an exhibition hall, and a café. The building was completed ahead of schedule and under budget. The main reason for this schedule performance was that the team worked collaboratively, using an integrated approach, which greatly reduced the amount of rework. A second reason was that the use of a 3D model increased the ability for the team to visualize and improve the construction process. A third important source of a faster schedule was that the use of BIM allowed many of the structural components to be prefabricated.

Phase 2 was completed in 2010 and included an additional 63,000 SF of educational and production space in four buildings: School of Cinematic Arts Buildings B, C, D and E (SCB, SCC, SCD, and SCE). The construction was completed ahead of schedule. The primary reason for this was that the use of BIM allowed much of the steel to be prefabricated, which reduced the duration of construction by 30 percent.

Phase 3, Building F (SCF), is currently under construction as the case study was written. This phase includes about 80,000 square feet, consisting of primarily computer and media technology and instructional labs. The building will also be used for teaching and research in gaming and movie technology.

FIGURE 6.18 Replaceable steel fuse support system.
Courtesy Gregory P. Luth Associates

The complex of six buildings was designed to be energy efficient, earthquake resilient, and have highly flexible interiors. One of the most innovative features of the complex was the structural system for the multistory buildings. These were designed using a ductile hybrid system intended to withstand one major earthquake with repairable damage. This was achieved by using replaceable steel fuses to support the building loads (Figure 6.18). The façade is a concrete substrate, with ductile linked shear walls, rocking shear panels, and replaceable steel fuses. The concept to the fuses is similar to an electrical circuit breaker (or old electrical fuse). Under a large load, the replaceable steel fuse will yield and absorb the earthquake energy, without breaking, while the walls remain undamaged. This concept developed to exceed traditional building code requirements, which state that a building is to withstand an earthquake, but is designed to be sacrificial. With the use of the replaceable structural components, these fuses are sacrificed instead of the building. Thus, after a major earthquake, it is only necessary to replace the fuses, and not demolish and rebuild the entire building.

For the main building the design of mechanical systems was also innovative. Ceiling integrated radiant heating and cooling panels, and under-floor air distribution were used. Radiant panels were installed because energy analysis found that these systems could result in significant energy savings (using up to 30 percent less energy than required by the California energy code). It was found that after occupancy, however, that while the radiant systems were as energy efficient as projected, it was difficult to regulate the temperatures in spaces with intermittent heating and cooling loads, such as classrooms. Under-floor air distribution systems combined with radiant flooring were used in lobbies outside of the main screening rooms (rooms where movies are shown). Given the high ceilings in the lobbies, the radiant flooring provides both heating and cooling closer to the occupants, reducing the amount of air and overall energy required to cool or heat these spaces.

Phase 2 and 3 mechanical systems are standard variable air volume (VAV) systems. The only exception is an under-floor air distribution system is installed in a large theater. Thus, the mechanical systems in most of the buildings are standard system types.

GOALS FOR BIM FM IMPLEMENTATION

As mentioned earlier, the use of BIM was established as a requirement for the complex from the beginning. Many of the project team members were selected based on their previous experience with BIM, especially with its use for clash detection during design and construction. However, for many members of USC Facility Management Services (FMS), this was the first time they were exposed to BIM. One of the benefits realized early on was the ability to view in a single 3D model the mechanical, electrical, fire safety and plumbing systems, including their interrelationships and connections. This was valuable because it provided an immediate high-level understanding of these systems. This was particularly important to FMS because nearly all of the maintenance in a building is performed on the same systems. Additionally, when clash detection was being performed, it became apparent that the model contained a lot of information, much of which had the potential to be used for facility management decision making downstream.

As the project progressed, part of the long-term vision was the ability to take a tablet computer into the field and hold it up to a part of the building and "overlay" a 3D model to understand what is behind the finished surface.

When the project first started, no formal guidelines for the use of BIM across any phase of the project were in place. Thus, the USC team saw construction of this complex as an opportunity to determine how BIM could be used to support facility management processes, as well as an opportunity to improve the project delivery process through better communication among FMS, consultants, and contractors.

As the project progressed, the use of BIM increased. During Phase 1 construction, the FMS division started to gain an understanding of how BIM was used for design and construction. Some specific areas of understanding included:

- How BIM can provide accurate 3D representations of the building structure and building systems.
- How can BIM provide higher-quality documentation during design and construction to support coordination.

The use of BIM during Phase 1 informed the use of BIM during Phases 2 and 3. Although FMS was aware of BIM during Phase 1, they did not start to get actively involved in the process until construction. At this point, the team started to see some of the benefits of BIM FM and how BIM helped resolve challenges during the construction process. As a result, FMS established a committee to track the progress of the project with a focus on BIM, and to determine how it could be used to support FM. A key focus of the committee was to determine how BIM could be integrated with existing FM technologies and processes.

During Phase 3, one of the subcontractors, CSI Electrical Contractors, used Revit MEP to create shop drawings, including underground and overhead distribution, penetrations, and equipment layouts. The same software was used to model conduit 1.25 inches or greater in diameter, cable trays, and conduit support racks. Using the feeder scheduling capabilities within Revit MEP, it was also possible to more accurately determine the length of feeders so that more accurate labor and material budgets could be established. The same model permitted much greater use of prefabrication of conduit, cable trays, racks, and the like. Although CAD can also be used to support this process, it was found to be easier to accomplish using Revit MEP.

Another application of Revit MEP was to support fabrication and packaging of electrical components by area. For example, lighting fixtures within a specific area could be removed from the manufacturer's packaging and have a proper length of wire attached to the fixture. This increased the installation speed in the field and reduced on-site waste. Revit supports this process because the floor plans can be used to quickly identify the quantity of fixtures on a given floor.

PROJECT TEAM AND CONTRACTS

Project Team

The USC FMS division played a large part within the BIM FM implementation. FMS is a sister division with the USC Capital Construction Division (CCD). FMS is responsible for the day-to-day operation, and repair and maintenance of 13 million square feet of space within 220 university buildings spread across 261 acres on the University Park campus and 72 acres on a remote Health Science Campus. FMS has about 300 staff and processes about 40,000 work orders per year. CCD is responsible for the programming, design, construction, and handover of new or renovated facilities. FMS supports CCD by providing internal quality control, to ensure construction projects meet university standards and buildings are designed and constructed to allow for proper operations and maintenance. Additionally, FMS participates in the commissioning of all buildings on campus.

To complete the design and construction of the School of Cinematic Arts complex, the team of contractors and consultants included:

- Architect: Urban Design Group
- General contractor: Hathaway Dinwiddie (Phases 1 and 2), Matt Construction (Phase 3)
- Civil engineer: KPFF Consulting Engineers (Phases 1 and 2), Brando & Johnston (Phase 3)
- Mechanical, Electrical and Plumbing design engineers: IBE Consulting Engineers (Phases 1 and 2), TMADTad, Taylor & Gaines (TTG) (Phase 3)
- BIM integrator: View By View
- Structural engineer: Gregory P. Luth and Associates (GPLA), Inc.

Urban Design Group served as the architect and lead coordinator of the design team throughout programming, design, and construction, along with CCD. During all three phases, a BIM Integrator, View By View, was hired to support coordination and collaboration through the use of BIM. The main responsibility of a BIM Integrator is to coordinate all building information models of all disciplines, and across both the design and construction teams. Although clash detection is a part of this effort, it also includes understanding the needs of different members of the design and construction teams. In fact, a highly skilled BIM Integrator can help to address questions and resolve challenges, reducing such things as the number of RFIs. A successful BIM Integrator must be an effective communicator: as teams have a diverse set of personalities, it is often necessary to determine effective strategies to support cooperation and collaboration. Finally, a BIM integrator should be diplomatic and proactive, while being able to determine when it is necessary to bring the owner in to support a decision-making process.

As the use of BIM FM developed, View By View expanded their services to include FM. It was necessary for them to understand the technologies and processes required to use BIM and have enough design and construction knowledge to ask the right questions. When BIM FM is the goal, it is ideal if the same BIM integrator is involved in the project during design, construction, and turnover for the purpose of FM. This allows them to oversee the project from a BIM perspective and support the best interests of the owner.

As a BIM integrator is not a common role across all design and construction projects, when evaluating the need to hire a BIM integrator, one should consider:

- If the BIM integrator should be hired for one phase of the project or across the life cycle of the project. Two benefits of hiring the BIM integrator across the life cycle are that (1) it builds trust across the project team, and (2) it allows better information to be shared between the different phases of the project.
- The experience the BIM integrator has in the technologies that will be used and how they will foster team collaboration and can be trusted by various stakeholders on the project team.
- That the BIM integrator is not meant to replace or take on the responsibilities associated with the BIM managers of design and construction team. These roles are usually employees of lead consultants and contractors who are responsible for the final deliverables.

Contract Structure

Historically, USC has used a gross maximum price (GMP) contract. This type of contract normally includes a negotiated fee with a general contractor (GC) for preconstruction services. The GC works with USC to develop the GMP budget, which then serves as the basis for the construction contract. Additionally, some design assist activities are often put in place. Figure 6.19 documents the contract structure and the members of the project team.

The GMP structure and principles of an integrated approach were leveraged for all three phases of the School of Cinematic Arts complex. The architect, Urban Design Group, was familiar with integrated delivery approaches as it is part of their common business practice. On this project, an integrated approach was observed to increase the level of cooperation between the architects, engineers, and contractors. It encouraged them to work concurrently so that insight about constructability was provided during early design.

Collaboration

As each phase of construction was completed, the use of collaboration tools increased. During Phase 1, face-to-face team collaboration was the most common method of collaboration. During Phases 2 and 3, virtual methods of collaboration, such as GoToMeeting, were used to supplement face-to-face collaboration. The

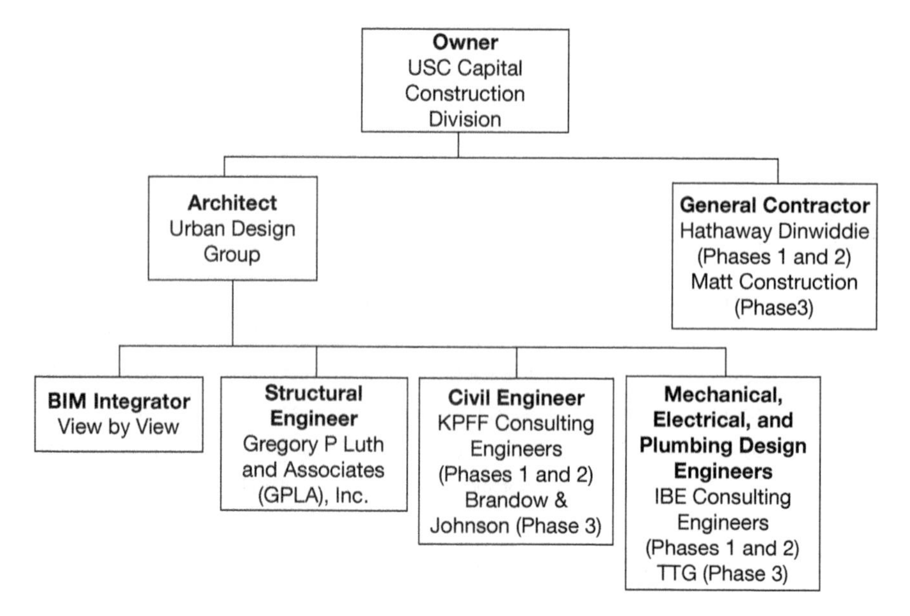

FIGURE 6.19 Gross maximum price contract structure showing team members.

team shifted to approximately monthly face-to-face collaboration meetings, with the remainder of these meetings occurring virtually. Although virtual collaboration was found to be very effective, it was acknowledged that using only virtual collaboration was not desirable. Some collaboration is best accomplished through face-to-face communication. Without periodic face-to-face communication, project teams can become disconnected.

SOFTWARE USED

Many different software packages were used throughout the course of all three phases. These can be categorized as either (1) BIM authoring, (2) fabrication, (3) collaboration, (4) middleware, or (5) facility management. In this case study, all of these are discussed in detail. Specific software used includes the following:

- BIM authoring
  - Autodesk: Revit Architecture, Revit MEP, Revit Structure, AutoCAD Civil 3D
  - Tekla Structures
- Detailing/Fabrication
  - AEC CADpipe and CADduct
- Collaboration software
  - e-Builder
  - GoToMeeting

- Middleware
  - Navisworks
  - EcoDomus
- Facility management
  - Accruent: FAMIS (CMMS)
  - Honeywell: Enterprise Building Integrator (BAS)
  - BlueCielo: Meridian Enterprise (DMS)

BIM Authoring Software

During Phase 1, a combination of BIM and 2D CAD packages were used to complete the design and construction documents. The architectural and structural design drawings were created using Revit, while the MEP drawings were created using AutoCAD.

As the project entered Phase 2, it became a requirement that all documents be developed using accepted BIM authoring software. USC decided that Revit would be used, unless it was demonstrated that different BIM authoring software was justified and would provide a better result. An example of one exception was Tekla Structures, which was used for structural design. According to the structural engineer for all three phases, Tekla has been used by the industry worldwide for several years to create structural shop drawings for fabrication. When Tekla is used by both designer and contractors, it helps to improve communication and reduce the duplication of effort between the structural designers and construction contractors. Additionally, when the same software is used for design and construction, there is an increased opportunity for designers to enhance the quality of drawings beyond design intent, and to work with contractors, as part of preconstruction efforts, to consider constructability in their designs. With this approach, it is additionally important that designers and contractors take an integrated approach.

For nonstructural designers and contractors, a free viewer called Tekla BIM sight can be used to view Tekla Structure models. The viewer allows any member of the project team to view the entire structural BIM and take snapshots of the model. These snapshots can be used to help support coordination and communication when developing or responding to requests for information (RFIs).

Even though two different BIM authoring software products were used, Tekla and Revit, it was possible to coordinate the models using Navisworks (discussed later). During Phase 2, the designers provided fully coordinated construction documents, which included architectural, structural, civil, and MEP drawings. To eliminate conflicts in these drawings, it was often necessary to move the locations of ducts or conduit from their initial proposed location to a location better suited for the layout of all systems and more representative of where things could more practically be installed. The use of both the built-in BIM authoring software features (such as interference checks within Revit), and the use of Navisworks clash detection capabilities, allowed engineered documents to be more thoroughly coordinated.

The robustness of the BIM authoring tools evolved over the duration of the three-year construction phase. When the project first started, one of the significant limitations of BIM authoring tools was the handling of large model files sizes and the impact it had on performance. As the software developed, and methods to manage models improved, it became easier for users to manage data and graphical information. Examples of these developments include methods to link files and create worksets, as an alternative to checking files in and out to support multitrade coordination and remote file sharing.

As the project progressed towards the end of Phase 2, the requirements for BIM were further refined and a BIM Guideline was created. Part of the BIM Guideline includes a requirement that equipment and component schedules be generated from the BIM model using parameter attributes, as opposed to manually creating schedules in other tools such as Excel and pasting them or hard coding information into a spreadsheet table with no intelligence. Creating the schedules in BIM-authoring software using associated equipment families and their type or instance parameters, allowed this data to be exported into a middleware, and in the case of USC, further imported into their CMMS. At the time the case study was written, data could be exported from BIM and imported into EcoDomus (middleware). However, direct import into the CMMS (FAMIS), was still under development.

Creating the equipment schedules (based on family parameters) in Revit can be challenging because many equipment/component families are not available and need to be created by designers as part of their own standard libraries. In addition, when attempting to establish more user defined properties, to support the goal of automatically generating full schedules, knowledge of how to attribute more parameters to an object (family), at a level desired, is required. While many BIM authoring tools provide the graphical tools needed for design, their ability to manage and share information are not as well developed. To the extent that new objects are required in the BIM model, this increases the amount of time required to complete the design, and hampers standardized approaches to data generation from the model. The generation of schedules from Revit is important because it forces the proper use of BIM authoring tools, which can then be used to export data into standard file formats, such as IFC or one formatted for COBie (such as a spreadsheet). These can then be used as inputs to CMMS and other facility management information systems.

Given some of these current industry challenges, FMS created shared parameters files for the designers to use within Revit. Shared parameters files are templates that can be used by the facility management team to convey to the design team, what information should be collected about a building or a specific equipment/component object (family). In other words, shared parameter files can include attributes that defined the information required for each type of system and their equipment, such as air handling units. The type of information included in the shared parameters files is similar to the information typically found in equipment and component schedules within 2D drawing sets.

Initially FMS focused on high-level information, called master attributes, meant to be associated with all major equipment (see Figure 6.20). The importance of master attributes to USC is that they provide the necessary database "hooks," which are used to facilitate downstream integration with facility management information systems. While some of the USC defined "master attributes" do include data that is

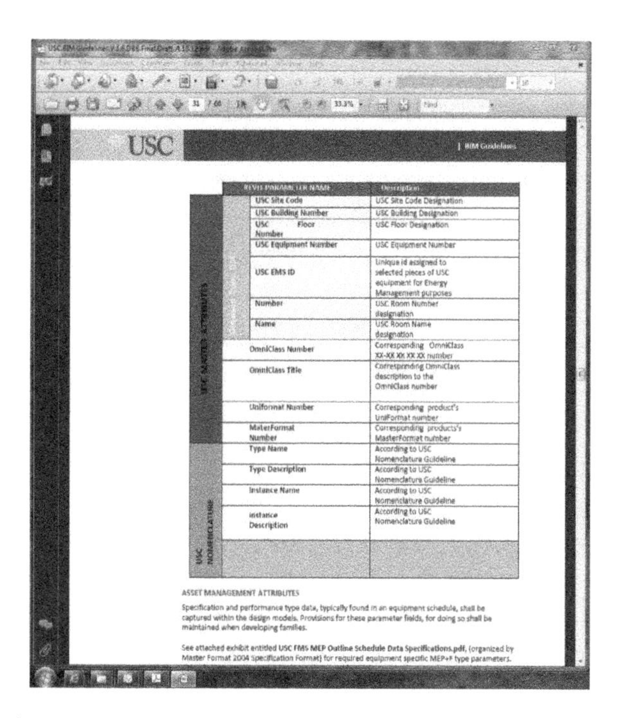

USC | BIM Guidelines

REVIT PARAMETER NAME	Description
USC Site Code	USC Site Code Designation
USC Building Number	USC Building Designation
USC Floor Number	USC Floor Designation
USC Equipment Number	USC Equipment Number
USC EMS ID	Unique id assigned to selected pieces of USC equipment for Energy Management purposes
Number	USC Room Number designation
Name	USC Room Name designation
OmniClass Number	Corresponding OmniClass XX-XX XX XX XX number
OmniClass Title	Corresponding OmniClass description to the OmniClass number
Uniformat Number	Corresponding product's UniFormat number
MaterFormat Number	Corresponding products's Masterformat number
Type Name	According to USC Nomenclature Guideline
Type Description	According to USC Nomenclature Guideline
Instance Name	According to USC Nomenclature Guideline
Instance Description	According to USC Nomenclature Guideline

USC NOMENCLATURE

ASSET MANAGEMENT ATTRIBUTES

Specification and performance type data, typically found in an equipment schedule, shall be captured within the design models. Provisions for these parameter fields, for doing so shall be maintained when developing families.

See attached exhibit entitled **USC FMS MEP Outline Schedule Data Specifications.pdf**, (organized by Master Format 2004 Specification Format) for required equipment specific MEP+F type parameters.

FIGURE 6.20 Contents of shared parameters file.
Courtesy USC FMS

standard to COBie, their intent is not to capture all COBie data. For example, some COBie data is also found in equipment schedules, but since the data categories outlined by FMS are not mutually exclusive, not all standard COBie data is found in equipment schedules. In an effort to organize data for the eventual management of an asset during the O&M stage, the following four categories were established: (1) Master Attributes, (2) Schedule Attributes, (3) Standard COBie Attributes, and (4) Owner-Extended Attributes. When evaluating how to classify data, it is important to recognize that a single piece of data can be classified in multiple ways. The purpose for these categories is to better communicate where and when this data is collected over the course the design, construction, and turnover of a project. The Master Attributes and Schedule Attributes were required to be captured within the design models, while the majority of data which fall into the remaining categories are captured at later stages in the project by contractors and those involved in project closeout.

Overcoming Model-Sharing Challenges

To support model sharing between project participants, the contract requirements state that USC owns all the models. This is believed to prevent design and construction teams from making claims that models cannot be shared among one another, due to legal issues or risk.

One challenge that was encountered during Phase 2 regarding model sharing occurred between the design and construction teams. After the design model was fully coordinated, it was turned over to the general contractor, only to realize that many of the construction subcontractors did not have a Revit license or a familiarity with this particular BIM authoring tool. To use the models to the greatest extent possible, 3D DWGs were exported from the design BIMs and then imported into subcontractor detailing software. Although the project moved forward effectively, an important lesson learned was that the software used by the design team is not necessarily the same software used by the contractors. This, of course, is an ongoing discussion in the industry and highlights the need for file interoperability.

Collaboration Software

To effectively manage submittals, requests for information, BIMs, and all other construction project documentation, e-Builder, a Web-based project management software, was being implemented during Phase 3 (Figure 6.21). The "document" portion of e-Builder acts as a digital exchange server accessed using an FTP site, that tracks and records when files are submitted and edited. E-Builder has more than file management capabilities, such as forms and processes built around USC's

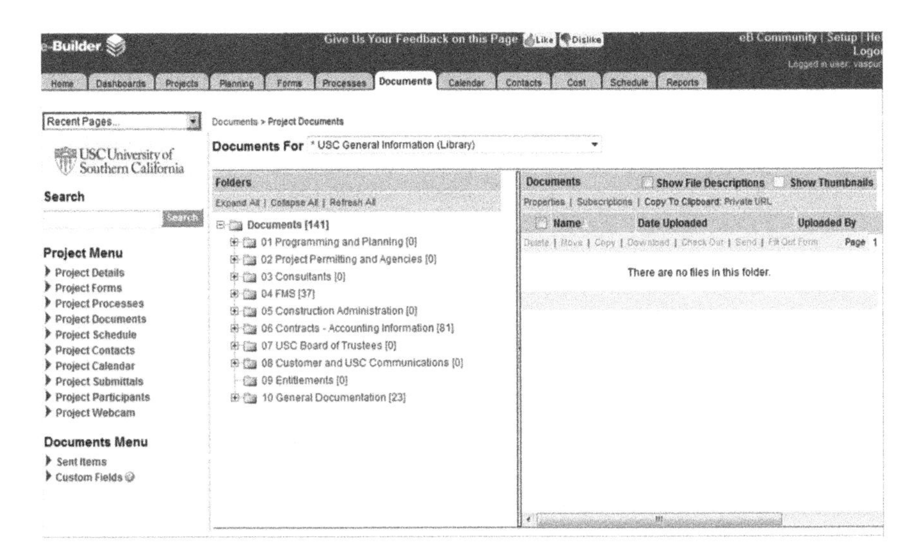

FIGURE 6.21 Screenshot of e-Builder, Web-based capital program and construction project management software.
Courtesy USC FMS

project management and communication standards. At the time of this case study, the university was investigating opportunities for e-Builder to further support BIM and possibly replace stand-alone digital exchange servers.

Middleware

Middleware is software that allows information from two different software packages to exchange information and connect applications. Since information to support FM is collected across the design and construction process, a middleware can be used to help gather and manage this information and package it for improved distribution or integration with facility management software. At the time the case study was written, the construction subcontractors were being trained how to use EcoDomus to collect information (such as equipment specification data). This data may supersede that originally entered in design models, for example, slight changes during the course of submittal approval. The goal was to provide subcontractors with a method to efficiently collect the data of important to USC. This data falls under the categories (1) standard COBie attributes, and (2) owner-extended attributes.

During the Cinematic Arts project, Navisworks was used to support clash detection and EcoDomus was used to export and manage information from BIM authoring software. These are described in the sections that follow.

Navisworks

Navisworks allows a team to receive design and construction BIM models in multiple file formats and combine them into a single master model. For example, files from CADpipe and CADmech and Revit can be combined into a single file format. The combined file can then be used for clash detection and collaboration.

During Phase 1, the project team also used Navisworks as a model viewer to create a *proof of concept* portal with links between equipment records and FM software: the FAMIS CMMS, the Honeywell BAS and Meridian Enterprise from BlueCielo document management system (DMS) (Figures 6.22, 6.23, and 6.24, respectively). Figure 6.22 shows the link between an air handling unit (AHU) in the Navisworks viewer and the AHU equipment record in the CMMS. Figure 6.23 shows the link between the viewer and the AHU graphic in the BAS. Figure 6.24 shows the link between the viewer and several documents that made up the operations manuals, which itself resided in the DMS. This specific data sheet shown provides information about the air handler, including pictures, type, description, and the unit fan curve. As shown, the intent of the links was to route the user from the Navisworks model viewer interface to one

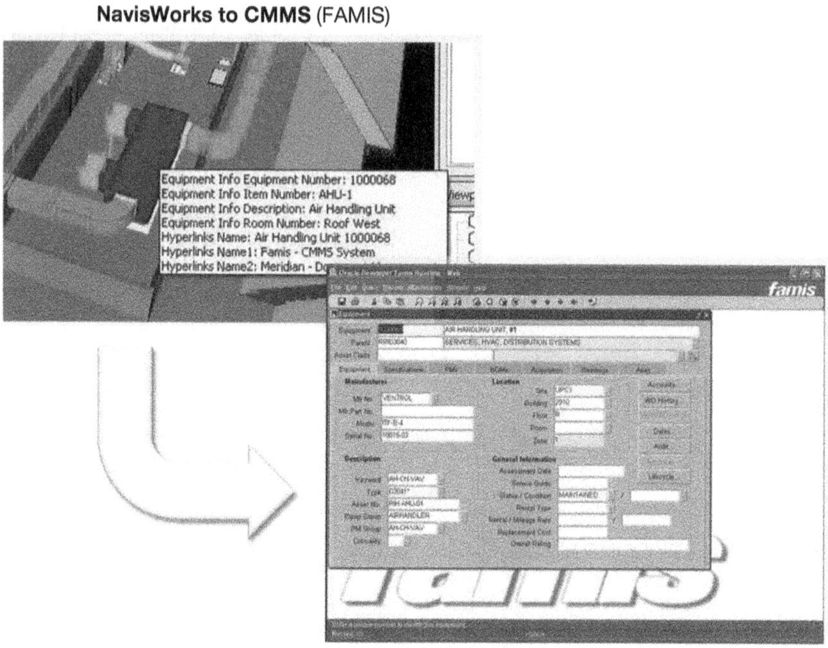

NavisWorks to CMMS (FAMIS)

FIGURE 6.22 Portal, linking Navisworks to CMMS.
Courtesy USC FMS

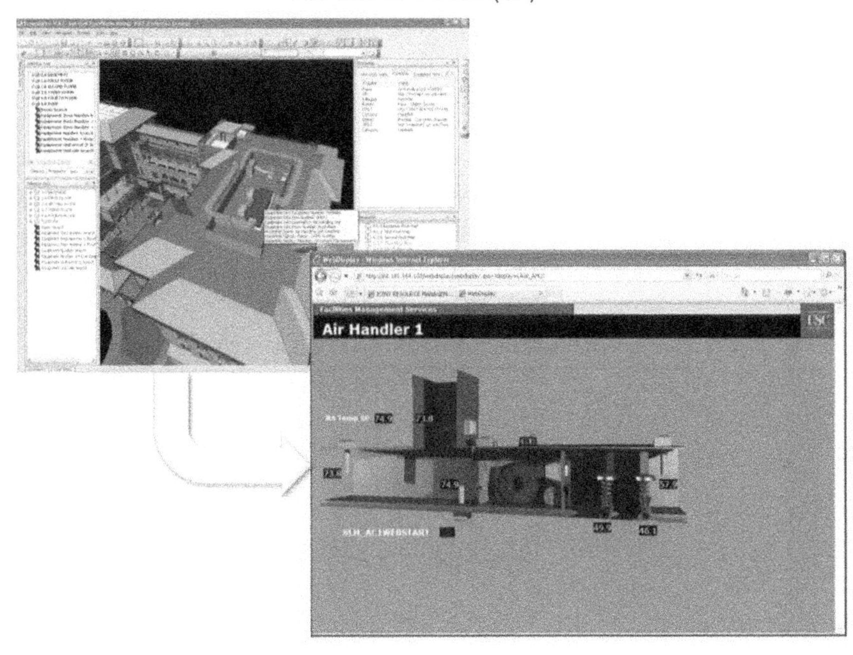

FIGURE 6.23 Portal, linking Navisworks to BAS.
Courtesy USC FMS

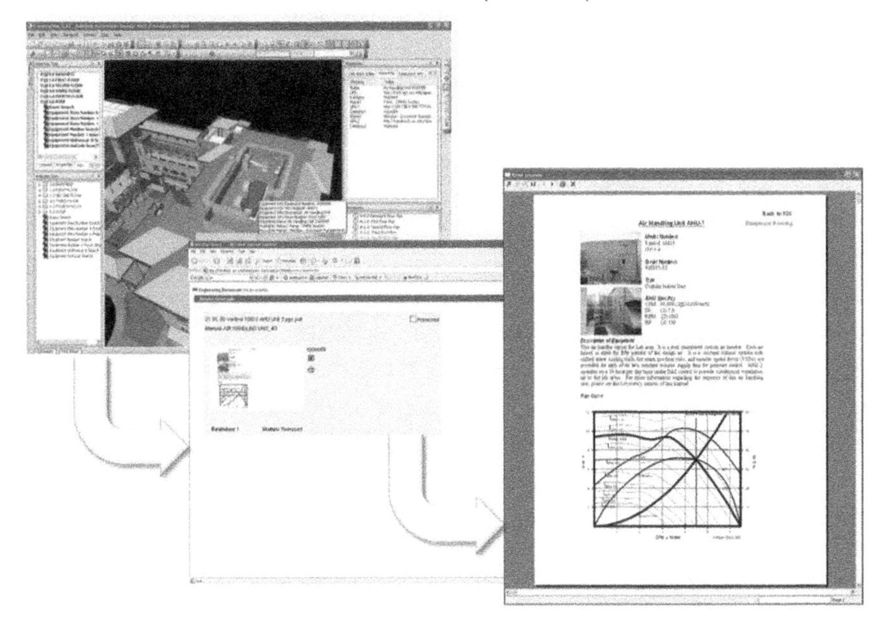

FIGURE 6.24 Portal, linking Navisworks to DMS.
Courtesy USC FMS

of the other three FM software systems: CMMS, BAS, or DMS. It is important to point out that none of the information acquired was "hard" attached to the Navisworks model viewer, but actually resided in the appropriate FM information system where this information can be continued to be maintained.

The portal could be accessed in two ways. The first way was by using a link on the front page of the listed FM information systems. The second way was using the Navisworks model viewer interface, as shown by the preceding three examples. It was anticipated that most users would use the second method, starting with the 3D viewer. The concept was, once the user accessed the viewer, it is possible to navigate to a location of interest, such as an air handling unit (AHU). As the user moves the cursor over the AHU, some high-level information would appear, such as equipment number, item number (such as AHU-1), equipment description, room number, along with links to separate FM information systems, the BAS, CMMS, and DMS.

After clicking a link, the user is directed to the software with the desired information, such as the warranty information for the air handler stored in the document management system. If the user clicks a link on the air handler to the BAS, the link directs the user to the graphic within the BAS for the air handler. Similarly, if the link to the CMMS were clicked, the user would be directed to the asset record for the air handler within the CMMS. In order for these processes to occur, each link had a built-in query that associated any information about an asset to the unique identifier for that asset. For example, all documents that reside in the DMS and are related to a specific air handler within a specific building will have building number and an asset unique identifier applied to them. See a later section for further discussion about this portal concept and the future direction of its development.

As each phase of the project was completed, the use of Navisworks evolved. For example, since FMS wanted to leverage the use of the coordinated models, FMS cleaned up the models through a set of steps that included making sure color-coding of systems, file naming, component hierarchies, and component naming was correct. Although it was the initial vision that the contractors should provide cleaned-up models, it was observed that common industry practice is not to provide models with the requested level of color-coding and naming. Instead, current industry practice is to use the models primarily for clash detection and to meet the specific needs of subcontractors to complete their detailing and fabrication efforts. Thus, it was determined that it was necessary to have the BIM integrator work with FMS to clean up the models to meet the formatting requirements, the effort of which is now outlined within the USC BIM Guideline. Understanding the difference between initial expectations and current practice provided an opportunity for FMS to be recognized as a leader, challenging the status quo.

EcoDomus PM

EcoDomus PM is a middleware solution that was tested during Phase 2 and used during Phase 3 to support data collection and integration between software. It can also be used as a central registry and repository of documents, to be subsequently turned over to an owner. Once collected, the information can either be retained in its database or exported elsewhere, such as to an FM information system. It uses COBie to implement a quality control and data validation process to improve the likelihood that correct data is collected in the correct format. The use of standards, such as COBie, provides a structure to determine what information should be collected, in terms of both minimum data and documents. EcoDomus imports data from many software systems, such as different BIM authoring tools, and then stores them in a SQL database. The data from a BIM can be exported from the model and then stored in a database outside the BIM to reduce the file size of the BIM. For example, before project closeout, the designers and contractors can attach information to records in EcoDomus, which can then be used to export the information into an FM system.

For a variety of other purposes, such as data/document quality control and progress reporting, USC proposed to leverage Ecodomus PM from design through construction and closeout. This provided a means to collect all categories of data, and validate such data before exporting to another system, primarily the CMMS. Much effort continues to take place with FMS software technology partners towards achieving more seamless data integration with BIM authoring and middleware packages. Ecodomus PM and FM are separate systems, and while there may be benefits to transitioning from PM to the FM offerings of Ecodomus, they both can stand alone and have distinct goals in their application. In terms of the classic definition of a middleware (go between for data and document transfer), PM falls in this category. Further discussion will focus on the partnership with USC to inform the ongoing development of Ecodomus FM, and leverage as a proof of concept for achieving integration with FM information systems (see discussion of the Phase 2 portal below).

EcoDomus FM

EcoDomus FM proposes to provide for bidirectional data flow with other software packages, such as FM information systems (see www.ecodomus.com/ecodomusfm.html). For example, it can consume data from a BAS server, which itself is managing and displaying sensor and meter data, and then display this data together with a BIM model.

To link data between different FM software, two methods can be used:

- Hyperlinking
- Data integration

Although EcoDomus can be used to hyperlink, this functionality was not the end goal for USC. Data integration is a method of exchanging data between software. For example, the BAS can display the outdoor air temperature. If it were necessary for a user to see this same outdoor air temperature in EcoDomus, the same data could also be viewed directly through a field within EcoDomus as a result of data integration. Viewing the data through EcoDomus instead of the BAS saves time because the user does not need to navigate to the BAS. This illustrates further the power of "portal solution" which can be, from a data perspective, integrated and synchronized, with other FM information systems. Figure 6.25 provides a second example. Within the figure, the viewer portion of EcoDomus shows an inline fan. On the right, general information about the fan is provided (this being information that resides with the CMMS). On the left, the operations and maintenance manual for the fan is shown, a document that resides within the DMS. This interface also includes a BAS-related pane, which is intended to display conditional data traditionally managed and accessed by the BAS.

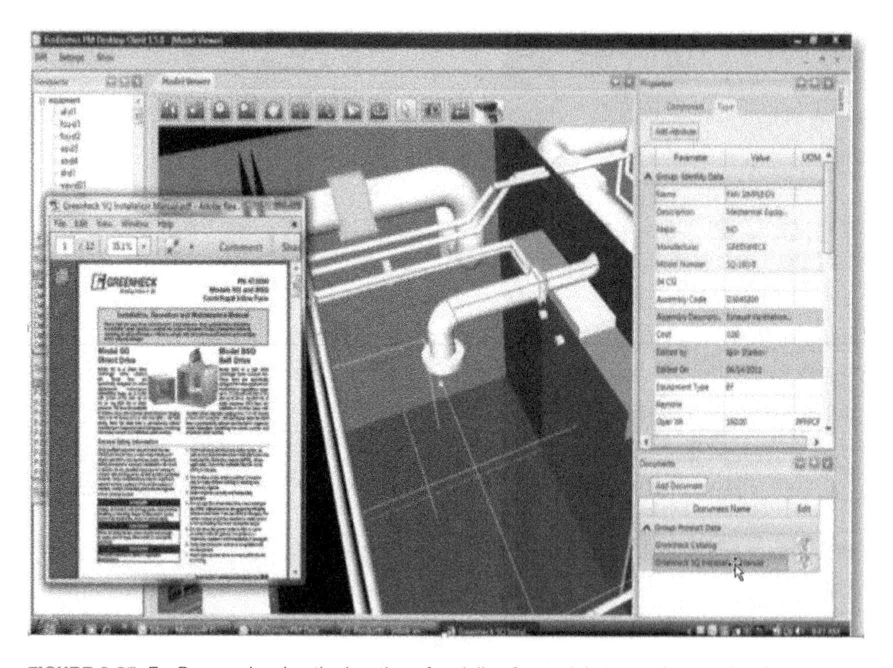

FIGURE 6.25 EcoDomus showing the location of an inline fan and the operations and maintenance manual.
Courtesy USC FMS

EcoDomus started to get involved with this project in summer 2009, during Phase 1. However, work between EcoDomus and UCS officially started during Phase 2 when the FMS team was trying to determine what information they wanted to have in the BIM and what data could be used for facility management. Through feedback from interviewing staff from multiple O&M divisions, USC helped inform the further development of Ecodomus FM. Specifically, they specified the major components of an interface for FM functions. The conclusion was to provide a "light" version of each of the FM information systems for data and document review purposes, combined with some level of model viewer and graphic controls for visualization. The final source of data was to be the individual FM information systems. The function of Ecodomus FM was to synchronize with these systems and allow access and display of current data.

Facility Management Systems

The facility management software systems discussed in this section are those commonly used by large facility management organizations: CMMS, BAS, DMS and CAFM.

Computerized Maintenance Management System (CMMS)

An Accruent FAMIShas been used at USC for about the last 14 years and is used for asset management, inventory control, generation of service requests, management of preventive maintenance work orders, and tracking the time and costs of services and materials used to complete work orders. FAMIS uses an Oracle database and is integrated with the financial database to capture employee records. Figure 6.26 is a screenshot of FAMIS, showing an equipment record for an air handling unit. The majority of O&M shop personnel, alongside the FMS division, which receive maintenance service requests (Customer Resource Center), interact primarily with FAMIS to assign and manage the time, materials, and labor required to process and close them.

Asset location records in the CMMS are categorized by campus, building, floor, and room. They are also classified by system and type of equipment. The level of detail is generally at the equipment level, such as AHU, pump, or chiller. However, there are a few exceptions, such as the gas burners for boilers. The exceptions are determined based on the frequency of component replacement, compared to the parent piece of equipment. For example, for an air handler, separate asset records are not kept for cooling coils, heating coils, filters, fans or motors. If information about the components of a system is available, such as information about a supply fan, it may be listed by specification section as part of the asset record for the air handler.

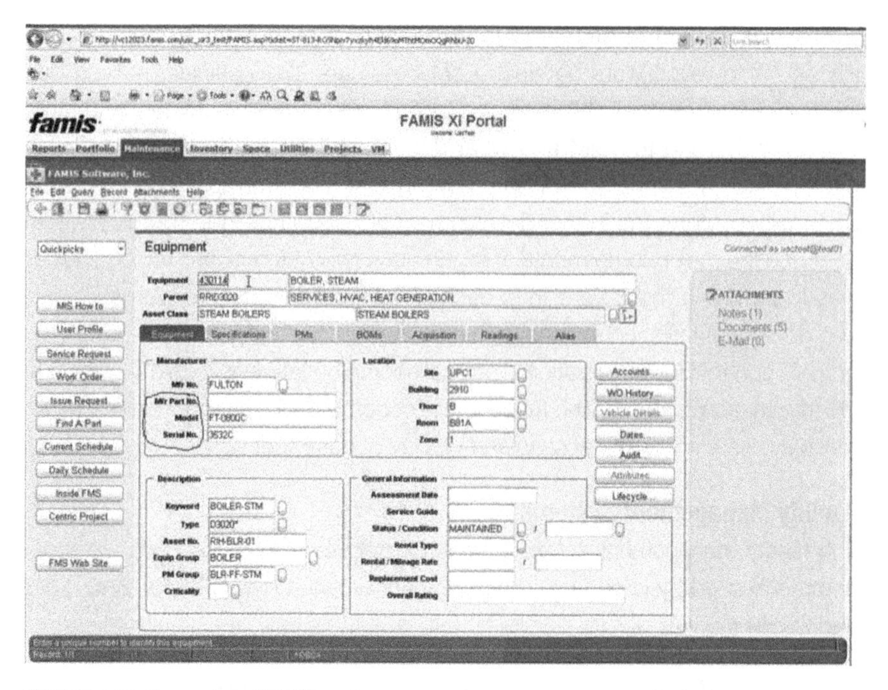

FIGURE 6.26 Screenshot of FAMIS equipment record.
Courtesy USC FMS

At the time FAMIS was originally set up, a consultant helped FMS determine that UniFormat standards should be used to classify assets. Today, UniFormat is still used to a sublevel that FMS has found to be appropriate. When a new building is built on the USC campus, a script is run to automatically populate FAMIS with generic asset records for typical types of equipment normally associated with a the new building. The script includes about 110 asset records and respective fields that are automatically created after the script is run for a new building. Most of these records are for HVAC and plumbing equipment and systems. The script contains a hierarchy of fields, which allow for three tiers of data to be associated with a specific equipment record, so to track "child" component relationships with its parent equipment "asset."

Building Automation System (BAS)

A Honeywell Enterprise Building Integration (Honeywell BAS) system is used at USC, which provides control, monitoring, alarming, and trending of major HVAC systems across the campus. The Honeywell BAS is used in nearly all buildings

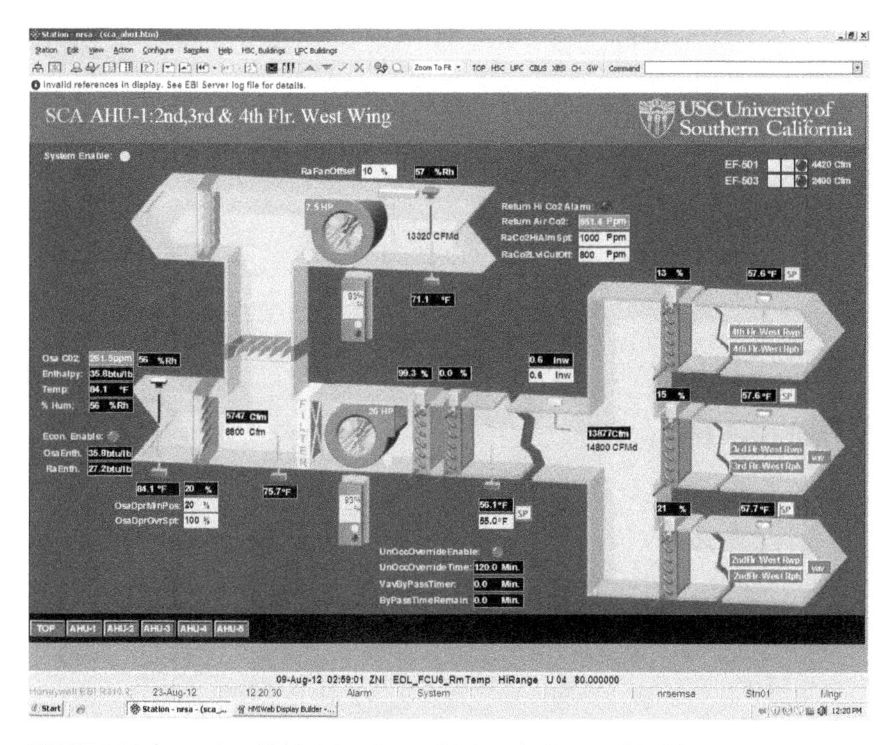

FIGURE 6.27 Screenshot of BAS air handler graphic from the Honeywell BAS System.
Courtesy USC FMS

for building automation. This can be an advantage for integration because there is only one BAS vendor's products to integrate with. In addition, it offers FMS the advantages of common-service relationships, staff familiarity with the system, and common part supply channels. Finally, it makes it easier to expand the use of this BAS with the upgrading and growth of campus buildings. At the time the case study was written, the integration of BIM and BAS was in its infancy. FMS continues to explore how to further benefit from this integration through partnerships with Honeywell and Ecodomus to allow for access of real-time data associated with the operating conditions of major pieces of equipment. The relevant data would be that which is displayed within the BAS hosted graphics, and refreshed at a higher frequency than most database applications. Figure 6.27 shows a screenshot of the Honeywell BAS graphic of an air handler. The graphic shows the operating status of the supply and return air fans, temperature, relative humidity and enthalpy of the supply and return air, system static pressure, percentage open of the valves at the heating and cooling coils, and many other parameters that define the current operating conditions of the air handler.

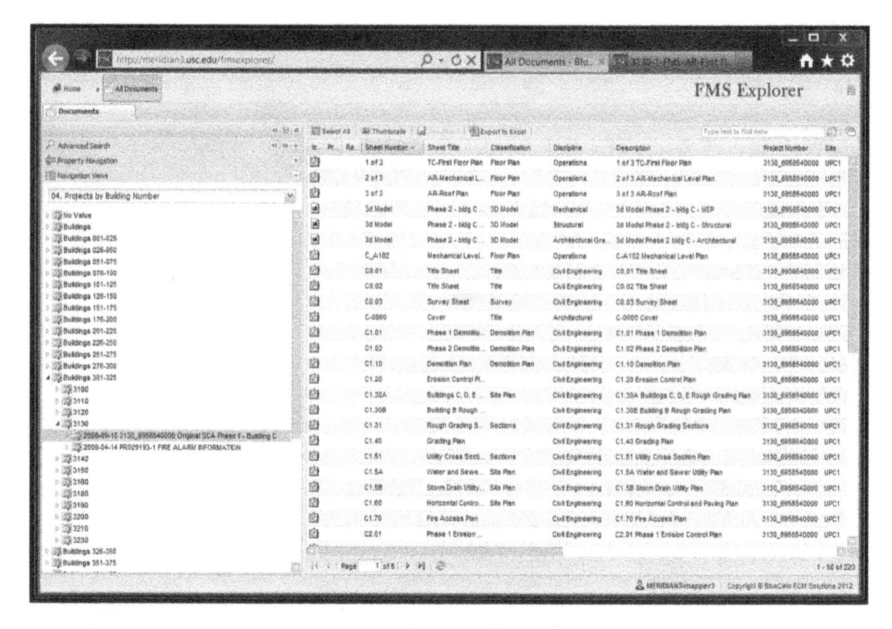

FIGURE 6.28 Screenshot of DMS listing projects by building.
Courtesy USC FMS

Document Management System

Meridian Enterprise Systems' document management system (DMS) is used, which serves as the master repository of all electronic building information on campus, including but not limited to O&M manuals, drawings, and warranty information. The DMS is a database that can be queried to find data and organize documents and is managed by the CAD manager. As shown in Figure 6.28, the DMS can be used to organize project documents by building. The DMS is integrated with the CMMS, linking the two systems. For example, a document from the DMS can be attached to an asset, project, or location record in the CMMS. As a practical example, a work order in the CMMS is assigned to a location and a piece of equipment. The attachment function of the CMMS has a tab that can be clicked to launch the DMS using a separate login to automatically query the documents attached to the equipment record of interest. Within a session, it is only necessary to log in once to the DMS when the first query to the CMMS is completed.

Computer-Aided Facility Management System (CAFM) for Space Management

At USC, space management is handled by Financial and Business Services, and thus it is not a responsibility of FMS. Space is managed by keeping accurate records of room numbers, departments that own the space, and other space data. To update space records, 2D CAD drawings are used by drawing polylines around room boundaries and associating these polylines with multiple layers of space data thus creating thematic maps of these spaces (e.g., color-coding by department versus by function). Clearly, these spatial data could be extracted from BIM to more efficiently create these thematic maps and further integrate with CAFM systems or other related financial management software. FMS CAD division is responsible for field surveying and maintaining accurate architectural floors plans for all buildings, which then become the basis for the area information needed by the University CAFM system. These architectural plans are called "operationals." The creation and upkeep of these files with the use of BIM authoring tools versus standard 2D CAD products was a use case that was quickly realized and achieved. These benefits will become scalable as more existing buildings are retroactively modeled, and new buildings continue to follow the established BIM Guidelines.

USC BIM GUIDELINES

At the time this case study was written, CCD and FMS had recently released a final version of the USC Building Information Modeling (BIM) Guidelines for Design Bid Build Contracts, version 1.6, which were used for Phase 3 of the project (their first use). These guidelines will be used on a second project that was under way on the USC campus when this case study was being written (USC 2012).

The purpose of the USC BIM guideline is to define the BIM deliverables for new USC construction projects, major renovations, and other projects. Some of the key topics include:

- Definition of USC responsibilities for reviewing and verifying the content of the BIMs.
- Defining the requirements of the BIM execution plan.
- Documenting the requirements for BIM authoring tools.
- Use of COBie, including the data required.
- Documenting the requirements at each project stage, including schematic design, design development, construction documents, bidding, construction, and turnover.

The appendices of the guidelines contain a lot of detailed, useful information, such as what elements should be modeled and the desired level of detail, information about the Revit shared parameters files, a discussion about naming and classification nomenclature and an outline schedule data specification.

DETERMINING WHAT DATA TO COLLECT

During Phase 2 of the project, the understanding of BIM as an information-centric process started to become clear. At the same time, BIM authoring tools were becoming better able to support more detailed levels of information capture. At the time the case study was written, the team was still determining specifically what data to collect from the model. This was complex because:

- There are a lot data in the model and asking for all of it was determined to not be the correct approach.
- Different members of the project team require different information to complete their job functions, thus recommendations of what data is required vary by role.
- It is necessary to determine what naming convention to use.
- Each asset type requires a separate decision regarding the appropriate level of detail and types of data to collect.

Despite these challenges, it was concluded that the data (not the 3D model) from BIM had the greatest value for BIM FM. However, to capture these data, it was necessary to revise current design and construction processes to support data collection. These issues are discussed in a later section.

As a starting point, the data stored in current FM software was evaluated. Data collection templates were created by asking the following questions:

- Is the component critical to the health of the overall MEP system and/or the building?
- Does the asset require regular maintenance? If so, what maintenance is required to prevent disruption of services provided by the asset and what kind of information is needed for that maintenance?

When reviewing the data, it was found that some of the data was static, while other data was likely to change over the life of the asset and/or building. For example, an equipment number, such as AHU-1, should be kept static over the life of the building. However, other information, such as the flow rate a chilled water pump operates at over a given day will vary based on the required cooling load for a building. A second example of dynamic data is the date a filter in an AHU was changed. Although this information changes less frequently than the flow rate of a pump, such information needs to be managed differently than static information. As data was defined to be static or dynamic, the following questions were considered:

- What data are required? Who is responsible for capturing this information?
- When should this information be captured?

- What should the format of the data delivered to the FM be?
- What data are part of the BIM process, versus already part of the traditional delivery process?

To help address such questions, the BIM integrator hosted workshops. Some of the workshops specifically focused on determining what information is needed, why the information is needed, and what information should be collected. The hardest question was determining what nomenclature to use. A decision was made to use OmniClass Table 23 for equipment naming and the National CAD Standard version 3.1 for equipment abbreviations, types, and instances. An example of an equipment abbreviation is VAV, which stands for "variable air volume." An example of a type is VAV box with reheat. An example of an instance is VAV-D01, which indicates a variable air volume box of a specific size within building D. The numbering and lettering convention used within the instance is determined by the mechanical engineer.

A key conclusion was that much of the necessary information was provided in equipment schedules within the construction documents issued by engineering consultants. It was important to consider how the information in the equipment schedules would be used to perform maintenance, troubleshooting, and replacement.

In addition, the information found in the bill of materials was helpful because it identified what components should be kept in inventory at the university because of lead times longer than two days. Warranty information was also important and not found on equipment schedules. In some cases, replacement part and warranty start and end dates can be particularly important.

Prior to this project, USC received rolls of drawings and binders of information after turnover of a building. Although this information could be potentially useful for FM decision making, it was concluded that the large amount of time required sorting through, understanding, and organizing this information made it too difficult to use the information in this form.

A number of lessons were learned from the decisions regarding what data to collect:

- It was determined that BIM can make design and construction data more accessible.
- FM organizations can provide guidance to designers and construction contractors about what information to include in the BIM considering what is required for MEP schedules, replacement parts, and warranties.

- The most important part of the process is documenting what information is most critical as decisions are made. One way to document the required information is to create a template such as a shared parameter file.
- Realizing that the first step is *not* determining what technology should be used to manage the information. It is necessary to first determine what information is critical and the processes necessary to manage this information. Only then can the appropriate technology be determined.

Model Elements and Level of Detail within BIM

As a result of determining what data to collect, the BIM Guidelines have begun to define the types of elements that are to be modeled for each discipline, mainly major equipment with many components and equipment that requires significant maintenance. These include architectural, structural, HVAC systems, electrical systems, plumbing and fire protection, critical specialty equipment, and site utilities. The level of detail (LOD) increases going from the design to the construction stages of the project. The required LOD for modeling of elements determines the geometric levels of accuracy and the proper definition of connections to critical equipment (families) that distribute services to and from these systems (air, water, etc.). Further discussion about level of detail is found in a later section.

Data Attributes

As previously noted, in an effort to organize data for the eventual management of assets during the O&M stage, four major categories were established by FMS, the rationale of which are as follows:

- *Master Attributes* (discussed earlier). These are required in the design BIM model.
- *Schedule Attributes:* It was found to be highly probable that all specification information typically found within equipment schedules would be eventually needed to perform maintenance, troubleshooting, and eventual replacement of a particular asset. Thus, all of these attributes should be collected and defined as parameters associated with modeled equipment (families). Owners may also request that these attributes be expanded.
- *Standard COBie Attributes:* All attributes considered part of standard COBie worksheets are important to FMS. Examples include warranty-related information, and to some degree, bill of material data. FMS does not require that COBie attributes that are not normally included in the design model be added to the model.
- *Owner-Extended Attributes:* This is the category for all other attributes required to complete the (per asset) data templates defined by FMS, but that do not fall

into any of the other categories. These are in essence completely "user defined," and would not be expected to be found within the design BIM models. These could follow the structure upon which COBie allows for extended attributes.

These four categories allowed FMS to communicate (1) when, (2) where, and (3) how of data was to be collected over the course design, construction, and turnover of a project. In the case of USC, Master Attributes and Schedule Attributes were required to be captured in the design models. The majority of data in the remaining two categories are captured by contractors during construction and project closeout.

Data Standards and Guidelines

The decision about what naming and classification standards to use is complex.The process that the FMS team was going through at the time the case study was written was similar to that used about 15 years ago when FAMIS was implemented using UniFormat. Thus, the project members used UniFormat to name and classify information within the design and construction documents. UniFormat continues to have a place and value to FM organizations and is also leveraged by construction professionals for such things as; assembly level estimating and scheduling. However, as the project progressed, it was realized that other standards, such as OmniClass, the National CAD Standard, MasterFormat, and COBie should be further evaluated.

- MasterFormat is believed to be a bridge to a standard used primarily by A&E consultants.
- OmniClass has the potential to be a robust means for classifying data, more suited to machine language, and the managing data within relational databases. In providing a link between UniFormat and MasterFormat, OmniClass appears to also offer a translation for different industry stakeholders familiar with one versus the other, as such, potentially offering a bridge to unify stakeholders.
- National CAD standard offers a consistent and well-recognized means for naming of typical MEP system components.

One of the hardest questions was determining what nomenclature standard to use when naming equipment. A decision was made to use OmniClass Table 23 for equipment naming and the National CAD Standard Version 3.1 for equipment abbreviations and their types. An example of an equipment abbreviation is VAV, which stands for variable air volume. An example of a type is VAV box with reheat. An example of an instance is VAV-D01, which indicates a specific variable air volume box within building D. The numbering and lettering convention used within the

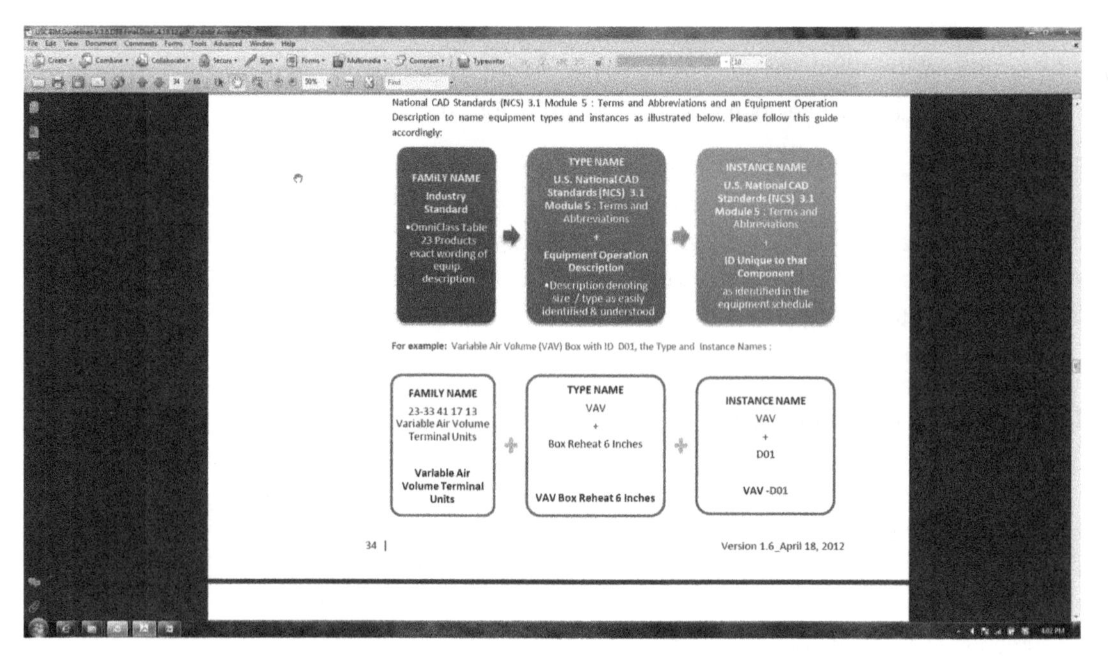

FIGURE 6.29 Relationship between OmniClass and the National CAD standard.
Courtesy USC FMS

instance is determined by the mechanical engineer. As shown in Figure 6.29, decisions were made to use the National CAD standard and OmniClass. As UniFormat and MasterFormat are both part of OmniClass, both of these standards are also part of naming and classification structure.

COBie

FMS first became familiar with COBie during Phase 2 and applied it during Phase 3. The project team recognized COBie as a consistent, recognizable framework for multiple stakeholders across the project team to collect information that could be used for facility management. Thus, COBie was included as part of the USC BIM Guideline. As shown in Table 6.5, the guidelines require an increasing amount of COBie data as the project moves through design and into construction.

The USC BIM Guidelines require that the design team submit design data in a COBie-compliant Excel file. To meet this requirement, they can either enter the data directly into an Excel file or use EcoDomus to automate the extraction of the COBie data from the Revit models. The second alternative is much more accurate and secure for large amounts of data. After the data are provided,

TABLE 6.5 COBie Data Requirements per Project Stage

	Project Phase			
COBie Data	**Schematic Design**	**Design Development**	**Construction Documents**	**During Construction**
Attribute			X	X
Component		X	X	X
Contact	X	X	X	X
Document			X	X
Facility	X	X	X	X
Floor	X	X	X	X
Job				X
Resource				X
Space	X	X	X	X
Spare				X
System		X	X	X
Type		X	X	X
Zone	X	X	X	X

USC checks the quality of the data against the COBie requirements. The USC BIM Guidelines also require the construction team to submit their portion of the required COBie data. To meet this requirement they enter the data directly into a COBie-compliant Excel file.

FMS is currently testing the use of Ecodomus PM to automate the extraction of COBie data from the Revit models. This provides an easier and more accurate method of collecting this data so long as it has been correctly entered in the Revit model.

To further organize the COBie data, the USC BIM Guidelines create three information tiers:

- Tier 1 data are anticipated to be found and maintained within the design model over the duration of the project.
- Tier 2 is the balance of the required COBie "standard" information that would not normally be contained in a model. This information will be collected and maintained in the COBie worksheets over the duration of the project.
- Tier 3, closeout documentation, is documents that are required by COBie, such as an O&M manual. Prior to this project, USC received rolls of drawings and

binders of information after turnover of a building. Although this information could be potentially useful for FM decision making, it was concluded that the extensive time required to sort and organize this information made it very difficult to use. This usually means a significant delay in coming up to speed on a facility and entering this important data in the CMMS. The COBie framework enables the timely and correct collection of documentation, and provides tools for ensuring the quality control of these data through the course of construction. These are important benefits to FMS.

Per the BIM Guidelines, it is anticipated that a master COBie-compliant worksheet will be created and it will be updated at the following project stages:

- 100 percent design documents
- Issuance for construction
- 75 percent substantial completion
- Commissioning complete
- Project closeout

AIA Document 202: Building Information Modeling Protocol Exhibit

To define the LOD at each project state, AIA Document 202, Building Information Modeling Protocol Exhibit, was used (available from AIA web site). As stated by the document:

- LOD 100 was used to develop schematic design documents.
- LOD 200 was used to develop design documents.
- LOD 300 was used to develop the construction documents.

Although AIA 202 has levels 400 and 500, they were not included in the USC BIM Guideline because it was thought that LOD 300 is adequate for the development of construction documents. Instead, the additional level of detail required by USC was focused on the extensive data parameters needed to describe the major building systems. Additionally, FMS found that not all information in the model is needed for facility management, nor was a very detailed level of geometric modeling required to achieve FM goals. While there are some modeling practices that are advocated by FMS to ensure connectivity of systems, the geometric modeling requirements focused on acceptable dimensional tolerances, proper placement and configuration of these, and the creation of "smart" connectors for all services, as related to equipment (families). In the future, FMS may require a greater LOD to allow for specific analysis capabilities such as energy modeling.

Decision to Use Industry Standards

Although the university could have elected to develop an internal standard, USC finds industry standards provide integrity and have a documented history. As staff turnover occurs, an industry standard has more longevity because new FMS staff is more likely to be familiar with an industry standard. The same thing can be said of design and construction teams. Using owner-specific standards can increase the costs and expose the owner to additional risks from lack of proper compliance.

Data Storage

One unresolved industry challenge is where information from the BIM should be stored after construction has been completed. USC determined that because BIM authoring tools are for developing BIM models and not storing data, BIM data should be managed in a database. Using this strategy, the information from the BIM can then be used by traditional FM systems, including CMMS, BAS, and DMS. The use of the DMS helps to provide a structure to store FM documentation without needing to create links between documents and the CMMS or any other applications, as the documents can be stored directly in the DMS. Although it is possible to attach documents or static links from a model to specific documents, a more effective approach is to query a DMS for documents associated with a specific equipment or system.

An important lesson learned about data storage is that just because a tool can be used for more than the original function does not mean it should. Similarly to BIM authoring tools, middleware such as EcoDomus, which was used to import and export information between software, was found not to be the long-term solution for information storage.

USE OF BUILDING INFORMATION MODELING FOR FACILITY MANAGEMENT

As Phase 3 progressed, the vision of BIM FM integration that started to evolve during Phase 2 continued to take shape. Embracing the vision also required the BIM models from all disciplines, including HVAC, electrical, plumbing, fire protection, architectural, and structural be combined into one master model and fully coordinated. Additionally, it was necessary to provide guidance to the BIM integrator about how to organize and consolidate design models from all BIM authoring tools, to achieve what would become a basis for an FM model viewer.

One of the goals for the use of BIM within building operation is to help troubleshoot hot/cold calls. Currently, when such a call is received, the customer call center will route the information to an operator, who will then look at the BAS to determine if the call is the result of an incorrect temperature setpoint or faulty sensor. If this does not identify the problem, a work order is issued. The work order is dispatched to a technician, who will go out into the field to determine how to solve the problem. However, it can be difficult to find the root cause. Thus, the technician may conclude that more information is needed and it is necessary to review the HVAC drawings to better understand the system. Since it can be difficult to find all the necessary information about the HVAC system on as-built drawings, the technician may still not be able to find the information needed. If this is the case, the root cause of the problem may remain unresolved, leading to additional customer complaints.

In contrast, when a 3D model is available, the work order clerk could provide more information to the technician when routing the work order. For example, the use of the model could help to determine that the room where it is too hot or cold is served by air handler AHU-1 located on the second floor and that the room with the hot/cold call is located near the end of a run of ductwork. With this information, it may be possible for the technician to understand the root cause of the problem even before he/she starts to resolve the problem in the field. The information provided may help to conclude the system balance has been compromised, or that there is an issue at a system level that is impacting all the zones on a particular air handler. The result is faster and more accurate resolutions of these problems with far less effort.

A second goal for the use of 3D models is to help inform tradesmen about the type of systems and location of systems in new buildings. Compared to common practice, where tradesmen are provided a written narrative or a list of systems, the 3D models can be used to visually describe them. The 3D models are shared with tradesmen either through formal training or project coordination meetings. When the information has been shared through project coordination meetings, it was determined that the tradesmen appreciated the opportunity to learn about the systems but could not be part of the detailed coordination discussions because of time constraints. Instead, they preferred to provide a checklist of items for the contractors, subcontractors, and BIM integrator to use to support the coordination process. As the meetings generally took two to four hours, the tradesmen found the meetings took away too much time from the field. Another alternative might be to have shop supervisors participate in these meetings, who could then convey feedback to and from their front-line technicians.

At the time the case study was written, a training program for tradesmen using the 3D models was being piloted. The training used the 3D models to visually communicate about the types of systems installed in the new Phase 3 building. As part of the training, the trainer navigates through the model while students observe and learn how to manipulate the system. This training was part of a much larger training effort for tradesmen to help engage tradesmen earlier in the design and construction process at USC.

BIM FM Workflows

To implement BIM FM processes, it is necessary to understand current FM workflows, as well as what changes may be necessary to further utilize information within BIM. To support this need, during Phase 2, FMS created a BIM execution framework in the form of a process map. The process map included the lessons learned from the project and illustrated key components of the BIM FM strategy. The overall goal of the process map was to help define the stakeholders and their roles within the process and information exchanges between parties. The BIM Guidelines, discussed earlier, were informed by the process map. Because this map is too detailed to include in the case study, key aspects are summarized:

- Development of guidelines for the design and construction team to use for reference.
- Establishment a feedback loop with all major consultants to support model coordination.
- All major design trades are required to perform clash detection before the models are released to ensure a minimum level of document coordination.
- A requirement that design models must be developed at the level of detail requested by the owner.
- Design models are to be handed over to the contractor so they can be used in their native format, such as 3D .dwg files.
- Documentation about how initial data transfers, including what data and the format, should be agreed upon. Decisions about how the data will be captured and maintained are also necessary.
- Documentation about how, after detailed shop and fabrication drawings are approved, they should be provided to the design teams to update the design documents. This process includes clash detection between the design and construction models using model mashup techniques to identify variations between the two models. The design teams are to adjust their drawings to match the construction drawings. This process included reconciling equipment, system layouts, and data associated with systems and equipment.

- After submittals are approved, data within design models, especially equipment parameter attributes, are updated to by the design team, to reflect the actual equipment procured and installed on site. The design team is required to issue a monthly bulletin that documents owner-requested changes to a project. The contractor shall determine what BIM model changes are necessary.
- Documentation that clash detection of detailing and fabrication drawings is to occur over the duration of construction.
- Documentation that all models are to be turned over to FMS. The models are verified for completeness by FMS.
- Documentation that all worksheets, such as COBie, are to be turned over to FMS to verify for completeness.

CREATING A FACILITY MANAGEMENT PORTAL

The development of a portal using Navisworks was discussed earlier. This section further discusses the portal concept, with a focus on the development of the portal across all three phases of the project. The overall goal of the portal is to make it easier to find documentation, particularly for staff that does not regularly access FM systems. Both the 3D models and the information from the BIM are part of the portal concepts. The portal was developed to meet the needs of facility management user groups, particularly facility managers and technicians. Thus, many discussions took place internally between the members of the facility management team to determine the requirements for the portal.

As discussed in more detail below, the Phase 1 portal, while not implemented, was used to inform the Phase 2 portal. A key point to recognize is that a BIM FM portal is complex and it would be unrealistic to expect that all of the challenges and needs would be identified during the first phase of development. The work of USC to develop the portal during Phase 2 is forward thinking when one considers that implementation of FM software, such as CMMS and CAFM, often fail to meet the initial expectations of users.[2]

Phase 1 Portal

The concept of the portal was developed during Phase 1 by a committee that championed the use of BIM. This Phase 1 portal used links between Navisworks, the CMMS, DMS, and BAS. By clicking on a link, the user was redirected to the login screen of the facility management software that would allow the user to view the contents of the link. The portal allowed queries to be performed to

[2] A study by the Standish Group (Standish 1995), a research firm that tracks IT implementation, found that "66 percent of all IT projects fail to meet the needs and expectations of users."

search for specific documents or information about a specific system or piece of equipment.

As Navisworks Manage (Navisworks) was used for clash detection, which is a point of integration between design and construction models, it may seem appropriate that it could also be used to integrate construction and facility management. Contractors who are familiar with Navisworks understand that it has the ability to create links to documents, which can add value to facility management. However, multiple challenges were identified with this approach:

- If changes were made to the building geometry, the links to the 3D geometry need to be updated in Navisworks. This would make it difficult to maintain as-built drawings in the portal without a significant time investment to maintain the links.
- The Navisworks files provided by the contractors were not at the level of detail and quality needed for 3D as-built models. In order for the drawings to be at the level of detail and quality necessary before the links were added, FMS would have needed to spend a significant amount of time reviewing and editing the files.
- The Navisworks platform requires training to understand. In contrast, the portal was intended to support multiple roles within FMS without requiring specialized training.

Additionally, and perhaps most importantly, it was recognized that using Navisworks would require the user to always start an information search using the model viewer. Although this makes sense for some users, it was not ideal for others. Troubleshooting was an example where viewing the model first worked well. The conventional workflow, when troubleshooting, is to look at the drawings first and then look at other information such as trend logs from the BAS, O&M manuals, and maintenance histories. Thus, the portal could effectively replace a set of paper drawings. An example of where starting with the model did not work well its a BAS, CMMS, or DMS technician, who, as a result of his familiarity with an individual FM tool, would prefer to start from the bottom up.

The Phase 1 portal was a useful proof of concept from which many valuable lessons were learned:

- The Navisworks portal provided little value to leverage data rich models. A portal that allowed the data from the models to be leveraged was needed.
- The portal needed to have more than one workflow: users need to be able to start by having access either the 3D model or information, depending on their needs.

- To use 3D models within an FM portal requires a significant time investment to clean up the models in-house to align with naming and color-coding standards.
- Navisworks is not the best tool to use for updating drawings as a result of renovations or other changes to the building geometry to maintain BIM models after construction.
- Navisworks was not created to be a facility management operations and maintenance management software tool; it is a tool primarily developed to support the construction coordination process. Thus, it was concluded that decisions about what software to use for an application should be based on reviewing the primary functions of the software.

In addition, a series of guiding principles for further development of a portal were defined:

- A connection to existing FM software should be the primary goal of the portal.
- BIM should not be expected to replace existing FM systems, but instead integrate and complement them.
- Strategies implemented need to be flexible enough to address future changes to the building and its building systems over the life of the building.
- Clear opportunities to maximize the use of available data from BIM models to populate existing FM software should be identified.

Although the Phase 1 portal was never implemented, it provided some important insights that informed the portal development in Phase 2.

Phase 2 Portal

During Phase 2, a new portal was developed based on lessons learned from Phase 1, definitions of several use cases, insight from technology partners, and observations of team members. A key requirement was that the portal interface needed to be simple and flexible so it could be used by a wide range of users. Additionally, the 3D model should not be the main point of entry. Benefits of the portal should include:

- High-level information can be viewed directly from inside the portal, instead of users' needing to access it from multiple systems. This can save time because the information can all be viewed at once from the same screen.
- It is not necessary to become familiar with multiple FM software packages, just the portal.
- The portal can be used to understand the relationships between systems and equipment through a network tree, have simple model graphics navigation and view control, and provide an integrated version of FM information systems,

in the form of a window into these systems. This would give the user the ability to access information that natively resides outside of the portal (in the DMS, CMMS, and BAS).

Developing this portal was a very time-consuming effort. It took significant time to determine what high-level information should be exchanged between systems and how to create the necessary links between the portal and the FM systems. A key action that led to the success of this portal was defining the key roles of its users through the development of the use cases.

Development of Use Cases to Define Portal Requirements

A use case is a written description that formalizes a process that identifies, defines and documents specific data elements that are exchanged between participants to support the activity being described (ASHRAE 2010). Use cases are commonly used by software developers. During Phase 2, multiple use cases were developed by a core group of USC users working with their technology partners, including Honeywell, FAMIS, Autodesk, and BlueCielo through shared business interests. Formal contracts between USC and the technology partners were not put in place to develop the use cases. The overall goal was to create a dialog between USC and the technology partners to determine how the software currently used by USC could meet the developing BIM FM needs. Four of the role use cases included:

- CAD project specialist
- Energy management administrator
- Commissioning manager
- HVAC maintenance manager

A role use case is a description of how a specific professional role would use a software product. These were developed by conducting a series of interviews with specific individuals within FMS. The goal of the interviews was to determine the core daily tasks of a professional, and what could be done to better equip them to carry out these responsibilities.

The use cases helped to answer the following questions:

- Who and how should users interface with existing facility management information systems?
- What information from the design and construction process would add value to facility management processes?
- Where and in what format can this information be found?
- How sophisticated should the user interfaces be?

- What role, if any, should facility management staff play during the design and construction process?
- How can technology and process improvements help facility management staff to perform their job duties more efficiently?

The development of these use cases subsequently helped to define three categories of users:

- *Administrators:* Those responsible to find answers to integration questions between software and manage the data and the individual FM information systems where this data resides.
- *Contributors:* Those responsible for making suggestions for the processes used for collecting and turning over information.
- *Consumers:* Individuals who can confirm how data and the portal would be used for specific applications.

The development of the use cases was a powerful exercise for the FMS team and the technology partners because it helped to determine what the software interfaces should look like, what information is truly needed, and who would use the different interfaces and associated information.

Data Quality

High-quality data are accurate and can be used for decision making. To ensure that data are of sufficient quality for an FM portal, it is necessary to define what the "source of truth" will be. The source of truth should be a primary (governing) source where the information is stored. If information is stored in more than one location, as may be the case with a middleware used to help transfer data, it is important that only one source of truth be defined. If a middleware continues to be used during a building's operational stage, there should be automatic synchronization capabilities to ensure that these systems stay in sync as changes are made. This is to avoid unmanaged duplication or loss of data, which can lead to lack of confidence in their accuracy. FMS determined that the source of truth for information shall be their respective FM information systems. This is not to suggest that a middleware cannot be used in the process to update information, for instance, when a remodel is undertaken, but after a space goes back into operation mode, the source of truth shall be returned to the respective FM information systems.

The Uses of Record BIM Models

The processes that require the use and updating of as-record BIM models have not yet been well defined. As-built models, as delivered by contractors, are considered snapshot in time, and, because of modifications to the building and its systems, often have very little value over the life of a building. There are many challenges that are yet to be solved, including:

- Construction BIMs have a lot of detail, such as pipe and duct hangers, that is not relevant for FM.
- It is necessary to spend a significant amount of time cleaning up design and construction BIM models before they can be used for FM.

To reduce the time necessary for cleaning up models, a detailed BIM Guideline, including requirements for nomenclature and model requirements, can help.

Part of the record BIM process is to make sure the design models reflect actual conditions at the level of detail required for FM. This level of detail, from a geometric standpoint, is usually no greater than that required to develop design documents which specify the location and layout of systems within a specific tolerance. For items found in a fabrication model, such as hangers and supports, additional detail may not be of practical importance to FM staff when navigating through a model of the building systems.

Part of the process for delivering the record models is called model mashup. This superimposes the design and construction models on top of each other to identify where changes were made as a result of construction coordination. This is shown in Figure 6.30. In this figure, the model with more valves (darker model) is from

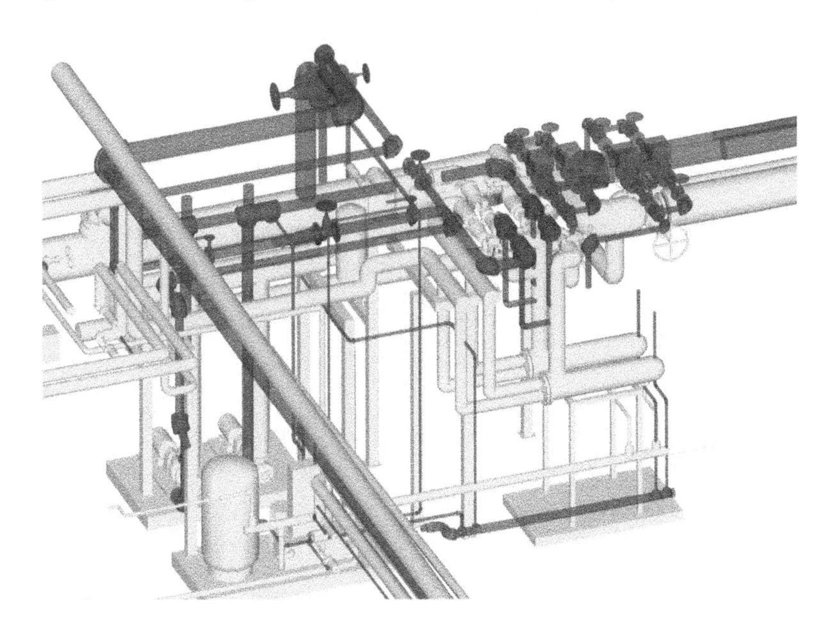

FIGURE 6.30 Model mashup, superimposed design, and construction models.
Courtesy USC FMS

construction, while the other model with the heat exchangers and pumps is the design model. The differences between the steam and hot water distribution piping between the two models are clearly revealed.

After the record models are turned over to FMS, it may be necessary to further clean up the models. This includes making sure that:

- Systems are properly color-coded.
- Files are named correctly.
- Components are named correctly.
- Component hierarchies are correct.
- Proper system connections and directions of flows are confirmed.
- Families are created correctly, including smart connectors.

The intent of the as-built BIM models was to keep them as record drawings, just as 2D CAD drawings have been used for past projects. Thus, as more buildings are built and renovated using BIM, it will be the responsibilities of the CAD manager to receive, update, and use the BIM authoring tools. As more BIM models are received, it is anticipated that the challenge of keeping BIM models up to date will be similar to those experienced in keeping as-built drawings up to date.

NECESSARY EDUCATION AND SKILLS

The use of BIM FM requires an understanding of new and evolving tools. This means that there is a need for all members of the project team to acquire new skills and think about solving problems in new ways. This includes a basic understanding or BIM by key personnel. Examples are discussed in the following sections.

UNDERSTANDING AND MAKING THE CRITICAL DECISIONS

All projects have critical decisions that may impact a project's success. Some of the critical decisions on this project are summarized here.

- From the perspective of a service provider, the most critical decision is for the owner to define the deliverables. Sometimes these are too vague. When this occurs, it is up to the service provider to actively engage members of the facilities group, to solicit end goals, and help define the deliverables. This is particularly important when BIM is new to the facility management team.
- Another critical decision is deciding what BIM authoring tools to use. This is a critical because it impacts the success of the information exchanges between

applications, coordination of information among disciplines, and eventual transfer of data for FM information systems.

- The format of the information and specific information to collect are critical decisions. This includes selecting a mechanism (such as COBie) to help collect and communicate data. COBie allows data to be collected by a variety of tools (as simple as spreadsheets) because it is an open standard.

Owner Education Requirements

The primary owner requirement is to have a clear picture of what business objectives are needed from BIM FM. These can be articulated in terms of reduced operating and maintenance cost, improved service delivery, streamlined processes, and better support for future building modifications. Given the findings of this case study, the main owner education requirements can be defined as process and technology. Technology aspects include the need to understand software, including new types of software and software terminology. Some terms to understand include *middleware, interoperability,* and *use cases.* When learning about software, it is important to understand what type of data can be collected during design and construction. It is also important to understand current FM processes and how they can be optimized using BIM FM.

LESSONS LEARNED

Many lessons were learned by the project team across the three phases of the project. Key lessons learned are summarized in the following categories: overall lessons learned, lessons learned about technology, technology users, information from models, and BIM FM processes.

Overall Lessons Learned

Lessons learned that apply to all stakeholders include the value of information compared to the 3D model, the importance of starting with the end in mind, the importance of setting goals, and the importance of not just replicating existing processes and technology.

One of the largest challenges with BIM FM is evaluating how the 3D and information components of the BIM should be used. The USC team concluded that the most important part of BIM FM is the data, not the 3D model. Specifically, it is most important to capture and deliver high-quality data that can be used for facility management. Although accurate geometric models are important, they are a second priority to the data.

The most significant benefit of BIM FM is the ability to have the proper information to support better FM processes. To achieve this, it is necessary to have buy-in from those who would benefit from use of the data. In some cases, this may require understanding the details of current workflows and how they could be improved if better information was easily available. When decisions are made about what data to collect and the format, it is important to get feedback from the team members who are providing and using the data. The earlier the feedback can be sought, the greater the opportunity to collaborate and determine what is possible and practical.

Starting with the end in mind is also critical. It is important for the facility management team to understand what they want to achieve, what resources are available to achieve the goals, and what are the critical functions of the facility management team. This is important because an extensive effort will be needed to collect data. Furthermore, if the accuracy of the data is not maintained over the life of the project, the initial data collection effort may not have been worth the investment.

When setting goals where it is necessary to implement new processes, it is important to set achievable goals. Setting small, achievable goals is more effective than setting a large goal that does not motivate using BIM and may even decrease the likelihood for success. Use each new project to identify new lessons learned that can be recorded and applied on the next project. As they are applied and new opportunities are identified, it is important to recognize that the process of developing standards will not stop.

It is important to realize that new technologies and processes are needed to implement BIM FM integration. The old approaches to capturing and using data will lead to additional expense and poor results. In some cases, new tools may be required. However, existing tools, such as CMMS and DMS, should not be overlooked. Finally, recognize that BIM FM is in its infancy—as one team member stated, "We are still learning."

Lessons Learned about Technology

Existing tools may already provide the necessary functionality. For example, CMMS and CAFM systems have been used in the facility management industry for many years. Although many of these systems are not fully utilized, this alone is not a reason to suggest they should be abandoned. The type and amount of data stored within existing tools, as well as current facility management processes, should be carefully evaluated before concluding that new tools are needed. Technology decisions impact facility managers, designers, and contractors.

Two key lessons learned for facility managers and technology relate to user interface design and data integration. Specific to user interface design, it is important to recognize that the decision about what a user interface should look like and what systems should be integrated are interrelated but separate decisions. It is not necessary for all decisions about integration to be made before decisions about what the user interface should look like. Decisions about what to integrate are difficult and take time. All stakeholders have different goals and require different information. Decisions about what to integrate, and why, are much more challenging than the technical effort required to complete the integration. When using new tools, including new software and middleware, it is important to be careful not to reengineer current facility management software, such as CMMS and DMS.

Procuring software licenses and having trained staff within an FM organization to efficiently use and keep up with various construction and fabrication software tools is unrealistic. It was concluded for this project that construction contractors and subcontractors could use any tool that met their needs, as long as it met the requirements for clash detection between trades. However, designers were required to use BIM creation software that met owner record BIM requirements. This is important because the record BIM models will be maintained and provide value over the life of the building.

Lessons Learned about Technology Users

In order for FM teams to receive the information they want from BIM deliverables, the FM team must clearly define these requirements. One way that this can be done is by creating shared parameter files for designers to use. These files specify what information is required and can help to ensure that equipment schedules are created in a manner that allows the data to be exported from the BIM authoring software for FM use.

When BIM is being used for FM, the design team is more engaged with the project during construction. This is a significant change from current practice. In addition, the design models are updated over the duration of construction to create as-built models, as opposed to waiting until construction is complete. The goal should be for the record models to be available on the first day that a building is operational.

Lessons Learned about Information from Models

One of the largest challenges of implementing BIM FM is justifying to designers, contractors, and financial decision makers the value of data and the need for integration. Construction budgets are always tight; thus, the data from the design and construction process is seen as less valuable than the physical building. However, having the right information is critical to make effective FM decisions.

When determining what information should be collected, it is important to make decisions from the frame of reference of the user. Thus, questions about how information should be used and who will use it are important. Determining what data to collect about equipment is much more complex than determining what space data to collect. Equipment data involves more stakeholders and requires a technical understanding of the data. At USC, the process to collect equipment data started with determining what equipment records existed in FAMIS for large equipment, such as boilers, chillers, and air handling units. Information determined to be most important included equipment name, manufacturer, specification section number, model number, and serial number. Part of the decision process also included determining where the information should be stored long term: in the BIM, within middleware, or within facility management software.

Lessons Learned about BIM FM Processes

It is important to recognize that BIM FM is not an "out-of-the-box" product. It requires new processes and new channels of communication. Thus, BIM FM provides an opportunity to revisit and review current facility management workflows to identify areas to improve efficiency. Process mapping can be an effective method to evaluate workflows. To succeed when making process changes, it is important to have buy-in from the leaders within the facility management organization because time and resources are needed to document process changes, gain buy-in across the facility management organization, and make changes to existing contracts.

Determining what software tools will be used to collect data is challenging. It was found that contractor fabrication models are not well suited for sharing data across the project team. Fabrication models are created based on assemblies of individual parts and not created as systems. For example, each piece of ductwork is created as a separate component within fabrication software. Thus, each duct elbow, reducer, and straight run of duct is a separate element in the construction model. In contrast, Revit can connect individual parts to create an assembly. Thus, with Revit, it is much easier to draw a duct system because the components can easily be connected. Although some fabrication software used by contractors has the capabilities to group individual components as a system, this is not a common practice by contractors because it is not a necessary step to fabricate components.

From the perspective of the design and construction teams, some of the most important lessons learned include the importance of carefully listening to the FM team from the start of the project and understanding their requirements. These can be very different than those for using BIM for visualization and construction coordination. Finally, as BIM FM requires collaboration and data exchanges between roles, all members of the project team must be willing to work together.

REMAINING CHALLENGES

Any project that challenges the status quo will have unique problems. Over the course of the Cinematic Arts project, the team encountered and resolved many challenges. Two of the largest are summarized here. One challenge is to determine who will manage the record BIM model after construction is complete. On a traditional project, the CAD manager is responsible for as-built documents. At the time this case study was written, management of the BIM model had not been resolved. Two alternatives were being considered: the CAD manager and the controls technicians. FMS was evaluating how the BIM could be used to support building operation troubleshooting.

An ongoing challenge is finding dedicated resources to make the progress needed to implement BIM FM. Making decisions about resources requires an understanding of the time and cost necessary to complete BIM FM tasks. During design and construction, the School of Cinematic Arts was fortunate to have a very generous donor that recognized the value of BIM. However, for many projects BIM FM work can be seen as an additional cost, even if benefits over the long term can be demonstrated. Often, decisions are made based on time and resources available in the short term, say one year. Additionally, if it is necessary to develop a business case to justify a need, collecting the data needed to quantify the benefits can be challenging, particularly since it may take several years to validate the effectiveness of implementing BIM FM. Hopefully, this case study will provide an understanding of challenges that need to be addressed and support the very real benefits resulting from the implementation of BIM within an FM organization.

USC and the BIM FM work completed during the School of Cinematic Arts project is viewed as a successful effort. This can be attributed to starting out with the end in mind and having excellent support from top management. This understanding was greatly influenced by top leadership, who understood the value of BIM FM. This reduced the time needed to make important decisions and allowed FM staff to become more familiar with the new building and more prepared to contribute to their effective operation.

SUMMARY

The University of Southern California School of Cinematic Arts complex is a leading example of BIM FM practices. The case study summarizes the progression of BIM to BIM FM across three phases of construction. The case study demonstrates the importance of focusing on information within the BIM process, as well as the need for integration and the user interfaces necessary to support the uses of this information for effective decision making.

REFERENCES

ASHRAE. 2010. *Guideline 20-10: Documenting HVAC&R Work Processes and Data Exchange Requirements.* Atlanta, GA: ASHRAE,

Standish. 1995. *Standish Group Report,* www.bing.com/search?q=Standish+Group+Project+Failure&FORM=QSRE1.

USC. 2012. *Building Information Modeling (BIM) Guidelines for Design Bid Build Contracts,* Version 1.6. Final Draft, April 18, 2012. USC Capital Construction Development and Facilities Management Services, www.usc.edu/fms/technical/cad/BIMGuidelines.shtml

ACKNOWLEDGMENTS

This case study could not have been completed without the insights from the following individuals from Facilities Management Services, University of Southern California: John Welsh, associate vice president of facility management services, Jose Delgado, CAD manager; and John Muse, management information management systems associate director. The following consultants and contractors also provided insight to develop the case study: David Kang, project engineer, CSI Electrical Contractors; France Israel, president, View by View, Inc.; Ray Kahl, principal, Urban Design Group; Igor Starkov, president, EcoDomus Inc.; Gregory P. Luth, president, Gregory P. Luth & Associates, Inc.; and Cliff Bourland.

This study would not be possible without the hard work and diligence of many operations and administrative departments that make up Facilities Management Services. Furthermore, the vision and support of the leaders for both Facilities Management Services and Capital Construction Development were crucial in the success of this endeavor.

It should be noted that the information in this case study has been shared to help educate readers about BIM FM. The use of names of vendors and service providers included within the case study does not imply that the University of Southern California endorses any of the software or service providers discussed.

Case Study 4: Implementation of BIM and FM at Xavier University

Elijah Afedizie, Rebecca Beatty, Erica Hanselman, Eric Heyward, Aisha Lawal, Eric Nimer, Laura Rosenthal, and Daryl Siman

MANAGEMENT SUMMARY

This case study describes the use, integration, and delivery of BIM through all stages of construction in Xavier University's latest construction projects. The major players in delivering the completed project were Messer Construction Co., Shepley Bulfinch, Richardson & Abbott, Michael Schuster Associates, and the Xavier Facilities Maintenance department. This project was the largest and most costly expansion in the school's history—adding 25 percent to the total portfolio (from approximately 2 million GSF to 2.5 million GSF) and four new campus buildings: Smith Hall (housing the Williams College of Business), Conaton Learning Commons, Central Utility Plant, and Bishop Fenwick Place.

The chosen BIM program, Autodesk Revit, was utilized to facilitate design and construction. However, the subcontractors modeled the mechanical, electrical, plumbing, and fire protection systems in various CAD-based software products. The CAFM system, FM:Interact by FM:Systems, is used to manage space and occupancy and track architectural finishes. The CMMS system, WebTMA by TMA Systems, is used to manage maintenance and track building system assets. While a thoroughly vetted cost/benefit life-cycle analysis is not yet available, Xavier estimates that over a person-year of data entry was avoided by leveraging data in the BIM. Also, initial estimates reveal that the use of BIM on these projects will generate significant cost savings for facility management over the life cycle of the buildings. Additionally, data from the models assisted Xavier in forecasting life-cycle facilities costs—helping the facilities department increase their renewal and replacement budget from $750,000 per year to $12 million per year, which represents approximately 2.3 percent of the total replacement value of the campus facilities.[3]

[3] The Current Replacement Value (CRV) Index of 2.3 percent would place this facility among the top 80 percent of all the buildings surveyed by IFMA in their 2009 Maintenance Cost Survey (see p. 48, http://www.ifma.org/resources/research/reports/pages/32.htm). The report comments that "... this year's measurement, an average of 1.55%, demonstrates a continuing decline in the CRV index compared to previous reports."

The additional budget will fund projects that allow the facilities department to reduce deferred maintenance and support a vibrant campus environment.

As Xavier's first attempt at using BIM on a large-scale project, it was not completed without challenges. Most important, the FM department was not involved in the early phases of the project. This led to additional costs to revise the models to support FM integration. In addition to these added modeling costs, the CMMS used for these buildings (WebTMA) is not currently easily linked to the BIM software. As a result, Xavier had to work with traditional methods to populate their CMMS asset inventory. Even with these added costs, Messer's use of BIM on the project led to construction being completed under budget and ahead of schedule—more than compensating for the BIM-FM integration efforts.

Furthermore, Xavier's FM department feels confident that the benefits of BIM use on future projects will continue to grow as university personnel become more comfortable working with these software applications and their processes evolve. In addition to the learning curve benefits of completing their first BIM project, Xavier also learned that it is important for the owner to specify the BIM data requirements as early as possible in the process to ensure the appropriate stakeholders are entering the required information in the proper way.

After full immersion in the project life cycle with the use of BIM for FM, the Xavier staff is convinced of the added value, ease of use, and lifecycle cost savings associated with the tool. They intend to implement its use in future projects as well as for existing facilities on campus.

GENERAL DESCRIPTION

Xavier University was founded in 1831 in Cincinnati, Ohio. This university is one of 28 Jesuit colleges and universities nationwide and is proud to be the sixth-oldest Catholic university in the nation, as stated in their profile on their web site.

The following list illustrates the school's educational program:

- 3 colleges
- 85 undergraduate majors
- 54 undergraduate minors
- 11 graduate programs
- 7019 total students
- 4368 undergraduates (www.xavier.edu/about/)

TABLE 6.6 Buildings Covered in This Case Study

Building	Start Date of Design	Completion Date of Construction	Area (sf)	Cost per sf
Smith Hall	September 2008	August 2010	88,000	$303.97
Conaton Learning Commons	October 2008	July 2010	84,000	$326.37
Bishop Fenwick Place	February 2010	August 2011	245,000	$237.00
Central Utility Plant	September 2008	June 2010	19,160	$528.03

This case study explores the use of BIM on four main projects on Xavier's campus. Table 6.6 provides a quick overview of each project; Figures 6.31 through 6.34 show the buildings listed in Table 6.6.

The construction site formerly contained old houses that the university owned and used as offices. The houses were demolished in order to begin construction. Xavier's projects were funded through a combination of bonds, donations, and gifts.

FIGURE 6.31 Smith Hall.
Courtesy Xavier University.

FIGURE 6.32 Conaton Learning Commons.
Courtesy Messer Construction Co.

FIGURE 6.33 Bishop Fenwick Place.
Courtesy Xavier University.

FIGURE 6.34 Central Utility Plant.
Courtesy Xavier University.

The materials used in the construction projects are a combination of brick veneer and cast-in-place concrete. There were no prefabricated structures included in the construction; however, some cladding was used.[1]

Xavier emphasized sustainability in the design of the building systems. The buildings feature high-efficiency boilers and chillers, two-pipe systems, fan coil units, central utilities; which generate their own heat and mechanical areas designed for expansion. Electrical systems installed also have sustainable characteristics. The projects meet LEED silver requirement by using high-efficiency lighting and a central utilities port. The central utilities provide one central meter for the campus, which then transfers the electric power to transformers assigned to individual buildings. The use of BIM did not play a role in achieving LEED silver.

Construction was carried out under schedule and as a result there was no need to implement any fees associated with liquidated damages (Meyer interview).

[1]Student interview with Greg Meyer, March 21, 2012; hereafter cited in text as "Meyer interview."

The modeling of the buildings began after the architectural programming stage. Xavier worked with Messer Construction Co., construction manager on the project, to gather and consolidate the various models and integrate them with the space management modules of FM:Systems' FM:Interact product (Xavier University Master Plan). At the time of this study, the models were connected to a test FM:Interact site. Xavier and Messer are in process of connecting the models to Xavier's production FM:Interact site where the data from the new buildings will be joined with data from the existing buildings on campus (Meyer interview).

ROLE OF OWNER AND FM STAFF IN SETTING BIM AND FM REQUIREMENTS

In the fall of 2009, Messer presented two project delivery approaches to Xavier. The first was a traditional approach (design/bid/build) where an architecture and engineering team designed the building completely and then the design was put out to bid with the lowest bidder being awarded the project. The estimated completion date for this option was December 2011 (Meyer interview).

The second option was a relatively new project delivery system that leveraged principles of integrated project delivery (IPD). From a project scheduling point of view, the team planned to design and build the project approximately six months faster than if a traditional approach was used. In actual fact, the use of BIM and IPD led to a project completion date two and a half weeks earlier than anticipated (Meyer interview).

The primary goal for BIM and FM integration on this project was to minimize required manual data entry of FM data for the new buildings. Greg Meyer was responsible for creating a 10-year comprehensive facility plan for the campus that covered all aspects of facility renewal and replacement. Buildings categorized for renewal and replacement are still functioning and still operationally sound if the university addressed deferred maintenance needs.

Although Xavier and Messer knew BIM would play a significant role in the construction of these buildings, no specific BIM requirements were part of the contract documents. However, in future projects for the university, they will document the procedures used in these projects in their BIM deliverable guidelines and execution plan. Greg Meyer believes that the proper communication of FM data requirements will drive additional value in future projects.

CONTRACTS USED ON PROJECT

Xavier University chose the IPD-inspired method in order to complete the projects as quickly and efficiently as possible. IPD encourages all parties involved in the project to collaborate early so everyone has a full understanding of both the entire project and their specific deliverables. To select their subcontractors, Messer released a request for proposal (RFP) to a list of prequalified firms, including the mechanical, electrical, and fire protection subcontractors. The selected firms then held a contract with Messer. The subcontractor agreements were written as a design/build, shared profit. This incented the project team to reduce costs and timeframes because all parties equally shared the benefits of project cost savings. The design team, including the mechanical designer, structural engineer, and architect, were contracted directly by Xavier University but acted as a part of the design/build team throughout the project. (Chris Speier, Messer Construction Co., project manager, personal communication, April 17, 2012). As the construction manager for the project, Messer modeled the Central Utility Plant building, while Sheply Bullfinch, Richardson & Abbott provided models for the other three buildings; however, Xavier University owns the models, while Messer maintains them. While Xavier keeps their procurement methods confidential, one reason they chose Messer as their construction manager was the firm's record and expertise in BIM (Meyer interview).

IPD, in conjunction with BIM, helped the construction manager, owner, designers and key subcontractors to work together with one goal in mind, to deliver the best project for the least cost in the shortest time. Contractors suggested and used new construction techniques throughout the project, such as backfilling the underground pipe trenched with gravel and using these same trenches to create an under-drain system instead of digging separate trenches for under-drains. Constant communication between the designers and builders reduced the number of formal requests for clarification from above 50 percent over a project of similar size and complexity, and significantly reduced the time needed to approve product ordering. This in turn allowed them needed to order major equipment with long lead times at least three months earlier than expected, which reduced the risk of supply chain issues impacting the project schedule (Meyer interview).

DESCRIPTION OF PROJECT TEAM

The firms associated with the projects are summarized in Table 6.7. The team had minor variations on some of the buildings.

TABLE 6.7 Key Members of Project Team

Architects:	Main: Shepley Bulfinch Richardson and Abbott, Boston, MA
	Associate: Michael Schuster Associates, Cincinnati, OH
	Landscape: Brown Sardina, Inc.; Boston, MA
Engineers:	Structural: Steven Schaefer Associates, Inc., Cincinnati, OH;
	MEP AKF Engineers
	Civil: Kleingers & Associates, West Chester, OH
	Code: Rolf Jensen & Associates, Framingham, MA
Consultants:	Audio/Visual: Acentech, Cambridge, MA
	Architectural: Campbell-McCabe, Inc., Waltham, MA
	Geotechnical: Thelen Associates, Inc., Cincinnati, OH
Construction Manager:	Messer Construction Co., Cincinnati, OH
Commissioning Engineers:	Thermal Tech Engineering, Cincinnati, OH

MAJOR DESIGN INNOVATIONS AND THEIR IMPACT ON BUILDING LIFE CYCLE

Although BIM played an integral role in streamlining the design and construction of these buildings, it did not lead to any specific design innovations. Xavier used the project as a learning experience: testing the capabilities of BIM, obtaining a level of comfort with BIM tools and processes, and learning how they could use BIM to enhance future projects. In efforts slated for the next several years, Xavier will continue to use more of BIM's capabilities. This will include evaluating different design options and testing design innovations during the project's schematic and design development phases. This will help Xavier select the alternative that provides the best solution based on the requirements established during programming. As discussed in the Lessons Learned section of this case study, Xavier now understands that all parties on the project, especially the architectural firm and the general contractor, need to have BIM experience, which Xavier will require in all future contract documents (Meyer interview).

The university did not use BIM simulation tools to analyze energy usage, sustainability or other environmental aspects. However, Xavier will look more closely at using these tools in the future, especially given the new 20,000–square-foot Central Utility Plant that provides heating and cooling for the campus. This plant was built by Messer within the scope of this project. Also, as the university has generation capacity and distributes its own electricity campus-wide, Xavier wants to perform simulation and environmental impact studies as it constructs new buildings and renovates older ones. This will help the university better plan future capacity needs and better understand the financial impact of adding new buildings. Also, this will allow the FM department to estimate the cost savings seen from replacing outdated mechanical systems in the older buildings on campus. Energy simulation also becomes more important as the university has committed to follow LEED standards for future construction efforts on campus, and the results derived from energy simulation tools will forecast the results expected from these designs (Meyer interview).

The university was involved with the design of the building from programming until it was handed over to the facility team to operate and maintain. The specific team from the university included the users of the facilities. However, the facility maintenance staff was not involved during the design phase, which was a great loss because their input would have added valuable insight into the final designs of each of the buildings and avoided added costs (Meyer interview).

Since the buildings are new, there is limited data on how these buildings have performed to date. However, Xavier conducted a formal analysis that looked at this project along with the entire inventory of facilities owned and maintained by Xavier to help plan for the future. This analysis included the components of new construction efforts, reduction of deferred maintenance of existing buildings, and the ongoing renewal and replacement of Xavier's Central Utility Distribution plant. Specifically looking at its current inventory of buildings, Xavier wants to reduce the amount to be spent on the ongoing maintenance of its existing buildings, while also enhancing their Facility Condition Index (FCI). FCI measurement is a benchmarking process that Xavier uses to compare the relative condition of all campus facilities. To calculate a building's FCI, the total cost of all deferred maintenance and capital renewal projects for the facility is divided by its current replacement value. A low value for this index indicates that the facility is in better condition, while a high value indicates a building in worse condition. For example, if a building had only $1 million in total repair and replacement projects, but it would cost $50 million to replace the entire building, its FCI would be 0.02 and Xavier would consider the facility to be in good condition. Xavier has developed a 10-year plan to reduce its deferred maintenance from $110 million dollars to $37 million dollars in the 2021–2022 fiscal year. It will accomplish this goal through new construction efforts that will replace some of the existing underperforming buildings. This strategic plan will help decrease the FCI from 0.21 (poor) to 0.06 (good) (Meyer interview).

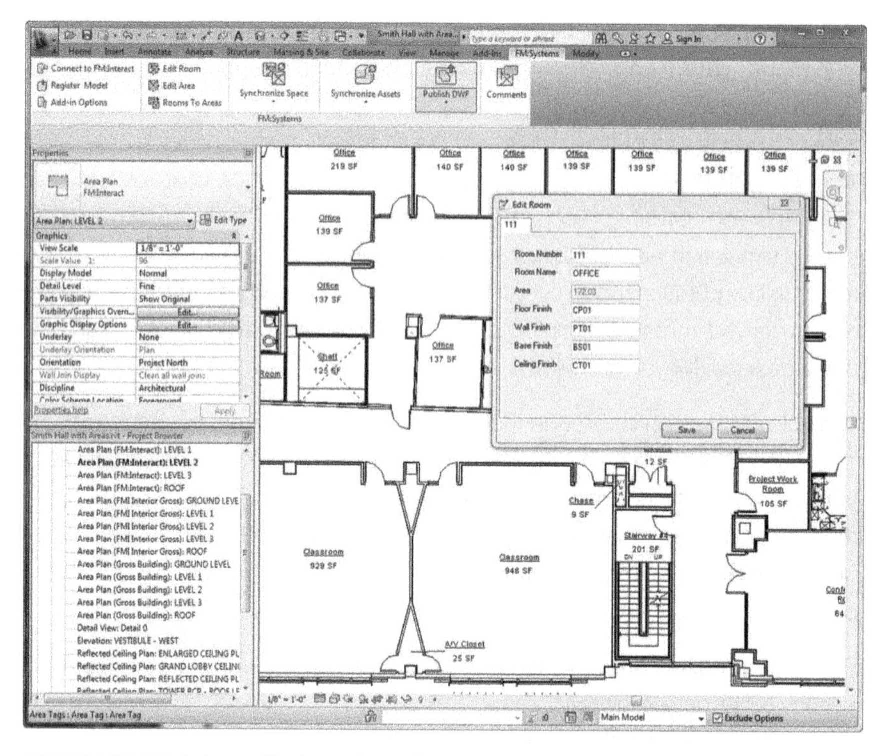

FIGURE 6.35 Link between 2D plan and room finish data for this space.
Courtesy FM:Systems

ROLE OF BIM IN SUPPORTING FM REQUIREMENTS

Messer is still in the process of connecting the models to the computer-aided facility management (CAFM) software, the FM:Interact Workplace Management Suite. This software is a workplace management product accessible via the Web that directly integrates with Revit. Revit users can synchronize room and area element data in Revit with the FM:Interact Space Management module. Figure 6.35 illustrates the link between a 2D floor view from the BIM and the room finish data for this space. Also, Revit users can synchronize any building component from the Revit models with the building systems data in the FM:Interact Facility Maintenance Module. Figure 6.36 illustrates how the flooring data can be integrated with the life-cycle data. As BIM data from design, construction, and renovations is input and updated, it is immediately synchronized with FM:Interact.

Xavier learned that BIM data entered for design and construction purposes can also be valuable for facility management. For example, Xavier's FM department spent two person-years collecting facility information to support its ten-year facilities plan. The facilities team walked through each building to identify the room finishes

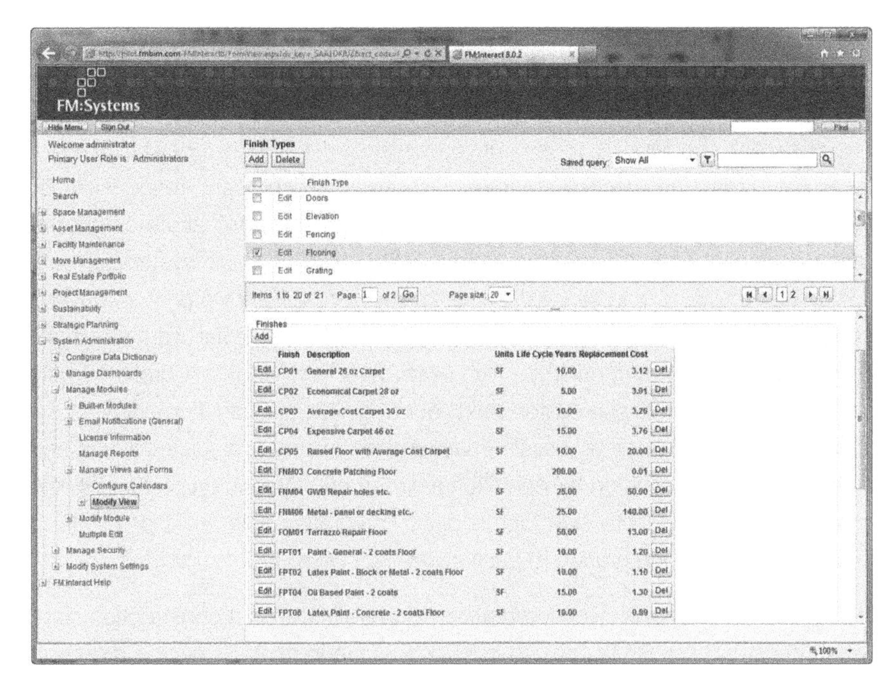

FIGURE 6.36 Link between flooring data and life-cycle data.
Courtesy FM:Systems

(floor finish, wall finish, etc.) used and to estimate the amount used and the installation date. Xavier then used that data to calculate the remaining useful life of the finish and estimate the replacement cost for its facilities plan. During construction, Xavier's FM department found that the architect had used Revit to document the finishes to be used in each room in order to communicate design intent to the contractor. As a result, Messer could synchronize this room data with FM:Interact. This allowed Xavier to avoid manually gathering and entering the finish data and saving an estimated person year of data gathering and manual calculations. (Greg Meyer)

However, because the BIM-FM integration process was started late in the project life cycle (postconstruction) and the subcontractors did not use a BIM solution that integrates with Revit, Xavier is still unsure of how much data Revit can provide and what data the FM department must enter manually into FM:Interact. Xavier believes that better documentation of FM data requirements and earlier involvement in the project life cycle will help them avoid even more data-entry effort. The connection between the two will allow for better space management, energy efficiency, preventative maintenance, reduction in cost for renovations and retrofits, and better life-cycle management (FM:Systems 2012).

There are still technical obstacles facing Xavier University. First, the university currently uses two different systems for facility management and maintenance management. The facility management team, responsible for space management, facility condition assessment, and planning campus renewal projects, uses FM:Interact as its CAFM system. The physical plant team, responsible for preventive maintenance and service requests, uses WebTMA as its computerized maintenance management system (CMMS). While a single system for both CAFM and CMMS would be ideal, Xavier implemented WebTMA prior to realizing the potential value of integrated BIM and FM workflows. Xavier wants to make these two systems communicate with each other and Revit. Integration would allow the two teams to share information about building assets. For example, the facilities team could see an asset's maintenance history and related costs and factor use that information for condition assessment. Integration of the systems may be achieved if TMA develops a direct integration with Revit or by using FM:Interact's Revit integration to pass asset data from Revit to TMA.

Another obstacle that slowed integration because of the post construction start, was converting the BIM's for use in Facility Management. Since the modeling has been completed, Messer has furnished Xavier with all of the as-constructed models for the buildings. For future projects, the facility management team will provide detailed requirements and participate early in the project lifecycle to avoid this step.

Third, at the start of the BIM-FM integration effort, neither Xavier nor Messer were familiar with the FM:Interact software. Xavier began its implementation of FM:Interact in 2011 and the system went live in 2012. As Messer integrates the BIM data with FM:Interact, the users will need to be trained on how to properly and efficiently use it. As its Revit integration is still fairly new, FM:Systems sponsored a BIM+FM Working Group in which Xavier and Messer participated. Messer is finding kinks as the integration progresses that require software vendor support (Meyer interview).

The integration of BIM data into FM:Interact is an ongoing process. With the new software for the facility management team, BIM will play a vital role in any FM requirements. FM:Interact is directly connected to Revit, so as the models are updated or errors fixed, the facility managers will be able to better manage the spaces involved. The major foreseeable challenge will be integrating TMA Systems with Revit and FM:Interact to enable one source for all the information. (Meyer interview).

TECHNOLOGY USED ON PROJECT

The Xavier University Hoff Academic Quad project team leveraged several software products in to successfully complete the project. The team put considerable thought into finding tools that could support the entire project life cycle, while also ensuring that each practitioner could effectively manage his/her project phase according to Xavier's expectations. Major considerations such as cost, availability, and familiarity of new technology played an important role in software selection. The key products selected for this project were Revit, Navisworks, and FM:Interact. Xavier purchased and implemented WebTMA prior to the software selection for this project. Revit and Navisworks assisted the contractor in project coordination, 2D drawing translation, and project status tracking; FM:Interact, a workplace management suite with strong BIM integration, served as the facilities management software, dealing with strategic planning and space management (Meyer interview).

Using BIM proved to be instrumental in integrating project documentation, sequencing activity across multiple construction disciplines, clash detection, design interpretation, change management, and facilities management. Leveraging these compatible technology products eased the exchange of information and provided the FM Department with accurate and complete as-constructed drawings (Meyer interview).

The upfront due diligence in selecting the BIM tools for the construction phase has been of great value to the entire project team. Basing the technology selection criteria on cost, availability, and familiarity facilitated easy adoption by the project team and owner alike. Most important, the selection process ensured that a well-thought-out approach to the project technologies was established, and the operations and maintenance considerations were addressed. There is strong reason to believe that the selection, implementation, and use of Revit, Navisworks, and FM:Interact led to the successful completion of this project (Meyer interview).

COLLABORATION

The collaboration for the Hoff Academic Quad Project was facilitated by Messer's Project Management and Collaboration software application.[4] This gave all key stakeholders the ability to share documentation and information, payment submission and management, external communication management, online bid entry, and many other important project communications. The emphasis on effective

[4] This software package is not integrated with BIM, but is described here because of its use on this project by the CM and others in the project team.

collaboration was evident in the ability for the owner to expedite the scheduling approach, without significantly impacting the coordination of the activities, payments, and documentation versioning (Meyer interview).

The ability to successfully collaborate with project stakeholders was extremely important, as many of the design teams were located out of town. Project teams would meet from three to four times a week during the peaks of the project to one to two times a month during lulls in the project. This meant that project team members needed to stay vigilant in the way they collaborated and disseminated information, as mistakes, miscommunications, and follow-ups would all be delayed if limited only to project meetings (Meyer interview). In general, the collaboration tools worked well on this project and allowed the project team to stay closely aligned.

LESSONS LEARNED

As with any large project, there are many lessons learned, which will help improve the management of future projects. From Xavier's perspective, the lessons learned from the construction of these four buildings included:

- Provide detailed BIM requirements in contract documents for all parties.
- Provide data standards to all parties at outset of project.
- Involve the facilities department in earliest phases of design.
- Require all project team members to use BIM workflows and methodologies.
- Use BIM and FM integration to gather data to support strategic facility goals.
- Use LEAN principles.

The first lesson was that all future contracts for general contractors, architects, and engineers will have specific BIM requirements. Although Xavier did not specify detailed BIM requirements in Messer's contract, Messer's extensive knowledge of BIM was invaluable to the success of this effort. Messer's team helped Xavier realize that the models were not only useful during construction, but would benefit them greatly when the facilities were turned over for operation and maintenance. As a result, Xavier's future contracts will have specific BIM conditions that each project participant will need to demonstrate. These will include an indication of how they use BIM, what documentation they will supply, and details from past experiences using BIM on similar projects. This requirement will become more important as additional data from all campus buildings is entered and stored in FM:Interact. Xavier's BIM requirements will help make sure the BIM documentation supplied by these parties can easily be integrated into their facility management systems. Also, they will want to make sure that the general contractor, architect, and engineers have the same level of experience with BIM and can properly use that tool to communicate issues and changes that will help shorten the project schedule and help find potential problems earlier in the project, so expensive cost overruns can be avoided (Meyer interview).

The second lesson learned was the need to provide details regarding the materials required by the university for use on all campus facilities and unique codes used to identify each material. At the start of the project, the architectural firm was not given the design standards and finish codes for exterior and interior materials and finishes. So the design documents were inaccurate and led to confusion among the parties about the specific materials to be used. Also, because the finish codes are used to join data from the Revit models with other information in the facility management system, the contractor had to take time to update models with the proper finish codes to make sure all project documentation was correct (Meyer interview).

The third lesson learned was that the FM staff should have been involved in the very earliest stages of the project. Their involvement in the programming activity could have provided valuable information, since they have the main responsibility of maintaining the exterior and interior of each facility, including the building envelope, roofing system, mechanical systems, landscape, and hardscape. Their input could have provided insight into why certain design elements would not work in the facility because of the procedures in place for maintaining these buildings. The FM staff is often overlooked as being a valuable stakeholder in the process, but their involvement is critical due to the fact that they have the major responsibility of managing the building during the building's life cycle (Meyer interview).

The fourth lesson learned was that all project team members should use BIM tools and workflows if possible. Because the subcontractors for key building systems (mechanical, electrical, plumbing, and fire protection) used a variety of different CAD-based tools, there was no clear workflow to get equipment data into Revit and then into FM:Systems. As a result, the capture and handover of some equipment data was an opportunity that was missed on this project. Xavier will address this issue in future projects as part of their more detailed BIM requirements and contracts.

The fifth lesson learned was that detailed BIM data can help facilities professionals achieve strategic goals. For Xavier, their strategic goal was to reduce deferred maintenance and improve the condition of facilities campus-wide. Xavier used BIM data entered for design and construction purposes to support their 100-year comprehensive facilities plan. This plan was critical in winning the support of the university administration to dramatically increase facilities funding.

Finally, a sixth lesson learned concerned the use of reverse phase scheduling and its value in expediting the schedule. Reverse phase scheduling involves creating a schedule that works backwards from the anticipated completion date. This makes deadlines harder to push back and creates more urgency among the project participants to complete their activities, particularly those on the critical path. If one subcontractor misses their deadline, it negatively impacts the schedule of those subcontractors that are dependent on the completion of that task. However, it makes the team members think of more creative solutions for those issues that could impact the project timeline, leading to more innovation (Meyer interview).

CONCLUSION

During the past few years, Xavier has been extremely active with several large capital projects to enhance its campus. The university has increased the size of the campus by 25 percent with the addition of Smith Hall, Conaton Learning Commons, Central Utility Plant, and Bishop Fenwick Place. The successful completion of the projects was a direct result of the partnership of Messer, Sheply Bulfinch, Richardson & Abbott, Michael Schuster Associates, and key internal departments within Xavier University.

Throughout design and construction, a wide range of both BIM and CAD-based tools were used to document the project. As its first BIM effort, Xavier worked with Messer and FM:Systems to better understand the value of BIM for the building life cycle. Not only did they learn how it enhanced design and construction, but how BIM data could be integrated into Xavier's CAFM and CMMS systems, to help improve the ongoing operation and management of their facilities. Although there is still some work ahead to realize the full value of integrating BIM and FM data, the university is already seeing benefits. Also, Xavier realizes the use of BIM will enhance future capital and renovation efforts, which will continue to become more complex due to sustainability, technology, and energy efficiency. Although it has not been an easy road for Xavier to embrace BIM, it has been a path that has greatly aided them on these efforts and will continue to aid them as they move forward with future construction projects.

ACKNOWLEDGMENTS

The Xavier University case study presented in these writings are the collective, collaborative, and direct effort of the following students from the graduate program in the School of Building Construction at Georgia Institute of Technology: Elijah

Afedizie, Rebecca Beatty, Erica Hanselman, Eric Heyward, Aisha Lawal, Eric Nimer, Laura Rosenthal, and Daryl Siman.

All findings, explanations, and conclusions of work were conducted under the guidance of Kathy Roper, associate professor. This case study was the final course requirement for demonstrating competence and integration of all topics covered in the Institute's Building Construction 6400: Facility Planning, Project Management and Benchmarking class. The entirety of the data used, facilities tour, and Q&A were generously provided by the Xavier FM staff. Most notably, Greg Meyer, Xavier University's assistant director for facilities assessment, contributed a great deal of his time, effort, expertise, and knowledge. Special thanks also to Chris Mealy of Messer. Marty Chobot of FM:Systems provided indispensable help in reviewing and clarifying this case study.

REFERENCES

FM:Systems. 2012. *The FM:Interact Building Information Modeling (BIM) Integration Component*, viewed April 12, 2012, www.fmsystems.com/products/bim_revit.html.

Xavier University. 2011. *Xavier University Facility Master Plan*, updated 2011.

Case Study 5: State of Wisconsin Bureau of Facilities Management, Division of State Facilities, Department of Administration

Angela Lewis, PE, PhD, LEED AP
Project Professional with Facility Engineering Associates

MANAGEMENT SUMMARY

The State of Wisconsin Bureau of Facilities Management, Division of State Facilities, Department of Administration, started implementing a BIM FM pilot program in 2011. This case study captures the processes and lessons learned of two of the four BIM FM pilot projects completed between 2011 and 2012. The first project is a residential hall on the University of Wisconsin River Falls (UWRF) campus. The primary phases of the life cycle captured were design and facility management. Thus, the main contributors to the BIM FM efforts were the WI Division of State Facilities, the UWRF facilities team, and SDS Architects. The second project is the Wisconsin Energy Institute, located on the University of Wisconsin Madison campus. The primary phases captured were construction and facility management. Thus, the main contributors to the BIM FM efforts were the Wisconsin Division of State Facilities and M. A. Mortenson Company.

The use of technology was important to both projects. Both projects used both 2D and 3D object-based parametric modeling software, as well as collaboration software and a computerized maintenance management system (CMMS). Autodesk Revit was the most commonly used 3D modeling software. Collaboration software used by the UWRF project included Submittal Exchange, LogMeIn, and an FTP site. The main collaboration software used by the Wisconsin Energy Institute project was Skier Unifier. Several processes to support collaboration on the Wisconsin Energy Institute were also performed, including the plan of the day, having a computer with a large monitor on the job site, and the use of a BIM protocol manual. A TMA Systems CMMS was used at UWRF, while AssetWorks was used on the UW Madison campus.

Comparing the two projects, it is clear that the members of the project team have a large impact on the information flows, availability of information for facility management from design through construction, and the format in which the information is handed over to the facility management team. Although many of the details between the two projects are different, the major challenges and most important lessons learned were similar. Major challenges for both projects included:

- The architecture and engineering design communities across the state of WI are still transitioning from 2D to 3D object-based parametric modeling software. Thus, the learning curve for how to use 3D object-based BIM parametric modeling software, as well as for understanding the value of linking information to object-based parametric models, is very steep.
- Communication across the different phases of the project life cycle is uncommon. Thus, many project team members were unfamiliar with the processes and vocabulary of other disciplines. In order for BIM FM to be implemented more effectively, it will be necessary to increase communication and understanding of the different phases of the project life cycle by designers, constructors, and facility managers.

Considering both projects, the most important lessons learned were:

- Well-written BIM FM specifications and guidelines are necessary for the facility management team to receive the information in a format that is most useful for FM. However, the development of such requirements is difficult when it is necessary to keep the requirements general enough that they can be applied across the entire state, while also being sufficiently specific to ensure that the information provided is of value.
- Each BIM FM project needs to have at least two champions, one who is either a member of the design or construction team and one who is a member of the facility management team. In the case of the residential hall, the architect served as one of the BIM champions, while the general contractor served as one of the BIM champions for the Wisconsin Energy Institute.

INTRODUCTION

The State of Wisconsin Bureau of Facilities Management, Division of State Facilities (DSF), Department of Administration, started implementing building information modeling on April 11, 2006, when Governor Jim Doyle signed Executive Order 145. The executive order (EO) required that all state buildings meet high environmental and energy efficiency standards. To meet the EO, integrated processes were to be used to conserve energy and improve the sustainability of capital projects. Early in adoption of the EO, the state realized that the use of BIM would be necessary to meet the EO requirements (Napier 2008).

BUREAU OF FACILITIES MANAGEMENT, DIVISION OF STATE FACILITIES (DSF), DEPARTMENT OF ADMINISTRATION

The DSF manages the state of Wisconsin's real estate portfolio, staffs the State of Wisconsin Building Commission, and provides facilities for all state programs through capital projects and leased space. Specific functions of the DSF include facilities planning, engineering services, real estate acquisition, architectural and engineering design, design and construction project supervision, energy management, heating plant fuel management, fuel procurement, building contract administration, and ensuring compliance with the Americans with Disabilities Act (ADA) in state buildings (DSF 2011).

The state of Wisconsin manages about 80 million square feet, which includes office buildings, laboratories, college campuses, and power plants, as well as various other building types used by 22 different state agencies and 13 University of Wisconsin campuses. Many of the facility management teams across the state have common needs, such as asset tracking, maintenance, and document management. However, the agencies have different levels of capacity and resources. Some facility management teams have a fully staffed facility management department, while other agencies may have a single facility management staff person who relies on consultants and other staff. The range of technologies used across the agencies spans from paper and pencil, spreadsheets, and sophisticated software applications (Beck 2011a).

AE BIM Guidelines and Standards

In June 2009, the DSF released a report about the current state of BIM technologies and recommendations for implementation (Napier 2009). The report summarizes what BIM is; provides an overview of why BIM is relevant to owner/operators, A/E designers, and constructors; and makes multiple recommendations for how BIM should be adopted and used by the state of Wisconsin. Recommendations and results of this report became the foundation for the state of Wisconsin "Building Information Modeling (BIM) Guidelines and Standards for Architects and Engineers," released July 1, 2009 (Napier 2009). The "Guidelines and Standards," as the name implies, contains information most relevant to architects, engineers, and constructors, such as the use of BIM authoring software, work effort and compensation schedule, and objectives for the use of BIM from predesign to construction close-out. Content that is most relevant to the use of BIM for FM includes IFC compliance, use of open standards for interoperability, and detailed lists of what elements should be modeled. The lists are specific to each discipline. For example, the HVAC system model should include, but is not limited to, equipment, distribution ductwork, diffusers, pipes greater than 2 inches (outside diameter), and clearances for access.

For space planning and management, the document states that BIM authoring software should be used to compare and validate the program requirements with the actual design solution. As a result, the assignable areas (ASF, assignable square feet) and nonassignable areas (NaSF, nonassignable square feet) data should be able to be automatically generated from the model.

During the bidding, construction, and A/E contract closeout phases, the models are to be updated to reflect as-built physical conditions. A full model is to be submitted at A/E contract closeout, which starts prior to substantial completion.

The "Guidelines and Standards" must be followed for all projects advertised or starting on or after July 1, 2009, that meet the following criteria:

- All construction (new and addition/alteration) with total project funding of $5 million or greater
- All new construction with total project funding of $2.5 million or greater
- All new addition/alteration with total project funding of $2.5 million or greater where the cost of the addition is 50 percent or more of total project funding

Projects that do not meet these criteria are encouraged, but not required, to follow the BIM guidelines and standards.

Mission and Vision of BIM FM

The mission of the DSF FM handover program is "to advance the quality, timeliness and cost-effectiveness of facility information" (Beck 2011a). The mission can be achieved through "the creation of a digital record of planning decisions, operational assumptions, design intentions, dates, costs, installed components, tests, potentially everything about the facility; the documentation of the information as it is created or becomes known; saving it in a useable, interoperable, searchable format, accessible by a variety of tools; and having all of it available on day-one of occupancy" (Beck 2011a). Although the program has been piloted by the Bureau of Facility Management within DSF, it is envisioned that the process can be adopted statewide for all state facilities.

The vision shared by all Wisconsin state agencies for BIM FM is timely access to accurate information. To work toward this vision, DSF plans to monitor developing technologies and methods used by other owners and incrementally develop policies and procedures to use new technologies. The state also acknowledges that to move towards the vision, cultural, business model, and legal changes will be necessary (Beck 2011a).

2.3 Transitions

As with many other public and private organizations seeking to implement BIM FM, many transitions in current processes are necessary. A few specifically relevant to DSF include:

- Changing mind-sets from project-centric to asset-centric information
- Moving from paper-based processes and documents to digital processes and documents
- Changing the perspective of team members to see themselves as part of an overall team process, not just part of their immediate coworkers and colleagues
- Collaborative knowledge building and information development that will result in new delivery models
- Increasing need for knowledge and comfort levels using computers

Across the DSF, some of the resistance to transition to digital documents and processes is due to lack of familiarity with computers and concerns about the security of data on computers. To overcome these challenges requires providing team members with the opportunity to use the new technologies and helping them to understand the additional cost, inefficiency, and risk of continuing to use paper-based processes and documents. These challenges are greatest across building operators and maintenance mechanics.

OVERVIEW OF TWO PILOT PROJECTS

By mid-2012, four pilot BIM FM projects were completed or were in final stages of completion. The four projects included two academic buildings, a residence hall at a university, and a state laboratory. The two projects discussed within this chapter are a residence hall located on the University of Wisconsin River Falls (UWRF) campus in River Falls, Wisconsin, and the Wisconsin Energy Institute, located in Madison, Wisconsin (Figure 6.37). The projects were selected from 20 possible projects, considering:

- Projects should be spread across multiple state agencies, BIM platforms, CMMS software, various AE firms, and construction contractors.
- Project team was already using the 2009 AE BIM Guidelines.
- Team members, including architects, engineers, contractors, and local facilities teams were willing to support the project.

FIGURE 6.37 Map of state of Wisconsin showing locations of pilot BIM FM projects.

- Building or campus where the building would be located already had a CMMS in place.
- Building was part of the current construction schedule.

The purpose of the pilot projects is to help define the requirements for BIM FM handover. Some of the items that need to be determined and verified include (Beck 2011b):

- What should be included in the BIM deliverables
- How the information should be delivered
- Development of methods
- How BIM can be used as an as-built facility management tool

The goals of each pilot project were to (Beck 2011b):

- Extract all available data from the construction BIM to evaluate if and how it could be used for facility management
- Use standards whenever possible
- Import data into CMMS
- Import data into space and/or maintenance management system
- Complete the pilots at the lowest cost possible, as the projects selected for the BIM FM pilots were already in progress, and little funding within the existing budgets was available to support the BIM FM efforts

As the scope of each pilot project was formed, teams had the option to use one or more of the following:

- COBie
- IFC exports
- Third-party processing of data

During the first three BIM FM projects, the DSF was unclear about COBie compliance and how it aligned with design stages of a project, and thus, COBie was not used. Specifically, it was unclear if the facility management software the pilot projects had was compliant with COBie. The use of IFC exports appeared to be part of standard BIM platforms, and exports from current models seemed easy to obtain. However, the format and large amount of data available resulted in some challenges. To overcome these challenges, IFC data was imported in a piece-by-piece fashion. As the IFC import process was understood, it was possible for DSF to use the same process on future projects. Third parties were not used to process the data (Beck 2011a).

The use of pilot projects was extremely helpful because defining the requirements and determining the processes and technologies to use included many unknowns. Some of the unknowns included:

- Equipment lists
- Equipment properties
- Data formats and file types
- Data management processes, including consideration for different processes, knowledge levels, and software platforms across multiple agencies
- Data import processes, including consideration for different processes, knowledge levels, and software platforms across multiple agencies
- Methods of data exchange

As the pilot projects were completed, the definition of an ideal pilot project emerged:

- Well-developed A/E BIM model.
- Contractor BIM model, with details, is available.
- Technologically savvy owner agency.
- Owner agency has software to import the data.
- All team members willing to participate and realize that the team would be working through a new process.

After the series of pilot projects is complete, the composite findings will be used to update the AEC BIM Guidelines and create Contractor BIM Requirements (issued in July, 2012, and available at www.doa.state.wi.us/dsf/masterspec_view_new .asp?catid=61&locid=4). A BIM for FM Guideline will be issued at a later date.

PILOT 1: RESIDENTIAL HALL AT UNIVERSITY OF WISCONSIN AT RIVER FALLS

The University of Wisconsin at River Falls (UWRF) campus is located on a 226-acre site in northwestern Wisconsin. Founded in 1874, UWRF was initially a state normal school to train rural teachers. Today, enrollment is around 7,000 students annually, with about 40 percent of students living on campus.

The residence hall discussed within this case study is located on the east side of the UWRF campus (Figure 6.38). The project kickoff to start the design of the building occurred in October 2009, while construction started in March 2011. The building is anticipated to open July 2012. The 82,000 gross square foot building will house 240 residents and also provide space for a single-story living learning center. The four-story residential area of the building is divided into 12 residential pods. There are two styles of pods, one of which is ADA compliant. Eleven of the pods have 12 bedrooms, typically two students per room. Each pod includes a lounge with kitchen, several showers, toilets, and sinks. Each floor of the residence hall includes

FIGURE 6.38 Exterior rendering of residential hall.
Courtesy SDS Architects

a main lobby with a study and laundry facilities. One pod houses mechanical rooms and two apartments for full-time staff members. One of the staff members lives in the building to provide support for half of the residential buildings on the campus.

The approved project budget was $18.9 million dollars. The construction bid came in under budget, allowing 16 solar thermal panels to be installed, instead of only 6, which were initially included in the construction bid. To adjust for more time being spent at earlier phases of the design, minor adjustments were made to the compensation process for BIM-based project delivery.

The living learning center will function as a conference center with flexible multipurpose rooms that can seat up to 150 people. The living learning center has a commercial kitchen that will be used to support catering and special events within the building. The living learning center interior features wood beams and limestone finishes and is served by a single air handling unit.

The penthouse contains an air handling unit to provide ventilation air for the residence halls, and also water storage tanks for the solar thermal hot water system used for domestic water heating. To control heating and cooling systems, a Johnson Controls Metasys building automation system was installed. A Metasys system was installed because it is the primary BAS vendor used on campus.

Heat for the building is provided by the campus high-pressure steam system. The high-pressure steam is reduced to low-pressure steam and then circulated through a heat exchanger to generate hot water for the building. The heating water is supplied to fan coils, VAV boxes, reheat coils, unit heaters, and fin tube radiation. Cooling is provided by the campus chiller plant. Ventilation air is provided by a dedicated outdoor air unit that serves both the living learning center and the residence hall. A VAV recirculating air handling unit is located on the first floor to meet the space conditioning requirements for the living learning center. Within the residence hall, four-pipe fan coil units with unit-mounted controls condition the air in each room. Additionally, the building has operable windows to allow for natural ventilation.

A small solar thermal system was installed to supplement the domestic hot water as an energy savings measure. The system was designed to include up to 51 panels. However, as stated earlier only 16 were installed initially. As it is anticipated the remaining panels will be installed, the mounting infrastructure has already been put in place (Figures 6.39 and 6.40).

The structural system for the entire building is load-bearing concrete masonry rain screen wall construction with a brick exterior and precast concrete floor planks for floors two to four. A brick and limestone exterior was selected to match the other

FIGURES 6.39 (top) and 6.40 (bottom) Solar thermal system with mounting infrastructure for additional panels; close up of solar thermal panel.

Courtesy SDS Architects, Inc.

buildings on campus. The interior walls of the building were constructed of concrete masonry, steel studs with gypsum board, decorative wood and metal panels, and limestone.

Sustainable Aspects of the Building

The project is anticipated to be certified as U.S. Green Building Council Leadership in Energy and Environmental Design for New Construction (LEED-NC) Silver, but may be able to achieve Gold under LEED Version 3. Some of the LEED features include building commissioning and storm water retention.

Addressing stormwater management was an important part of the project. During the construction of an adjacent building completed several years prior to the new residence hall, only minimal design and construction was included to manage storm water. Thus, with the increased amount of impervious surfaces, it was necessary to include a significant amount of stormwater management infrastructure within the project, to prevent localized flooding after large rain events. The design included constructing several swales to retain water (Figure 6.41).

FIGURE 6.41 Swales to help manage storm water flow rates.

Courtesy SDS Architects, Inc.

Contract Structure and Project Team

The project used a typical design/bid/build contract structure (Figure 6.42). Micron Construction Co., Inc., based out of Neenah, Wisconsin, served as the general contractor. The architect was SDS Architects, based in Eau Claire, Wisconsin. The mechanical, electrical, and plumbing (MEP) design team was KJWW Engineering Consultants, based out of Madison, Wisconsin. The architect was a large contributor to the BIM FM efforts. The MEP designers used Revit, but not to its full capacity. The general contractor did not use BIM on the construction site, but would periodically request BIM files to generate shop drawings. Thus, the construction contractor delivered 2D drawings.

SDS Architects started using Autodesk Revit in early 2000, partially because it was required by the state of Wisconsin. Today, Revit is the office standard for design. Thus, the process of designing the residential hall was not different from non-BIM FM projects. The design process included:

- Drawing the main building components as a 3D object-based parametric model that defined the shape, volume, and usable area for occupants within the building and locations of MEP equipment
- Entering information into the schedules directly in Revit

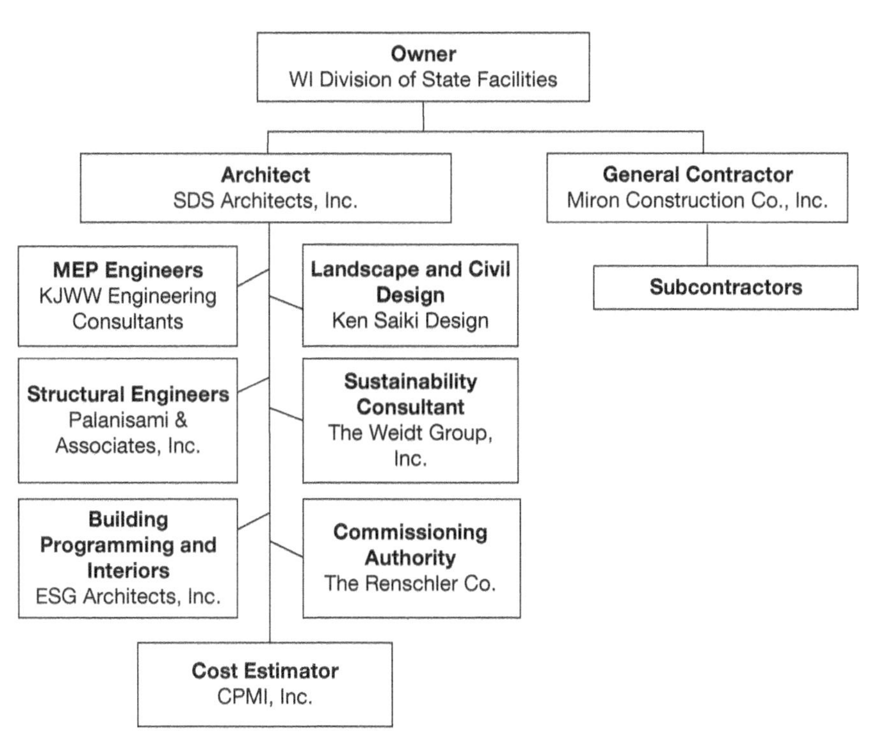

FIGURE 6.42 Design/bid/build contract structure with key stakeholders identified.

Thus, the information included within the BIM was driven by the type of information required to generate the schedules. For example, windows as a component were scheduled, but not the glass within the windows. Additionally, performance criteria, such as U-values and R-values, to calculate the heating and cooling loads were not entered into the BIM.

Revit is still evolving as a tool for use by all design disciplines, with Revit MEP developed after Revit for architecture. This resulted in MEP designers adopting Revit after some architects were already fluent with the software. One of the challenges of using Revit architecture and Revit MEP is that it is necessary to understand how to automatically generate schedules from the model. The model and schedules are linked. Thus, information, both text and dimensions, can be entered by the designers in either the model or the schedules. When information is included within Revit, it can be exported as an IFC, allowing the data to transfer to the CMMS. In contrast, if the schedule information is typed into an Excel file and pasted into the Revit file, it cannot be exported to upload within the CMMS. Although the architects generated their schedules automatically, the MEP designers created their schedules using Excel files and pasted them into Revit.

During the design of the building, the campus planner served as the point of contact for UWRF with the architect. Once the project reached 90 percent complete construction documents, the campus planner turned the project over to the UWRF facilities team. The facilities team managed the project through the end of construction. After construction, the project was turned over to UWRF FM.

Commissioning

The commissioning process was monitored by the architect, using a Web-based file management software program, Submittal Exchange, sold by a division of Textura Corporation. The primary purpose of Submittal Exchange is to track the submittal process between disciplines during construction. This includes the management of shop drawings and submittal forms.

Submittals are generated as PDFs and stored as a series of logs. Instead of using a paper-based process that can take two to three days to complete to mail the submittal, redline it five times (as five hard copies are required) and mail it back; the process is done completely electronically, including stamping drawings. In many cases the electronic process can be completed in less than half a day. In addition to saving a significant amount of time in sending the submittals to the respective trade, it greatly reduces the amount of paper used, and allows the redline process to be completed more quickly because only one copy needs to be generated.

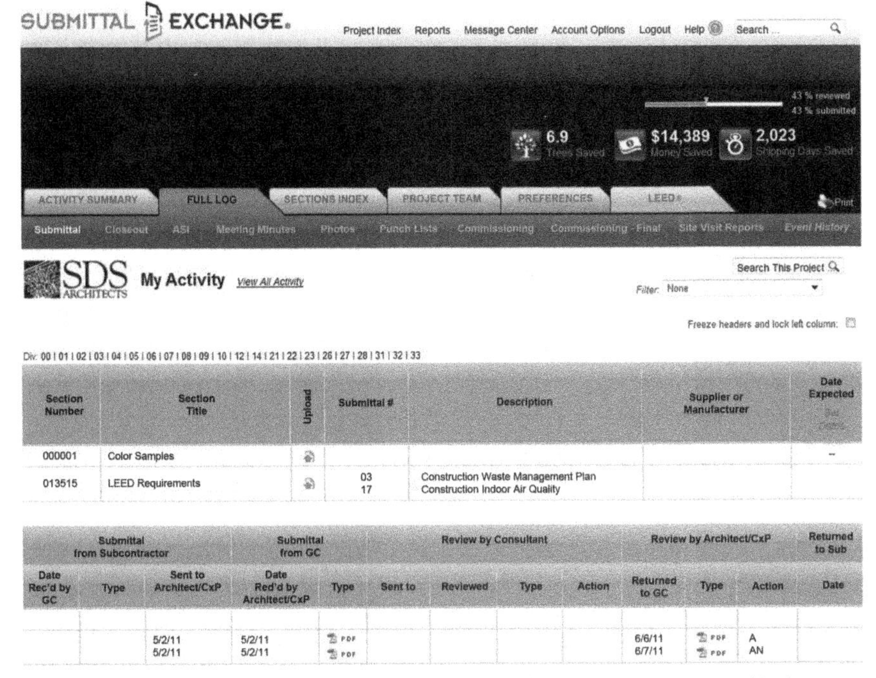

Image altered to fit printed page. Actual log is a continuous row, as opposed to two stacked rows.

FIGURE 6.43 Screenshot of Submittal Exchange software.
Courtesy SDS Architects and Submittal Exchange

As shown in Figure 6.43, the software quantifies the total cost, paper, and days of shipping saved from its use. Additionally, the figure shows key sections of the log management process, including the title of the submittal section, submittal number, submittal description, key dates, and the path of the the submittal through the process. The key dates, which correspond to the submittal process, include the date the submittal was received by the general contractor, date sent to the architect or commissioning agent, date sent to the consultant, date reviewed by the architect, and date returned to the general contractor.

In order for a project team to use Submittal Exchange, the project administrator sets up the project so that all team members who processed submittals have access to the system. For the residence hall project, design consultants, construction contractors, and their subcontractors had access to Submittal Exchange. When one member of the team uploads a submittal for review by another team member, an email is automatically generated to notify the team member that a submittal needs to be reviewed. To process the submittal, drawings are marked up electronically.

BlueBeam PDF Revu or Adobe Acrobat was used as a markup tool. To help indicate which discipline or trade marked up the drawing, different colors were used. The architect used red, while the general contractor used blue. To keep the submittals organized, each submittal was named using the submittal number. However, considering the life cycle of the information, it was determined during the project that the naming convention that is most helpful to the design and construction team may not be equally useful to the facility management team. After construction is complete, submittal numbers are less significant. However, since this was the naming structure used during design and construction, it was also the naming structure used when delivering as-built information to the facility management team on a memory stick. A key lesson learned from this process is that if the facility management team wants electronic content delivered using a specific format and indexing scheme, it is important to clearly determine this early in the project, so it can be used across the project life cycle.

Submittal Exchange was also used to manage the commissioning documentation. Because the construction verification forms were organized by the construction subcontractors, the goal of the facilities team was for the information to be organized into folders by CSI specification section. Additionally, each file was to be placed in a folder and labeled with the equipment tag number. This would allow the construction documentation to be turned over to the facility management team in an organized manner to support linking the construction data to equipment records within the CMMS.

Although the contractors agreed to place the documentation into folders by specification section, the files were not labeled as requested because this requirement was not clearly stated within the project requirements. Although the information was not as organized as desired, the UWRF FM team concluded that what was provided was better than what is often provided at the end of many construction projects: a memory stick with the available construction information in a single, unsearchable PDF.

One challenge encountered was the collection of commissioning data for equipment that required sign-offs by multiple trades, due to the structure of the construction verification forms and numbering structure provided by the state. For example, commissioning a pump required sign-off from the mechanical, electrical and plumbing subcontractors on the same form. The use of a single form to collect all three signatures was cumbersome and difficult to coordinate. Therefore, the architect worked with the state to create separate sign-off forms for each trade, resulting in multiple sign-off sheets per piece of equipment. The lesson learned in this process was that the more granular the data needed for facility management, the more construction verification forms were required.

One of the limitations of some of the PDFs generated during the commissioning process was that the PDF form was printed out, filled out by hand in the field, scanned, and then uploaded as a new PDF. Although the information was captured electronically, it was not in a searchable format. The PDFs generated were delivered from the commissioning process to the facility management team on a memory stick. In order for the PDFs to be uploaded to the CMMS, each needed to be manually reviewed and attached to a CMMS record.

Two lessons learned from the commissioning efforts were:

- In the next version of the BIM guidelines, requirements to name PDFs by equipment tag number need to be clearly stated.
- The contractors' primary focus is to build the building and install the systems, not document management. Therefore, changes in the contractors' management efforts will be needed to improve the quality of the construction documentation received. Specific change management practices will include helping contractors to understand the value of handing over information in a format that is useful and searchable by the facility management team, as opposed to binders and rolls of drawings or a single, unorganized PDF with all of the project documentation.

Team Collaboration

During design, the team collaborated through face-to-face workshops, design team meetings, GoToMeetings, and electronic data and file exchange methods, such as the use of an FTP site and Submittal Exchange. Additionally, LogMeIn remote access software was used to coordinate the design between the architect and the interior designer. The architect and interior designer both needed to work simultaneously in the architectural model and physically did not work in the same office. The architect installed LogMeIn on a computer in the architect's office so the interior designer could log in remotely to work the architect's Revit model. Although this worked very well for the architect and interior designer, this level of coordination with all disciplines would cause the model to be very large, decreasing the speed at which it can run on a computer. Therefore, the team set up individual models for each of the other design disciplines. These models were referenced back to a central model.

Facility Management Systems

The primary software systems used by the facility management team to manage information are the TMA Systems CMMS and the Johnson Controls Metasys building automation system. TMA Systems was selected as the CMMS because it met the needs of the campus and is also used by many other state of Wisconsin agencies. The CMMS is used to manage work orders, track preventive maintenance, assign charge backs, manage inventory, and run reports. The inventory module of the CMMS allows parts used to complete a work order to be automatically deducted from the computer-based inventory system. Work orders are generated to perform time-based preventive maintenance and customer service calls. All work orders are tracked and stored in a database. Currently, work orders are completed by technicians using a paper-based process. At the end of the day, the work orders are turned in to the human resources department, which enters the information into the CMMS. Although the benefits of transitioning to an electronic work order management process are recognized, it is first necessary to help the technicians gain a better understanding of and comfort level with using computers. To do this, the human resources department is transitioning the time reporting and requesting leave processes from paper to electronic.

Equipment records within the CMMS include floor-scrubbing machines, elevators, door alarms, motor starters, air handling units, air compressors, backflow preventers, and pumps. Equipment records include equipment tag number, description, location ID, and maintenance priority code. In some cases, the equipment model number is also included. Within the CMMS, charge backs are used to track the cost of maintenance work for a project on campus that was built and operated using program revenue, as opposed to state tax dollars. Residence halls are one example of a UWRF facility funded by program revenue.

All equipment records are classified by an equipment type. Equipment type classifications include:

- Architectural
- Building miscellaneous
- Chiller/cooling tower
- Compressed air
- Controls and instruments
- Custodial
- Electrical
- Elevators
- Emergency generators
- Fire or safety
- Grounds
- Grounds equipment
- HVAC
- Heating equipment
- Heating plant
- Kitchen/walk-in coolers
- Locks and door openers
- Meters
- Miscellaneous
- Motor pool fleet
- Plumbing
- Pool
- Roofs
- Testing

A Dean Evans and Associates event management system is used to manage space and schedule events on campus. Although the FM team is starting to consider how the event management system could be linked to the BAS to help schedule when buildings should be heated and cooled, each system is currently used as a stand-alone system.

BIM Handover from Construction to FM

The BIM handover process from construction to facility management is highly dependent on the structure of the data requested by the FM team and the type of information within the BIM. This will be illustrated in the following sections.

Export from Revit to IFC

The first part of the handover process was for the design team to update the drawings to create as-built drawings. Data was gathered from RFIs, construction bulletins, and change orders to update the graphical parts of the drawing set. The submittals and shop drawings were provided to the facility management team to document equipment that was installed. Equipment schedules were not updated to include as-built information. Although this is possible, it was not part of the contract requirements.

The second part of the handover process was that the architect delivered IFC file exports from Revit to the facility management team. Generating an IFC is very similar to saving an MS Word file as a PDF; it is just a matter of selecting the desired file format. One IFC file was generated for the entire project. The exports were generated as flat files and delivered to the FM on a memory stick. The IFC file was then processed using a SQL database to extract object types from the file. The file processing takes several hours to complete, and requires a computer with a large amount of memory, such as a PC with a quad core processor with 8GB of memory running on a 64-bit Microsoft 7 operating system. It was determined that processing small portions of the data was helpful so that the information could be reviewed to determine what was most useful.

The third part of the handover process was to review the data that was included within the model, and determine if the data could be used and the quality of the data. The first level of the data review required someone knowledgeable about building systems because large portions of the data were not uniformly labeled and not labeled in a manner that identified the equipment by type. For example, two of the objects from the model were labeled "A. O. Smith_Commercial Gas" and "KJWW_FP-BFP_DC 2.5-10 Inch." Although it is possible to deduce from the vendor name, A. O. Smith, that the first object is a commercial gas water heater, the nomenclature of the second name is much less clear. A larger sample of object names is found in Figure 6.44.

'Fire Pump-6×8:6×8 Fire Pump:6
'Floor Drain – Round:5" Strain
'Floor Drain – Round:HD-2:HD-2
'Floor Drain – Round:MB-1:MB-1
'Generic Duplex Water Softener
'Inline Pump:1.5":1.5":1213707
'Inline Pump:1.5":1.5":2277361
'Inline Pump:1.5":1.5":3128613
'Inline Pump:1.5":1.5":3194595
'KJWW_B & G ROLAIRTROL Air Sep
'KJWW_B & G SU Heat Exchanger-
'KJWW_Balancing Damper – Recta
'KJWW_Balancing Damper – Round
'KJWW_Cab Heater-Horizontal Re
'KJWW_Circiut Setter 0.5-2 Inc
KJWW_Circulation Pump-High He

FIGURE 6.44 Sample of object names from mechanical system IFC export.
Courtesy KJWW Engineering Consultants

To overcome the lack of standardization with the naming of equipment, it is anticipated that the equipment data types will be defined for future projects to support the use of a standard naming convention.

After a general understanding of what type of data was provided, it was necessary to determine if the data could be used. Two additional criteria that needed to be evaluated were:

- How can the data be used?
- Will using the data save time?

To answer these two questions, it was necessary to review the data from both an information technology (IT) and an FM perspective. The IT perspective was important to determine if the data could be uploaded into the CMMS, and if so, if the uploading would take less time, even if large amounts of time were required to clean up the data, compared to manual entry of the data. The FM perspective was important to determine what data is needed for maintenance activities, such as work orders and preventive maintenance.

In order for the data from the BIM to be uploaded smoothly when using a TMA systems CMMS, it is important that the equipment and room types be clearly defined. The types provide a structure of how the data is imported in the CMMS. The BIM data received for equipment was not very clean; thus, it required some manual entry of data. Additionally, it was necessary to create some crosswalks to align the naming conventions used.

Use of Submittal Data for FM

As previously stated, the resulting file format of the submittals was PDFs. It was understood by both the architect and the facility management team that the PDFs could be attached to equipment records within the CMMS. However, as stated, to match equipment records within the CMMS with PDFs of submittals, it is necessary to review each individually, as the PDFs are named using the submittal number.

Information from the BIM

Information from the BIM that was determined to be useful for facility management included room numbers, room area, department that uses the room, door, and door hardware. (See Figure 6.45 for a sample of this information.) The foundational information from the BIM is the room numbers and names. Having this information provides a structure to assign equipment to a location.

The locations of the doors assigned to the adjacent rooms within the BIM were found to be useful to help identify equipment locations. Although door hardware information is not the most frequently used information for preventive maintenance,

Element ID	Room Number	Area	Department	Name
#79462	'100'	1416.96	'CIRCULATION'	'CORRIDOR'
#79190	'100A'	111.40	'COMMON SPACE'	'VEST'
#79311	'100B'	98.42	'COMMON SPACE'	'VEST'
#81146	'100C'	341.30	'CIRCULATION'	'CORRIDOR'
#78879	'100D'	368.78	'CIRCULATION'	'CORRIDOR'
#79914	'101'	498.46	'MISC.'	'LOUNGE'
#277	'102'	1164.16	'MISC.'	'MULTI-PURPOSE'
#80635	'102A'	25.57	'COMMON SPACE'	"
#80082	'103'	308.51	'MISC.'	'MULTI-PURPOSE'
#80200	'104'	927.71	'MISC."	MULTI-PURPOSE'
#80756	'104A'	25.57	'COMMON SPACE'	"
#80352	'105'	134.88	'MISC.'	'MULTI-PURPOSE'
#80465	'106'	936.43	'MISC.'	'MULTI-PURPOSE'
#39317	'106A'	526.53	'SERVICE AREAS'	'STORAGE'

FIGURE 6.45 Excerpt of room data information.
Courtesy SDS Architects, Inc.

it is useful for performing preventive maintenance on automated door openers, to provide detailed records of door hardware if a component needs to be replaced and to help populate the key management module within the CMMS. Although the BIM included some detailed door information, some of the door information, such as the lockset information, was only included in the specifications. Within the BIM, the information in the specifications was assigned to each door, using a schedule. However, the codes used to represent a lockset type are only useful if the lockset schedule is available. This resulted in an important lesson learned: it is important to specify the equipment types that should have the BIM objects populated with information. The equipment types that are likely of most value are HVAC, plumbing systems, and elevators because the most preventive maintenance is performed on these equipment types.

The largest benefit of having the information from the BIM is so that technicians, supervisors, and purchasing agents can use the information. Having the information within the CMMS will reduce time spent performing administrative tasks and increase staff efficiency because data will be more readily available.

Although some of the data from the BIM was useful, some of the data were either not useful for facility management, missing, or were default values that would need to be deleted to prevent importing of incorrect data into the CMMS. For example, the air flows for the air handling units were generally not listed. Although the state had asked for the MEP equipment schedules to be created from the Revit model, this was not done. Instead, the MEP schedules were created using standard methods.

When using information from the BIM, it is also important to clearly determine if the information in the model is the basis of design information or as-built information. It is very common for the piece of equipment or component installed to be from a different vendor than the one that was used for the basis of design. Given this difference, it is necessary to determine what information should be entered into the BIM, when, and to require that the information entered reflect as-built conditions accurately.

CMMS Test Site

A very important part of understanding how the data could be used and how it could be imported into the existing CMMS was to have a test site. Although the information from the BIM would eventually be stored in the same database as the other asset information, it was necessary to first evaluate it using a test site. A test site, sometimes also called a sandbox, is a mirror image of the CMMS database that can be used to try new processes and methods to use the data without making undesired changes to the actual database. Although a test site is not difficult to set up, managing the test site and determining what to test require the understanding of data management processes and the desire to experiment with new processes and data use methods.

Streamlining the Process of Building Turnover

When a building is turned over to the maintenance staff, if BIM has not been used, it is necessary for one or more maintenance staff members to spend a significant amount of time in the building, identifying each piece of equipment, determining if preventive maintenance should be performed on it, and putting a tag on it. If some of the information about the equipment is available within the BIM, this process can be completed much faster because some of the information determined during the walk-through can be completed ahead of time. Although floor plans can be used to help plan the walk-through, the use of floor plans is very time-consuming, and they may not be in a format that aligns with the CMMS.

Information within the BIM

The goal of the pilot project was to determine what data would be provided by the architect, engineers, and construction contractors. Thus, specific requirements about what data to include in the model were intentionally not specified. This allowed the facilities team to understand what the A/E and contractors were willing and able to provide. At the time this case study was written, the facility management team thought that if detailed lists of required data to support BIM FM were provided to the design and construction teams, the requested information would not be provided. This conclusion was drawn because the facility management team's perspective of the industry was that the procedures necessary to collect and organize the requested data were not currently in place.

For future projects, it is anticipated that a list of specific equipment types will be requested. Although the level of detail required for all equipment types will not be specified, having the data provides the opportunity to determine what information is useful for facility management. Thus, the state prefers to get more data than what will actually be used, because it is easier to delete data than to collect it in the field.

BIM Data Ownership

The state contracts document that the state owns the BIMs and the information within them. The state has found that ownership of the BIM has not been an area of resistance; instead, liability for the accuracy of the model is of greater concern. This has resulted in an increased number of legal agreements between the A/E and the construction contractors. When BIMs are transferred from the architect to contractors, it is important that it be clear whether the information in the BIM is the basis of design or what is actually installed in the building.

At this point in the implementation of BIM FM, the primary benefit is the data from the model. Although the 3D model will be very valuable for any future remodeling or renovation efforts, the 3D model will not be updated over the life of the building. In the event of a renovation, the 3D model would be given to the A/E. It is anticipated that providing this model would reduce the amount of field time required to document as-built conditions. Additionally, the 3D models are anticipated to be useful for understanding how a potential change will look, and they can be shared with individuals who are not familiar with reading floor plans and elevations. Thus, the BIM is really seen as a one-time hand-off process between construction and facility management. After the construction data is handed off, it will be maintained in the CMMS—not the BIM.

Characteristics of a Good Pilot Project

When evaluating various projects, characteristics that made UWRF a good pilot project included:

- The FM team was interested in participating in the effort.
- The CMMS IT manager was interested in the project and open to new ideas.
- Architecture and engineering BIM were available in Revit.
- The Submittal Exchange software provided an opportunity to structure the data collected from the construction and commissioning processes.

Owner Education Requirements

As this project was a pilot, the processes and methods used were learned through trial and error and thinking outside of the box how to do something new. For future projects, it will be necessary to provide training to help members of the facility management team understand how to capture and process the data.

Metrics

Although the facilities team did not formally quantify possible time savings from having data within the CMMS to use when performing preventive maintenance, it is estimated that time savings will be significant. For example, a plumber was looking for information about a part from 1976. Although the manual was available as a hard copy, to order the part, it was necessary for the plumber to work with a facilities team member who understood how to use the scanner to send the information to the vendor. The scanning process alone took 30 minutes. If the document had already been available electronically, 30 minutes would have been saved. Because technicians often prefer to fix things, as opposed to searching for information, having the information available electronically will reduce the time spent searching for information—increasing wrench time.

Lessons Learned and Challenges

As demonstrated through the case study, it is necessary for both the design and FM teams to work together towards a common goal of using BIM for FM. Thus, it is important to highlight some lessons learned that are relevant to designers, facility managers, and both stakeholder groups.

Three key lessons learned that directly impacted designers included:

- The design community sees Revit as a graphics tool, not an information tool. Thus, in order for BIM FM to be further implemented, it will be necessary for Revit to be seen as both a graphics and an information tool.
- As the use of BIM for FM evolves, the role of the architect will be impacted. The architect may be required to manage more information and provide data entry services.
- One of the challenges of learning a 3D modeling software program is that it requires a different thinking process than 2D CAD, which requires thinking about each part of the building as a line between two points. However, to correctly model an object in 3D requires knowing the start and end point of each line, as well as the height and information about the properties of the object. For example, adding a wall in a 3D modeling program requires knowing the length, height, and thickness of the wall, as well as what the wall is made of. At schematic design, it is more challenging using 3D modeling software because the project requirements are in the process of being defined.

Key lessons learned for facility management include:

- As more data becomes available for technicians to use, it will be necessary to implement a change management plan to demonstrate how the data can be used, where to find the data, and basic computer skills training.
- Naming of information across the project life cycle is important so that it can be understood by stakeholders as the information is handed over from construction to facility management.
- It is important to have a CMMS test site to understand the value of BIM information and determine how to use it most effectively.

Lessons learned that impact both designers and facility managers include:

- It is important to be open to new ideas and doing things differently. There are a lot of possible ways to use BIM, but it takes time to figure out what they are.
- To use COBie within the project, it was suggested that it would have been necessary to adopt it very early in the process. As the design team was not familiar with

COBie, it would have first been necessary for team members to gain a working knowledge of this open information exchange standard.

- Populating the data into the model is challenging because there is a lack of standard families to populate the model quickly and consistently.
- Architects and designers use equipment information as a basis of design that is not necessarily from the same vendor as the equipment installed. Thus, it is necessary to determine what level of detail information should be provided at the end of design, within construction documents and the as-built models.

Summary of Residence Hall Pilot Project

The use of BIM FM for the residence hall on the UWRF campus was positively impacted by the use of BIM by the architect. The BIM was used for FM to gain perspective on what is currently possible given standard industry practices, and to start to establish the processes and requirements that will be needed to further implement BIM FM. It is anticipated that many of the lessons learned from this pilot project will be used to inform future BIM FM projects across the state of Wisconsin, including the next version of the "BIM Guidelines and Standards" (issued in July 2012).

PILOT 2: WISCONSIN ENERGY INSTITUTE

The case study for the Wisconsin Energy Institute was completed while the building was in 50 percent construction. Construction started December 2010 and is anticipated to be complete December 2012. The project demonstrates a construction process that supports the delivery of a BIM with detailed project data to the facility management team. The focus of the state of Wisconsin was similar to that of the UWRF case study: to determine what information would be available from the BIM and then determine how to use the information for facility management. Within this case study, the processes needed to support data collection during construction to support FM processes are emphasized.

The Energy Institute (Figure 6.46), located on the UW Madison campus at 1552 University Avenue, will serve as a research facility for the school of engineering. Bio-energy, wind, and battery research will be conducted within the building. The bio-energy research will focus primarily on the use of nonedible ethanol sources, such as corn stalks, for fuel. The 107,000 square foot, $46 million (U.S. dollars), four-story building contains labs, meeting rooms, and offices. The lower level of the building will have a nuclear magnetic resonance (NMR) reactor, the emergency generator, and some electrical rooms. The first floor will include public spaces, meeting rooms, and several offices. The second to fourth floors

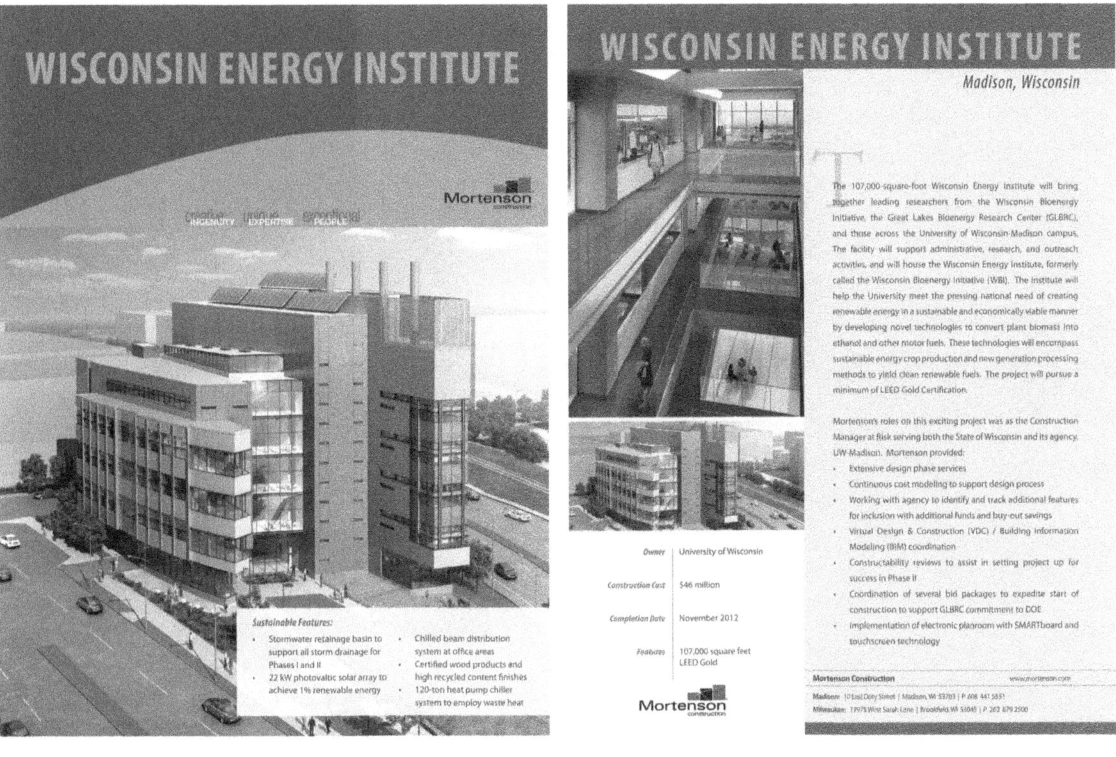

FIGURE 6.46 Rendering of exterior of Wisconsin Energy Institute.
Courtesy Potter Lawson/HOK

will house labs and offices. Additionally, the building was designed to accommodate a future expansion, which would allow the building to double in size.

The structural system is structural steel for the office half of the building, while the lab half is reinforced, cast-in place concrete. The transition between structural systems will be very transparent aesthetically once the building is complete, because each half of the building has different, yet blended, architectural features (Figure 6.46). The structural system of the lab portion of the building was driven by state requirements. Structural steel cannot be used for labs because of vibrations produced by the laboratory equipment. The office portion of the building was built of structural steel to reduce cost.

To increase the amount of natural light that enters the building, the two sections of the building are connected by a light well and are oriented in an east-west direction. The light well will serve as a gathering space on the ground floor and as

FIGURE 6.47 Chilled beam.
Courtesy M. A. Mortenson Company

community gathering spaces on the lab floors. The community gathering spaces include small kitchens and seating areas with views to the center of the building and of University Avenue.

The heating and cooling are provided to the building by the campus steam and chilled water plants. Ventilation to the labs is provided by variable air volume (VAV) air handling units, while offices are conditioned by 280 passive chilled beams (Figure 6.47) and ventilated by dedicated outdoor air units. To increase the energy efficiency, a 120-ton heat pump chiller system, located in the penthouse, will be used to precondition the outside air using waste heat (the air exhausted from the building).

Sustainable features of the building include:

- Stormwater retention basin to support all stormwater drainage
- Use of certified wood products and high recycled content finishes
- East-west orientation to maximize use of daylighting
- Occupancy control sensors used to vary the air changes per hour within the lab spaces

It is anticipated that the building will achieve at least a LEED-NC Gold rating.

Contract Structure and Project Team

Although the project was designed and constructed using BIM, it is important to note that the architect was awarded the project in December 2008, six months before the "BIM Guidelines and Standards" were put into place. Thus, it was not contractually required for any of the design to be completed using BIM. Thus, the construction manager was bound to 2D documents for construction.

The project was completed under a construction manager at risk (CMAR) contract, held between the construction contractor and the state of Wisconsin. Under this contract structure, M. A. Mortenson Company served as the construction manager for the project, managing 54 subcontractors, while the state held one contract with Mortenson (Figure 6.48). A larger number of subcontractors were required compared to many typical construction projects because:

- Lab buildings are more complex, and have more systems and equipment that needs to be procured and installed.
- The building had more detailed finishes.
- LEED points required local procurement, resulting in an increased number of subcontractors and suppliers that needed to be engaged.
- The state of Wisconsin has a 5 percent minority requirement to award a project (although the project goal of 10 percent was met).

Part of the construction manager's responsibilities was to review the design models and model components necessary to support construction coordination.

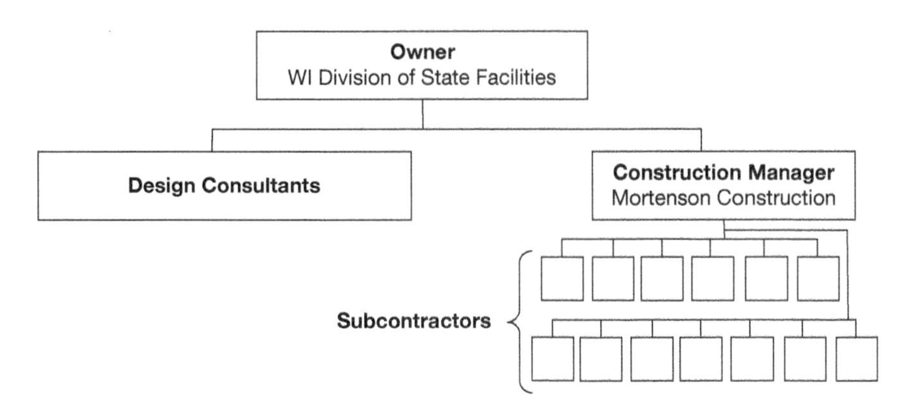

FIGURE 6.48 Construction manager at risk contract structure with key stakeholders identified.

Mortenson, the construction manager, often uses CMAR contracts because they allow:

- For relationship-based decision making. Instead of making construction decisions based solely on the contractual requirements, the owner and the construction manager can work together to make decisions that are best for the project during the course of construction.
- The construction manager to maintain control of how BIMs are created and managed by multiple subcontractors.
- Innovative ideas to be implemented during the project, as the construction manager determines is appropriate.
- For high-quality results to be delivered for design/build projects. Within the contract structure, the construction manager can set specific requirements for the level of BIM expertise that subcontractors must be able to demonstrate.

Although the contract does not state that it is required to turn the as-built BIM over to the state of Wisconsin at the end of the project, this is a standard practice for Mortenson.

Mortenson has been constructing buildings using 3D models for almost 15 years. The first 3D-model-based construction project Mortenson completed was the Walt Disney Concert Hall, designed by Frank Gehry, located in Los Angeles, California. The project was designed, and then several contractors determined that it could not be built because it had too many complex features; each member of the steel frame was unique. After the project had been shelved for three to four years, Mortenson, working with Stanford's Center for Integrated Facility Engineering (CIFE) and Disney's Imagineering team, determined that it was possible to build the building by using Catia, a 3D modeling software program (not typically used for building design), to create a construction model of the building. As a result of completing this project, Mortenson started to determine the benefits of using 3D modeling and using BIM tools to provide construction services.

As the construction manager, Mortenson worked with many of the design consultants and construction subcontractors, including:

- Architect: Potter Lawson, Inc., Madison, WI, where HOK partnered to provide lab-planning expertise
- Vertical circulation design architect: American Design, Inc., Milwaukee, WI
- Structural engineer: Arnold and O'Sheridan, Madison, WI
- Mechanical and electrical engineer: Affiliated Engineers Inc., Madison, WI
- Plumbing engineer: PSJ Plumbing, Milwaukee, WI

- Civil engineer and landscaping: Ken Saiki Design, Madison, WI
- Energy modeling and daylighting design: Weidt Group, Minnetonka, MN
- Vertical transportation design: American Design Inc., Milwaukee, WI
- Metal panels, soffit panels, and interior architecture panels: CS&E Construction Supply and Erection, Germantown, WI
- Steel subcontractor: Endres Manufacturing, Waunakee, WI
- Mechanical subcontractor: North American Mechanical Inc., Madison, WI
- Electrical subcontractor: Pieper Power, Madison, WI
- Plumbing subcontractor: Hooper Plumbing, Madison, WI
- Fire protection subcontractor: J. F. Ahern, Madison, WI
- Elevator subcontractor: Otis Elevators, Madison, WI

Design consultants that used only 2D drawings included:

- Civil engineer and landscaping
- Plumbing engineer
- Mechanical and electrical engineer

Design consultants and subcontractors that used a combination of BIM and 2D drawings included:

- Architects
- Structural engineer
- Vertical transportation design
- Construction manager
- Steel subcontractor
- Mechanical subcontractor
- Electrical subcontractor
- Plumbing subcontractor
- Fire protection subcontractor
- Elevator subcontractor
- Civil engineer and landscape designer

When both 2D and 3D were used, the 3D models were most commonly used to help the user visualize other aspects of the project to support the conceptualization of their work. From the perspective of the construction manager, this is a common industry practice because it is easier to look at a 3D model than a drawing set. Additionally:

- The learning curve to understand how to navigate a 3D model is easier than designing using 3D modeling software.

- Many free viewers, such as Design Review and Adobe 3D PDF viewer, are available to view Revit files, but the cost of a Revit license can be expensive for small companies.
- As in the UWRF case study, it was found that modeling in 3D requires knowing more parameters than 2D, such as wall thickness and material types.

Most of the construction model was developed using the design documents as a starting point; for example, the locations of the walls from the architectural model were used. However, because the mechanical, electrical, and plumbing engineers were contracted to provide only 2D drawings, it was necessary for the construction manager to turn the 2D drawings into 3D models. One current industry challenge is receiving 3D modeling information from the design team that contains the correct information to use for fabrication. Thus, for this project, it was necessary to create 3D models from 2D line drawings. This process included reviewing the 2D construction documents as PDFs and the specifications, and using the 2D CAD backgrounds to develop 3D models that could be used for fabrication.

To test the capabilities of the subcontractors to transform 2D drawings into 3D models, a simple building was designed in 2D by the construction manager and provided to the subcontractors to demonstrate their capabilities, as part of the bidding process. This also allowed the construction manager to determine if the modeling software used by the subcontractors was interoperable and if any additional processes needed to be put in place. The BIM was used to support the fabrication of ducts, plumbing systems, electrical systems, and some concrete work.

Team Collaboration

A BIM room (Figure 6.49) is housed in a job trailer. This room is used by all of the trades for construction coordination. This saves significant amounts of time because the different trades can discuss coordination items as they arise, instead of needing to make multiple phone calls. In some cases, coordination that would previously take several days can be completed in a few hours. The room includes a large screen that can be used to project the BIM, allowing the model to serve as an instant narrative, instead of first needing to describe what a team member is looking at, so the other person(s) can see within the model.

A second method of coordination and collaboration is the "plan of the day." Each day, the construction manager identifies part of the construction that requires coordination. The purpose of these meetings is to raise the awareness of the team members onsite of what other trades are doing. This helps to notify team members of necessary safety precautions that must be taken and also increases construction

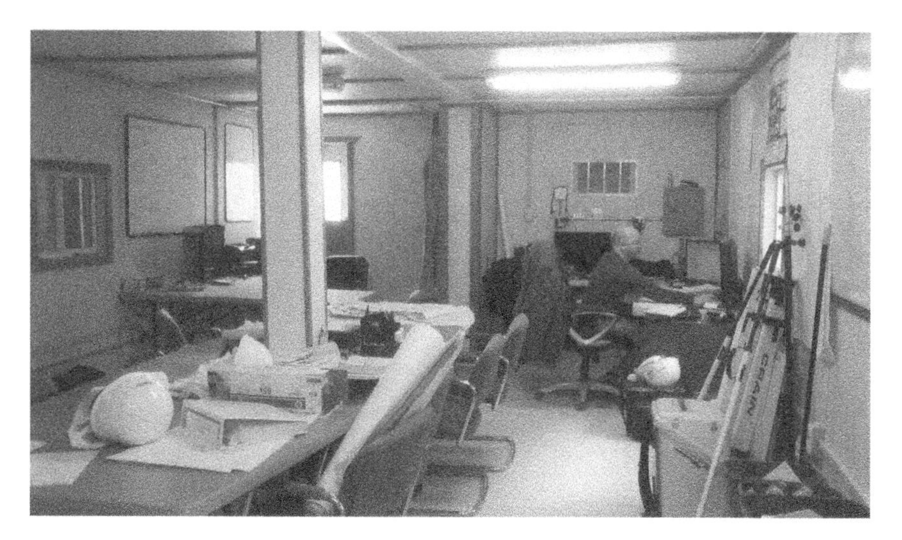

FIGURE 6.49 BIM room, located in construction trailer.

efficiency because equipment, such as overhead cranes, that is shared by subcontractors can be sequenced and scheduled.

One additional benefit of the plan of the day is that it allows best practices and lessons learned to be collected by the construction manager. These practices are then organized into a database so that the information can be shared with project teams across Mortenson. This is advantageous for facility managers because it helps to reduce construction errors, identify constructability and warranty challenges, mitigate unanticipated challenges, and improve the quality of the information that can be handed over to the FM.

To access the plan of the day (Figure 6.50), the tower crane schedule, 2D construction drawings, specification sections, and 3D construction models, a 46-inch computer monitor is located within a gang box within the building while it is under construction (Figure 6.51). The computer can be accessed by any of the subcontractors and the construction management team. Having the computer on-site is one of the first steps to transitioning to a paperless construction site. To find electronic documents quickly, all of the drawings, models, and specifications are organized using Excel worksheets that are set up as a table of contents with links to PDFs of each document (Figure 6.52). PDFs are viewed using BlueBeam. Although it takes time to set up this structure, it allows the construction team to quickly scan a list to find necessary information, saving a lot of time searching for information in the field.

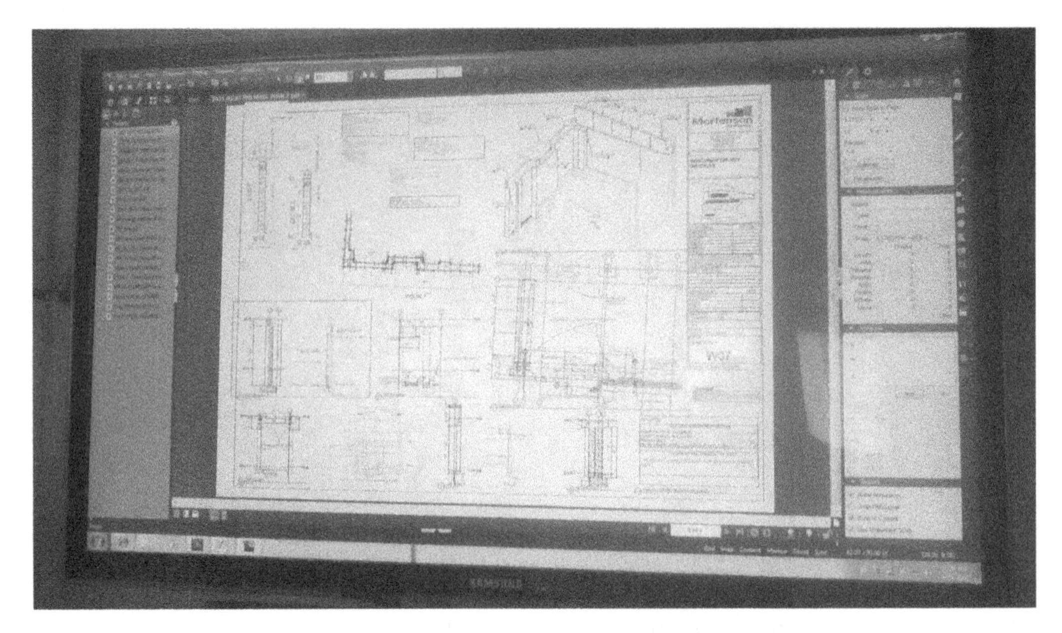

FIGURE 6.50 Sample plan of the day, viewed from the computer on the construction site.

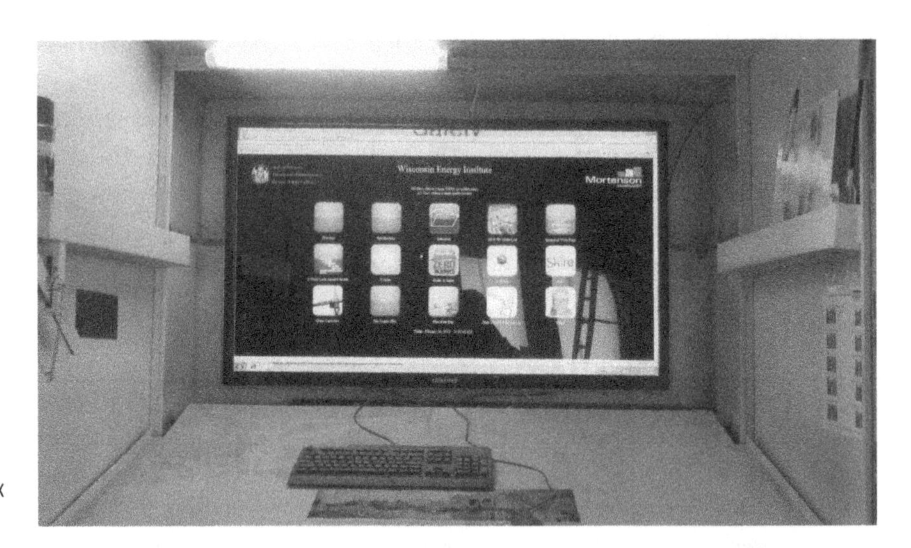

FIGURE 6.51 46-inch monitor located in a gang box on the construction site.

A third method of collaboration and coordination during construction is the use of an electronic submittal exchange system, Skier Unifier, which is an Internet-based document management system. It is similar to Submittal Exchange, mentioned in the UWRF case study, but includes additional functionality. Mortenson uses Skier Unifier to manage RFIs, submittals, change orders, and pricing information provided from subcontractors. To use Skier Unifier as needed by Mortenson, some

01 Specifications — WISCONSIN ENERGY INSTITUTE

Section	Title	Date
05 51 00	Metal Stairs	05/26/11
05 52 13	Pipe & Tube Railings	05/26/11
05 58 00	Formed Metal Fabrications	05/26/11
05 58 13	Column Covers	05/26/11
05 73 13	Glazed Decorative Metal Railings	
05 75 09	Metal Base	05/26/11
06 10 00	Rough Carpentry	05/26/11
06 40 00	Architectural Woodwork	05/26/11
06 42 00	Wood Paneling	05/26/11
07 10 90	Waterproofing and insulation systems for Utilities	
07 14 00	Fluid-Applied Waterproofing	05/26/11
07 18 00	Traffic Bearing Waterproofing	
07 21 00	Thermal Insulation	05/26/11
07 27 26	Fluid-Applied Membrane Air Barrier	05/26/11
07 42 13	Metal Wall panels	05/26/11
07 42 43	Composite Wall Panels	05/26/11
07 53 23	Ethylene-Propylene-Diene-Monomer Roofing	05/26/11
07 61 00	Sheet Metal Roofing Specialties	05/26/11
07 72 00	Roof Accessories	05/26/11
07 81 00	Applied Fireproofing	05/26/11
07 84 13	Penetration Firestopping	05/26/11
07 84 46	Fire-Resistive Joint System	05/26/11
07 92 00	Joint Sealants	03/10/11
08 11 13	Standar Hollow Metal Doors & Frames	05/26/11
08 11 29	Fire Rated Door & Frame Assemblies	05/26/11

Specifications Log

FIGURE 6.52 Table of contents structure used to access specification sections in the field.
Courtesy M. A. Mortenson Company

customization was necessary. One of their future goals is to integrate Skier Unifier with Revit. To do this will require resolving multiple interoperability challenges. Until this functionality is added, drawings are issued as 2D PDFs and 3D models using both the software with which the models were developed and a viewer version of the software. The viewer version models are primarily used to review and monitor the data within the files, without the ability to edit the files.

To support collaboration between the design team and the construction team, a BIM protocol manual was developed. The BIM protocol manual included:

- Overview of the concepts of BIM and 3D modeling
- Key members involved in the BIM efforts
- List of BIM software used
- List of plug-ins, file formats, and viewers used
- Recommendations for hardware to use
- Lessons learned and initial concerns
- Project standards, including file exchanges procedures, data exchange procedures, and file standards
- Information flows descriptions

- Project closeout procedures
- High-level file-naming conventions
- Revit coordinates
- Revit naming conventions
- Building clash flowchart

To support collaboration and information sharing through the construction to FM handover, the BIM protocol manual was redeveloped to serve as a BIM closeout manual. The purpose of the closeout manual is to provide the FM team with the information necessary to operate and maintain the building from a BIM perspective. The closeout manual is further discussed later in the chapter.

Facility Management Systems

The UW Madison campus uses an AssetWorks CMMS across the entire campus. As each CMMS is proprietary, the data structure required to import the IFC exported from Revit is different from the UWRF TMA System data structure. Thus, it is necessary to develop a data structure for each CMMS vendor used across the state of Wisconsin, unless open standards are used.

BIM Handover from Construction to FM

The information within the BIM provided as-installed information on a memory stick. The structure of the information is all of the drawings and PDFs organized by specification section. The PDFs will be searchable. To generate an organized set of PDFs, the construction manager requires that all subcontractors submit the PDFs named by specification section and within a structure that aligns with the specification sections. It is part of the culture on the job site to have the person who generates the PDF name it as required. Additionally, to ensure that procedures are completed as required, subcontractors must submit operations and maintenance documents by the 60 percent billing stage of construction. This gives the construction manager time to check to make sure that the documents are complete and in the proper format. Additionally, it prevents delays at the end of the project caused by the gathering and organization of project documentation.

Some of the information included within the model was plumbing components, door hardware, and wood blocking. While the building was still under construction, a subset of plumbing component information (Figure 6.53) was provided to the facility manager to determine how it could be used. One idea determined was that the data could be used to order replacement parts, as accurate as-built data was provided.

Door hardware information was populated within the BIM because the architectural team included a door hardware expert that provided a lot of design details.

Element ID	Element Name	'Host'	'K Coefficient'	'Level'	'Mark'
#2249157	'Backflow_Preventer-RP-Zurn_Wilkins-Model_375_	'Level : 02	NULL	'02)HC_1st Floor'	'227'
#1191191	'Balancing Valve - Straight - 0.5-2 Inch – Threade	'Level : 02	31.28	'02)HC_1st Floor'	'116'
#1191309	'Balancing Valve - Straight - 0.5-2 Inch – Threade	'Level : 02	31.28	'02)HC_1st Floor'	'117'
#1295409	'Balancing Valve - Straight - 0.5-2 Inch – Threade	'Level : 02	31.28	'02)HC_1st Floor'	'171'
#1296192	'Balancing Valve - Straight - 0.5-2 Inch – Threade	'Level : 02	31.28	'02)HC_1st Floor'	'181'
#1296279	'Balancing Valve - Straight - 0.5-2 Inch – Threade	'Level : 02	31.28	'02)HC_1st Floor'	'182'
#1298878	'Balancing Valve - Straight - 0.5-2 Inch – Threade	'Level : 02	31.28	'02)HC_1st Floor'	'190'
#445171	'Basket Strainer - 2-12 Inch - Flanged:4":4":85942	'Level : 01	5.23	'01)HC_Basement'	'22'
#197098	'Check Valve - 0.5-4 Inch - Threaded:3":3":733265'	'Level : 00	0.32	'00)HC_Underground'	'2'
#197206	'Check Valve - 0.5-4 Inch - Threaded:3":3":733463'	'Level : 00	0.32	'00)HC_Underground'	'3'
#451814	'Gate Valve - 2-12 Inch:2":2":862066'	'Level : 01	0.34	'01)HC_Basement'	'29'
#2703363	'Gate Valve - 2-12 Inch:4":4":1341511'	'Level : 01	0.16	'01)HC_Basement'	'346'

FIGURE 6.53 Sample of plumbing data exported from the construction BIM.
Courtesy Wisconsin Department of Administration

However, the door hardware expert was unfamiliar with BIM and provided the schedules in Excel. As the construction manager found this information to be of value to FM for key management, they entered the information into the BIM. If this had not been done, it would be necessary to look at the drawings to identify the location of the door, look at the door schedule, and then look at the door hardware specification to find the information needed. With the information in the BIM, the lock shop will only need to look in the model, not four different documents.

Wood-blocking information was also entered into the BIM. Because the building had a lot of case work, and laboratory spaces are often reconfigured over the life of the building, it is often necessary to mount new equipment or move equipment from one wall to another. Since a lot of lab equipment is very heavy, it is important that proper blocking be located in the wall. When the blocking information is included within the BIM, it is easy to quickly identify where blocking exists, resulting in quickly determining proper locations for mounting equipment.

The BIM delivered to the FM will include 2D and 3D closeout models and PDF closeout files. The 3D closeout Revit and AutoCad 3D models will include all coordination and construction models and 2D attachments to the 3D models. The 2D closeout models will include all AutoCAD files used during coordination and construction. The PDF closeout files will include all files associated with the 2D and 3D closeout models. It is anticipated that the BIM data will be sorted and then stored in a SQL database before it is formatted to be imported into the CMMS. The data will be sorted by reviewing small datasets.

BIM Closeout

To help transfer the information within the BIM to FM, as well as transfer knowledge about how to navigate and use the BIM for FM, a BIM closeout manual was developed for the owner. This allowed all pertinent information to be included in one document, including project contact information. The manual included the contents of the BIM protocol manual, as well as contact information for each team who developed models using BIM software and a list of software used on the project. Providing contact information allows the FM team to contact the modelers to ask how and where to find specific information within the model. Providing the list of software is useful because it can help to resolve interoperability problems as well as determine what software should be provided. Additionally, the closeout manual included:

- Names of construction firms and subcontractors, including the name of the technology leader
- List of software used by each firm
- Processes to post project files and requirements for files
- List of required documents that must be turned over at project closeout
- High-level list of naming conventions for drawing submittals in both PDF and AutoCAD formats
- Revit naming conventions

Although the specific uses of the BIM for FM and BIM software that would be used had not been determined, the construction manager had been working with FM staff to help them understand how to use BIM for the last year and a half. To help reduce the learning curve, the construction manager will provide views from the model with relevant filters turned on so the contents of the model can be viewed without needing to understand how to navigate within the model or understanding the level of detail included within the model.

Use of BIM for FM

As previously stated, at the time of the case study, it was not certain how the BIM would be used for FM. However, the construction manager and the FM team were working together to evaluate what information is available within the BIM and how the information could be used. Key questions that were being researched included:

- What information is in the model?
- How can information within the model be found?
- What information is not included within the model?

Although Mortenson had the ability to link equipment schedule, submittal, original equipment manufacturer, and sequence of operation information for the control of

HVAC systems to the BIM, it was outside of the construction contract, and thus not delivered to the FM team.

BIM Data Ownership and Right of Reliance

It was stated in the CMAR contract that the state of Wisconsin owns the BIM and the data within in it. As the model is transferred between the designers and construction managers, one common challenge is the right of reliance: The construction manager cannot contractually rely on the accuracy of the design BIM. Instead, contractually, the construction contractor can only rely on the accuracy of the 2D drawings. As the use of 3D modeling software to generate 2D drawings increases, this should become less of a concern because the graphical content of both the 2D and 3D deliverables should be the same. Over time, the level of trust across the industry should increase.

Owner Education Requirements

As described earlier, a construction management at-risk contract structure was used. For owners and facility management teams not familiar with this type of contract structure, this is an area where owners will need to be educated.

A second area of owner BIM education is providing an overview of BIM and the value of BIM across the facility life cycle. The construction manager provided training to architectural planners at the university. Only planners were trained because it was concluded that they would be responsible for providing training to the craftsmen, and the training provided to the planners was a train-the-trainer format. One training opportunity identified, but not pursued, was how to navigate BIMs and find content within them. Although the 3D models will be provided to the state of Wisconsin, the state currently does not have plans to use them for FM.

Lessons Learned and Challenges

The lessons learned include those relevant to BIM FM, as well as some that are more aligned with the construction process. Thus, as the construction process provides the data source for the BIM FM handover, having a well-managed and coordinated construction process increases the opportunity for the FM team to receive the information.

FM Lessons Learned

During the Wisconsin Energy Institute project, four key lessons learned for facility managers were identified. First, data within the BIM delivered during facility management handover is mainly driven by the data in the construction model, since the data is used for construction functions. Although the FM may receive a model with large amounts of data, much of it will not be relevant to FM. For example, information about concrete forms or the size of rebar within a concrete column is not required for FM. Thus, the data must be cleaned to determine what is really of use for FM. Similarly, although well-developed design BIM models create a stronger foundation for the construction BIM to be developed, the FM needs information primarily based on what is installed, not on what was used as the basis of design.

When determining what data to include in the BIM for FM, it is important to look at the big picture and determine the overall goals for importing BIM information into the CMMS. Just because data was useful for one stakeholder group does not mean it is useful for another. For example, a facility manager wants information on replacement parts for a pump, while the contractor wants the information to procure the pump.

One way for the FM to determine what data is relevant is to start by evaluating relevant specification sections and then ask the contractor to provide IFC data for only the requested specification sections. For example, it may be relevant to request information about pumps and air handling units, but not pipe hangers. To further evaluate data, an important question to ask, regardless of the phase of the project, is: What is the value of adding the information? If value cannot be demonstrated for any team(s) that will use the model, it is unlikely that this information should be added. A large challenge within the industry, currently, is to answer this question for each discipline involved in the life cycle of a building.

The third lesson learned is that subcontractors will generally not provide data desired by the FM until it is contractually required. Thus, it is important to specify what data is needed and in what format the data should be delivered. The final lesson learned is that contracts should clearly state relationships and requirements about how BIM should be used and the level of detail with which building elements are to be modeled.

Construction-Focused Lessons Learned

Two key lessons learned were identified specific to the construction process. Facility managers should take note of these lessons learned because they will impact the success of the facility management team's efforts to achieve their goals.

First, when submitting or responding to RFIs during construction, it is challenging to convey current as-built conditions in the BIM in real time. The ability to convey this information in real time helps to resolve RFIs more quickly. When it was possible for as-built conditions to be conveyed using the model, the designers were able to better visualize the challenge that needed to be resolved on the construction site. It was suggested that future efforts to coordinate in real time should require a narrative summarizing the changes in the model. The main goal of the narrative should be to describe the changes at the level of detail necessary to prevent those using the revised model from searching the model to determine what changes were made. The process of determining when narratives should be written and the level of detail they contain should be well defined. Future projects should also emphasize the need for more verbal and written communication, to ensure team members clearly understand the changes to the model because just posting an updated model can cause confusion.

Second, two effective strategies were determined to support coordination in real time.

1. GoToMeeting was used to help resolve RFIs.
2. A member of the design team wrote a script to automate updates to the models using the Newforma FTP site to allow an automated exchange between the designers, and construction manager's models. The model updates would be sent through the Newforma FTP site at midnight, and in the morning the script would download the most current model, so each day the design team and construction team had the most current version of the model. Although it proved valuable to have the most current version, as design could be completed more quickly, it added confusion when a portion of the design was left incomplete. If a narrative were written and provided each morning, it would be easy to understand that a portion of the design was still in progress.

Overall Project Lessons Learned

More broadly, two key lessons learned apply to both the facility management and construction teams. First, at the beginning of the project, the requirements must carefully define which disciplines and trades should use 2D and 3D software, and what components should be included in the 2D and 3D deliverables. Without these requirements clearly defined, it is more difficult to coordinate the model, and this can result in duplication of effort.

Second, every project has unique software challenges. Often the scope of work was assigned on the basis of software use. This was especially true for the architectural design, because there were three different architectural firms involved in the project, each using different design software and having varied skill sets with BIM: HOK, Potter Lawson, and American Design, Inc. Although it will never be possible for design software to be standardized across an entire project, the more different software products are used, the more challenging it becomes to create an interoperable BIM.

Summary of Wisconsin Energy Center Pilot Project

The use of BIM FM for the Wisconsin Energy Institute was positively impacted by the use of BIM by the construction manager. The BIM and the processes used by the construction manager helped the facility management team gain further perspective about how different design and construction teams can greatly impact the type, quality, and amount of information delivered. This understanding validates the need to develop an updated version of the "BIM Guidelines and Standards."

SYNTHESES OF FINDINGS OF TWO CASE STUDIES

As each pilot project was completed, the current state and use of BIM tools across the building life cycle were further understood. Although the case studies discussed within this chapter were different building types, used different contract structures, and used BIM at differing degrees (Table 6.8), many of the lessons learned were relevant across all of the pilot projects. Since the director of the Bureau of Facility Management was involved with all the pilot projects, the lessons learned were applied across all the projects. Two lessons learned that are relevant to both projects discussed within this chapter are summarized in the following material.

TABLE 6.8 Comparison of Case Study Characteristics

	UW River Falls	Wisconsin Energy Institute
Type of building	Residence hall	Laboratory and offices
Project budget	$18.9 million	$46 million
Contract structure	Design bid build	Construction manager at risk
Team members who used BIM[a]	Architect MEP designers	Architects Civil engineer and landscape designer Construction manager Electrical subcontractor Elevator subcontractor Fire protection subcontractor Mechanical subcontractor Plumbing subcontractor Steel subcontractor Structural engineer Vertical transportation design
CMMS vendor	TMA Systems	AssetWorks

[a] In some cases, both BIM and 2D drawings were used.

First, to further implement the use of BIM FM, it is necessary for designers, contractors, and facility managers to better understand each other's roles, needs, and responsibilities. To do this, it is important for disciplines to cross-pollinate. This will require the establishment of new lines of communication and the willingness of each discipline to understand the terminology of the other.

Second, the data structure used by each CMMS vendor is different because each system was developed using proprietary methods. Thus, to import data into each CMMS, it is necessary for the data to be structured to meet proprietary requirements. If open standards could be used with both CMMS, the same data structure could have been used for both UWRF and the WI Energy Center.

Applying the Lessons Learned across the State

One of the key goals of the pilot projects was to determine how to improve the processes to make further BIM FM projects more widely implemented across the state, using standardized processes.

One lesson learned was the importance of having well-written specifications. Well-written specifications are especially important when requesting data that will be imported into the CMMS. Because general specifications are written on a statewide level, it is important that BIM FM specification content be specific enough that the data provided can be imported into the CMMS. Yet, the specification must be written generically enough that it can be used by most state agencies without major edits to accommodate differences in CMMS vendors and data structures.

A second lesson learned was to understand what A/E teams could provide, which influenced what the state should ask for within the next version of the "Guidelines and Standards," as well as the specifications. Four listening sessions were held across the state, where members of the state FM team invited A/E teams to discuss their current experience and skill sets using BIM. The purpose of these sessions was to prevent asking for something within the specifications, guidelines, and standards that could not be delivered. Over all, the A/E experience with BIM ranged widely, from fairly experienced to some firms stating that the State of Wisconsin 2009 "BIM Guideline and Standards" were too strict. A significant finding from the listening session held in Milwaukee was that none of the 45 people in attendance, representing 35 firms, had heard of COBie. This caused the state to question whether to include COBie as part of the next version of the guidelines and standards. However, in order for firms to adopt it, they must first be aware of it. Thus, it is challenging to determine whether the state should require something the industry is unfamiliar with, or wait to see what the industry adopts as standard practice.

In both projects, the amount of as-built information in the BIM was driven by the processes and requirements used by the general contractor and/or construction manager. Although both projects delivered information in the BIM, a large task of the FM was to clean up the data and determine the data structure required to upload it into the CMMS. As the use of BIM continues to evolve across the entire industry, it is important to be actively engaged with new developments from both a technology and a process perspective.

The strongest finding from the pilot projects was that to receive consistently populated BIM for use within FM, it is important to clearly define the quality and level of detail of the data that must be provided. To convey this information, it is necessary to update the BIM guidelines and standards to include which building elements should be modeled and what information should be associated with each element. However, this is not a small task. Given the number of assets within even a single building, it is necessary to develop these requirements in phases. Both FM and IT staff should be involved in this process to ensure that the required information is collected and that it is in a format that can be uploaded into the CMMS.

SUMMARY

The two pilot projects described in this case study used different technologies, had different project teams, and were different building types. However, they share a common vision: to provide easy access to information, increased productivity, and greater certainty of data through improved data quality for facility management (Napier 2009).

The implementation of BIM FM across the state is in the early stages. However, the state of Wisconsin strongly supports this: "With governmental leadership, early adopter architectural leadership, education support and business process leadership clearly pointing the way to success, Wisconsin's BIM initiatives clearly demonstrate the state motto: 'Forward'" (Napier 2008). The BIM FM work completed across the state so far has established a foundation that will help the industry move the BIM FM vision forward.

REFERENCES

Beck, K. 2011a. *Digital Facility Management Information Handover: Current DSF Practices, Industry-wide Movement, Future Directions*. A Research, Findings and Recommendations Report for the State of Wisconsin, Department of Administration, Division of State Facilities. DSF Project Number: 08H3M. Accessed December 27, 2011, at ftp://doaftp04.doa.state.wi.us/master_spec/DSF%20Digital%20FM%20Handover/FM%20Findings&RecRpt.pdf.

______. 2011b. *Building Information Modeling FM Handover*. Washington DC: EcoBuild America.

Division of State Facilities. 2011. Accessed December 27, 2011, at www.doa.state.wi.us/index.asp?locid=4.

Napier, B. 2008. "Wisconsin Leads by Example." *Journal of Building Information Modeling*, pp. 30–31. www.wbdg.org/pdfs/jbim_fall08.pdf.

______. 2009. *Building Information Modeling, a Report on the Current State of BIM Technologies and Recommendations for Implementation*. DSF Project Number: 08H3M. Accessed December 27, 2011, at ftp://doaftp04.doa.state.wi.us/master_spec/DSF%20BIM%20Guidelines%20&%20Standards/BIM%20Findings%20and%20Recommendations%20Report.pdf.

ADDITIONAL RESOURCE

State of Wisconsin Executive Order that Led to the State Requiring BIM.

Executive Order 145: https://docs.legis.wisconsin.gov/code/executive_orders/2003_jim_doyle/2006-145.pdf.

ACKNOWLEDGMENTS

This case study could not have been completed without the insights from the following individuals:

Keith Beck, director, Bureau of Facilities Management, Wisconsin Department of Administration; Susan Bischof, IS Technical Services senior, and Michael Stifter, director of facilities management of the University of Wisconsin, River Falls; Matthew Long, architect of record, and Paul Kouba, Revit manager, of SDS Architects; and M. A. Mortenson Company, including Todd Hoffmaster, senior integrated construction coordinator; Jeff Madden, general manager; Rob Weise, construction executive; and Craig Wacker, project manager.

Case Study 6: University of Chicago Administration Building Renovation

Angela Lewis, PE, PhD, LEED AP Project Professional with Facility Engineering Associates

MANAGEMENT SUMMARY

The University of Chicago Administration Building renovation case study focuses on the information handover between construction and facility management (FM). Thus, the major players were the construction manager (CM), M. A. Mortenson Company, and the University of Chicago. A large portion of the case study discusses the transition from construction to facility management, including determining the level of detail with which data should be collected; discussions with decision makers about how they would use the data; and collecting, organizing, and structuring data.

The most important insight from this case study was that the processes to support the use of technology within BIM FM are in their infancy. Skills that are needed to advance process development within the industry include the ability of more professionals to communicate across industry specialties and more knowledge among professionals about computerized maintenance management system (CMMS) databases. Thus, leadership from owners, designers, builders, software companies, and FM consultants is necessary to help advance the industry's vision for BIM FM.

The primary challenges addressed by the case study include:

- Determining to what level of detail information should be collected to support facility management processes and decision making
- Understanding how the 3D BIM could be used for facility management and how to determine what software, if any, should be procured to support the use of 3D models by the University of Chicago
- Aligning and leveraging the varying team member' skill sets to deliver a valuable FM tool for the university

The construction and FM teams both used a variety of different technologies. Software used by the design and construction team included Autodesk Revit, Autodesk Navisworks, and 3D MEP fabrication software. Additionally, the use of laser scanning was very important to help verify the existing as-built drawings because of the limited space available to run ductwork, piping, and electrical systems. Maximo is the primary facility management software discussed within this case study. The use of Archibus for space management and eBuilder for project management and procurement is briefly discussed.

The largest benefit resulting from the project was the creation of a process that will be of benefit to future renovation and new construction projects: a process to capture data during construction so that it can be used for operations and maintenance over the life of the building.

INTRODUCTION

The University of Chicago is located about six miles from downtown Chicago and about half a mile from the Lake Michigan lakefront. Twenty-eight thousand people work or attend classes within the 15 million square feet of buildings located on the 211-acre campus.

The University of Chicago Administration Building (Figure 6.54) is located at the center of campus, known as the Main Quadrangles. Built in 1949, the 15,000-square-foot

FIGURE 6.54 Exterior of Administration Building at the University of Chicago.
Courtesy M. A. Mortenson Company

prominent campus building houses the executive officers of the university. The structure and building are typical of many other academic administrative buildings. The structural system is cast-in-place concrete. Chilled water and steam are provided by the campus central plant. New air handlers were installed in the lower-level mechanical room to replace the existing units. The existing variable air volume (VAV) boxes with electric reheat were replaced with VAV boxes with hot water reheat.

In 2011, part of the building was renovated to modernize the office areas, add additional restrooms, and upgrade the mechanical systems. It was necessary to perform the work in two phases to keep the building fully operational during the renovation. The first phase of the renovation included 9 offices on the north side of the first floor and 10 offices on the south side of the second floor. Work was performed on opposite sides of the building to allow for adequate swing space. Renovation work was also completed on the lower level within the mechanical rooms. At the time of the case study, Phase 2 of the renovation for the building was in conceptual design.

Given the location of the building, there were many restrictions regarding construction activity, including parking, vehicle access, and deliveries. Additionally, it was necessary to plan how old mechanical systems would be taken offline and new mechanical systems would be brought into the building. For example, it was necessary to bring the air handlers in through exterior area wells in four sections.

The building was renovated to meet the Chicago energy code, and included concepts to maximize the amount of sunlight entering the building, and the installation of variable frequency drives and occupancy sensors.

Goals for BIM for FM Implementation

At the start of the project, specific requirements for BIM FM were not established. Instead, an opportunity was recognized for the BIM FM initiative during the development of the BIM protocol manual and further refined throughout the early phases of the project. It was determined that this complex, yet small, renovation would make an excellent pilot project to begin developing a historical database of FM data that could be used to populate Maximo and determining the necessary supporting processes. Selecting a smaller construction project for the pilot has multiple benefits:

- Modifications to the dataset were easier because the dataset, as well as the size of the project team, was smaller.
- Changes could be made more quickly because the organizational structure of the team was well integrated, requiring fewer levels of communication and approval. This was especially important because new ideas and processes were often being developed and refined over the duration of the project.

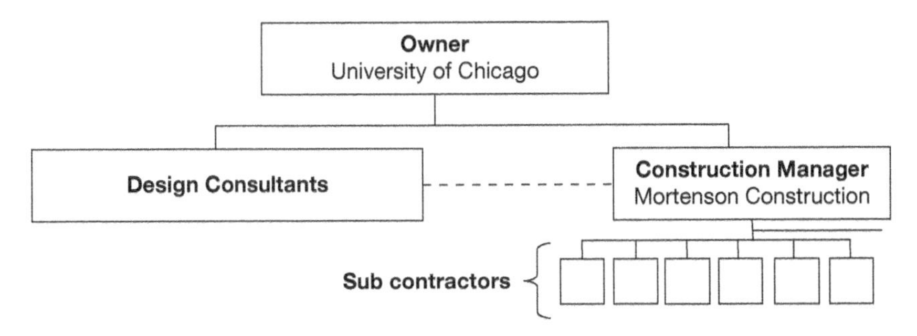

FIGURE 6.55 Construction manager at risk contract structure with key stakeholders identified.

Contract Structure

From initial programming and design through construction and turnover, the $3.3 million (U.S. dollar) construction project was completed in 20 months, starting in January 2010 and ending in October 2011. The project was completed using a construction management at risk contract held by M. A. Mortenson Company. The owner for the project was the University of Chicago, and the architect of record was Gensler. The relationships among the architect, a design consultant, and the construction manager is described in later sections of this case study. The MEP engineering was completed by dbHMS. The structural engineering was completed by ROCKEY Structures LLC. An organizational chart describing the contractual relationships is found in Figure 6.55. The dashed line between the design consultants and the construction manager indicates an informal relationship between the two parties.

The contract did not require that the construction manager use BIM, or that any BIM information be turned over to the FM team. However, it is Mortensen's standard practice to use BIM, and the University of Chicago is starting to use BIM for most new construction and capital projects. This was the first project where BIM was used for a small renovation at the University of Chicago. The collective team recognized an opportunity to improve the efficiency and effectiveness by which the university manages its buildings.

PROJECT TEAM

The selection of the project team members was very important. The selected designer had demonstrated commitment to BIM and excellence in the use of BIM on previous projects, as well as a history of collaboration and knowledge of facility management. The selected contractor used BIM as an integral part of the construction process and had in-house BIM expertise.

Collaboration

The design, construction, and university teams collaborated over the duration of the project. During some phases of the project, there were significant collaboration efforts among the university, construction manager, Autodesk, and BIM. Specifically, Autodesk provided training to the project team about COBie and the challenges that exist when integrating Revit and Maximo.

One method of collaboration implemented by Mortenson involved the use of a local computer and computer monitor on the construction site. A screenshot of the home screen, showing the different resources available through the computer, is shown in Figure 6.56. As shown, this computer was available to project teams to access contract drawings, coordination models, submittals, approved shop drawings, the project FTP site, and other project-specific resources, directly on the job site. Building strong collaborative relationships during construction allowed the construction manager and FM team to successfully implement the BIM FM handover solution.

Subcontractor Prequalification

Mortenson routinely uses a prequalification process to select subcontractors who demonstrate basic BIM skills. The prequalification process includes the use of a trial model whereby the potential subcontractors need to demonstrate how to transform a 2D model into a 3D coordination model. The submissions of the

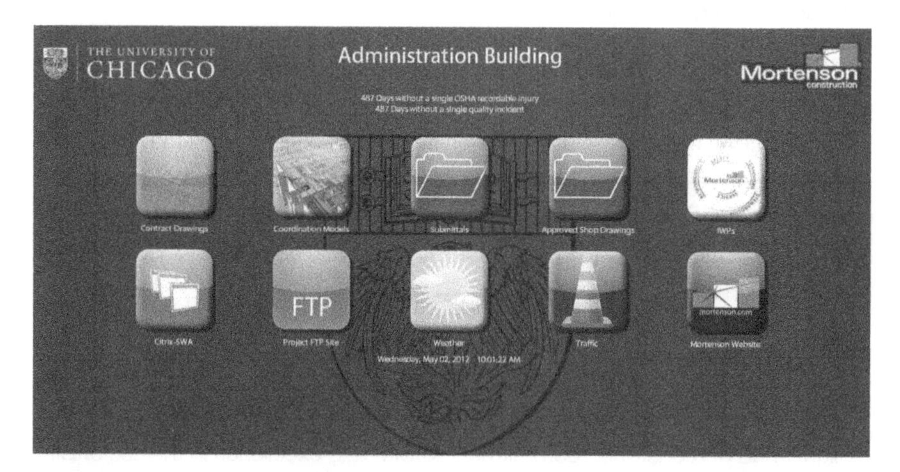

FIGURE 6.56 Screenshot of computer on construction site to support team coordination and collaboration.

Courtesy M. A. Mortenson Company

prequalification process are looked at carefully to determine the skill sets of the subcontractors.

The combination of a small project scope and focus on participation of local minority- and women-owned businesses resulted in multiple trade bidders not having the necessary BIM experience for such a complex, intricate renovation. As neither the university nor Mortenson wanted BIM to prevent local subcontractors from submitting proposals for the project, Mortenson and Autodesk provided BIM training sessions for local contractors (Figure 6.57). The training ranged from helping subcontractors understand the value of using computers to the benefits of using BIM, connecting firms with local software and hardware vendors, and answering questions about how to get started using BIM.

Key points of the training included:

- Overview of BIM and virtual design and construction (VDC)
- BIM benefits to owners
- Live demonstrations of Navisworks and MEP BIM fabrication software
- An overview of the BIM FM process and goals
- How to get started using BIM in the format of a panel of local subject matter experts

FIGURE 6.57 BIM training session for subcontractors.
Courtesy M. A. Mortenson Company

FACILITY MANAGEMENT SYSTEMS

The University of Chicago currently uses Maximo and Archibus for asset and space management, respectively. While both systems have been fully implemented, there is a strong desire for additional efficient and effective methods to more fully integrate the two systems to support the daily operations. Beyond routine work order and maintenance tracking, capturing and analyzing asset data from new perspectives may lead to improved cost savings and overall team productivity. For example, having the asset data populated into the CMMS before the warranty period ends would allow reminders to be set up in Maximo before expiration of the warranty period, helping to resolve warranty problems at the expense of the vendor or installer—not the university.

The FM team uses Archibus for space management; Maximo for asset management, maintenance management, and work orders (Figure 6.58); and eBuider for project management and procurement. Maximo and Archibus are integrated to allow data exchange of space information from Archibus to Maximo. Archibus houses building names, room numbers, departments assigned to each room and/or building, usable height of spaces, and room area in square feet. This data established a foundation from which the Maximo database can pull, to assign assets to spaces. However, eBuilder is not integrated with either software program. eBuilder is used to manage RFIs, change orders, submittals,

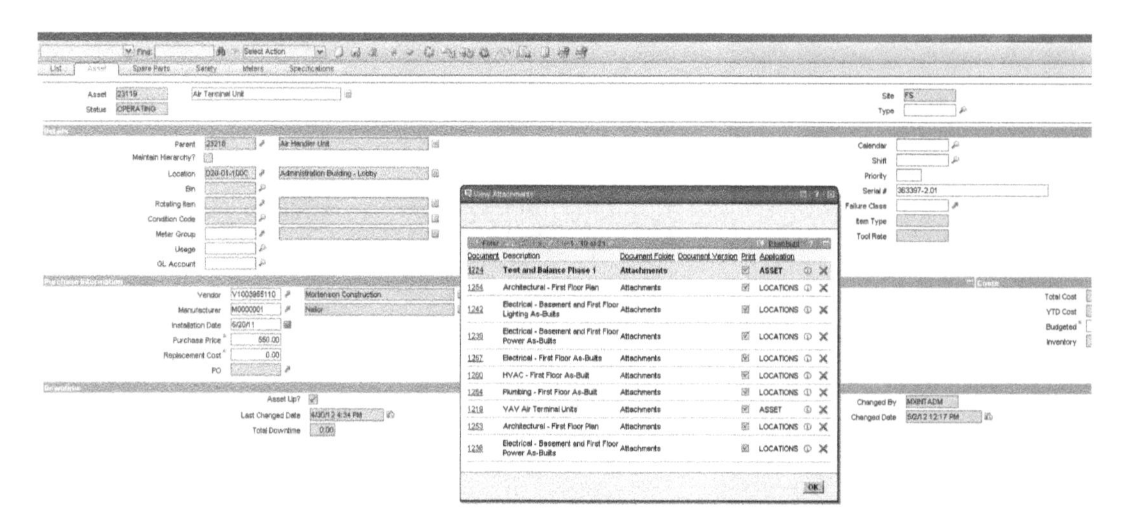

FIGURE 6.58 Maximo screenshot, used for asset management.
Courtesy M. A. Mortenson Company

invoices, scheduling, and cost summaries. At the time of the case study, the project team was focusing primarily on how to properly gather, format, and import asset project data into Maximo.

DOCUMENTING AS-BUILT CONDITIONS AND DEVELOPMENT OF THE BIM

Gensler, the architect, created the design model in Revit, using the original as-built drawings from 1947 (Figure 6.59). Numerous renovation projects since 1947 prompted the team to use laser scanning to document actual as-built conditions in areas where construction was to be performed. The MEP systems, as well as the walls, were the primary focus of the laser scanning.

The construction manager completed the laser scanning, converted the 3D images into an Autodesk Revit model, and worked with the architect to align the design Revit model with the actual field conditions determined through the laser scanning process (Figure 6.60).

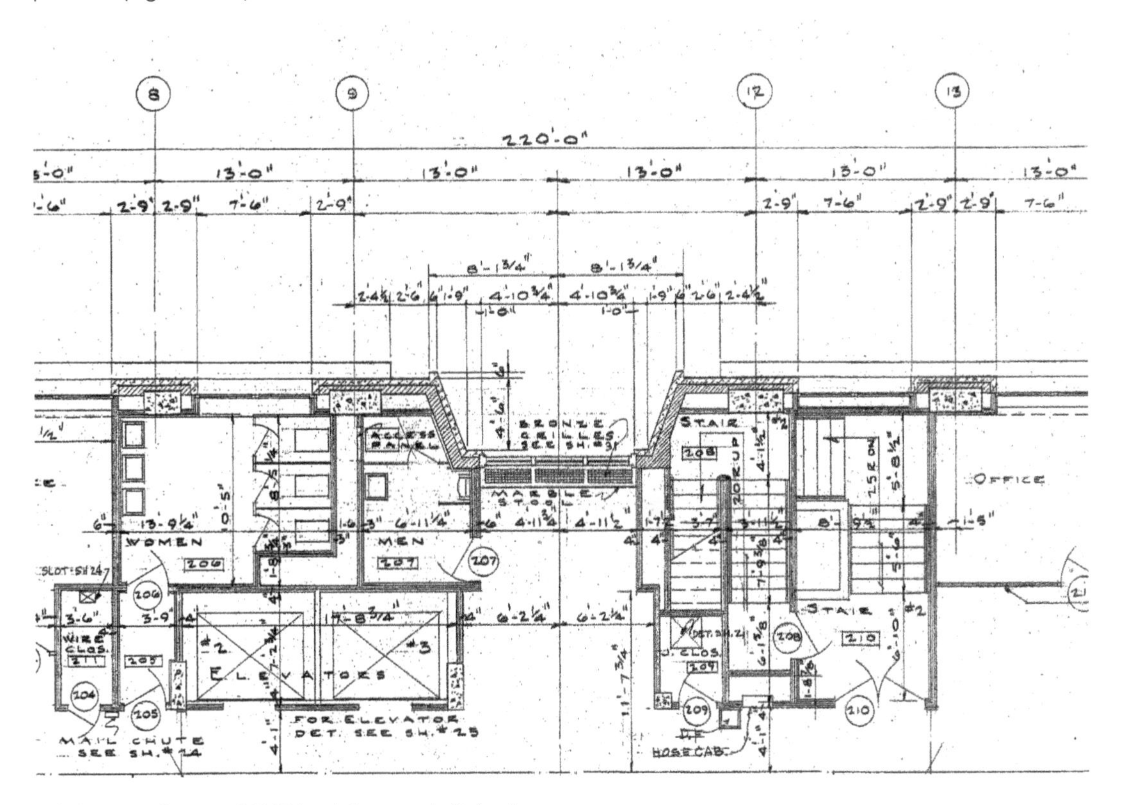

FIGURE 6.59 Excerpt of 1947 hand-drawn as-built drawings.
Courtesy M. A. Mortenson Company

FIGURE 6.60 Laser scan overlay with design BIM.
Courtesy M. A. Mortenson Company

FIGURE 6.61 Construction manager performing laser scanning.
Courtesy M. A. Mortenson Company

Laser Scanning

The art of laser scanning requires an understanding of BIM and surveying (Figure 6.61). It is important that the personnel completing the laser scanning have a clear understanding of what components will be modeled and also be able to align the field coordinates with those in the model.

Although laser scanning is very useful, the level of accuracy can sometimes create challenges when comparing the scans to the BIM. For example, if a wall has settled, causing the wall to be at a slight angle, this will be identified in the laser

FIGURE 6.62 Tight clearances on the first floor. Courtesy M. A. Mortenson Company

scan. These conditions must be carefully evaluated when developing the as-built model. Evaluation factors include the level of accuracy needed and the amount of time required to model a specific condition.

Determining the Level of Detail within the BIMs

The 3D construction model included the level of detail necessary to perform the renovation with minimal clashes. For example, ductwork, including the insulation, was modeled, as well as electrical conduits, plumbing piping, mechanical piping, and fire protection piping. This was especially important because the space to reconfigure the ductwork and run the other utilities was very tight within the existing spaces (Figure 6.62).

To help determine what should be included in the BIM and by whom, a level of development (LOD) matrix based on AIA Document E202–2008: Building Information Modeling Protocol Exhibit was developed to define the extent to which elements should be modeled. The E202 document defines five levels of progressively detailed completeness for the models. The five levels are generally described as:

- LOD 100: Overall building massing, including area, height, volume, location, and orientation
- LOD 200: Generalized systems and assemblies with approximate quantities, size, location, and orientation
- LOD 300: Specific systems and assemblies with accurate information for quantities, size, location, and orientation

- LOD 400: Specific systems and assemblies with accurate size, shape, location, quantity, and orientation that will allow fabrication, assembly, and detailing to be completed
- LOD 500: As-constructed assemblies with accurate size, shape, location, quantity, and orientation information

LOD 200 is the first level to which nongeometric information is recommended to be added to the model.

For the project, LOD 500 was used for facility management, and LOD 300 was used for most other project phases (Figure 6.63).

After the Revit design models were created, the subcontractors developed 3D coordination models and subsequent 2D fabrication drawings. The construction manager led periodic model reviews using Navisworks. These reviews highlighted clashes in the model and facilitated how these would be resolved.

			Schematic Design	Design Development	Construction Documents (IFC)	Construction Model (Coord.)
		Project BIM Lead	Gensler			Mort
A. SUBSTRUCTURE	Foundation	Standard Foundations	100	200	NA	NA
		Special Foundations	100	200	NA	NA
		Slab on Grade	100	200	300	300
	Basement Construction	Basement Excavation	NA	NA	NA	NA
		Basement Walls	100	200	300	300
B. SHELL	Superstructure	Floor Construction	100	200	300	300
		Roof Construction	NA	NA	NA	NA
	Exterior Enclosure	Exterior Walls	100	200	300	300
		Exterior Windows	100	200	300	300
		Exterior Doors	100	200	300	300
	Roofing	Roof Coverings	NA	NA	NA	NA
		Roof Openings	NA	NA	NA	NA
C. INTERIORS	Interior Construction	Partitions (Exisiting & New)	100	200	300	300
		Interior Doors	100	200	200	200
		Ceilings (Existing)	100	200	200	200
		Ceilings (New)	100	200	300	300
	Stairs	Stair Construction	100	200	300	300
		Stair Finishes		100	100	100
	Interior Finishes	Wall Finishes		100	100	100
		Floor Finishes		100	100	100
		Ceiling Finishes		100	100	100

FIGURE 6.63 Portion of level of development matrix used for the project.
Courtesy M. A. Mortenson Company

BIM HANDOVER

The building information modeling handover process consists of two primary data transfers—from design to construction and from construction to facility management. Both of these handover processes are discussed next.

Handover of the Model between Design and Construction

As Mortensen and Gensler have a well-established partnering relationship, there was a level of trust between the architect and construction manager to share the design BIM. Sharing of the model supported a more integrated approach, even though the construction manager was not involved until the construction documents were substantially complete. One of the limitations of having the construction manager brought on board later in the project was that opportunities to perform design phase clash detection were lost. Few MEP clashes were found during design because the MEP design was completed in 2D, which did not permit 3D clash detection.

Handover from Construction to Facility Management

The handover process from construction to facility management started with a desire to use COBie and integrate the Revit model with Maximo. Initially, a partnership was established among the university, Mortenson, Autodesk, and BIM to determine how to integrate Revit and Maximo. The initial work started with a proof of concept developed by Autodesk. From the start of the effort, Autodesk provided valuable training about both the structure and use of COBie. After preliminary research and end-user interviews, the team developed a three-phase strategy:

- *Phase 1: Asset Creation:* Populate assets from Revit into Maximo with key information required to perform maintenance management in the facility.
- *Phase 2: Asset Visualization:* Integration visualization to support and enhance service requests and work order execution.
- *Phase 3: Asset Reconciliation:* After data exchanges are made in Maximo, reconcile these changes in the Revit model.

The collective team agreed on the focus of Phase 1: Asset Creation. Through the use of a Revit COBie template provided by Autodesk, Mortenson was able to add representative data into a Revit MEP model and extract data from COBie. However, as work on Phase 1 progressed, significant hurdles prevented the team from developing an efficient interface between Revit and the university's Maximo

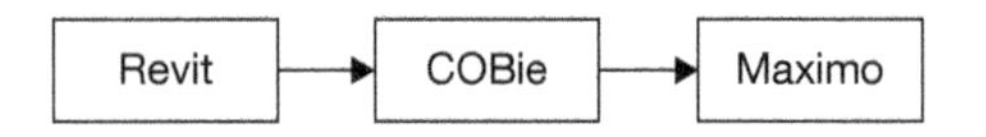

FIGURE 6.64 Envisioned information flow.

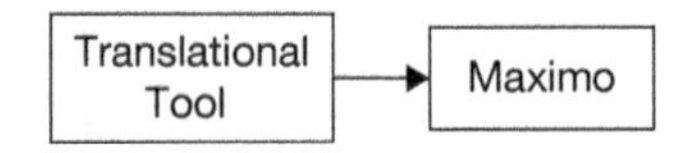

FIGURE 6.65 Possible information flow.

database. Given the limited project schedule, the team decided to revise its strategy and focus strictly on gathering information from the construction process and organize it in a uniform structure that could be populated into Maximo. Thus, the flow of data was changed from Figure 6.64 to 6.65. To assist with this project, a third-party database consultant was hired by the construction manager. The role of the third-party database consultant was to help determine what data to collect, determine how to organize the data within an Excel spreadsheet, and how to map the data so it could be uploaded successfully into Maximo.

A translational tool (modified version of COBie in the form of a spreadsheet) was eventually created to collect information during the construction process and import it into Maximo. Fields that did not align with the university's needs were eliminated, and new fields were added to address information requirements that were not included in COBie. The translational tool included 4 tabs, compared to the standard COBie, which contains 19. While the current translational tool is recognized as a valuable tool for the university, future versions of the tool will include additional tabs for information such as room dimensions and preventative maintenance (PM) procedures. Various FM information was collected, including (Figures 6.66 and 6.67):

- Asset name
- Installation contractor
- Vendor information
- Warranty information
- Purchase price
- Expected equipment life
- Asset location
- Serial number
- Bar-code number

Name	Design Manufacturer	Design Model Number	Installed Manufacturer	Applicable Vendor	Warranty Duration	Expected Life
Air Terminal Unit	Nailor	NAILOR-D30HQW	M0000001	M0000001	2	10 Years
Air Handler Unit	McQuay	McQuay-CAH017GDAC	M0000002	M0000002	2	10 Years
Split A/C Unit	Carrier	Carrier-40MVC012	M0000003	M0000003	2	5 Years
Supply Fan	Carrier	AirFoil AFMV01181	M0000003	M0000003	2	5 Years
Return Fan	Carrier	AirFoil AFMV01181	M0000003	M0000003	2	5 Years
Hot Water Recirculation Pump	Armstrong	Armstrong 1.25B 1050-001	M0000004	M0000004	2	10 Years
Silencer	Vibro-Acoustics	EXPD-MHV-F1-L11165	M0000005	M0000005	2	20 Years
Air Cooled Condenser	Carrier	Carrier-3BMVC012	M0000003	M0000003	2	10 Years
F1	Lightolier	LIGHTOLIER CFH2GPF217UNVP2	M0000006	M0000006	2	2000 Hours
F1A	Lightolier	LIGHTOLIER CFH2GPF217UNVP3	M0000006	M0000006	2	2000 Hours
F2	Lightolier	LIGHTOLIER D6132BU-8021CLW	M0000006	M0000006	2	1000 Hours
F3	Lightolier	LIGHTOLIER PTS7T254E8UP2, PTS7248E8UP2, PTS7EP	M0000006	M0000006	2	1000 Hours
F4	Axis	AXIS CUB-F-4-T8-2-AP-X-X-P-UNV-1-CA36	M0000007	M0000007	2	1000 Hours
F5	Lightolier	LIGHTOLIER SS3S125HPFUNVP2	M0000006	M0000006	2	1000 Hours
F6	Lightolier	LIGHTOLIER KW4A232UNVP2	M0000006	M0000006	2	1000 Hours
F7	Lightolier	LIGHTOLIER 22MC6WH	M0000006	M0000006	2	2000 Hours
F8	Lightolier	LIGHTOLIER 6003NWH, 6001NWM	M0000006	M0000006	2	1000 Hours
F9	Kurt Versen	Kurt Versen H8432	M0000008	M0000008	2	50,000 Starts
F10	Kurt Versen	Kurt Versen H8455	M0000008	M0000008	2	50,000 Starts
F11	Lumetta	Lumetta P2094	M0000009	M0000009	2	2000 Hours
X1	Lightolier	LIGHTOLIER MJES2RW23	M0000006	M0000006	2	3 Years
Drinking Fountain	Elkay	Elkay EDFPBMV117C BI-LEVEL	M0000010	M0000010	2	15 Years
Urinal	Toto	TOTO TEU1UN w/ Vitreous China Urinal	M0000011	M0000011	2	10 Years
Water Closet	Toto	TOTO CT708E w/ Vitreous China Elongated Bowl	M0000011	M0000011	2	10 Years
Lavatory	Kohler	Kohler K-2610	M0000012	M0000012	2	10 Years

FIGURE 6.66 Portion of asset types tab of translational tool.

Courtesy M. A. Mortenson Company

Asset Name	Asset Type	Asset Location	Asset Status	Bar Code	Commissioning Date	Bin Number
VAV-001	Air Terminal Unit	D20-00-004	OPERATING	23120	6/1/2011	
VAV-101	Air Terminal Unit	D20-01-100C	OPERATING	23119	6/1/2011	
VAV-102	Air Terminal Unit	D20-01-121-1	OPERATING	23121	6/1/2011	
VAV-102	Air Terminal Unit	D20-01-121-2	OPERATING	23121	6/1/2011	
VAV-102	Air Terminal Unit	D20-01-121-3	OPERATING	23121	6/1/2011	
VAV-102	Air Terminal Unit	D20-01-121-4	OPERATING	23121	6/1/2011	
VAV-102	Air Terminal Unit	D20-01-121-5	OPERATING	23121	6/1/2011	
VAV-102	Air Terminal Unit	D20-01-121-6	OPERATING	23121	6/1/2011	
VAV-102	Air Terminal Unit	D20-01-121-7	OPERATING	23121	6/1/2011	
VAV-102	Air Terminal Unit	D20-01-121-8	OPERATING	23121	6/1/2011	
VAV-102	Air Terminal Unit	D20-01-121-9	OPERATING	23121	6/1/2011	
VAV-102	Air Terminal Unit	D20-01-121-10	OPERATING	23121	6/1/2011	
VAV-102	Air Terminal Unit	D20-01-121-11	OPERATING	23121	6/1/2011	
VAV-102	Air Terminal Unit	D20-01-121-12	OPERATING	23121	6/1/2011	
VAV-102	Air Terminal Unit	D20-01-121-13	OPERATING	23121	6/1/2011	
VAV-103	Air Terminal Unit	D20-01-120	OPERATING	23122	6/1/2011	
VAV-104	Air Terminal Unit	D20-01-121-7	OPERATING	23123	6/1/2011	
VAV-105	Air Terminal Unit	D20-01-121-13	OPERATING	23124	6/1/2011	
VAV-106	Air Terminal Unit	D20-01-121-13	OPERATING	23125	6/1/2011	
VAV-107	Air Terminal Unit	D20-01-121-13	OPERATING	23126	6/1/2011	

FIGURE 6.67 Portion of assets tab of translational tool.

Courtesy M. A. Mortenson Company

- Performance units, such as CFM or GPM
- Installation date
- Commissioning date

The equipment included in the spreadsheet was limited to air terminal units, air handling units, split systems, supply and return fans, hot water recirculation pumps, air-cooled condensers, drinking fountains, urinals, water closets, lavatories, and lighting fixtures. Pick lists were created to help standardize the asset naming, including spelling, capitalization, and number of spaces between words, as well as make the spreadsheet easy to use.

An important benefit for the university resulting from this process was the incorporation of bar coding within the construction process. The University of Chicago team places bar codes on every operable piece of equipment for tracking maintenance. It was determined that Mortenson could more efficiently install the bar codes for the university as the equipment was installed in the field. Figure 6.68 shows a university bar code provided to Mortenson and placed on the equipment by the installation contractor during construction.

FIGURE 6.68 University bar code provided during construction.
Courtesy M. A. Mortenson Company

A second valuable result of the process was the integration of operations and maintenance documents and as-built data into Maximo. As documents were turned over to the university in an electronic format, the translational tool was used to align assets with the turnover documentation names. This linking exercise allowed university personnel to immediately access the operations and maintenance information within Maximo.

CMMS Test Site

As the process to upload the data into Maximo was developed, a test site was used to make sure the data was uploading and mapping correctly before the data was uploaded into the live database. Without the use of a test site, it is possible that incorrect data could override existing data, erasing valuable data and requiring rework to restore correct information.

Naming Conventions

In order to have the documents correctly imported into Maximo using the translational tool, it was necessary to align the naming conventions used by the design and construction teams with those used by the space and facilities management teams. Drop-down menus were created to allow the use of pick lists to reduce data entry errors.

Anticipated Cost Savings through Changing the Process

There is significant opportunity for cost savings when collecting asset data and bar coding equipment during design and construction. The key to recognizing this need is to determine how to streamline the asset inventory data collection process by performing activities at the most opportune time. Postoccupancy asset inventories represent waste and rework that contradict industry movement towards lean processes and optimized efficiency. When the asset inventory can be performed during construction, it is a manner of shifting responsibility for asset data collection, not creating additional work.

To determine the potential cost savings for performing an asset inventory during construction, as opposed to after occupancy, the cost of performing a typical asset inventory and bar coding by a third party after a building is occupied can be used. A typical asset inventory and bar coding effort can cost between *$0.30 and $0.60 per square foot*.

A typical asset inventory includes thousands of rows of data with multiple data items. After an asset inventory is completed, it is still necessary for the university to manually enter the data. Thus, when the asset data can be automatically populated into the CMMS, significant time savings occur. Additionally, when an asset inventory is performed during postoccupancy, it can cause disruptions to the building occupants.

USE OF BUILDING INFORMATION MODELING FOR FACILITY MANAGEMENT

The concepts of BIM provide many potential benefits for future construction and renovation projects at the University of Chicago. While 3D visualization models have not yet been integrated with Maximo, the ability to link views of the model to assets within Maximo would be valuable for the university engineers and technicians. In advance of asset visualization, the recently completed Phase 1: Asset Creation will be of value for future projects, whether or not BIM is used. The translational tool has proven to be successful for information collection. Two other benefits of using BIM for FM include (Black, Wilson, et al. 2011):

- Better management of building assets and information, improving the accuracy and value of data
- Streamlined project turnover and transition to operations because it is possible to collect FM data during construction and import it directly into facility management software

One of the challenges that the project team encountered was that it is necessary to determine what format of the model to maintain. At this time, software such as Navisworks does not allow all BIM information to be updated and coordinated as a single model. Thus, the project team determined it was not possible, because of the current capabilities, to procure multiple different software packages and allow the team to use BIM for FM.

Necessary Skill Sets

As the concepts and processes of BIM FM are still evolving, it is important to carefully consider the concepts and skills that team members bring to the project. Some of the necessary skills include an understanding of what contract structures will best support innovation, such as the early partnering that accompanies construction management at risk contracts. Team members must also be flexible and have the capacity to develop new processes with limited information. Team member(s) who are responsible for establishing data collection processes must be invested in solving problems that arise. At least one person on the team must be versed in CMMS, from both a facility user perspective and a programming perspective. Specific skills for the project described in this chapter included familiarity with database management and Maximo integration. Finally, as the use of information within

FM and the handover of information between construction and FM increases, it will be necessary for more individuals within the FM organization to have database management skills.

LESSONS LEARNED AND CHALLENGES

The lessons learned and challenges identified during this case study center on people, processes, and software. Specific challenges and lessons learned within these areas are described in the following sections.

Team and Process Challenges and Lessons Learned

One of the primary challenges with BIM FM integration processes is the number of departments and individuals involved in planning, design, construction, operations, inventory, procurement, maintenance management, contracts, and information systems. Every stakeholder has valuable input that must be collected. The time and effort required to capture this information should not be underestimated. For example, the bar-coding initiative discussed earlier required sharing ideas across departments. This effort was motivated by the potential to identify new and more efficient processes. The success of the effort was dependent on the leaders within the departments promoting collaboration for the overall benefit of the institution.

Regarding process improvement, it is important that an executive-level FM professional understand the BIM strategy for a project and have the ability to communicate priorities of the FM team members. It is also very important that one member of the team be recognized as the designated BIM FM champion. It is important to find team members with the right skill sets. In the event that a necessary skill set is not represented within the team, look for a way to engage such a team member and provide necessary training.

The implementation of BIM FM is in its infancy. Therefore, looking for FM teams and service providers who have worked on similar projects is challenging. A potentially larger challenge is quantifying the productivity advances that would occur if cultural changes were made to use data for facility management decision making.

Software Challenges and Lessons Learned

Successful deployment of software depends largely on the processes that have been defined and the familiarity of the project team members with the software. Within this case study, the two primary software products were Revit and Maximo. The design and construction teams were familiar with Revit. The facility management team was familiar with Maximo. No single team member was proficient with both software products. When seeking to integrate two software programs, it is important to recognize that information systems and information technology departments play an important role. Part of the integration process includes determining:

- How information will be stored
- Where information will be stored
- Who has rights to access the data

One of the key lessons learned was the importance of database management within any BIM FM strategy. Industry experts have emphasized the "I" in BIM, information. However, as designers, builders, and owners are trying to leverage the value of information, the value of database expertise becomes ever more important.

FUTURE EFFORTS

As the concept of how to use BIM for FM evolves at the University of Chicago, there are varying possibilities for how the BIM could be leveraged within Maximo. Beyond Phase 2: Asset Visualization, and Phase 3: Asset Reconciliation, one possible use would be to capture static 3D images of the BIM model within work orders generated by Maximo. This would allow users to see these images from the model without requiring the skills necessary to navigate the model. This would help maintenance technicians understand where an item is located in the building, what tools may be necessary to bring to perform a repair, and/or if the equipment is behind a door, above a ceiling, or requires a specific key or access card.

SUMMARY

The University of Chicago case study summarizes how an initial concept of leveraging BIM FM evolved into a streamlined initiative to capture relevant asset data during design and construction to support ongoing operations and maintenance of the Administration Building at the University of Chicago. COBie served as the guiding standard at the beginning of the effort. As the project progressed, the input from various stakeholders was collected. The format of the data capture evolved into a custom solution for the university. At the completion of the initiative, the university developed a translational tool that will be used on future projects for collecting asset information efficiently prior to building turnover. This tool will be of value, regardless of whether BIM is used or not.

With the successful completion of Phase 1: Asset Creation, two additional phases remain to be proven. Both Phase 2: Asset Visualization and Phase 3: Asset Reconciliation are future use cases that will be investigated by the university and evaluated for the value they may add to the long-term operations and maintenance strategy of the university.

Key lessons learned included:

- Small projects create great opportunities to advance the use of BIM and information handover between construction and facility management.
- The use of laser scanning early in the design process can help to create accurate as-built drawings, while also significantly reducing the time needed to verify as-built conditions.
- It is necessary to clearly define what data drives FM decisions. Because large amounts of accurate data have not been historically available for facility management teams for decision making, the potential value of data for data-driven FM decisions remains unknown.
- Educating team members about BIM, including what it is and its benefits, is important because, although many individuals within the industry have heard of BIM, few can define it.

Although the project team faced many challenges, the resulting translational tool provides a strong foundation for future construction to facility management information handover efforts within the University of Chicago.

REFERENCES

American Institute of Architects. 2008. AIA Document E202–2008: Building Information Modeling Protocol Exhibit.

Black, B., P. Wilson, A. LoBello, and A. Stapleton. 2011. *Next Steps with BIM: Use on Renovation Projects and Team Selection Tips. A Case Study of the University of Chicago Administration Building*. Construction Owners Association of America (COAA), 2011 Fall Owners Leadership Conference, Las Vegas, November 10, 2011.

ACKNOWLEDGMENTS

This case study could not have been written without the detailed information provided, and site visit conducted, by Andy Stapleton, LEED AP, director of project development of M. A. Mortenson Company; and Patrick Wilson, project manager, Capital Project Delivery, the University of Chicago.

Appendix A

List of Acronyms

Acronym	Meaning
2D	Two-dimensional
3D	Three-dimensional
4D	BIM model with associated time information as a fourth dimension
5D	BIM model with associated time and budget data as fourth and fifth dimensions
ADA	Americans with Disabilities Act
A/E	Architect/engineer
AEC	Architectural, engineering, and construction (industry segment)
aecXML	A markup language that uses Industry Foundation Classes to create a vendor-neutral means to access data generated by building information modeling
AGC	Associated General Contractors of America
AIA	American Institute of Architects
ANSI	American National Standards Institute
API	Application programming interface

(Continued)

Acronym	Meaning
As-built BIM	Editable copy of the record BIM that is constantly updated to represent the current building and systems configuration
ASF	Assignable square feet
ASTM	American Society for Testing and Materials
BAS	Building automation system
BEP	BIM execution plan
BIM	Building information model or building information modeling
BIM FM	Integration of BIM and FM-related system
BOMA	Building Owners and Managers Association
bSa	buildingSMART alliance
CAD	Computer-aided design (normally 2D)
CAFM	Computer-aided facility management (can incorporate CMMS functions in addition to asset management, human resource management, condition assesment, and other functions)
CF	Cubic feet
CFM	Cubic feet per minute
CIFE	Center for Integrated Facility Engineering, Stanford University
CM/GC	Construction manager/general contractor
CMA or CMa	Construction manager as agent
CMAR	Construction manager at risk
CMC	Construction manager as contractor
CMMS	Computerized maintenance management system
COBie	Construction Operations Building information exchange
Construction BIM	BIM model typically representing a single building system created for purposes of planning, scheduling, coordinating, fabricating components, and executing construction. Model elements are accurate in terms of size, shape, location, quantity, and orientation and may include fabrication, assembly, detailing, and nongeometric information. MEP/FP systems models include primary keys that link them to the COBie data. Construction BIMs are maintained in the native format of the authoring software.

(Continued)

Acronym	Meaning
Coordination BIM	Composite model that includes multiple design or construction BIMs, registered spatially, used for the purposes of interference checking (clash detection), visualization, and 4D applications during construction. Coordination BIMs are maintained in the native format of the coordination software.
CQC	Construction Quality Control plan
CRV	Current replacement value
CUP	Central utility plant
CxA	Commissioning agent
DBIA	Design Build Institute of America
Design Intent BIM	Building information model(s) created by and conformed to the bid addenda by the A/E. Elements are accurate in terms of quantity, size, shape, location, and orientation. The design intent BIM includes the Spatial Program model. Elements also contain primary keys that link them to the COBie data. The Design Intent BIM must be submitted in both .ifc and native format.
DMS	Document management system
DSF	Division of State Facilities (in Wisconsin)
EAM	Enterprise asset management
EDMS	Electronic document management system
EDRC	Engineering Research and Development Center
EMS	Energy management system
ERP	Enterprise resource planning
EUL	Equipment useful life
FAR	Federal Acquisition Regulation
FCI	Facility Condition Index
FISMA	Federal Information Security Management Act of 2002
FLCM	Facility Live Cycle Manamagement
FM	Facility management
FMSP	Facilities Management and Services Program
FP	Fire protection
GC	General contractor
GIS	Geographic information system
GPM	Gallons per minute

(Continued)

Acronym	Meaning
GSA	General Services Administration, U.S. Government agency responsible for office space, goods and services to other federal agencies
GSAR	General Services Acquisition Regulation
GSF	Gross square feet
GUID	Globally unique identifier for an item that does not change over its life
HVAC	Heating, ventilating, and air conditioning
IaaS	Infrastructure as a service, refers to the IT infrastructure services offered by cloud providers
IAI	International Alliance for Interoperability
IFC	Industry foundation classes: an object-oriented neutral file format with a data model developed by buildingSMART (International Alliance for Interoperability, IAI) to describe, exchange and share information
IFC BIMs	Building information models compatible with IFC data standard
ifcXML	Industry Foundation Classes: specifically the "ifcXML" format, defined by ISO 10303-28 ("STEP-XML"), having file extension ".ifcXML". This format is suitable for interoperability with XML tools and exchanging partial building models.
IFX	IFC-XML (see XML below)
IPD	Integrated project delivery
ISO	International Organization for Standardization
IT	Information technology
IWMS	Integrated workplace management system
LEED	Leadership in Energy and Environmental Design, standard for green building design
LEED-NC	Leadership in Energy and Environmental Design for New Construction
LOD	Level of detail or level of development
MEP	Mechanical, electrical, plumbing
MEP/FP	Mechanical, electrical, plumbing, and fire protection
MHS	Department of Defense's Medical Health Service
NaSF	Nonassignable square feet

(Continued)

Acronym	Meaning
National 3D-4D-BIM Program	In 2003, the U.S. General Services Administration (GSA) Public Buildings Service (PBS) Office of Design and Construction (ODC) established the National 3D-4D-BIM Program (see http://www.gsa.gov/portal/content/105075).
NBIMS	National Building Information Model Standard
NIBS	National Institute of Building Sciences
NIST	National Institute of Standards and Technology
NMR	Nuclear magnetic resonance
O&M	Operations and maintenance
OCA	Office of the Chief Architect
ODBC	Open database connectivity
ODC	Office of Design and Construction, part of the GSA
OmniClass	The OmniClass Construction Classification System (known as OmniClass™ or OCCS) is a classification system for the construction industry.
P-100	Facilities Standards for the Public Buildings Service
PBS	Public Buildings Service
PM	Preventive maintenance (performed before an item fails)
POR	Program of requirements
QSP	Quality service plan
Record BIM	Multiple construction BIMs, organized by building system and floor and registered spatially, that represent the final as-constructed building and components configuration, including architectural
RFI	Request for information
RFID	Radio-frequency identification
ROI	Return on investment
RSF	Rentable square feet
SaaS	Software as a service, refers to applications are hosted on the Web and accessed by subscription users via a browser
SBS	Smart building systems integrate major open building systems on a common network. Smart building systems share information and functionality to improve energy efficiency, operational effectiveness, and occupant satisfaction.

(Continued)

Acronym	Meaning
SDM	Spatial Data Management, GSA's national effort to create, update, and maintain its spatial data and associated computer-aided design (CAD) floor plans to accurately reflect the national federally owned inventory
SEPS	The Space and Equipment Planning System (SEPS) is a health facility planning tool.jointly developed by the Department of Defense and the Department of Veterans Affairs.
SEPS BIM Tool	A Revit add-in that automates the creation, placement, and validation of medical equipment within a BIM model
SF	Square feet
SOW	Statement of work
SPie	Specifiers' Properties information exchange
UniFormat	A method of arranging construction information based on functional elements, or parts of a facility characterized by their functions, without regard to the materials and methods used to accomplish them. These elements are often referred to as systems or assemblies. This system is trademarked by the Construction Specifications Institute (CSI). See www.csinet.org/uniformat
UW	University of Wisconsin
UWRF	University of Wisconsin River Falls
VA	Department of Veterans Affiars
VAV	Variable air volume
VDC	Virtual design and construction
VR	Virtual reality
XML	Extensible Markup Language

Appendix B

Software Cross References

Software name	Company and Website	References to software items
Adobe Acrobat	Adobe Systems, Inc. www.adobe.com/products/acrobat.html	Chapter 6, case study 5
AEC CADduct	Technical Sales International, Inc. http://aec-apps.com/content/cad-duct	Chapter 6, case study 3
AEC CADpipe	Orange Technologies, Inc. www.cadpipe.com/	Chapter 6, case study 3
AiM™ Maintenance Management	AssetWorks, Inc. www.assetworks.com/products/aim-maintenance-management	Chapter 6, case studies 2 and 5
Archibus Space Inventory and Performance	www.archibus.com/index.cfm/pages.content_application/template_id/847/section/Space%20Inventory%20&%20Performance/path/1.3.29.92/menuid/93	Chapter 6, case study 6
AutoCAD	Autodesk, Inc. http://usa.autodesk.com/autocad/	Chapter 6, case studies 1, 3, 4, and 5
BlueBeam PDF Revu	BluBeam Software, Inc. www.bluebeam.com/us/products/revu/standard.asp	Chapter 6, case study 5

(Continued)

Software name	Company and Website	References to software items
eBuilder Document Management	www.e-builder.net/products/document-management	Chapter 6, case study 6
EcoDomus FM	EcoDomus, Inc. www.ecodomus.com/ecodomusfm.html	Chapter 3 Chapter 4 Chapter 6, case studies 2 and 3
Enterprise Building Integrator	Honeywell Inc. https://buildingsolutions.honeywell.com/Cultures/en-US/ServicesSolutions/BuildingManagementSystems/EnterpriseBuildingsIntegrator/	Chapter 6, case study 3
FAMIS (CMMS)	Accurent LLC, www.accruent.com/products/enterprise-facility.html	Chapter 6, case study 3
FM:Interact	FM:Systems, Inc. www.fmsystems.com/	Chapter 6, case studies 1 and 4
GoToMeeting	Citrix Systems, Inc. www.gotomeeting.com/fec/	Chapter 6, case studies 1 and 3
LogMeIn	LogMeIn, Inc. https://secure.logmein.com/products/central/	Chapter 6, case study 5
Maximo Asset Management	www-01.ibm.com/software/tivoli/products/maximo-asset-mgmt/	Chapter 6, case study 6
Meridian Enterprise	BlueCielo www.bluecieloecm.com/en/products/bc-meridian-enterprise/	Chapter 6, case study 3
Metasys®: Building Management System	Johnson Controls, Inc. www.johnsoncontrols.com/content/us/en/products/building_efficiency/building_management/metasys.html	Chapter 6, case study 5
Navisworks Manage	Autodesk, Inc. http://usa.autodesk.com/navisworks/	Chapter 6, case studies 1, 3, and 4
Onuma System	Ounuma Systems, Inc. www.onuma.com/products/OnumaPlanningSystem.php	Chapter 3 Chapter 6, case study 2

(Continued)

Software name	Company and Website	References to software items
Revit Architecture	Autodesk, Inc. www.autodesk-revit.com/	Chapter 2 Chapter 6, case studies 1, 2, and 3
Revit MEP	Autodesk, Inc. http://usa.autodesk.com/revit/mep-engineering-software/	Chapter 6, case study 3
Revit SEPS BIM Tool	Developed by Design and Construction Strategies www.dcstrategies.net/resources/seps-bim-tool	Chapter 2
Revit Structure	Autodesk, Inc. http://usa.autodesk.com/revit/structural-design-software/	Chapter 6, case study 3
Skire Unifier	Skire is an Oracle Company http://www.skire.com/index.php/solutions/capital-projects/	Chapter 6, case study 5
Submittal Exchange	Textura Corp. www.submittalexchange.com/public/	Chapter 6, case study 5
Tekla Structures	Tekla is a Trimble Company www.tekla.com/us/products/full/Pages/Default.aspx	Chapter 6, case study 3
Telka BIMsight	Tekla is a Trimble Company www.teklabimsight.com/	Chapter 6, case study 2
TOKMO	EcoDomus, Inc. www.ecodomus.com/ecodomuspm.html	Chapter 6, case study 1
Vela Mobile Systems	Autodesk, Inc. www.velasystems.com/construction-field-software-products/#vela-mobile	Chapter 2
WebTMA	TMA Systems, Inc. www.webtma.com/Products/WebBasedSolutions/WebTMAClientHosted.aspx	Chapter 6, case studies 4 and 5

Index

NOTE: Page numbers in *italics* indicate figures and tables.

Established in 1990 as a nonprofit 501(c)(3) corporation, the IFMA Foundation works for the public good to promote research and educational opportunities for the advancement of facility management. The IFMA Foundation is supported by the generosity of the facility management community, including IFMA members, chapters, councils, corporate sponsors and private contributors who are united by the belief that education and research improve the facility management profession. To learn more about the good works of the IFMA Foundation, visit www.ifmafoundation.org. For more information about IFMA, visit www.ifma.org.

Contributions to the IFMA Foundation are used to:

- Advance FM education—increase the number of colleges and universities offering accredited FM degree programs worldwide and to keep facility managers up to date on the latest techniques and technology
- Underwrite research—to generate knowledge that directly benefits the profession
- Provide scholarships—to support education and the future of the facility management profession by encouraging FM as a career of choice.

Without the support of workplace professionals, the IFMA Foundation would be unable to contribute to the future development and direction of facility management. If you care about improving the profession and your career potential, we encourage you to make a donation or get involved in a fund-raising event. Donations can be made at www.ifmafoundation.org.

IFMA FOUNDATION SPONSORS AT PUBLICATION:

Major Benefactor

Corporate Facilities Council of IFMA

Platinum Sponsors

A&A Maintenance
Atlanta Chapter of IFMA
Bentley Systems
East Bay Chapter of IFMA
FM:Systems
Greater Philadelphia Chapter of IFMA
Greater Triangle Chapter of IFMA
Herman Miller
ISS
Milliken
Utilities Council of IFMA

Gold and Silver Sponsors

Aramark
Boston Chapter of IFMA
Capital Chapter of IFMA
Central PA Chapter (Pennsylvania)
CORT Furniture
Denver Chapter of IFMA
DTZ a UGL Company
Emcor
Houston Chapter of IFMA
New York City Chapter of IFMA
Public Sector Council of IFMA
Silicon Valley Chapter of IFMA
Sodexo
Steelcase
Teknion
Academic Facilities Council of IFMA
Autodesk
Canadian Chapters of IFMA
Charlotte Chapter of IFMA
Dallas / Fort Worth Chapter of IFMA
Fire Detection, Inc.
FMN (Facility Management Netherlands)
Graphic Systems, Inc.
Greater Louisville Chapter of IFMA
Indianapolis Chapter of IFMA
Manufacturing Council of IFMA
New Jersey Chapter of IFMA
Orange County Chapter of IFMA
Kayhan International
Sacramento Valley Chapter of IFMA
San Antonio Chapter of IFMA
San Diego Chapter of IFMA
San Francisco Chapter of IFMA
Southeast Michigan Chapter of IFMA
Southeast Wisconsin Chapter of IFMA
Staples Advantage
Suncoast Chapter of IFMA
West Michigan Chapter of IFMA

Additional copies of this book and other IFMA Foundation and IFMA publications can be ordered through the IFMA bookstore online at www.ifma.org.